THE
HITTITE DICTIONARY
OF THE ORIENTAL INSTITUTE OF THE UNIVERSITY OF CHICAGO

VOLUME 3

Editorial Staff

THE HITTITE DICTIONARY

OF THE ORIENTAL INSTITUTE OF THE UNIVERSITY OF CHICAGO

Edited by
Hans G. Güterbock and Harry A. Hoffner

Published by
THE ORIENTAL INSTITUTE OF THE UNIVERSITY OF CHICAGO
1980

ISBN 0-918986-27-3
(Set 0-918986-26-5)
Library of Congress Catalog Card Number 79-53554

The Oriental Institute

The preparation of this volume of the Chicago Hittite Dictionary was made possible in part by grants from the Program for Research Tools and Reference Works of the National Endowment for the Humanities, an independent Federal Agency.

Text typeset by Eisenbrauns in Times
Cover and title pages typeset by The University of Chicago Printing Department in Janson
Printed and bound in the United States of America by Braun-Brumfield

FOREWORD

It is a pleasure and privilege to inaugurate the first published fascicle of the *Chicago Hittite Dictionary*. A fitting introduction to the new volume may be to sketch the history of the project that gave it birth.

In 1963, the year in which he received his doctorate from Brandeis University, Harry Hoffner began assembling Hittite lexical files as a tool for personal research. The files were compiled according to the *Chicago Assyrian Dictionary* method of transliterating extensive contexts and reproducing multiple file copies for parsing individual words. From 1964 to 1973, while teaching at Brandeis and Yale, Hoffner put on file about 65% of the published Hittite material. In autumn 1972, he spent a sabbatical term with Heinrich Otten at Marburg. Through Otten's generosity, Hoffner was able to use the lexical file at the Marburg Seminar for completion of his book *Alimenta Hethaeorum*. Learning that Otten's plans to produce a Hittite thesaurus were likely to be delayed for many years, Hoffner began to appreciate the need for a Hittite-English lexical tool of intermediate length that could be completed over the next few decades.

When Hoffner was invited in 1973 to come to the Oriental Institute in Chicago, he and Hans Güterbock saw the opportunity for a long hoped-for collaboration. Güterbock had extensive experience in Hittite lexical studies, but no files. Hoffner had files, but felt the need for an experienced and learned colleague with Güterbock's background. It was an ideal combination, and both men agreed to set the plan in motion. After Hoffner had come to Chicago in 1974, he was given a part-time student assistant and the equipment necessary to house and expand his files. In 1975 a formal application was submitted to the National Endowment for the Humanities to fund a full-scale dictionary project.

With the award of a substantial three-year grant from the National Endowment for the Humanities at the beginning of 1976, the Hittite Dictionary project was able to hire a full-time research associate, Howard Berman, and several graduate-student assistants. The files were rapidly augmented, colleagues were advised of the new status of the project, and the decision was made to begin the dictionary with the letter "L" to avoid immediate overlap with Annelies Kammenhuber's Hittite-German work. In 1977, Emmanuel Laroche agreed to read and criticize selected articles as an outside consultant, and the first drafts of many "L" words were written. By 1978 sufficient progress had been made to have Eisenbrauns prepare offset samples of dictionary articles and to apply for a second three-year grant from the National Endowment for the Humanities.

Now in 1979, as the Oriental Institute prepares to celebrate its sixtieth anniversary, the National Endowment for the Humanities has renewed its grant support; and the first fascicle of the *Chicago Hittite Dictionary* is ready to go to press.

In a multifaceted project such as this, acknowledgements are due in many quarters. First a deep debt of gratitude is owed to the editors and their staff. Professor Hoffner is to be thanked for over ten years of unassisted labor, out of which grew the main dictionary file of the project, and for his continuing painstaking service as Executive Editor. In the latter capacity he has been responsible not only for writing and editing the dictionary articles but also for negotiating the National Endowment for the Humanities grants and supervising the work of the junior staff. The Senior Editor, Professor Güterbock, has brought to the project a rare expertise born of many years of philological and archeological work reaching back to the days when the field of Hittitology was in its infancy. Besides writing and criticizing manuscripts, he has provided a mine of information on all aspects of Hittite language, history, and culture freely drawn on by the staff. Dr. Howard Berman, as Research Associate, has provided a careful philological approach to Hittite combined with a valuable background in linguistics and a study of the historical reconstruction of Proto-Indo-European. Finally the world of scholarship must acknowledge the indispensable support of the National Endowment for the Humanities, Research Tools Division, without whose aid this dictionary could not have appeared. It is the unique combination of all these efforts that has produced the present work.

September 18, 1979

John A. Brinkman
Director, Oriental Institute
University of Chicago

PREFACE

The Hittite language is the earliest preserved member of the Indo-European family of languages. It was written on clay tablets in central Asia Minor over a five hundred year span (c. 1750-1200 B.C.) which witnessed the rise, the floruit and the decline of many political powers in the Near East. It is studied today for a wide variety of reasons. Historical linguists seek information in Hittite texts to elucidate the interrelationships between the various member languages of the Indo-European family, as well as the probable structure of their common parent, Proto-Indo-European. Historians find in Hittite annals, treaties, royal edicts and political correspondence information of great value in reconstructing the sequence of events on the international scene of mid-second-millennium Western Asia. Anthropologists, mythographers, and students of comparative religion mine the riches of Hittite religious texts: myths, magic rituals to cure ailments, festivals to worship the gods of the empire. Students of the history of law discover ancient precedents for legal procedures which have survived to this day. All of these interested researchers share a dependence upon the written texts. None can penetrate further than our limited understanding of this language allows.

The vast majority of Hittite tablets derive from the ruins of the ancient Hittite capital Ḫattuša located near the modern Turkish town of Boğazkale (earlier name: Boğazköy) about 210 kilometers east of Ankara. Scientific excavation of these ruins by a German team began in 1906. About 10,000 clay tablets inscribed with the familiar Assyro-Babylonian script came to light. Although some were written in the Akkadian language and could be read immediately, most were in an unknown language, correctly assumed to be Hittite. Within ten years the language had been deciphered, and a sketch of its grammar published. Gradually, the international community of scholars, led by the Germans, extended the boundaries of the known. The number of common Hittite words which one could translate with reasonable certainty increased steadily. Glossaries published in 1936 by Edgar Sturtevant (in English) and in 1952 by Johannes Friedrich (in German) admirably served the needs of their contemporaries. Yet today, sixty years after the decipherment, there still exists no complete dictionary of the Hittite language.

Certain conditions must be met before a Hittite dictionary can be written. Fundamental to all the others is the first: a sufficient percentage of the excavated tablets and tablet fragments must be published or at least made available to the dictionary editors. At this writing twenty-six volumes of the KBo series have appeared, forty-eight of the KUB series, three of the IBoT, and four singly published volumes. Thus eighty-one volumes of published Hittite texts exist, each containing on the average fifty plates of copies, totalling 4050 plates of Hittite texts. Although the total number of Hittite fragments with excavation or museum numbers may amount to 30,000, most of these are quite small in size. It is therefore quite likely, when measured in terms of lines of Hittite text, that more than half the total number of excavated tablets has been published. This remarkable achievement over a period of half a century is a tribute to the work of Ehelolf, Figulla, Goetze, Güterbock, Klengel, Walther, Weidner and others, who labored at the task of copying texts, but especially in recent years to Heinrich Otten, who copied all or large parts of over twenty volumes of texts.

Lexical surprises still come from newly published texts. But as the published corpus grows, the frequency of such surprises diminishes, and dictionary editors with prepublication knowledge of the lexical content of unpublished texts enjoy a measure of protection. The *Chicago Hittite Dictionary* (CHD) is fortunate that Güterbock, by virtue of his long association with the Boğazköy excavations, has knowledge of and permission to use unpublished texts. But since his access to these texts is limited, we do not claim a complete coverage, as we do for published texts.

A second condition is sufficient progress in the editing of texts. Although the decipherer Hrozný himself wrote the first edition of a Hittite text in 1919, it was Ferdinand Sommer who in 1925 founded the first series to publish editions of Hittite texts, the Hethitische Texte subseries of the Mitteilungen der Vorderasiatisch-ägyptischen Gesellschaft. Modern series of Hittite text editions are H. Otten's Studien zu den Boğazköy-Texten (StBoT) and A. Kammenhuber's Texte der Hethiter, which to date have produced 32 volumes.

Indispensible to the text editions are the discussions of the meanings of Hittite words. These discussions are found in the philological commentary appended to the transliteration and translation of the texts under study. Such lexical studies and others which appeared in separate articles or books formed the basis of the first two glossaries of the Hittite language, those of Sturtevant (1936) and Friedrich (1952). The bibliography of lexical studies appearing in the two aforementioned glossaries indicates the degree of our indebtedness to Ehelolf, Friedrich, Goetze, Güterbock, Laroche, and Sommer, whose contributions are most frequently cited.

It would be difficult to conceive of writing a Hittite dictionary without a tool such as E. Laroche's *Catalogue des textes hittites* (CTH), first published in 1956-58 and now in a thoroughly revised and augmented second edition of 1971. This systematic classification of the published Boğazköy tablets allows each Hittitologist to utilize all known copies of a given composition to create his own critical edition, or to supplement and correct an older published edition by means of more recently found evidence. The usefulness of CTH is universally recognized. The front matter of each new volume of cuneiform copies now often identifies each published fragment by its CTH number. Discoveries of additional joins or duplicates are regularly reported and related to the CTH numbering system. As in the assembling of a jigsaw puzzle, the identifying and placing of new pieces becomes easier as the picture grows more complete. The contribution of such work to lexical study is obvious. Joining and thus reconstructing tablets from their fragmentary remains affords full contexts in passages where the words occur. Identification of duplicates often leads to the discovery that a syllabically written Hittite word in one copy is written with a Sumerogram or Akkadogram of known meaning in its duplicate. Therefore it is no mere coincidence that Laroche's preparation of the first edition of his *Catalogue* was carried out concurrently with his significant lexical studies of 1947 and 1958.

No dictionary of a language written over a span of four centuries would be serviceable without reliable criteria for determining the dates of the texts on which it is based. There must be an agreed upon basis for distinguishing earlier from later compositions and — in the case of traditional, transmitted texts — the earlier from the later copies of the same composition. Indeed the date of the original composition of some texts can be determined on the basis of named authors, in most cases a king. But for the majority of religious and administrative texts not datable by this means the following methods have been developed. The copy is dated by noting the latest palaeographic features of its script. The original composition is dated by noting the oldest orthographic, grammatical, and lexical features to be found in its copies. In the CHD we have chosen to abbreviate our conclusions in the form OH/NS, which is to be interpreted as "deriving from OH archetype, but showing New Script and often considerable linguistic modernization". Although we distinguish Old Script (Otten's "typisch alt" and "alt"), Middle Script (Otten's "ältere Schrift", "ältlich", etc.), and New Script, we have refrained from differentiating early and late forms of NS, although such a differentiation is certainly possible. When dating texts attributable to specific kings of the empire period, we have usually made no comment about the script. But the reader should not conclude from such words as "prayer of Murš. II" after a citation that the copy cited was necessarily made during that same king's reign. But a Ḫattušili III copy of Muršili II composition is not as likely to show significant grammatical innovations as a Ḫattušili III copy of a Ḫattušili I text.

In matters of text dating we concur in the main with the judgments of the Marburg School. For two reasons we have decided not to include here a complete listing of the Old and Middle Hittite corpora according to our point of view. First, provisional lists are available with which we are in general agreement. And secondly, we deem it wiser to continue to refine our own dating scheme and to print it on a later occasion. Since evidence will continue to accumulate, our opinions will certainly change. It is inevitable that not all datings in this volume will be retained in future ones. In most cases, however, changes will be minor, such as discovering from a newly published OS duplicate that a text which we previously called NH was in reality OH/NS. Users of the CHD can easily accommodate such developments.

Although published lexical studies provide a broad base of information about the occurrence of certain Hittite words, no dictionary could be written without extensive lexical files. The main lexical file of the CHD, consisting of over 600,000 cards, now gives complete coverage to over 90 percent of published texts and will soon include 100 percent. It is based upon the personal lexical file of H. A. Hoffner built up from 1963 through 1975, augmented and corrected by Hoffner and Berman working under the first National Endowment for the Humanities grant 1976-79. A much smaller, but significant, source is the personal lexical file of Güterbock, which contains references to unpublished texts.

Since we believe that the conditions for the writing of a Hittite dictionary have been met, we have embarked upon the production of the CHD.

While in many ways we have consciously imitated the organization, procedure, and format of our sister dictionary, the *Chicago Assyrian Dictionary* (CAD), the much smaller size of the Hittite text corpus insures that the CHD will be more limited in size and scope. We attempt to give complete coverage of the representative occurrences of each Hittite word, but we will not seek to be exhaustive.

Although Hittite dictionary and thesaurus projects have been initiated in Germany by A. Kammenhuber, we do not consider our work a mere duplication. The CHD is primarily designed for English-speaking scholars and students, who truly need and deserve an up-to-date Hittite dictionary in their own language. Our procedure, organization, and views on text dating differ from Kammenhuber's. In no way do we wish to disparage her work; we welcome it and profit from it. But while we are eager to learn from her experience, we have adopted distinctive operating procedures and do not intend to model our dictionary upon hers.

The specific ways in which the CHD approach will differ from HW^2 have already been outlined by Hoffner in his review of its first fascicle in Bibliotheca Orientalis 35:242ff. The user will now be able to observe in our dictionary articles the results of applying these methods. We aim to give the user a maximum of usable information, allowing him to see not only our conclusions but the basis for them. The CHD does not attempt to determine the Proto-Indo-European origins of Hittite words. In that sense it is not an etymological dictionary. Words borrowed into Hittite from some identifiable foreign source will be noted as such. In many cases (exceptions are marked with a dagger †) our dictionary does not list all known occurrences of a particular form or a semantic usage, but adduces those which are representative of a time period (OH, MH, NH), of a text genre (myth, ritual, law), or of an ethno-cultural milieu (Hurrian, Hattian, Luwian). When other considerations are equal, we prefer to cite a well-preserved passage rather than a broken one.

The alphabetization scheme for the dictionary's entries is essentially that used by HW. The consonant alternations *b/p*, *d/t*, and *g/k/q* have been merged and alphabetized as *p*, *t*, *k*. Consonantal doubling is ignored. Also adjacent *i* and *y* or *u* and *w* are alphabetized as single *i* or *u*.

It is well-known that the vowels *e* and *i* often interchange in the spelling of Hittite words. It is quite likely that the two vowels, still kept distinct in Typical Old Script, began to merge in later Old Hittite, and certainly had completed their merger by the Empire period. In order to avoid unnecessary use of cross references (such as "*zenna-* see *zinna-*") we have decided to consider these two vowels equivalent for purpose of alphabetization and to list them in the *i* position.

When different spellings are attested for the stem of a word (*laḫlaḫḫeškinu-*, *laḫḫilaḫḫeškinu-*), we have alphabetized according to that form of the stem which allows the entry to appear closest to its cognates.

In the morphological section we have sought to adduce at least one example of each spelling of the form under consideration. We have usually refrained from citing more than two or three locations for the same spelling. Line numbers in parentheses indicate that the form cited is partially broken.

The morphological terminology is that used conventionally by our colleagues with one exception: we have called the nominal case in *-a* the "allative" in preference to either "directive" or "terminative". Our objections to "directive" are those adduced by F. Starke in StBoT 23 (1977) 23 with note 12. In addition, the standard complete dictionary of American English, *Webster's Third New International Dictionary of the English Language Unabridged*, attests no use of "directive" as a designation of a noun case. Although "terminative", once suggested by Hoffner and advocated by Starke, is not unacceptable to us, in English it occasions some confusion, since its well-established usage with verbs in the sense of perfective (see F. Josephson, *The Function of Sentence Particles in Old and Middle Hittite*, page 33) beclouds its more recent employment to describe noun case. "Allative", on the other hand, enjoys a clear usage in noun-case terminology, being defined in *Webster's New International Dictionary of the English Language Second Edition Unabridged*: "Designating or pertaining to a case which expresses the relational idea of motion to or toward". Its symmetry with other case designations such as ablative and illative (the latter not needed in Hittite grammar) also favors its adoption. Our choice of English terms is not to be regarded as a rejection of the argument or conclusions of Starke as to the functions of this case. For another opinion see Kammenhuber in *Hethitisch und Indogermanisch*, Neu and Meid, eds., 115ff.

Within the morphological section of each article we have indicated our estimate of the date of archetype (i.e., OH, MH, NH) and copy (OS, MS, NS), but not the genre (e.g., fest., rit., hist.). For while genre of text is often an important datum in the area of semantics, it is usually irrelevant in considerations of spellings. Occasional exceptions are cult inventories and oracle texts. If given a choice, we have preferred to cite well-preserved rather than broken examples of each spelling. If we cite a line to locate a form which is partially broken, we place the line number in parentheses. If we cite a line to locate a form which requires emendation, we place an exclamation point after the line number. Such exclamation points do not, therefore, indicate a correction of the line count. Normally in the morphological section we employ the line count of the cuneiform copy rather than a cumulative one from an edition.

Bilingual evidence has been assigned a location between morphological and semantic sections, although bilingual passages may be cross-referenced at a point in the semantic section appropriate to their semantic content or usage.

The significance of the number and letter hierarchy of the CHD in its semantic section is essentially the same as that of the CAD. In those articles where the Hittite word requires a different English translation in each of its principal usages the highest level of the hierarchy (i.e., the primary division) is represented by Arabic numerals, which correlate with translations in the article heading. In those articles where the Hittite word may be uniformly translated in all its usages the primary division of the article is represented by lower case letters of the alphabet.

Within the semantic section wider contexts are indicated by means of English translations (in quotation marks) or paraphrases, while a minimal significant context is given both in Hittite and English. Only the key word is transliterated; other Hittite words are rendered in broad transcription. When it is deemed necessary to indicate morpheme boundaries within a Hittite word cited in broad transcription, the mark ⸗ is used in preference to the simple hyphen (e.g., *keššaruš⸗muš⸗a* "and my hands"). In all cases text references are to the cuneiform copies with additional information about cumulative line count in published editions. We indicate line count as follows. In the case of vertically joined tablet fragments, if there is a difference between separate and cumulative line count and there is a need for indicating both, the separate is given first followed by cumulative, e.g., KBo 3.8 ii 34-35 (= KUB 7.1 + KBo 3.8 ii 68-69). Otherwise only the separate will be given, as regularly in the morphological section. Lateral joins are indicated KUB 31.4 obv. 15 + KBo 3.41 obv. 14. Some elaborate and complex tablet reconstructions are simpler to cite in a standard cumulative line count, e.g., Otten's line count for the Vow of Puduḫepa adopted from StBoT 1 and used, e.g., in our *laman* article. Following the text references appears information about text type, date, and published studies.

Suspect readings are indicated *-ta*(sic)-, emended readings *-ga*!-, and collations *-ga*(coll.)-. Unpublished texts derived from published references are noted, e.g., Bo 3348 i 6 (StBoT 15:24). Those with no annotation should be assumed to come from transliterations made by or entrusted to Güterbock with authorization to use them in his personal research and publication. Such unpublished texts have been cited only when important information which they provide is not obtainable to our knowledge from a published source.

Transliteration follows the conventions of Hittitology, which in turn were derived from Assyriology. We have tried to avoid a faddish striving to incorporate the very latest values proposed for Sumerian words. Like the CAD, we do not hesitate to use what might look like an outmoded writing of these words. Since this is not a Sumerian dictionary, we have had as our primary concern the unambiguous representation in transliteration and transcription of the actual signs which occur on the Hittite tablets. Our second consideration is the obvious value of using writings familiar to Hittitology itself. We do not wish to make it difficult to correlate earlier editions of Hittite texts with our dictionary renderings. For all these reasons we have kept our adjustments and innovations to a bare minimum. We wish to avoid the subscript x-values. Therefore, since Borger (*Assyrisch-babylonische Zeichenliste*, AOAT 33, 1978) gives a numbered value for EN×GÁNA (BURU$_{14}$), and for GEŠTIN as a Hittite syllabic sign (*wi*$_{5}$), we have adopted these. We have also followed him in reading ^{GIŠ}KIRI$_{6}$ for GIŠ.SAR, and ^{LÚ}SAGI(.A) for ^{LÚ}QA.ŠU.DU$_{8}$(.A). We have retained SAL in preference to MUNUS since it is so frequent, and we prefer a shorter form to conserve space. Because we use Arabic, not Roman numerals, we have avoided ^{d}X and ^{d}XXX for the Stormgod and Moongod. And since ^{d}U and ^{d}*SIN* are familiar writings in our discipline, we have decided to continue to use them rather than the unfamiliar ^{d}10 and ^{d}30. Hittitologists understand that these signs are conventional designations for Stormgod and Moongod and do not pretend to identify the deities with Adad or Sin. Since we will never read the other Moongod designation ^{d}EN.ZU as ^{d}*SIN*, no confusion is likely to arise. Unfortunately, Borger did not assign index numbers to the "ZU" value of the sign KA×UD, the "LI" value of LIŠ, the "D/TAN" value of DIN, the "SUR" value of SAG (in SAG.DÙ.A^{MUŠEN}), or the "UḪ" value of U+KAK at Boğazköy. Götze (NBr 14) was of the opinion that the U+KAK sign derived from the same prototype as the sign normally used for *aḫ/iḫ/uḫ* in Hittite texts, but that its different shape was preserved for the logographic representation of *alwanzatar* "sorcery". Indeed the lexical entry [*ú-uḫ*] [AḪ] = [*ki-iš-pu*] = (Hitt.) *al-wa-an-za-tar* S^{a} Voc. B 8′ is cited in CAD K 454. But the AḪ (number one) sign confidently restored is not preserved for us to observe its shape. The usual Sumerogram for Akkadian *kišpū* is UḪ$_{4}$ (KA×BAD). Although

U+KAK is probably a variant shape of AḪ/UḪ (number one), we have chosen to assign it the value UḪ$_x$ to avoid confusing it with the regular shape of UḪ (number one). We realize that such orthographic decisions are in large measure arbitrary and make no claim that our procedures are "better" than those adopted by others. We wish to avoid confusion, however, by stating at the outset what our symbols mean.

We express our appreciation to the curators and directors of the archaeological museums whose Hittite tablets we have been allowed to collate and photograph: Raci Temizer (Ankara), Necati Dolunay, Aykut Özet, Veysel Donbaz and Fatma Yıldız (Istanbul), Liane Jakob-Rost and Horst Klengel (Berlin), Edmund Sollberger (London), Pierre Amiet (Paris), W. W. Hallo (Yale University, New Haven), Erle Leichty and Åke Sjöberg (University of Pennsylvania, Philadelphia), and J. A. Brinkman (Oriental Institute, Chicago). We also remember the kindnesses extended to us by the late R. Meyer (Berlin) and Nezih Fıratlı (Istanbul).

We are indebted to E. Laroche, who as our outside consultant read and commented upon a number of articles, although ill health prevented him from as extensive an involvement in the work as he and we had hoped for.

To the University of Chicago and its president, Hanna H. Gray, and to the Oriental Institute and its director, John A. Brinkman, who provided partial financial support and a wide variety of services and resources which furthered our work, we express our thanks.

Graduate student assistants with a Hittitological concentration who gave a great deal of assistance were Richard Beal, Barbara Knowles, and George Moore. Other graduate student assistants over the past three years were Terence Ahern, Elizabeth Bailey, Cynthia Bates, Woodford Beach, Robert Englund, Alice Figundio, Ronald Gorny, Susan Griffin, John Leavitt, John McDonald, John Mooney, Mark Osgood, Mitchell Reep, Margaret Rogers, Jo Ann Scurlock, and Paul Zimansky.

Especially to the National Endowment for the Humanities, its former director Mr. Ronald Berman, and its present director Mr. Joseph Duffey, we are grateful for generous financial support in the form of a three-year initial grant. Under this grant we were able to supplement the main lexical file and to produce the first fascicle of this volume.

The Editors
October, 1979

PROVISIONAL LIST OF ABBREVIATIONS

1. Texts, Authors, Literature

A	lexical series á A = *nâqu*
AAA	Annals of Archaeology and Anthropology — Liverpool
AASF	Annales Academiae Scientiarum Fennicae
AASOR	Annual of the American School of Oriental Research — Cambridge, Massachusetts
ABAW	Abhandlungen der Bayerischen Akademie der Wissenschaften (numbers refer to Philosophisch-historische Abteilung)
ABoT	Ankara Arkeoloji Müzesinde bulunan Boğazköy Tabletleri — Istanbul 1948
ACh	C. Virolleaud, L'astrologie chaldéene — Paris 1908
ACME	Annali della Facoltà di Filosofia e Lettere dell'Università Statale di Milano
AfK	Archiv für Keilschriftforschung
AfO	Archiv für Orientforschung
AHw	W. von Soden, Akkadisches Handwörterbuch
Ai	lexical series ki.KI.KAL.bi.šè = *ana ittišu* (MSL 1)
AION	Annali dell'Instituto Universitario Orientale di Napoli
AJA	American Journal of Archaeology
AJPh	American Journal of Philology
AJSL	American Journal of Semitic Languages and Literatures
Akurgal	E. Akurgal, The Art of the Hittites — London 1962
Alakš.	Treaty of Muwatalli with Alakšandu, ed. SV 2:42-102
AlHeth	H. A. Hoffner, Jr., Alimenta Hethaeorum (AOS 55) — New Haven 1974
Alp, Beamt.	S. Alp, Untersuchungen zu den Beamtennamen im hethitischen Festzeremoniell — Leipzig 1940
—— Siegel	—— Zylinder- und Stempelsiegel aus Karahöyük bei Konya (TTKYayın 26) — Ankara 1968
AM	A. Götze, Die Annalen des Muršiliš (MVAeG 38) — Leipzig 1933
AMAVY	Anadolu Medeniyetlerini Araştırma Vakfı Yayınları — Ankara
An	lexical series An = *Anum*
An.	Ankara Museum, inventory numbers of tablets
Anadolu	Anadolu. Revue des études d'archéologie et d'histoire en Turquie — Paris
Anadolu/ Anatolia	Anadolu/Anatolia. Journal of the Institute for Research in Near Eastern and Mediterranean Civilizations of the Faculty of Letters of the University of Ankara — Ankara
Anatolica	Anatolica (Institut historique et archéologique néerlandais à Istanbul) — Leiden
AnDergi	Ankara Üniversitesi Dil ve Tarih-Coğrafya Fakültesi Dergisi
ANEP	J. B. Pritchard, ed., Ancient Near Eastern Pictures Relating to the Old Testament, 2nd ed., with suppl. — Princeton 1969
ANET	J. B. Pritchard, ed., Ancient Near Eastern Texts Relating to the Old Testament, 3rd ed., with suppl. — Princeton 1969 (Hittite texts tr. A. Goetze)
AnOr	Analecta Orientalia — Rome
AnSt	Anatolian Studies (Journal of the British Institute of Archaeology at Ankara) — London
Antagal	lexical series antagal = *šaqû*
AnYayın	Ankara Üniversitesi Dil ve Tarih-Coğrafya Fakültesi Yayınları — Ankara
AO	Der Alte Orient — Leipzig
AOAT	Alter Orient und Altes Testament — Neukirchen-Vluyn
AOATS	AOAT, Sonderreihe
AOF	Altorientalische Forschungen — Berlin
AOS	American Oriental Series — New Haven
APAW	Abhandlungen der Preussischen Akademie der Wissenschaften
ArOr	Archiv Orientální
AT	D. J. Wiseman, The Alalakh Tablets (unmarked number refers to text, p. indicates page in the volume) — London 1953
A-tablet	lexical text, see MSL 13:10ff.
Athenaeum	Athenaeum — Pavia
AU	F. Sommer, Die Ahhiyavā-Urkunden (ABAW, NF 6) — Munich 1932
Bab	Babyloniaca — Paris

BagM	Baghdader Mitteilungen — Berlin
Balkan, İnandık	K. Balkan, İnandık'ta 1966 yılında bulunan eski Hitit çağına ait bir bağış belgesi (AMAVY No. 1) — Ankara 1973
BASOR	Bulletin of the American Schools of Oriental Research
BCILL	Bibliothèque des Cahiers de l'Institut de Linguistique de Louvain
BDB	F. Brown, S. R. Driver, and C. Briggs, A Hebrew and English Lexicon of the Old Testament — Oxford 1907
Bechtel, *-SK-*	G. Bechtel, Hittite Verbs in *-sk-* — Ann Arbor 1936
——	*see also* Chrest.
Beckman, Diss.	G. M. Beckman, Hittite Birth Rituals (diss., Yale University) — New Haven 1977
Bel Madg.	*Bēl Madgalti* instr., ed. Dienstanw.
Belleten	Türk Tarih Kurumu Belleten — Ankara
Berman, Diss.	H. Berman, The Stem Formation of Hittite Nouns and Adjectives (diss., University of Chicago) — Chicago 1972
Bildbeschr.	C.-G. von Brandenstein, Hethitische Götter nach Bildbeschreibungen in Keilschrifttexten (MVAeG 46.2) — Leipzig 1943
Bilgiç, App.	E. Bilgiç, Die einheimischen Appellativa der kappadokischen Texte — Ankara 1954
Bin-Nun	*see* THeth
BiOr	Bibliotheca Orientalis — Leiden
Birds	B. Bruun and A. Singer, Birds of Europe — New York 1970
Bittel, Boğazköy	K. Bittel, et al., Boğazköy, I-V — Berlin 1935, 1938, 1957, 1969, 1975
—— Yaz	—— Yazılıkaya (WVDOG 61) — Leipzig 1941 (Osnabrück 1967)
—— Yaz^2	—— Das hethitische Felsheiligtum Yazılıkaya — Berlin 1975
—— Hattusha	K. Bittel, Hattusha: Capital of the Hittites — New York 1970
—— Hethiter	—— Die Hethiter (Universum der Kunst) — Munich 1976
BM	Tablets in the collections of the British Museum
Bo	Inventory numbers of Boğazköy tablets excavated 1906-12
Bo year/...	Inventory numbers of Boğazköy tablets excavated 1968ff.
Boissier, Mant.	A. Boissier, Mantique babylonienne et mantique hittite — Paris 1935
Borger, AOAT 33	R. Borger, Assyrisch-babylonische Zeichenliste (AOAT 33) — Neukirchen-Vluyn 1978
Bossert, Heth.Kön.	H. T. Bossert, Ein hethitisches Königssiegel — Berlin 1944
BoSt	Boghazköi-Studien — Leipzig
BoTU	E. Forrer, Die Boghazköi-Texte in Umschrift (WVDOG 41/42) (unmarked numbers following BoTU refer to texts pub. in translit. in BoTU 2, pages in BoTU 1 or 2 will be indicated by p(p).) — Leipzig 1922, 1926
van Brock, Dér.Nom.L	N. van Brock, Dérivés Nominaux en L du Hittite et du Louvite (RHA XX/71, 69-168) — Paris 1962
von Brandenstein	*see* Bildbeschr.
BSL	Bulletin de la Société de Linguistique de Paris
Burde	*see* StBoT
CAD	The Assyrian Dictionary of the Oriental Institute of the University of Chicago — Chicago 1956ff.
CAH	The Cambridge Ancient History, 3rd ed. — Cambridge 1970, 1971, 1973, 1975
Carruba, Pal.	O. Carruba, Beiträge zum Palaischen (PIHANSt 31) — Istanbul 1972
—— Part.	—— Die satzeinleitenden Partikeln in den indogermanischen Sprachen Anatoliens — Rome 1969
——	*see also* StBoT
Carter, Diss.	C. Carter, Hittite Cult Inventories (diss., University of Chicago) — Chicago 1962
CCT	Cuneiform Texts from Cappadocian Tablets in the British Museum
CH	Codex Hammurabi
CHD	The Hittite Dictionary of the Oriental Institute of the University of Chicago — Chicago 1980ff.
CHM	Cahiers d'Histoire Modiale — Paris
Chrest.	E. H. Sturtevant and G. Bechtel, A Hittite Chrestomathy — Philadelphia 1935
Cor.Ling.	Corolla linguistica (FsSommer) — Wiesbaden 1955
Couvreur, Ḫ	W. C. Couvreur, De hettische Ḫ — Louvain 1937
CRRAI	Compte rendu de la . . . Recontre Assyriologique Internationale (cited by date of congress, not date of pub.)
CT	Cuneiform Texts from Babylonian Tablets in the British Museum
CTH	E. Laroche, Catalogue des textes hittites, 2nd ed. — Paris 1971
DAB	R. C. Thompson, Dictionary of Assyrian Botany — London 1949
DACG	R. C. Thompson, Dictionary of Assyrian Chemistry and Geology — Oxford 1936
Dalman	G. H. Dalman, Aramäisch-neuhebräisches Wörterbuch — Frankfurt am Main 1901
Darga, Kadın	A. M. Darga, Eski Anadolu'da Kadın — Istanbul 1976
Deimel	*see* ŠL
del Monte	*see* RGTC 6
DEP	*see* Plants

Dergi	*see* AnDergi
Diakonoff, Hurr.u.Urart.	I. M. Diakonoff, Hurrisch und Urartäisch — Munich 1971
Dienstanw.	E. von Schuler, Hethitische Dienstanweisungen für höhere Hof- und Staatsbeamte (AfO Beiheft 10) — Graz 1957
Diri	lexical series diri DIR *siāku* = (*w*)*atru*
DLL	E. Laroche, Dictionnaire de la langue louvite — Paris 1959
Dressler, Plur.	W. Dressler, Studien zur verbalen Pluralität (SÖAW 259, 1) — Vienna 1968
Drohla, Kongruenz	W. Drohla, Die Kongruenz zwischen Nomen und Attribut sowie zwischen Subjekt und Prädikat im Hethitischen — Marburg 1934 (mimeographed)
DŠ	H. G. Güterbock, The Deeds of Šuppiluliuma as Told by his Son, Muršili II (JCS 10:41ff., 59ff., 75ff.) — New Haven 1956
Dupp.	Treaty of Muršili II and Duppi-Tešub, ed. SV 1:1-48
Ea	lexical series ea A = *nâqu*
EA	J. A. Knudtzon, Die El-Amarna-Tafeln (VAB 7) (quoted by text numbers) — Leipzig 1915
EHGl	H. A. Hoffner, Jr., An English-Hittite Glossary (RHA XXV/80:1ff.) — Paris 1967
Erimḫuš	lexical series erimḫuš = *anantu*
Erimḫuš Bogh.	Boğazköy version of Erimḫuš
Erman-Grapow	A. Erman and H. Grapow, Wörterbuch der aegyptischen Sprache — Leipzig 1925-1931(-1955)
Ertem, Coğrafya	H. Ertem, Boğazköy metinlerine geçen coğrafya adları dizini — Ankara 1973
—— Fauna	—— Boğazköy metinlerine göre Hititler devri Anadolu'sunun Faunası — Ankara 1965
—— Flora	—— Boğazköy metinlerine göre Hititler devri Anadolu'sunun Florası — Ankara 1974
FHG	Fragments hittites de Genève (RA 45: 183-94; RA 46:42-50) — Paris 1951-52
Finkelstein Mem.	Essays on the Ancient Near East in Memory of Jacob Joel Finkelstein. M. Ellis, ed. (Memoirs of the Connecticut Academy of Arts and Sciences 19) — Hamden, Connecticut, 1977
Forrer	*see* BoTU, Forsch.
Forsch.	E. Forrer, Forschungen — Berlin 1926-29
Friedrich	*see* HE, HG, HKL, HW, HW 1., 2., 3. Erg., HW², SV
Friedrich-Kammenhuber	*see* HW²
Frisk	H. Frisk, Griechisches etymologisches Wörterbuch I-III — Heidelberg 1960-72
FsFriedrich	Festschrift J. Friedrich zum 65. Geburtstag gewidmet — Heidelberg 1959
FsGordon	Orient and Occident: Essays Presented to Cyrus H. Gordon (AOAT 22) — Neukirchen-Vluyn 1973
FsGüterbock	Anatolian Studies Presented to Hans Gustav Güterbock on the Occasion of his 65th Birthday (PIHANSt 33) — Istanbul 1973
FsLaroche	Florilegium Anatolicum: Mélanges offerts à Emmanuel Laroche — Paris 1979
FsMeissner	Altorientalische Studien Bruno Meissner zum 60. Geburtstag gewidmet (MAOG 4) — Leipzig 1928-29 (1972)
FsMeriggi	Studi in onore di Piero Meriggi (Athenaeum NS 47, fasc. 1-4) — Pavia 1969
FsMeriggi 2	Studia Mediterranea Piero Meriggi ottuagenario — 1980
FsOtten	Festschrift Heinrich Otten — Wiesbaden 1973
FsSalonen	StOr 46 — 1975
FsSommer	*see* Cor.Ling.
FuF	Forschungen und Fortschritte — Berlin
FWgesch.	Fischer Weltgeschichte: Die Altorientalischen Reiche — Frankfurt am Main 1965ff.
GAG	W. von Soden, Grundriss der Akkadischen Grammatik, with suppl. (AnOr 33/47) — Rome 1969
Gamkrelidze, Laryngale	T. V. Gamkrelidze, Hittite et la théorie laryngale — Tiflis 1960
Garelli, AC	P. Garelli, Les Assyriens en Cappadoce — Paris 1963
Garstang and Gurney	*see* Geogr
Gelb, Alishar	I. J. Gelb, Inscriptions from Alishar and Vicinity (OIP 27) — Chicago 1935
—— HH	—— Hittite Hieroglyphs 1-3 (SAOC 2, 14, 21) — Chicago 1931-42
—— HHM	—— Hittite Hieroglyphic Monuments (OIP 45) — Chicago 1939
Geogr	J. Garstang and O. R. Gurney, The Geography of the Hittite Empire — London 1959
Gesenius-Buhl	Hebräisches und Aramäisches Handwörterbuch
Gilg.	Gilgameš epic
Gl.Hourrite	E. Laroche, Glossaire de la langue hourrite (RHA XXXIV-XXXV) — Paris 1976-77, pub. 1978-79
Glotta	Glotta — Göttingen
Goetze, Kl	A. Goetze, Kleinasien, 2nd ed. — Munich 1957
——	*see also* AM, Ḫatt., Kizz., Madd., NBr, Pestgeb., Tunn.
Gordon, UT	C. Gordon, Ugaritic Textbook (AnOr 38) — Rome 1965

Gröndahl	F. Gröndahl, Die Personnamen der Texte aus Ugarit (Stud.Pohl 1) — Rome 1967
GsBossert	Anadolu Araştırmaları (JKF) vol. II 1-2 — Istanbul 1965
GsKretschmer	ΜΝΗΜΗΣ ΧΑΡΙΝ (mnēmēs charin): Gedenkschrift Paul Kretschmer — Vienna 1956
Güterbock	*see* DŠ, Kum., SBo, Ullik.
Gurney, AAA 27	O. R. Gurney, Hittite Prayers of Muršili II (AAA 27) — Liverpool 1941
——— Schweich	——— Some Aspects of Hittite Religion (The Schweich Lectures 1976) — Oxford 1977
———	*see also* Geogr
Gusmani, Lessico	R. Gusmani, Il lessico ittito — Naples 1968
——— Lyd.Wb.	——— Lydisches Wörterbuch — Heidelberg 1964
Haas, KN	V. Haas, Der Kult von Nerik (Stud.Pohl 4) — Rome 1970
Haas-Wilhelm, AOATS 3	V. Haas and G. Wilhelm, Hurritische und luwische Riten aus Kizzuwatna (AOATS 3) — Neukirchen-Vluyn 1974
HAB	F. Sommer und A. Falkenstein, Die Hethitisch-akkadische Bilingue des Ḫattušili I (ABAW, NF 16) — Munich 1938
Hahn, Naming	E. A. Hahn, Naming Constructions in Some Indo-European Languages (Philological Monographs of the American Philological Association 27) — Cleveland 1969
Ḫatt	A. Götze, Ḫattušiliš. Der Bericht über seine Thronbesteigung nebst den Paralleltexten (MVAG 29.3) — Leipzig 1925; Ḫatt. also abbreviates Apology of Ḫattušili III, cited by col. and line in Ḫatt., NBr, or Chrest. (Ḫatt. also abbreviates the royal name Ḫattušili, always followed by I, II, or III).
HbOr	Handbuch der Orientalistik (esp. Altkleinasiatische Sprachen) — Leiden
HE	J. Friedrich, Hethitisches Elementarbuch, 2nd ed. — Heidelberg, HE 1 1960, HE 2 1967
Heinhold-Krahmer	*see* THeth
Held, Rel.Sent.	W. H. Held, Jr., The Hittite Relative Sentence (Lg.Diss. no. 55; Lg. 33.4 part 2 suppl.) — Baltimore 1957
Hethitica	G. Jucquois et al., eds., Hethitica: vol. 1 (Travaux de la Faculté de Philosophie et Lettres de l'Université Catholique de Louvain); vol. 2 (BCILL 7); vol. 3 (BCILL 15)
Heth.u.Idg.	E. Neu and W. Meid, eds., Hethitisch und Indogermanisch: Vergleichende Studien zur historischen Grammatik und zur dialektgeographischen Stellung der indogermanischen Sprachgruppe Altkleinasiens — Innsbruck 1979
Heubeck, Lydiaka	A. Heubeck, Lydiaka. Untersuchungen zu Schrift, Sprache und Götternamen der Lyder — Erlangen 1959
——— Lyd	——— Lydisch (HbOr I.2.1/2.2, pp. 397-427) — Leiden 1969
Ḫg.	lexical series ḪAR.gud = *imrû* = *ballu* (MSL 5-11)
HG	J. Friedrich, Die hethitischen Gesetze — Leiden 1959, 2nd ed. 1971
Ḫḫ.	lexical series ḪAR.ra = *ḫubullu* (MSL 5-10)
HHB	H.-S. Schuster, Die hattisch-hethitischen Bilinguen I/1 — Leiden 1974
HHT	K. Riemschneider, Hurritische und hethitische Texte — Munich 1974 (mimeographed)
Hipp.heth.	A. Kammenhuber, Hippologia hethitica — Wiesbaden 1961
HKL	J. Friedrich, Hethitisches Keilschrift-Lesebuch 1, 2 — Heidelberg 1960
Hoffner	*see* AlHeth, EHGl
Houwink ten Cate	*see* Records
Hrozný, CH	B. Hrozný, Code Hittite provenant de l'Asie Mineure, I. — Paris 1922
——— HKT	——— Hethitische Keilschrifttexte aus Boghazköi in Umschrift, Übersetzung und Kommentar (BoSt 3) — Leipzig 1919
——— IHH	——— Les Inscriptions Hittites Hiéroglyphiques 1-3 — Prague 1933-37
——— SH	——— Die Sprache der Hethiter (BoSt 1-2) — Leipzig 1917
——— VSpr	——— Über die Völker und Sprachen des alten Chatti-Landes (BoSt 5) — Leipzig 1920
HSM	Harvard Semitic Museum, inventory number
HT	Hittite Texts in the Cuneiform Character in the British Museum — London 1920
HTR	H. Otten, Hethitische Totenrituale (VIO 37) — Berlin 1958
HUCA	Hebrew Union College Annual
Ḫuqq.	The Treaty of Šuppiluliuma with Ḫuqqana, ed. SV 2:103-63
HW	J. Friedrich, Hethitisches Wörterbuch — Heidelberg 1952(-54)
HW 1., 2., 3. Erg.	J. Friedrich, Hethitisches Wörterbuch 1.-3. Ergänzungsheft — Heidelberg 1957, 1961, 1966
HW^2	J. Friedrich and A. Kammenhuber, Hethitisches Wörterbuch, 2nd ed. —

	Heidelberg 1975ff.
IAK	Die Inschriften der altassyrischen Könige, ed. E. Ebeling, B. Meissner and E. F. Weidner — Leipzig 1926
IBoT	Istanbul Arkeoloji Müzelerinde Bulunan Boğazköy Tabletleri(nden Seçme Metinler) I-III — Istanbul 1944, 1947, 1954
Idg.Bibl.	Indogermanische Bibliothek
Idg.Gr.	Indogermanische Grammatik — Heidelberg 1968ff.
Idu	lexical series Á = *idu*
IEJ	Israel Exploration Journal — Jerusalem
IF	Indogermanische Forschungen
Igituḫ	lexical series igituḫ = *tāmartu*; Igituḫ short version, Landsberger-Gurney, AfO 18:81ff.
IM	Istanbuler Mitteilungen — Berlin
Imparati, Leggi	F. Imparati, Le leggi ittite — Rome 1964
Izi	lexical series izi = *išātu* (MSL 13:154-226)
Izi Bogh.	Boğazköy version of Izi (MSL 13:132-47)
JA	Journal asiatique — Paris
Jakob-Rost, Familienzwist	L. Jakob-Rost, Ein hethitisches Ritual gegen Familienzwist (MIO 1:345-79) — Berlin 1953
——	*see also* Mašt., THeth
JAOS	Journal of the American Oriental Society — New Haven
Jastrow	M. Jastrow, A Dictionary of the Targumim ... — London 1903
JBL	Journal of Biblical Literature
JCS	Journal of Cuneiform Studies
JEOL	Jaarbericht van het Vooraziatisch-Egyptisch Genootschap (earlier Gezelschap) "Ex Oriente Lux" — Leiden
JKF	Jahrbuch für kleinasiatische Forschungen — Heidelberg, Istanbul
Josephson, Part.	F. Josephson, The Function of Sentence Particles in Old and Middle Hittite (Acta Universitatis Upsaliensis. Studia Indoeuropea Upsaliensia) — Uppsala 1972
JNES	Journal of Near Eastern Studies
JRAS	Journal of the Royal Asiatic Society of Great Britain and Ireland
JSOR	Journal of the Society of Oriental Research — Chicago
Kagal	lexical series kagal = *abullu* (MSL 13)
Kammenhuber, HbOr	A. Kammenhuber, Hethitisch, Palaisch, Luwisch, und Hieroglyphenluwisch (HbOr I.2.1/2.2, pp. 119-357, 428-546) — Leiden 1969
—— HbOr Ind	—— Hethitisch, Palaisch, Luwisch, Hieroglyphenluwisch und Hattisch: Altkleinasiatische Indices zum Handbuch der Orientalistik (MSS, Beiheft 4) — 1969
—— Materialien	—— Materialien zu einem hethitischen Thesaurus — Heidelberg 1973ff.
—— MIO 2-4	—— Studien zum hethitischen Infinitivsystem I-IV (MIO 2:44-77, 245-65, 403-44; MIO 3:31-57, 345-77; MIO 4:40-80) — Berlin 1954-56
——	*see also* Hipp.heth., THeth, HW^2
Kaškäer	E. von Schuler, Die Kaškäer — Berlin 1965
KBo	Keilschrifttexte aus Boghazköi
Kikk.	Kikkuli text, ed. Kammenhuber, Hipp. heth. pp. 54-147
King	*see* HT, STC
Kizz.	A. Goetze, Kizzuwatna and the Problem of Hittite Geography — New Haven 1940
Klengel, Gesch.Syr.	H. Klengel, Die Geschichte Syriens im 2. Jahrtausend — Berlin 1965, 1969, 1970
KlF	Kleinasiatische Forschungen, ed. F. Sommer and H. Ehelolf, vol. 1 — Weimar (1927-)1930
KlPauly	Der kleine Pauly: Lexikon der Antike — Stuttgart 1964ff.
König	F. W. König, Handbuch der chaldischen Inschriften (AfO Beiheft 8) — Graz 1955-57
Kronasser, EHS	H. Kronasser, Etymologie der hethitischen Sprache I (fasc. 1-4), II (fasc. 5/6) — Wiesbaden 1963-65, 1966
——	*see also* Schw.Gotth.
KUB	Keilschrifturkunden aus Boghazköi
Kühne	*see* StBoT
Kum.	H. G. Güterbock, Kumarbi. Mythen vom churritischen Kronos (Istanbuler Schriften 16) — Zürich-New York 1946
Kümmel	*see* StBoT
Kup.	Treaty of Muršili II with Kupanta-^{d}KAL, ed. SV 1:95-181
Kupper, Nomades	J.-R. Kupper, Les nomades en Mésopotamie au temps des rois de Mari — Paris 1957
KZ	Zeitschrift für Vergleichende Sprachforschung ("Kuhns Zeitschrift") — Göttingen
Labat	R. Labat, Manuel d'Epigraphie Akkadienne (numbers refer to sign number, not page) — Paris 1976
—— AkkBo	—— L'Akkadien de Boghaz-Köi — Bordeaux 1932
Landsberger, Fauna	B. Landsberger, Die Fauna des alten Mesopotamien nach der 14. Tafel der ḪAR.RA = *ḫubullu* — Leipzig 1934
Lanu	lexical series alam = *lānu*
Laroche, HH	E. Laroche, Les hiéroglyphes hittites I (unmarked number following "Laroche" refers to sign) — Paris 1960

—— Myth.	—— Textes mythologiques hittites en transcription (RHA XXIII/77, XXVI/82) — Paris 1965, 1968
—— prière hittite	—— La prière hittite: vocabulaire et typologie (École pratique des Hautes Études, V^{e} section, Sciences Religieuses; Annuaire, tome 72) — Paris 1964/1965
—— Rech.	—— Recherches sur les noms des dieux hittites (RHA VII/46) — Paris 1947
——	*see also* CTH, DLL, Gl.Hourrite, NH
Lebrun, Samuha	R. Lebrun, Samuha, foyer religieux de de l'empire hittite (Publications de l'institut orientaliste de Louvain 11) — Louvain-la-neuve 1976
Leichty, Izbu	E. Leichty, The Omen Series Šumma Izbu (TCS 4) — Locust Valley, New York 1970
Lex.Aeg.	W. Helck and E. Otto, Lexikon der Aegyptologie — Wiesbaden 1975ff.
Lg.	Language. Journal of the Linguistic Society of America
Lg.Diss.	Language Dissertations — Baltimore
Liddell-Scott	H. Liddell and R. Scott, A Greek-English Lexicon — Oxford 1925-40(-68)
Löw, Flora	I. Löw, Die Flora der Juden — Vienna and Leipzig 1926-34
LS	K. Riemschneider, Die hethitischen Landschenkungsurkunden (MIO 6:321-81) — Berlin 1958
LSS	Leipziger semitische Studien
LTU	H. Otten, Luvische Texte in Umschrift (VIO 17) — Berlin 1953
Lu	lexical series lú = *ša* (MSL 12:87-147)
Madd.	A. Götze, Madduwattaš (MVAeG 32.1) — Leipzig 1928
Man.	Treaty of Muršili II with Manapa-^{d}U, ed. SV 2:1-41
MAOG	Mitteilungen der Altorientalischen Gesellschaft
Mašt.	Ritual of Maštigga against family quarrels (CTH 404); 2Mašt. cited according to the edition of L. Rost, MIO 1 (1953) 348-67
MAW	S. Kramer, ed., Mythologies of the Ancient World — Garden City, New York 1961
MDOG	Mitteilungen der Deutschen Orient-Gesellschaft zu Berlin
Melchert, Diss.	H. C. Melchert, Ablative and Instrumental in Hittite (diss., Harvard University) — Cambridge, Massachusetts 1977
Meriggi, HhGl	P. Meriggi, Hieroglyphisch-hethitisches Glossar, 2nd ed. — Wiesbaden 1962
—— Manuale	—— Manuale di eteo geroglifico I, II — Rome 1966-1975
MIO	Mitteilungen des Instituts für Orientforschung — Berlin
MRS	Mission de Ras Shamra — Paris
MSL	B. Landsberger et al., Materialien zum sumerischen Lexikon — Rome
MSS	Münchener Studien zur Sprachwissenschaft
MVAeG	Mitteilungen der Vorderasiatisch-ägyptischen Gesellschaft — Leipzig
MVAG	Mitteilungen der Vorderasiatischen Gesellschaft — Leipzig
Nabnitu	lexical series SIG_7+ALAM = *nabnītu*
NBC	Nies Babylonian Collection, Yale University
NBr	A. Götze, Neue Bruchstücke zum grossen Text des Hattušiliš und den Paralleltexten (MVAeG 34.2) — Leipzig 1930
Neu	*see* StBoT, Heth.u.Idg.
Neumann, Weiterleben	G. Neumann, Untersuchungen zum Weiterleben hethitischen und luwischen Sprachgutes in hellenistischer und römischer Zeit — Wiesbaden 1961
NF	Neue Folge
NH	E. Laroche, Les Noms des Hittites — Paris 1966
NHF	Neuere Hethiterforschung, ed. G. Walser (Historia Einzelschriften 7) — Wiesbaden 1964
Nigga	lexical series nigga = *makkūru* (MSL 13:91-124)
NPN	I. J. Gelb, P. A. Purves, A. A. MacRae, Nuzi Personal Names (OIP 57) — Chicago 1943
NS	Nova Series
NTS	Norsk Tidskrift for Sprogvidenskap — Oslo
OA	Oriens Antiquus — Rome
OED	The Compact Edition of the Oxford English Dictionary — Oxford 1971
Oettinger, Stammbildung	Norbert Oettinger, Die Stammbildung des hethitischen Verbums (Erlanger Beiträge zur Sprach- und Kunstwissenschaft, Band 64) — Nürnberg 1979
——	*see also* StBoT
OIP	Oriental Institute Publications — Chicago
OLZ	Orientalistische Literaturzeitung — Berlin
Oppenheim, Dreams	A. L. Oppenheim, The Interpretation of Dreams in the Ancient Near East (TAPS, NS 46.3) — Philadelphia 1956
Or	Orientalia — Rome
Oriens	Oriens. Journal of the International Society for Oriental Research — Leiden
OrS	Orientalia Suecana — Uppsala
Ose, Sup.	F. Ose, Supinum and Infinitiv im Hethitischen (MVAeG 47.1) — Leipzig 1944
OT	Old Testament

Otten, Luv.	H. Otten, Zur grammatikalischen und lexikalischen Bestimmung des Luvischen (VIO 19) — Berlin 1953
—— MGK	—— Mythen vom Gotte Kumarbi (VIO 3) — Berlin 1950
—— Puduḫepa	—— Puduḫepa: Eine hethitische Königin in ihren Textzeugnissen (Akademie der Wissenschaften und der Literatur, Abh. Geistes- u. Sozialw. Kl. 1975:1) — Mainz 1975
—— Tel.	—— Die Überlieferungen des Telipinu-Mythus (MVAeG 46.1) — Leipzig 1942
——	*see also* HTR, LTU, StBoT
Pap.	F. Sommer and H. Ehelolf, Das hethitische Ritual das Papanikri von Komana (BoSt 10) — Leipzig 1924
PD	E. Weidner, Politische Dokumente aus Kleinasien (BoSt 8-9) — Leipzig 1923 (1968)
Pestgeb.	A. Götze, Die Pestgebete des Muršiliš (KlF 1:161-251) — Weimar 1930
PIHANSt	Publications de l'Institut historique et archéologique néerlandais de Stamboul
Plants	J. C. Uphoff, Dictionary of Economic Plants — Lehre 1968
Pokorny	J. Pokorny, Indogermanisches etymologisches Wörterbuch — Bern-Munich 1959, 1965-69
Potratz	H. A. Potratz, Das Pferd in der Frühzeit — Rostock 1938
Practical Vocabulary Assur	lexical text (Landsberger-Gurney, AfO 18:328ff.)
Proto-Diri	*see* Diri
Proto-Ea	*see* Ea (MSL 2:35-94)
Proto-Izi	lexical series (MSL 13:7-59)
Proto-Kagal	lexical series (MSL 13:63-88)
Proto-Lu	lexical series (MSL 12:25-84)
PRU	Le palais royal d'Ugarit (subseries of MRS) — Paris 1955ff.
RA	Revue d'Assyriologie et d'Archeologie orientale
RAI	*see* CRRAI
Records	P. H. J. Houwink ten Cate, The Records of the Early Hittite Empire (C. 1450-1380 B.C.) (PIHANSt 26) — Leiden 1970
RGTC 6	G. F. del Monte and J. Tischler, Répertoire Géographique des Textes Cunéiformes, vol. 6 — Wiesbaden 1978
RHA	Revue hittite et asianique
RHR	Revue de l'histoire des religions
RIDA	Revue internationale des droits de l'antiquité, 3rd series
Riedel	W. Riedel, Bemerkungen zu den hethitischen Keilschrifttafeln aus Boghazköi — Stockholm 1949 (mimeographed)
Riemschneider, Omentexte	K. Riemschneider, Die hethitischen und akkadischen Omentexte aus Boğazköy (unpub. ms. in Oriental Institute)
——	*see also* HHT, LS, StBoT
RLA	Reallexikon der Assyriologie — Berlin
Rosenkranz, Luv.	B. Rosenkranz, Beiträge zur Erforschung des Luvischen — Wiesbaden 1952
Rost	*see* Jakob-Rost
RS	Ras Shamra Text, inventory number
RSO	Rivista degli Studi Orientali — Rome
Rüster	*see* StBoT
S^a	lexical series Syllabary A (MSL 3:3-45)
S^a Voc.	lexical series Syllabary A Vocabulary (MSL 3:51-87)
Salonen, Agric.	A. Salonen, Agricultura Mesopotamica nach sumerisch-akkadischen Quellen (Annales Academiae Scientiarum Fennicae B 149) — Helsinki 1968
SAOC	Studies in Ancient Oriental Civilization — Chicago
S^b	lexical series Syllabary B (MSL 3:96-128, 132-53)
SBo	H. G. Güterbock, Siegel aus Boğazköy I, II (AfO Beiheft 5, 7) — Berlin 1940, 1942 (1967)
von Schuler	*see* Dienstanw., Kaškäer
Schuster	*see* HHB
Schw.Gotth.	H. Kronasser, Die Umsiedlung der schwarzen Gottheit: das hethitische Ritual KUB 29.4 (SÖAW 241.3) — Vienna 1963
SCO	Studi Classici e Orientali — Pisa
Siegelová	*see* StBoT
Silbenvokabular	lexical series
Singer, Diss.	I. Singer, The Hittite KI.LAM Festival (diss., University of Tel Aviv) — Tel Aviv 1978
ŠL	A. Deimel, Šumerisches Lexikon — Rome 1925-50
SMEA	Studi micenei ed egeo-anatolici — Rome
SÖAW	Sitzungsberichte der österreichischen Akademie der Wissenschaft (numbers refer to Philosophisch-historische Klasse Sitzungsberichte) — Vienna
von Soden	*see* AHw, GAG, StBoT
von Soden-Röllig, Syll.	W. von Soden and W. Röllig, Das akkadische Syllabar, 2nd ed. with suppl. (AnOr 42/42a) — Rome 1967, 1976
Sommer, AS	F. Sommer, Ahhijavāfrage und Sprachwissenschaft (ABAW, NF 9) — Munich 1934
—— Heth.	—— Hethitisches 1, 2 (BoSt 4, 7) — Leipzig 1920, 1922
—— HuH	—— Hethiter und Hethitisch — Stuttgart 1947

——	*see also* AU
Sommer-Ehelolf	*see* Pap.
Sommer-Falkenstein	*see* HAB
Souček	*see* StBoT
SPAW	Sitzungsberichte der Preussischen Akademie der Wissenschaften — Berlin
Speiser, Intr.	E. A. Speiser, Introduction to Hurrian (AASOR 20) — New Haven 1941
Starke	*see* StBoT
StBoT	Studien zu den Boğazköy Texten — Wiesbaden
—— 1	H. Otten and V. Souček, Das Gelübde der Königin Puduḫepa an die Götten Lelwani — 1965
—— 2	O. Carruba, Das Beschwörungsritual für die Göttin Wišurijanza — 1966
—— 3	H. M. Kümmel, Ersatzrituale für den hethitischen König — 1967
—— 4	R. Werner, Hethitische Gerichtsprotokolle — 1967
—— 5	E. Neu, Interpretation der hethitischen mediopassiven Verbalformen — 1968
—— 6	E. Neu, Das hethitische Mediopassiv und seine indogermanischen Grundlagen — 1968
—— 7	H. Otten and W. von Soden, Das akkadisch-hethitische Vokabular KBo 1.44 + KBo 23.1 — 1968
—— 8	H. Otten and V. Souček, Ein althethitisches Ritual für das Königspaar — 1969
—— 9	K. K. Riemschneider, Babylonische Geburtsomina in hethitscher Übersetzung — 1970
—— 10	O. Carruba, Das Palaische: Texte, Grammatik, Lexikon — 1970
—— 11	H. Otten, Sprachliche Stellung und Datierung des Madduwatta-Textes — 1969
—— 12	E. Neu, Ein althethitisches Gewitterritual — 1970
—— 13	H. Otten, Ein hethitisches Festritual (KBo 19.128) — 1971
—— 14	J. Siegelová, Appu-Märchen und Hedammu-Mythus — 1971
—— 15	H. Otten, Materialien zum hethitischen Lexikon — 1971
—— 16	C. Kühne and H. Otten, Der Šaušgamuwa-Vertrag — 1971
—— 17	H. Otten, Eine althethitische Erzählung um die Stadt Zalpa — 1973
—— 18	E. Neu, Der Anitta-Text — 1974
—— 19	C. Burde, Hethitische medizinsche Texte — 1974
—— 20	C. Rüster, Hethitische Keilschrift-Paläographie — 1972
—— 21	E. Neu and C. Rüster, Hethitische Keilschrift-Paläographie II — 1975
—— 22	N. Oettinger, Die Militärischen Eide der Hethiter — 1976
—— 23	F. Starke, Die Funktionen der dimensionalen Kasus und Adverbien im Althethitischen — 1977
STC	L. W. King, The Seven Tablets of Creation — London 1902
StOr	Studia Orientalia (Societas Orientalis Fennica)
Stud.Pohl	Studia Pohl — Rome
Sturtevant, CGr	E. H. Sturtevant, A Comparative Grammar of the Hittite Language — Philadelphia 1933; 2nd ed., vol. 1 — New Haven 1951
—— Gl.	—— A Hittite Glossary, 2nd ed. — Philadelphia 1936
—— Suppl.	—— Supplement to A Hittite Glossary — Philadelphia 1939
——	*see also* Chrest.
SV	J. Friedrich, Staatsverträge des Hatti-Reiches in hethitischer Sprache (MVAeG 31.1, 34.1) — Leipzig 1926, 1930
Symb.Hrozný	Symbolae Hrozný. Symbolae ad studia Orientis pertinentes Fr. Hrozný dedicatae (ArOr 17-18) — Prague 1941-50
Symb.Koschaker	Symbolae Koschaker, Symbolae ad iura Orientis Antiqui pertinentes P. Koschaker dedicatae — Leiden 1939
Szabó	*see* THeth
TAD	Türk Arkeoloji Dergisi — Ankara
TAPA	Transactions of the American Philological Association
TAPS	Transactions of the American Philosophical Society — Philadelphia
Targ.	Treaty of Muršili II with Targašnalli, ed. SV 1:51-94
Taw.	Tawagalawa letter, ed. AU
TCL	Musée du Louvre Département des Antiquités Orientales; Textes Cunéiformes — Paris
TCS	Texts from Cuneiform Sources, ed. A. L. Oppenheim — Locust Valley, New York
Tel Aviv	Tel Aviv. Journal of the Tel Aviv University Institute of Archaeology — Tel Aviv
Tel.pr.	Telipinu proclamation
Tel.myth	Telipinu myth
THeth	Texte der Hethiter — Heidelberg
—— 1	G. Szabó, Ein hethitisches Entsühnungsritual für das Königspaar Tuthaliia und Nikalmati — 1971
—— 2	L. Jakob-Rost, Das Ritual der Malli aus Arzawa gegen Behexung (KUB 24.9 +) — 1972
—— 3, 4	A. Ünal, Hattušili III, Part 1: Hattušili

	bis zu seiner Thronbesteigung; vol. I: Historischer Abriss (THeth 3); vol. II: Quellen (THeth 4) — 1973
—— 5	S. Bin-Nun, The Tawananna in the Hittite Kingdom — 1975
—— 6	A. Kammenhuber, Orakelpraxis, Träume und Vorzeichenschau bei den Hethitern — 1976
—— 7	S. Heinhold-Krahmer, Arzawa: Untersuchungen zu seiner Geschichte nach den hethitischen Quellen — 1977
TTAED	Türk Tarih, Arkeologya ve Etnografya Dergisi — Istanbul
TTK	Türk Tarih Kurumu
TTKYayın	Türk Tarih Kurumu Yayınları — Ankara
Tunn.	A. Goetze, The Hittite Ritual of Tunnawi (AOS 14) — New Haven 1938
UF	Ugarit-Forschungen — Neukirchen-Vluyn
Ugar.	Ugaritica — Paris
Ugumu	lexical series (MSL 9:51-65)
Ugumu Bil.	lexical series (MSL 9:67-73)
Ullik.	H. G. Güterbock, The Song of Ullikummi. Revised Text of the Hittite Version of a Hurrian Myth (JCS 5:135-61; 6:8-42) — New Haven 1961-62
Ullik.	Ullikummi myth
Ünal	*see* THeth
Uruanna	pharmaceutical series uruanna = *maš-takal*
VAB	Vorderasiatische Bibliothek — Leipzig
VAT	Inventory numbers of tablets in the Staatliche Museen in Berlin
VBoT	Verstreute Boghazköi-Texte, ed. A. Götze — Marburg 1930
Ventris, Docs.	M. Ventris and I. Chadwick, Documents in Mycenaean Greek — Cambridge 1966
VIO	Veröffentlichungen des Instituts für Orientforschung der Deutsche Akademie Wissenschaften — Berlin
VS	Vorderasiatische Schriftdenkmäler der Staatlichen Museen zu Berlin
Walther, HC	A. Walther, The Hittite Code (J. M. Powis Smith, The Origin and History of Hebrew Law, App. IV) — Chicago 1931
Watkins, IESt	C. Watkins, Indo-European Studies, Special Report to NSF, Report HARV-LING-01-72, Dept. of Linguistics, Harvard University — Cambridge, Massachusetts 1972
—— IESt II	—— Indo-European Studies II, Report HARV-LING-02-75, Dept. of Linguistics, Harvard University — Cambridge, Massachusetts 1975
—— Idg.Gr	—— Idg.Gr 3.1 Formenlehre. Geschichte der indogermanischen Verbalflexion — Heidelberg 1969
Wb.Myth.	Wörterbuch der Mythologie, ed. H. W. Haussig — Stuttgart (1962-)1965
Webster	Webster's New International Dictionary of the English Language, 2nd ed. unabridged — Springfield, Massachusetts 1934
Weidner, Studien	E. Weidner, Studien zur hethitischen Sprachwissenschaft (LSS 7:1/2) — 1917
——	*see also* PD
Werner	*see* StBoT
West, Encycl.	G. P. West, ed., Encyclopedia of Animal Care, 12th ed. — Baltimore 1977
WO	Die Welt des Orient — Göttingen
WVDOG	Wissenschaftliche Veröffentlichungen der Deutschen Orient-Gesellschaft
WZKM	Wiener Zeitschrift für die Kunde des Morgenlandes
YBC	Tablets in the Yale Babylonian Collection
YOS	Yale Oriental Series, Babylonian Texts — New Haven
YOSR	Yale Oriental Series, Researches — New Haven
ZA	Zeitschrift für Assyriologie und verwandte Gebiete
ZDMG	Zeitschrift der Deutschen Morgenländischen Gesellschaft
Zimmern-Friedrich, HGes	H. Zimmern and J. Friedrich, Hethitische Gesetze aus dem Staatsarchiv von Boghazköi (AO 23.2) — Leipzig 1922
Zuntz, Ortsadv.	L. Zuntz, Die hethitischen Ortsadverbien *arḫa*, *parā*, *piran* als selbständige Adverbien und in ihren Verbindung mit Nomina und Verba (diss., Munich) — Munich 1936
—— Scongiuri	—— Un testo ittito di scongiuri — Venice 1937
.../a-.../z	Inventory numbers of Boğazköy tablets excavated 1931-67

2. General

abbr.	abbreviation
abl.	ablative
acc.	accusative
act.	active
adj.	adjective
adv.	adverb
Akk.	Akkadian
all.	allative
ann.	annals
apod.	apodosis
app.	appendix
Arn.	Arnuwanda
Ašm.	Ašmunikal
astron.	astronomical

bil.	bilingual
bk.	book
Bogh.	Boghazköy
cat.	catalogue
caus.	causative
cf.	compare
chap.	chapter
chron.	chronicle
col.	column
coll.	collated
coll. W.	collation of Arnold Walther entered in his personal copies of KBo, KUB, etc.
com.	common (gender)
comp.	compound
compl.	complement(ed)
conj.	conjunction
corr.	correspond(s), corresponding, correspondence
depos.	deposition (in court)
descr.	description
det.	determinative
det. annals	detailed annals
disc.	discussion
diss.	dissertation
dittogr.	dittography
div.	division
d.-l.	dative-locative
DN	divine name
dupl(s).	duplicate(s)
dur.	durative
e.	edge
ed.	edition, edited by
e.g.	for example
eras.	erasure
erg.	ergative
Erg.	Ergänzungsheft (supplement)
esp.	especially
etc.	et cetera
ex(x).	example(s)
ext.	extispicy
f(f).	following
fasc.	fascicle
fest.	festival
frag.	fragment
Fs.	Festschrift
gen.	genitive
gloss.	glossary
GN	geographical name
gram.	grammatical
Gs.	Gedenkschrift (memorial vol.)
HAH	Harry A. Hoffner
hapax	hapax legomenon
Ḫatt.	Ḫattušili
HGG	Hans G. Güterbock
hierogl.	hieroglyph(ic)
hipp.	hippological
hist.	historical
Hitt.	Hittite
Hurr.	Hurrian
ibid.	in the same place
i.e.	that is
imp.	imperative
impers.	impersonal
incant.	incantation
incl.	including
inf.	infinitive
infl.	inflection
inscr.	inscription
inst.	instrumental
instr.	instruction(s)
interj.	interjection
interrog.	interrogative
intrans.	intransitive
inv.	inventory
invoc.	invocation
iter.	iterative
Kizz.	Kizzuwatna
l.e.	left edge
lex.	lexical
lit.	literature, literary, literally
loc.	locative
loc. cit.	in the place cited
log.	logogram, logographic
Luw.	Luwian
lw.	loan word
masc.	masculine
med.	medical
MH	Middle Hittite
mid.	middle (voice)
misc.	miscellaneous
mng.	meaning
MS	Middle Hittite Script
ms(s)	manuscript(s)
Murš.	Muršili
Muw.	Muwatalli
myth.	mythological
n.	(foot)note, noun
neut.	neuter
NH	New Hittite
no.	number
nom.	nominative
NS	New Hittite Script
obj.	object
obv.	obverse
OH	Old Hittite
op. cit.	in the work cited
opp.	opposite
OS	Old Hittite Script
p.	page
Pal.	Palaic
par.	parallel
part.	participle
pass.	passive
pl.	plural
pl. tantum	plurale tantum (plural only)
PN	personal name

poss.	possessive
postpos.	postposition
pr.	proclamation
pres.	present
pret.	preterite
prev.	preverb(s)
pron.	pronoun
prot.	protasis
pub.	published
Pud.	Puduḫepa
purif.	purification
q.v.	which see
ref(s).	reference(s)
resp.	respectively
rest.	restored
rev.	reverse
rit.	ritual
RN	royal name
rt.	right
sc.	namely
sec.	section
sg.	singular
sim.	similar
s.v.	under the word
subst.	substantive, substitution
suff.	suffix
Sum.	Sumerian
sup.	supine
Šupp.	Šuppiluliuma
suppl.	supplement(ary)
syll.	syllable, syllabically
Tel.	Telipinu
TOS	Typical Old Script
tr.	translation, translated by
trans.	transitive
translit.	transliteration, transliterated (by)
Tudḫ.	Tudḫaliya
uncert.	uncertain
undecl.	undeclined
unkn.	unknown
unpub.	unpublished
v.	verb
var(s).	variant(s)
vers(s).	version(s)
viz.	namely
voc.	vocative
vocab.	vocabulary
vol.	volume
w.	with
wr.	written
x	illegible sign
yr.	year
×	indicates an inscribed sign
o	space within a lacuna for a sign
=	duplicates, lexical texts and bilinguals
§	new paragraph
□	introduces comment in semantic section
*	unattested form
[ ]	encloses material lost in break
[( )]	encloses material restored from a duplicate
⌜ ⌝	partly broken
<>	omitted by scribal error
<<>>	to be omitted
†	all known occurrences are cited
... / ...	end of line
.../...	alternation or possibilities
⸗	marking morpheme boundaries; also used for division of transcribed Hittite or Akkadian word at the end of a printed line
	single- or double-wedge marker ("Glossenkeil"), cf. OrNS 25:113ff.

L

la-, lai- v.; **1.** to unbind, untie, detach (wool, garments), (participle:) detached (exta), **2.** to untwine (cord, rope), **3.** to take off (shoes), **4.** to unhitch (draft animals), **5.** to release (birds, animals), **6.** to release from sorcery, to free from a spell (often with *appa*), **7.** to relieve (one's mind, body parts, nature), **8.** to dispel, remove (ailments, etc.), **9.** (adverb/preverb); from OH/OS; written syll. and DU$_8$.

pres. act. sg. 1 *la-a-mi* KBo 11.1 obv. 12 (Muw.), KUB 24.14 i 2, iv 28 (NH); KBo 3.5 i (5) (NH); **sg. 2** *la-a-ši* KUB 15.11 ii 7 (NH); DU$_8$-*ši* KUB 22.35 ii 7 (NH); **sg. 3** *la-a-i* KBo 17.54 i 6 (2x) (OH or MH/MS), IBoT 1.36 i 54 (MH/MS), IBoT 2.136 iv 68 (MH/NS), KBo 3.5 iv 20, 25 (NH); KBo 13.137:8, KBo 14.133 iii 7, 8 (NH); *la-a-iz-zi* KBo 17.105 iii 21 (MH/MS); KUB 35.19 (11) (NH); *la-a-i-iz-zi* KBo 17.105 iii 19 (MH/MS); **pl. 1** *la-a-u-e-ni* KBo 11.1 obv. 3, 5, 9 (Murš.); **pl. 3** *la-a-an-zi* KBo 18.141:5 (NH), KUB 36.83 i 26, KUB 39.57 i 8 (NH), and passim in the hipp. texts (Kammenhuber, Hipp.heth. 335); *la-an-zi* KBo 17.36 iii 8, with dupl. KBo 17.33:1 (OH/OS).

pres. mid. (all NH) **sg. 3** *la-it-ta-ri* KBo 2.2 iv 37, KBo 2.6 iii 48, 65, KUB 16.58 rev. 5; *la-a-it-ta-ri* KUB 16.77 ii 65; DU$_8$-*ta-ri* KBo 2.6 i 38; DU$_8$-*a-ri* KUB 46.37 rev. 48; DU$_8$-*ri* KUB 16.41 iii 14, KUB 16.77 iii 24; DU$_8$-*da* KUB 22.31 obv.? 14, KUB 22.56 rev. 24 (DU$_8$-*da*!).

pret. act. sg. 1 *la-a-nu-un* KBo 10.2 iii 19 (OH/NS), KUB 17.27 ii 34, KUB 29.7 rev. 36 (both MH/MS), VBoT 120 i 18 (MH/NS), KBo 19.145 iii 42, 43 (NH); *la-a-ú-un* KUB 7.1 iii 20 and passim (NH) in text with many scribal errors, to be preferred is the OH dupl. KUB 43.52, which has *la-a-ú* (q.v.) in all places; **sg. 2** *la-i-iš* KUB 9.34 iii 29 (NH); **sg. 3** *la-a-it* KUB 21.8 ii 10, KUB 34.110:(8) (both NH); DU$_8$-*it* KUB 27.29 i 30, 32, KBo 12.85 ii (1), (2) (both the same tablet, MH/NS), KUB 16.55 iv 4 (!?) (NH); **pl. 1** *la-a-u-en* VBoT 120 i 17, iii 3 (MH/NS); *la-a-u-e-en* ibid. 4, KBo 19.145 iii 40 (NH); **pl. 3** *la-a-ir* KUB 43.75 obv. (17) (OH/NS), KBo 12.85 ii 7 (MH/NS), KBo 11.1 rev. 10 (Muw.); *la-a-e-er* KUB 31.101:10 (if one may ignore the fact that the scribe left no word space between *warpi* and *laer*; coll.).

pret. mid. sg. 3 *la-at-ta-at* KBo 3.8 iii 21 (NH); *la-a-at-ta-at* ibid. 21, 22, 24, 26, 27, 29, 30, 31; *la-a-ad-da-at* ibid. 25, 28, 29; **pl. 3** *la-a-an-ta-at* ibid. 23.

imp. act. sg. 2 *la-a* KUB 36.75 iii 11 (OH/MS), KUB 43.23 obv. 14 (OH/MS); *la-a-a* KBo 11.14 ii 16, 18 (MH/MS); *la-a-i* ABoT 44 iv 11, 18 (OH/NS), KUB 31.66 i 28 (NH?); **sg. 3** *la-a-ú* KBo 17.54 i 8, 9, 10 (2x), 12, 14, 16, KUB 43.52 iii 15, (17) (NH); *la-a-ad-du* KUB 41.20 rev. 3, (4) (NH); **pl. 2** *la-a-at-te-en* KUB 24.4 obv. 24 (MH/MS); *la-a-at-ten* KBo 19.145 iii (46), 48 (NH), KUB 24.3 ii 36 (Murš. II).

imp. mid. sg. 3 *la-a-at-ta-ru* KBo 11.1 rev. 18 (Muw.).

part. nom. sg. com. *la-a-an-za* KUB 13.27 obv.! 20 (MH/MS), KBo 16.97 rev. (20) (NH), KUB 13.4 i 26 (NH), KUB 22.70 obv. 70 (NH); DU$_8$-*an-za* KUB 22.52 obv. 2 (NH), KUB 22.55 obv. 16, KUB 22.56 obv. 19, rev. 13, (20) (all NH).

verbal subst. nom. *la-a-u-wa-ar* KUB 24.5 obv. 18 + KUB 9.13:6; 17.32:(10); **gen.** *la-a-u-wa-aš* 291/f i 19, iv 8 (AfO 25:177), KUB 20.96 v (1).

inf. *la-u-an-zi* KBo 17.105 iv 25 (MH/MS).

iter. pres. act. sg. 1 *la-a-iš-ki-mi* KUB 17.27 ii 40 (MH/MS), KUB 26.86 iii 10 (NH), KUB 46.44 rev. 20 (NH); **sg. 3** *la-a-i-iš-ki-iz-z*[*i*] KBo 17.105 iv 19 (MH/MS).

(Akk.) *qablīšunu ipṭurma* "He unbelted their waists" KBo 10.1 rev. 12-13 = (Hitt.) *naš QABLĪŠUNU arḫa la-a-nu-un* "I unbelted their waists" KBo 10.2 iii 19 (bil. ann. of Ḫatt. I, OH/NS). □ On the meaning of this expression in Akk. see Oppenheim, OrNS 14 (1945) 239-41.

D[U$_8$-*it*] KBo 12.85 ii 1 = *la-a-i*[*t*] in dupl. KUB 34.110:8; in KBo 2.6 DU$_8$-*ta-ri* in i 38 alternates with *la-it-ta-ri* in iii 48, 65.

1. to unbind, untie, detach (wool, garments) — **a.** *arḫa lai-* with *-kan*, and object from which detached (opp. of *anda ḫamenk-* and *anda išḫiya-*): *ANA* ^{d}LAMMA ^{KUŠ}*kuršaššiš-šan kuiš* SÍG.BABBAR *anda ḫamankanza parḫuenašakan kuiš* DINGIR<-*LIM*>-*ni anda išḫiyanza naškan* SAL.ŠU.GI DINGIR-*LIM-ni arḫa la-a-i-iz-zi* "The Old Woman detaches from the god the white wool which was attached to (the statue of) ^{d}LAMMA of the shield and the *p.* which was tied to the god" KBo 17.105 iii 17-19 (rit., MH); *ANA* $^{\text{LÚ.MEŠ}}$MUŠEN.DÙ.ḪI.A-*yakan kuiš* SÍG.

BABBAR *INA* UZU GÚ-*ŠUNU anda ḫamankanza* GIŠ*kalmiššaniaššan kuiš* SÍG.BABBAR *anda ḫamankanza nušmašakan* SAL.ŠU.GI *arḫa la-a-iz-zi* "The Old Woman detaches from them the white wool which was attached to the augurs' necks and the white wool which was attached to the log(s)" ibid. 19-21.

b. (part.) detached (describing parts of the exta in oracle): GIŠTUKUL *la-a-an-za* "The 'weapon' is detached" KUB 22.70 obv. 70; [UZ]U[Z]É ZAG-*az la-a-a*[*n*]-*z*[*a*] "The gall bladder is detached on the right" KBo 16.97 rev. 20; *ta*!(*naniš*) DU₈-*an-za* "The *t.* is detached" KUB 22.52 obv. 2; □this translation is based on the meaning of Akkadian *paṭāru* (the reading of DU₈ in Akkadian omen texts) used in the stative to describe parts of the exta (von Soden, AHw 849).

2. to untwine, unravel (cord or rope) (opp. of *tarup-*): *išḫaminan-ma-an* GIM-*an arḫa la-a-nu-un* "I have untwined it (the words of sorcery; but note *-an* is com. gender) like a rope" KUB 17.27 ii 34 (rit. for DINGIR.MAḪ and dGulšeš); cf. *nu* SAL.ŠU.GI ŠU.SAR *dai nat* GÙB-*la la-a-i* ZAG-*nayat la-a-i* "The old woman takes the cord. She untwines it to the left and she untwines it to the right" ibid. ii 37-38; also *nat* ŠU.SAR-*aš iwar tarupta nat a*[-o o G]ÙB-*laz taruptat am*[*mug*]*at kāša* EGIR-*pa* ZAG-*az la-a-nu-un* "He twined them like a cord. They were twined [. . .] to the left and I have untwined them to the right" KUB 29.7 rev. 35-36 (rit. of Šamuḫa).

3. to take off (someone's shoes) (opp. of *šarkuwai-*): KUŠE.SIR BABBAR *la-an-zi* [. . .] KUŠE.SIR GE₆ *šarkuizz*[*i*] "They (the palace attendants) take off (the king's) white shoes [. . .] He puts on black shoes" KUB 34.118 rt. col. 6-7 (fest. frag.); "If a guard deserts his post and carries (his) spear off through the side door" *nan* LÚÌ.DU₈ *wašduli epzi nuššikan* KUŠE.SIR *arḫa la-a-i* "and a gatekeeper catches him in the act, he (the gatekeeper) will take off his (the guard's) shoes" IBoT 1.36 i 53-54 (instr., MH/MS).

4. to unhitch (opp. of *turiya-*): **a.** with horse as object: "In the fall when (the horse-trainer) lets the horses go out on the grass, he hitches them (to a chariot)". (He makes them walk and run,) *naš arḫa la-a-i* "and he unhitches them" KUB 1.13 i 3-6 (Kikkuli tablet I) and passim in Kikkuli; cf. *nuš turiyanzi nat* 1 DANNA *zallaz uwanzi nuš la-a-an-zi* KUB 29.40 ii 12 (hipp.) and passim in the Hittite horse-training manual; □the expression used by Kikkuli is *arḫa la-*. The Hittite horse-training manual uses simple *la-*, with the exception of KBo 14.63a iv 1: [*maḫḫa*]*nma* ANŠE.KUR.RA.ḪI.A *arḫa la-a-an-zi nuškan anaššiyan*[*zi* . . .] (Hipp.heth. 335).

b. with draft animal as implied object in a saying: *nu tariyandan la-a-at-ten* (var. *la-a-at-te-en*) *waršiyandanma turiyatten* "Unhitch the tired one, but hitch up the fresh one" KUB 24.3 ii 36-37 (prayer of Murš. II) with dupl. KUB 24.4 + KUB 30.12 obv. 24, ed. Gurney, AAA 27:99-101; *la-a-a dariyantan turiyama waršiyanta*[*n*] KBo 11.14 ii 18 (cf. 16-17).

5. to release (birds): with bird(s) as object: *kinu*[*nm*]*a kāša apun* MUŠEN *ier nan arḫa* ⌈*la*⌉-*a*-⌈*ir*⌉ "Now they have 'treated' that bird and they have released it" KBo 11.1 rev. 10 (prayer of Muw.), ed. Houwink ten Cate, RHA XXV/81 109, 118; MUŠEN.ḪI.A-*wannaškan warpi la-a-e-er* "They released for us the birds in/from the enclosure(?)" KUB 31.101:9-10 (letter about bird oracles); □coll. confirms copy, which shows no word division space between *warpi* and *lāer*; it is therefore possible that this is one word.

6. to release from sorcery, to free from a spell (often with the adverb *appa*) (opp. of *alwanzaḫḫ-*) — **a.** with humans as object: [*m*]*ān alwanzaḫḫantan* UN-*an* EGIR-*pa la-a-mi* "When I free a bewitched person from a spell (I do the following)" KUB 24.14 i 2 (rit. of Ḫebattarakki); cf. 1 SISKUR *mān alwanzaḫḫantan* EGIR-*pa la-a-mi* ibid. iv 27-28; *aškimakan anda* UḪₓ-*anda*[*n* U]N-*an* EGIR-*pa la-a-nu-un* "At the gate I freed the bewitched person from the spell" KUB 27.29 i 3 + VBoT 120 i 18 (= cumulative line 26) (rit. of Allaituraḫi); *aškikan anda alwanzaḫḫandan* SAL-*an la-a-nu-un ašk*[*ika*]*n anda alwanzaḫḫandan* LÚ-*an la-a-nu-u*[*n*] KBo 19.145 iii 41-43 (rit. of Šalašu), ed. Laroche, RHA XXVIII:60; *išḫiyantanmankan išḫiyalaz arḫa la-a-u-en* "We released from the bond him who was bound" VBoT 120 iii 2-3 (rit. of Allaiturahi, MH/NS); *išh[iy]an-tanwaran arḫa la-a-u-e-en* "We released him who was bound" KBo 19.145 iii 39-40 (rit. of Šalašu), ed. Laroche, RHA XXVIII:59; cf. *ki[tpa]ndalaz išḫi-yandan [l]a-a-at-ten* ibid. iii 45-46; *numu wašdulaš kat[t]an a[rḫ]a išḫiyandan* LÚ-*an mā[n] arḫa la-a* "(O my god), release me, (who am) like a man bound in sins" KUB 36.75 iii 9-11 (prayer); cf. EGIR-*pa UL la-a-u-wa-aš ḫukmain kiššan ḫukmi* "I recite the/an incantation from which one cannot be released" 291/f i 19, iv 8 (Otten, AfO 25:177).

b. with animals as object: [U]DU-*un la-a-i* GUD-*un la-a-i* "He (the Sungod) releases the sheep. He releases the ox" KBo 17.54 i 6 (incant.); for continuation of the context see below, mng. 8 a 1'.

c. In a myth told for purposes of magic (nature and animals that were "bound" are "released" through divine intervention): GAL-*iš* ÍD *ḫunḫumaz<zi>šit* EGIR-*pa la-a-at-ta-at anda* KU_6-*uš ḫantiyaraš la-at-ta-at* "The great river — its flood — was released, in it the ... fish was released" (there follow mountains, valleys, meadows, various animals and "the throne of ᵈLAMMA") KBo 3.8 iii 20-21 (third ritual on the tablet, called *ŠIPAT ḫami[nkuwaš]* "spell against 'binding'," KUB 7.1 iii 28 = KBo 3.8 + KUB 7.1 iii 62); in analogy, in order to release the "bound" (afflicted) body parts of a child, Ḫannaḫanna orders a midwife to pronounce spells (*ḫuekdu*) over those parts KUB 7.1 iii 10-19, whereupon she (the goddess or the midwife) says: *šeran* ᵁᶻᵁ*ḫupallaš la-a-ú-un nan šuppauš tetanuš la-a-ú-un* "Above I released his scalp(?), I released his pure hair" (etc.) KUB 7.1 iii 20-21 (text with many erasures), □OH dupl. KUB 43.52 iii 15, (17) with better readings has *la-a-ú* "let him/her release ...", ed. Kronasser, Die Sprache 7:157-59; Laroche, Myth 109-12.

7. to relieve (one's mind) (opp. *wišuriya-*): *nuza apaš* EN-*ŠU azzikkizzi akkuškizzi kuit naš* ZI-*an arḫa la-a-an-za* "Since his master eats and drinks, (in) his mind he is relieved" KUB 13.4 i 25-26 (instr. for temple officials); *mānma* GIDIM ZI-*an* DU_8-*ši* "If you, spirit of the dead, relieve (your) mind" KUB 22.35 ii 7 (oracle); [Z]I?-*TUM wišuriantan arḫa la-a-an-zi* "They relieve the oppressed [mi]nd" KUB 39.57 i 8 (rit.).

8. to dispel, remove (an ailment or an undesirable condition) — **a.** active — **1'** obj. an ailment: (The Sungod releases the sheep and ox [see above mng. 6b], then) *kedani[y]awakan antuḫši šer arḫa la-a-ú* SAG.DU-*aš [ḫ]uwal-taraman la-a-ú taraššanaš taškupiman la-a-ú* ZI-*naš impan la-a-ú* "(He says) 'and from upon this man let him remove (the following things): Let him remove the *ḫ.* of (his) head. Let him remove the screaming of (his) throat. Let him remove the burden of (his) mind'" KUB 17.54 i 8-10 and passim in this text (conjuration).

2' anger: *nu ŠA* ᵈU TUKU.TUKU-*an piran la-a-u-e-ni* "We dispel the Stormgod's anger" KBo 11.1 obv. 3 (prayer of Muw.), ed. Houwink ten Cate, RHA XXV/81:105, 114; *ŠA* DINGIR-*LIM* TUKU.TUKU-*an* DU_8-*it*(!) "Did she (the queen) dispel the anger of the god?" KUB 16.55 iv 4 (oracle).

3' sin; to remove (sin): *nuza* KUR.KUR.ḪI.A-*aš waštul*ᴴᴵ·ᴬ *maḫḫan* EGIR-*pa la-a-mi [natza k]i [a]rkuwar iyam[i] nat* ᵈU EN-*YA ištamašdu* "Let the Stormgod, my Lord, hear how I again remove the sins of the countries and make that into this plea" KBo 11.1 obv. 12f. (prayer of Muw.), ed. Houwink ten Cate, RHA XXV/81: 106, 115; *numu ḫarā[tar arḫ]a la-a-i* KUB 31.127 + ABoT 44 iv 11, cf. 18. (prayer, OH/NS).

b. (mid.) to be removed: *mānmannaš ŠA* ᵐ*Urḫi*-ᵈU-*up* ḪUL-*lu apiz* INIM-*za* DU_8-*ri* "But if the evil of Urḫi-Tešub will be removed from us by that word (let the oracle be favorable)" KUB 16.41 + 7/v iii 13-14 (Otten-Rüster, ZA 62:106); INIM ᵐᵈ*SIN*-ᵈU-*kan kez* INIM-*za* DU_8-*ta-ri* "(If) the matter of Arma-ᵈU will be removed by this word (let the oracle be favorable)" KBo 2.6 i 38; cf. *ŠA* INIM ᶠᵈ*IŠTAR-attinaškan apez m[e]-minaza la-it-ta-ri* "(If) the affair (lit. that of the word) of Š. will be removed from us by that word (let the oracle be favorable)" ibid. iii 47-48; also INIM ᶠᵈ*IŠTAR-attinaškan apez meminaza [l]a-it-ta-ri* ibid. iii 64-65.

9. Adverbs — **a.** *appa la-*: the adverb *appa* is used with *la-* to indicate the return to a previous state or condition. *appa la-* is especially frequent in mng. 6: "to release from sorcery, to free from a spell." See also mng. 2; see Josephson, RHA XXV/81 (1967) 129. — **b.** *arḫa la-*: the adverb *arḫa* is frequent with active forms of *la-* in all mngs. It does not appear to change the mng. of the simple *la-*. See esp. mng. 4 a. — **c.** *piran la-*: function unclear. See mng. 8 a 2′. On the adverbs with *lā-* see Josephson, RHA XXV/81 (1967) 128-29.

Usually the obj. from which something is loosed is indicated by loc. and *-kan* (1 a, 3, 5, 8 a 1′, 8 b), but once by abl. and *-kan* (6 a). The *-kan* is not required in the *mān* clause (8 b).

Hrozný, HKT 59 n. 5; Otten, HTR 123 (ad mng. 7).

Cf. *lauwar*, *latar* and DU₈.

lāḫ- A v.; to pour, pour out (liquids); OH, MH.†

pres. pl. 1 (The forms *la-ḫu-e-ni* and *la-a-*⌈*ḫu-e-ni*⌉ could derive from *lāḫ-* A or *laḫuwai-*; for refs. see *laḫuwai-*).

pret. sg. 1 *la-a-ḫu-un* KUB 29.7 rev. 49 (MH/MS).

imp. sg. 2 *la-a-aḫ* IBoT 2.128 rev. 5 (MH/NS), KBo 21.22:12 (OH/MS).

a. water: "Draw water seven or eight times and" *wātar 7-ŠU* [*našma 8-ŠU*] *la-a-aḫ* "pour out the water seven or eight times" IBoT 2.128 rev. 3-5 (MH/NS), cf. Otten, ZA 54 (1961) 124, 157; *witār katta* ᴰᵁᴳGÌR.KIŠ-*ya la-ḫu-e-ni* KBo 19.156 ii 15 + KUB 32.117 "rev." 7 (Pala rit., OH/MS), cf. KUB 35.93 obv.! 5 and KBo 17.25 obv. 9.

b. perfumed oil and honey: *kāšašmaš* Ì.DÙG.GA LÀL-*ya* EGIR-*anda la-a-ḫu-un* KUB 29.7 rev. 49 (Šamuḫa rit., MH/MS).

Adverbs: *appanda* (postpos./preverb) KUB 29.7 rev. 49 (above); *katta* (adv.) KBo 19.156 ii 15 + KUB 32.117 "rev." 7 (above).

Cf. *laḫ(ḫ)uwai-*.

laḫ- B v.; (mng. unkn.).†

pret. 3 (2?) *la-aḫ-ta* KBo 18.64:5, also KBo 18.11 obv. 10?.

In letters in broken context only, but apparently not the same as *lāḫ-* A.

laḫḫa- n. com.; **1.** military campaign, **2.** journey, trip, voyage; from OH/OS.

sg. all. *la-a-aḫ-ḫa* KBo 17.22 ii 6, KBo 25.100 ii 1-3 (both OH/OS), KBo 20.59:9 (OH/MS), KUB 14.1 rev. 13! (MH/MS) correct KUB after Madd. and photo; *la-aḫ-ḫa* KBo 6.2 + KBo 19.1 ii 27 (Law §42, copy A, OS); Otten and Souček AfO 21:4; the join does not allow for the additional *-a-*; *la-aḫ-ḫa* KUB 43.25:10 (OH/OS), KUB 33.60 rev. 10, KUB 1.16 ii 42, KBo 3.1 ii 17 (all OH/NS), KBo 16.47:6; KBo 16.25 i 31, KUB 23.77a rev. (9) (all MH/MS); KUB 1.16 ii 45!, KBo 3.1 i 5, KBo 12.5 ii 3 (all OH/NS); *la-aḫ-ḫa(-an)* KUB 11.1 ii 9 (OH/NS, var. of *la-aḫ-ḫa-ma* KBo 12.5 ii 3).

d.-l. *la-a-aḫ-ḫi*[(-) ...] KUB 40.76:12 (OH or MH/MS); *la-aḫ-ḫi* KBo 6.5 iv 7 (OH/NS), KBo 16.25 i 19 (MH/MS), KUB 19.10 i 12 (Murš. II), KUB 1.1 ii 71, with dupl. KBo 3.6 ii 51 (Ḫatt.).

abl. *la-a-aḫ-ḫa-az* KBo 20.59:10 (OH/MS); *la-aḫ-ḫa-az* KUB 9.16 i 1, KUB 25.12 vi 10, KUB 25.13 vi 7 (all OH/NS), KUB 23.77:91 (MH/MS), KUB 13.21 obv. 9 par. 26.11 iv (11) (both MH/NS), ABoT 14 v 12, KUB 22.12:2 (NH); ⌈*la-aḫ*⌉*-ḫa-za* KUB 25.14 vi 3 (OH/NS).

pl. acc. *la-a-aḫ-ḫu-u-uš* KBo 16.86 i 10 (OH/NS).

1. military campaign — **a.** with *pai-* — **1′** *laḫḫa pai-* go on an expedition/campaign, go to war: [(*mān*) ᵁᴿᵁ*Purušḫanda l*]*a-aḫ-ḫa paun* "When I went on a campaign [against P.]" (the men, [so B and C; A: 'man'] of P. brought me gifts) KUB 36.98b rev. 3 (Anitta, copy C, OH/NS), dupl. of KBo 3.22:73 (copy A), ed. Neu, StBoT 18:19f.; [*mān* M]U.3.KAM *naš la-aḫ-ḫa paiddu* "When it is the third year, let him (the young Muršili) go to war" KUB 1.16 ii 42 (HAB); *kuwat*=*taš la-aḫ-ḫa-ma paizzi* "But whenever he went on a campaign (he kept the enemy countries defeated)" KBo 3.1 i 4, 14 (Tel. pr., OH/NS) = BoTU 23A i 5, 15; *la-aḫ-ḫa-an* (var. B *la-aḫ-ḫa-ma*) *kuwatta* ERÍN.ME[(Š-*uš paizzi*)] "(But) wherever the troops went (lit. go) on a campaign (they did not return safely)" KBo 3.1 + 12.5 ii 3 (A) with dupl. KUB 11.1 ii 9 (B) transliterated in BoTU 23A and B; cf. ibid. ii 17.

2′ *laḫḫi pai-* (same mng.): *namma la-aḫ-ḫi QATAMMA paiwani* "In the same way we shall go on military expeditions" KUB 31.42 iii 18-19 (LÚ.DUGUD oaths, MH), ed. von Schuler, OrNS 25:228, 231; [*m*]*ān* ᵈUTU-*ŠI-ma la-aḫ-ḫi ukila UL paimi* "But if I, My Majesty, do not go on a campaign myself" KUB 13.20 i 16 (instr., MH); *la-aḫ-ḫi-ma-aš UL panza* "but he has not gone on a campaign" ibid. i 1 with par. KUB 26.11 iv 7; *nu* LUGAL-*uš la-aḫ-ḫi UL kuwapikki panza* "and the king has gone nowhere on a campaign" KUB 27.1 i 20f. (fest., NH), cf. par. LÍL-*ri paizzi* i 23; *natmu la-aḫ-ḫi kattan paišgauwan tier* "and they began to go with me on campaigns" KBo 5.8 ii 4f. (AM 152f.). KUB 40.76:12 could belong here or in b, 2′.

b. with *iya-* — **1′** *laḫḫa iya-* march on a campaign, go to war: *numu* ERÍN.MEŠ URU*Ura* ERÍN.MEŠ URU*Mutamutaši* [*kat⸗tan*] *la-aḫ-ḫa iyantari* "and the troops of U. and M. march with me to war" KBo 16.47 obv. 5f. (treaty, MH), ed. Otten, IM 17:56f.

2′ *laḫḫi iya-*: *nu mān* dUTU-*ŠI la-aḫ-ḫi apašila iyatta* "And if His Majesty himself is to march on the campaign" KUB 13.20 i 6 (instr., MH); *ABUYA-ia ANA ABI ABIYA la-aḫ-ḫi* GAM-*anpat iya*[*ttat*] "and my father marched with my grandfather on the campaign" KUB 19.10 i 12 (DŠ frag. 13), ed. Güterbock, JCS 10:65; *nat IŠTU* ERÍN.MEŠ-*ŠUNU* [(*ANA*)] *ABIYA Ù ANA ABA ABIYA la-aḫ-ḫi kattan* [*i*]*yantat ammugat kattan la-aḫ-ḫ*[*i*] *iyantatpat* KBo 5.8 iv 6-8 with dupl. KBo 16.8 iv 4-6 (AM 160f.).

c. *laḫḫi peḫute-* to lead a campaign, lead to war: *nu tuzzin la-aḫ-ḫi apāš peḫutezzi* "then that one (whom the king has appointed) will lead the army to war" KUB 13.20 i 17 (instr., MH); *nu* KARAŠ ANŠE.KUR.RA.MEŠ *kel ŠA* KUR-*TI ANA* ŠEŠ-*YA la-aḫ-ḫi INA* KUR URU*Mizri kattan peḫutenun* "I led the troops and chariots of this country on the campaign to Egypt along with my brother" KBo 3.6 ii 50-52 (Ḫatt.); *mān antuwaḫḫaš kuwapi tuzziuš la-aḫ-ḫi ANA* URU LÚKÚR *peḫutezzi* KUB 30.42 i 9f. (cat. entry, rit.), ed. Laroche, CTH p. 162.

d. *laḫḫaz appa uwa-* to return from an expedition/campaign, from war: *mānaš la-aḫ-ḫa-az-ma* EGIR-*pa uizzi* "But when he returned (lit. returns) from a campaign" KBo 3.1 i 7 (Tel. pr.); cf. i 17; for *laḫḫaz uizzi* in fest. texts cf. mng. 2.

e. other verbs: *mānkan* LÚ.SIG$_5$ *našma appezziš antuwaḫḫaš* (var. *antuḫšaš*) [(*la-aḫ-ḫa-az* KASKAL-*az*) EGI]R-*pa ḫuwāi* "If an officer or a lowly person runs back from (i.e. deserts) a campaign (or) a journey, (let his superiors not hide him)" KUB 13.20 i 3f., with dupl. KUB 13.21 obv. 8f. (instr., MH); *nušmaš* dUTU-*ŠI kuedani la-aḫ*[-*ḫi peḫutezzi mā*]*nma* dUTU-*ŠI la-aḫ-ḫa-az* EGIR-*pa neyar*[*i*] ERÍN.MEŠ-*ma arḫa INA* É-*ŠU* [*tarnā*]*i* "On whatever campaign His Majesty [will lead] you, [whe]n His Majesty turns back from the campaign, he will [let] the troops (go) home" KUB 13.27 rev.! 20f. + KUB 23.77 + KUB 26.40:91f. (Kaška treaty, MH); [*Š*]*A* NINDA.ERÍN.MEŠ *uttar kitpandalaz išḫiul eštu* [*maḫ*]*ḫan la-aḫ-ḫa nininkanzi* "Let the matter of bread rations (lit. soldiers' bread) from now on be (a matter of) binding regulations! When they mobilize for an expedition, (let the commanders inspect the bread rations and flour)!" KBo 16.25 i 30-32 (instr., MH); *nuwamu kuwapi* dUTU-*ŠI BELIYA la-a-aḫ-ḫa ḫalziššatti* "Whenever you, Your Majesty my lord, call me to an expedition" KUB 14.1 rev. 13 (Madd., MH), ed. Götze, Madd. 24f.

f. in figura etymologica: *la-a-aḫ-ḫu-u-uš laḫḫiškiuwan*[*zi*?] KBo 16.86 i 10 (OH); [*la-aḫ-ḫ*]*u-u-uš laḫḫeškit* KBo 14.4 i 4 (DŠ) (for context see *la*(*ḫ*)*ḫiyai-* 1 d).

2. (non-military) journey, trip, voyage — **a.** with *pai-*: *takku* LÚ.U$_{18}$.LU-*an kuiški kuššanizzi naš la-*⌜*aḫ-ḫa*⌝ (var. C: *la-aḫ-ḫi*) *paizzi n*[(*aš aki*)] *takku kuššan piyan šarnikzil* [NU.GÁL] (var. B and C: *nu UL šarnikzi*) *takku kuššana natta piyan* 1 SAG.DU [(*pāi*)] "If someone hires a person, and (this person) goes on an expedition and dies, if the hire has been paid, there is no compensation (var. B and C: he will not compensate), but if the hire has not been paid, he shall give one person" KBo 6.2 + KBo 19.1 ii 27-29 (Law §42, copy A, OH/OS) with dupl. KBo 6.3 ii 48-50 (B) and KBo 6.5 iv 7-9 (C); □later copies B and C add: "And as hire he shall pay 12 shekels, and as a woman's hire he shall pay 6 shekels." Even without this addition, the terms LÚ.U$_{18}$.LU in B and UN-*an* in C include both sexes; *mān la-a-aḫ-ḫa paiš*[*i* ...] "If you go on a journey" KBo 17.22 ii 6 (prayer, OH/OS); [d*Ḫ*]*annaḫannašašše appa tezz*[*i* MU.KAM-*t*]*i* MU.KAM-*ti la-aḫ-ḫa paiškaḫḫu*[*t*] "Ḫ. answers him: 'Year by year you must go on a trip'" KUB 33.60 rev. 9f. (myth., OH/NS), with dupl. KUB 33.61 iv 9f. and KUB 43.25:9f. (OS), ed. Laroche, Myth 94; cf. dIM-*aš la-a-aḫ-ḫa-az* [. . .] KBo 20.59:10 (myth., MH).

b. *laḫḫaz neya-*: ^{d}UTU-*ŠI-ma kuwapi la-aḫ-ḫa-az neyari* ABoT 14 v 12 (oracle); □according to ibid. v 3 and the par. KUB 22.27 iii this is the end of a cult voyage to various cities.

c. *laḫḫaz uwa-* in incipits and colophons of *nuntarriyašḫaš* fest. may refer to the return in the autumn from a military campaign or from a peaceful trip. The following exx. probably refer to the latter: *mān* LUGAL-*uš la-aḫ-ḫa-az zēni* $^{[U]RU}$*Arinnaz ANA* EZEN *nuntarriyašḫaš* $^{[U]RU}$*Ḫattuši uizzi* KUB 25.12 vi 9-13; cf. KUB 11.34 vi 46-49; *mān* LUGA[L] SAL.LUGAL ⌈*la-aḫ*⌉-*ḫa-za uwa*[*nzi*] KUB 25.14 vi 2f.; ambiguous: *mān* LUGAL-*uš la-aḫ-ḫa-az uizz*[*i*] KUB 9.16 i 1; KUB 25.13 vi 7f.

d. ambiguous in other context: [GI]M-*ankan* ^{d}UTU-*ŠI la-aḫ-ḫa-az* UGU *uizzi nuza* DINGIR.MEŠ DÙ-*zi* ŠE$_{12}$-*anzima* ^{d}UTU-*ŠI* SAL.LUGAL ^{URU}KÙ.BABBAR-*ši* "When His Majesty comes 'up' (to Ḫattuša) from an expedition and celebrates the gods, but His Majesty and the queen spend the winter in Ḫattuša . . ." KUB 18.12 i 1 (oracle); LUGAL-*uš kuwapi la-aḫ-ḫi* x x [o] *uddār* ^{LÚ}NAR-*aš ANA* ^{d}UTU ^{URU}*Arinna šuḫḫi* [*šer m*]*emiškizzi* "When the king is on an expedition, the singer recites [. . .] words to the Sungoddess of Arinna on the roof" KUB 30.43 iii 11-14 (cat. entry, rit.), ed. Laroche, CTH p. 177f.

Related terms: *ištu* KARAŠ *it-tù-ur* KUB 3.85:9 is free rendering "returned from the army" for *laḫḫazma* EGIR-*pa uizzi* of KBo 3.1 i 7 (Tel. pr.) = BoTU 23A i 8. There is no other indication that KARAŠ could be the logogram for *laḫḫa-*. Another term for "journey" is KASKAL, but this cannot be the logogram of *laḫḫa-* because of the complements in *-ša/-ši*, also because KUB 13.21 obv. 9 (above sub mng. 1 e) has *laḫḫaz* KASKAL-*az* side by side, evidently to differentiate between a military campaign and a trip.

Götze, ZA 34 (1922) 186, Ḫatt. (1925) 87; ad mng. 2: Kronasser apud Haase, Die Keilschriftlichen Rechtssammlungen in deutscher Übersetzung (1963) 68 n. 75 on non-military use; Neu, StBoT 18 (1974) 60 on spellings.

Cf. *laḫ(ḫ)iyai-*, *laḫḫiyala-*, *laḫḫiyatar*, *laḫḫema-*.

laḫanni- n. com.; (a bottle or pitcher often made of gold or silver); from MH; only in Hurr. fest. and rit.

pl. acc. *la-ḫa-an-ni-uš* KBo 21.34 i 8 and passim (MH/NS); *la-ḫa-an-ni-uš* $^{ḪI.A}$ ibid. 36 (MH/NS), KUB 39.100:6 (NH); *la-ḫa-ni-uš* VBoT 89 iv 24 (MH/NS?); *la-a-ḫa-an-ni-uš* KBo 21.34 i 29 (MH/NS), 24.7:(4); *la-a-ḫa-ni-uš* VBoT 89 iv 5 (MH?/NS).

(sg. or pl.) abl. *la-ḫa-an-na-az* KUB 46.47 obv. 22.

Akkadographic (*IŠTU*) *LA-ḪA-AN-NI* KBo 20.114 i 8, 9, etc. (MH/NS); (*IŠTU*) *LA-ḪA-A-NI* KUB 44.17:5.

a. in the *ḫišuwaš* fest.: EGIR-*ŠU-ma la-ḫa-an-ni-uš šipandanzi* KBo 15.49 iv 6; also ibid. (1), 4-5; KUB 46.47 obv. 18, 20, rev. 14, 16; KUB 47.72 iv? 16, 20, 26, 27; VBoT 89 iv 5; without EGIR-*ŠU-ma* KBo 15.61 i 14, 19; *namma* EGIR-*andama* ^{LÚ}SANGA-*ŠU IŠTU* 1 *LA-ḪA-AN-NI* KÙ.BABBAR *šipanti* LUGAL-*ušma IŠTU* 2 *LA-ḪA-AN-NI* KÙ.GI *šipanti* "Afterward his priest pours libations from one silver *l.*, and the king pours libations from two gold *l.*'s" KUB 32.128 i 22-23, and passim in this text and its dupls.

b. in the fest. for Tešub and Ḫebat of Lawazantiya: *našta* GAL ^{d}IM *šunnai la-ḫa-an-ni-uš-ša šipanti* "He fills the cup of the Stormgod. And he pours the *l.*'s" KBo 21.34 i 8 and passim in this text; EGIR-*ŠU-ma la-a-ḫa-an-ni-uš* EGIR-*pan danzi* ibid. i 29-30; [. . .] x GEŠTIN-*ya la-ḫa-an-na-az šipanti* "He (the king) pours a libation of . . . and wine from a *l.*" KUB 46.47 obv. 22; cf. ibid. obv. 18, 20, rev. 14 and 16.

c. in unidentified fest. and rit.: EGIR-*ŠU-ma la-ḫa-an-ni-uš šipanti* KUB 45.52 obv. 13, also 26; LUGAL-*ša IŠTU* 2 *LA-ḪA-AN-NI* KÙ.GI *šipa*[*nti*] KUB 27.19 iii 12; [*w*]*itenaš* KÙ.GI *la-ḫa-an-ni-uš* $^{ḪI.A}$ [. . .] KUB 39.100:6.

Probably a *Kulturwort*. Compare Akkadian *laḫannu* and Sumerian DUG.LA.ḪA.AN. References in Sum. and Akk. texts (CAD) indicate *laḫannu*'s made of clay and of glass, lapis lazuli, gold, and silver.

Friedrich, HW 124; CAD L "bottle".

laḫ(ḫ)anza(na)- n. com. (KUB 39.7 ii 8ff.); (a duck); from OH/NS.†

sg. nom. *la-ḫa-an-za* MUŠEN KUB 39.7 ii 8, 10, 13 (pre-NH/NS); *la-ḫa-an-za* KUB 39.7 ii 13, KUB 43.60 i 12 (OH/NS); *la-aḫ-ḫa-an-za* KUB 39.7 ii 12 (2x); [*la-a*]*ḫ-ḫa-an-za* KUB 39.8 i 6 (pre-NH/NS); [*la-a*]*ḫ-ḫa-an-za-aš* MUŠEN ibid. i 4; 10 *la-aḫ-ḫa-an-za* MUŠEN.ḪI.A KUB 39.7 ii 11; *la-aḫ-ḫa-an-za-ma* MUŠEN KUB 39.8 i 7; [*l*]*a*?-*ḫa-an-za-na-aš* KBo 1.34 obv. 8 (NH); **sg. d.-l.** *la-ḫa-an-za-ni* KUB 39.7 ii 9.

pl. acc. *la-ḫa-*[*a*]*n-zu-uš* KUB 39.7 ii 31; *la-aḫ-ḫa-an-zu-uš* KUB 39.7 ii 33, KUB 39.8 i 32; *la-aḫ-ḫa-an-zu-uš* MUŠEN KUB 39.7 ii 35; *la-ḫa-an-zi-uš* KUB 39.7 ii 24, 37; *la-aḫ-ḫa-an-za-nu-uš* MUŠEN.ḪI.A KUB 39.7 ii 19; *la-ḫa-an-za-nu-uš* 814/z rev. (1), 9, 10, 12; **pl. gen.** *la-ḫa-an-za-na-aš* KUB 39.6 obv. 17; *la-aḫ-ḫa-a*[*n-* . . .] KUB 39.8 iv 34; *la-ḫa-an-za-na-aš* MUŠEN.ḪI.A <<-*na-aš*!>> KUB 30.19 (pre-NH/NS) iv 29; **(sg. or pl.?) gen.** *la-aḫ-ḫa-an-za-na-aš* MUŠEN KUB 39.7 ii 7.

[za-la-ag] = [UD] = [. . .] = [*l*]*a*?-*ḫa-an-za-na-aš* KBo 1.34 obv. 8, MSL 3, 61, cf. Laroche, RHA XXIV/79 (1966) 161.

a. in royal funeral rit.: *INA* UD.13.KAM *našta* É-*ri and*[*a*] *la-aḫ-ḫa-an-za-na-aš*MUŠEN *ḫimuš iyanzi nu ŠA* GIŠ.ḪI.A 10 *l*[*a*]*-ḫa-an-za*MUŠEN *iyanza nuš IŠTU* KÙ.BABBAR *ḫališšiyanzi nu ANA* 5 *la-ḫa-an-za-ni*<<-*a*>> (var. [. . .-]*aš*MUŠEN) SAG.DU.MEŠ-*ŠUNU* KÙ.GI GAR.RA SÍG*iyatnašša* 10 *la-ḫa-an-za*MUŠEN (var. *la-a*[*ḫ-* . . .]) *iyanza išnašša* 10 *la-aḫ-ḫa-an-za*MUŠEN.ḪI.A (var. [*la-a*]*ḫ-ḫa-an-za-aš*MUŠEN) *iyanza naš* 30 *la-aḫ-ḫa-an-za ḫuišwantešša naššu* 5 (var. 4) *la-aḫ-ḫa-an-za našma* 6 *la-ḫa-an-za*MUŠEN (var. *la-a*[*ḫ-* . . .]) *appanzi ma-a-an la-ḫa-an-za-ma* (var. *la-aḫ-ḫa-an-za-ma*MUŠEN) *U*[*L*] *meḫur nu* MUŠEN *ḪURRI*ḪI.A *appanz*[*i*] "On the thirteenth day, they make models of the *l.*-birds in the house. Ten *l.*-birds are made of wood, and they inlay them with silver. On five *l.*-birds (representing the males?) the heads are plated with gold. Ten *l.*-birds are made of *iyatna-* (something of wool). And ten *l.*-birds are made of dough. There are thirty (artificial) *l.*-birds (in all). And they catch either five (var. four) or six live *l.*-birds. If it is not the *l.*-bird season, they catch shelducks" KUB 39.7 ii 7-14, with dupl. KUB 39.8 i 1-8, ed. HTR 36f., cf. UD.13.KAM *la-ḫa-an-za-na-aš* MUŠEN.ḪI.A<<-*na-aš*!>> (var. *la-aḫ-ḫa-a*[*n-* . . .]) *zinnanza* (var. *zinnanteš*) KUB 30.19 iv 29-30 (pre-NH/NS) with dupl. KUB 39.8 iv 34-35, ed. HTR 46f. In the funeral rit. 814/z rev. 1, 8-9 models of these birds and of MUŠEN *ḪURRI* are attached/bound (*anda ḫa*[*menk-*]) to objects.

b. in a rit.: *takku arunazma nat la-ḫa-an-za udau natšan pedišši dau* "If it is from the sea, let the *l.*-bird bring it (i.e. my *iyatar*) and put it in its place" KUB 43.60 i 12-13 (OH/NS).

Certain factors aid in determining the identity of this bird: (1) it was a sea or seashore bird; (2) there was a period of time each year (winter?) when it was absent from Ḫatti and the look-alike(?) MUŠEN *ḪURRI* (shelduck, scientific name: *Tadorna tadorna*) was present; (3) the males had a head color (represented by gold overlay on models) different from the females, while the body coloration of both could be represented by silver overlay. If the restorations used above for the lexical entry in KBo 1.34 ii 8 are correct, this entry too indicates a white or silver body plumage. The *laḫ*(*ḫ*)*anzana-*, like the MUŠEN *ḪURRI*, was a member of the duck family.

H. Otten, HTR (1958) 133 (no translation); cf. B. Landsberger, WO III/3 (1966) 262-66 for MUŠEN *ḪURRI* "Tadorna".

laḫḫi- n. com.; (mng. unkn.); NH.†

In a SALŠU.GI rit.: *la-aḫ-ḫi-ša-aš-ta kišaru naššikan anda tamektaru* "Let him become a *l.* and let him/it be fastened to it/him" KUB 9.4 ii 1-2.

Perhaps *la-aḫ-ḫi-ya-aš* (dupl. 50/a:10: [*la*]-*aḫ-ḫi-ya*) VBoT 128 ii 24, dupl. 50/a cited in Sommer, HAB 82 n. 1, (rit. frag.) is a form of this word.

Neu, StBoT 5 (1968) 164, 165 n. 7.

la(ḫ)ḫiyai- v.; **1.** (intrans.) to travel, go on an expedition, wander, roam, march, operate, go to war; **2.** (trans.) to attack, make war on, operate against; from OH.

pres. sg. 1 *la-aḫ-ḫi-ia-mi* KUB 21.5 iii 20 (Muw.); *la-ḫi-ia-am-mi* KUB 5.1 ii 17 (Ḫatt. III); **sg. 2** [*la-aḫ-ḫ*]*i-ia-ši* KUB 21.1 iii 7 (Muw.); **sg. 3** *la-aḫ-ḫi-ia-iz*(coll.)-*zi* KUB 26.17 i 4 (MH/MS); *la-ḫi-ia-iz-zi* KUB 5.1 i 5 and passim (Ḫatt. III).

pl. 2 *la-aḫ-[-ḫi-i]a-at-te-ni* KUB 21.47:21 + KUB 23.82 obv.! 26 (MH/MS); **pret. sg. 3** *la-aḫ-ḫi-ia-it* KBo 12.33 ii 5 (Arn. II), KUB 21.17 i 15 (Ḫatt. III); **imp. sg. 2** *la-aḫ-ḫi-ia-ia* (sic) KUB 27.67 iii 64 (NH); **pl. 2** *la-aḫ-ḫi-ia-at-ten* KUB 31.119:9, KUB 23.82 obv.! (19) (MH); **v. subst. gen.** *la-aḫ-ḫi-ia-u-wa-aš* KBo 16.25 i 33 (MH/MS); **inf.** *la-aḫ-ḫi-ia-u-wa-an-zi* KUB 23.11 iii 10 (MH/NS), KUB 34.33:6 + KBo 14.20 + KBo 14.44 i 20 (Murš. II), KUB 21.1 iii 8 (Muw.), KUB 22.39 iii 11 (NH?); *la-aḫ-⌜ḫi-u-wa⌝-an-zi* KUB 21.5 iii 22 (Muw.); *la-ḫi-ia-u-an-zi* KUB 5.1 iii 10, 28, iv 80 (Ḫatt. III); **part. sg. neut.** *la-aḫ-ḫi-ia-an* KUB 27.1 i 8 (NH); **iter. pres. sg. 2** *la-aḫ-ḫe-eš-ki-ši* KUB 21.5 iii 21; var. *la-aḫ-ḫi-ia-iš-ki-ši* KUB 21.4 i 28 (Muw.); **sg. 3** *la-aḫ-ḫi-iš-ki-iz-zi* KBo 12.59 i 5 (Tudḫ. IV), *la-aḫ-ḫi-ia-iš-ki-iz-zi* KUB 2.1 vi 3 (Tudḫ. IV); **pret. sg. 1** *la-aḫ-ḫe-eš-ki-nu-un* KUB 31.4 obv. 17 (OH/NS); **sg. 3** *la-aḫ-ḫe-eš-ki-it* KBo 14.4 i 4 (DŠ), KUB 27.1 i 7 (NH), *[la-a]ḫ-ḫi-ia-iš-ki-it* KUB 8.50 ii 9 (NH); **imp. sg. 2** *la-aḫ-ḫe-eš-ki* KUB 21.5 iii 23, var. *la-aḫ-ḫi-ia-iš-ki* KUB 21.4 i 31 (Muw.); **pl. 3** *la-aḫ-ḫe-eš-kán-du* KUB 40.40 ii 7 (NS) *-du* over erasure; **sup.** *la-aḫ-ḫi-iš-ki-u-wa-an* KBo 16.86 i 10 (OH/NS); **iter.-dur. pres. pl. 1** *la-aḫ-ḫi-ia-an-ni-iš-ga-u-e-ni* KBo 4.4 iii 50 (Murš. II).

(Akk.) *⌜a⌝-na* LÚKÚR *a-la-ki ul i-el-ʾi* "he could not march against the enemy" KUB 3.14 obv. 17 = (Hitt.) *nuza la-aḫ[-ḫi-ia-(u-wa-an-zi UL namma tarḫḫeškit)]* "he was no longer able to go to war" KUB 3.119 obv. 16, with dupl. KUB 21.49 obv. 13 (Dupp.).

1. intrans. — **a.** absolute: *mān* dUTU-*ŠI-ma kuwapi apašila la-aḫ-ḫi-ia-iz*(coll.)*-zi* "But if His Majesty at any time goes to war in person" KUB 26.17 i 4 (instr., MH/MS), □replaced by *nu mān* dUTU-*ŠI laḫḫi apašila iyatta* "goes on a compaign" in later version KUB 13.20 i 6; *mān* dUTU-*ŠI apiz*(!) KUR-*ea*[*z* ... (*la-aḫ-ḫi-ia-m*)]*i numu ziqqa QADU* ERÍN.MEŠ ANŠE.KUR.[(RA.MEŠ *kattan la-aḫ-ḫ*)]*i-ia-ši* (var. A 21: *la-aḫ-ḫe-eš-ki-ši*, B 28: *la-aḫ-ḫi-ia-iš-ki-ši*) *našma mān BĒLU kuinki k*[(*ez* KUR-*az*)] *la-aḫ-ḫi-ia-u-wa-an-zi* (var. A 22: *la-aḫ-⌜ḫi-u-wa⌝-an-zi*) *uiyami nu ap*[(*edaniya kattan la-a*)]*ḫ-ḫe-eš-ki-ši* (var. A 23: *la-aḫ-ḫe-eš-ki*, B 31: *la-aḫ-ḫi-ia-iš-ki*) "If I, My Majesty, go to war from that country ... you, too, with your troops and chariots shall go to war with me; or if I send some lord on a campaign from this country, then you shall go (var. go!) to war together with him, too!" KUB 21.1 iii 4-9, with dupl. KUB 21.5 iii 19-23 (A) and KUB 21.4 + KBo 12.36 i 27-31 (B) (Alakš.), ed. SV 2:66-69; *nuwadda kattan la-aḫ-ḫi-ia-an-ni-iš-ga-u-e-ni* "and we shall always go to war with you" KBo 4.4 iii 49f. (AM 130f.); *la-aḫ-ḫi-ia-u-wa-aš*(*-za*) [*išḫi*]*ul* "the obligation of going to war" KBo 16.25 i 33f. (instr., MH); [*n*]*uza kuitman* m*Tudḫaliyaš* LUGAL.GAL *INA* KUR URU*Aš-šuwa la-aḫ-ḫi-ia-u-wa-an-zi ešun* "While I, the Great King T., was in A. for military operations" KUB 23.11 iii 9f. (ann.); [*la-a*]*ḫ-ḫi-ia-u-wa-an-zi pāun* ibid. 14f.; cf. ibid. 23-26, 29; [*nušm*]*aš la-aḫ-ḫi-ia-u-a*[*n-z*]*i UL pāun* "I did not go to war against them" KUB 34.33:6 + KBo 14.20 i 20 (Murš. II), ed. Houwink ten Cate, JNES 25:169, 178; cf. KUB 3.119 obv. 16 above in bilingual section.

b. with allative, to operate against: *mān* dUTU-*ŠI kedani* MU URU*Tanizila la-ḫi-ia-iz-zi mān kuedani pidi la-ḫi-ia-iz-zi mānaškan* TA KARAŠ *ḫa-aš-ši-i* ÍD-*i paizzi* "If His Majesty in this year operates against T., if at the place at which he operates he goes from the camp (or: with the army?) to the ... river" KUB 5.1 iii 65-66 (oracle, Ḫatt. III); *parāma* URU*Kammama* URU*Šaqamaḫa la-ḫi-ia-iz-zi* "Shall he further operate against K. and Š.?" ibid. ii 62 (contrast URU*Kammaman* RA-*zi* and URU*Šaqamaḫan* RA-*zi* ibid. ii 56f.); dUTU-*ŠI-zakan* URU*Neriqan karpzi nu* EGIR-*pa* ḪUR.SAG*Ḫaḫarwa la-ḫi-ia-iz-zi nu* URU*Kamaman* ... RA-*zi* "Shall His Majesty 'lift' Nerik and again operate against (? or: on?) Mt. Ḫ. and attack (the towns of) K. etc.?" ibid. ii 66f., cf. ibid. i 40, iv 84, ed. (differently) THeth 4:38f., 60-63, 74f., 90f.

c. with acc. of extent: *ŠA* KUR URU*Ḫatti* ḪUR.SAG.ḪI.A *ḫumantaš* KUR-*eaš ḫumantaš* dUTU-*ŠI* m*Tudḫaliyaš kuēš la-aḫ-ḫi-ia-iš-ki-iz-zi* "To all the mountains of Ḫatti-land, of the whole country, over which His Majesty T. regularly travels" KUB 2.1 vi 1-3, cf. [*kui*]*n la-aḫ-ḫi-iš-ki-iz-zi* KBo 12.59 i 5 (both texts cult of dLAMMAs), ed. Archi, SMEA 16:113, 116f.; LUGAL-*ušma kuiēš gi-im-ri*(sic)*-uš la-aḫ-ḫe-eš-ki-it nu mašieš gimruš la-aḫ-ḫi-ia-an ḫarzi* "What regions the King used to travel in — however many (of these) regions he has traveled in" KUB 27.1 i 7-8 (Hurr. cult, NH); *īt la-aḫ-ḫi-ia-ia*(sic) ḪUR.SAG.ḪI.A GIŠ*laḫḫurnuzzi* "Go, roam the mountains (and their) vegetation" KUB 27.67 iii 64 (rit.); □(After *īt* one does not expect *-ya* "and". Dittography for **laḫḫiya* or **laḫḫiyai*?); *nu* ḪUR.SAG.M[EŠ(-) ... *la-a*]*ḫ-ḫi-ia-iš-ki-it* "he roamed the mountains"

KUB 8.50 ii 8f. (Gilg. epic), ḪUR.SAG.M[EŠ(-) . . .] is acc., contra Friedrich, ZA 39:22, who restored dat.-loc. pl. ḪUR.SAG.M[EŠ-*aš an-da*]; . . . *mān la-aḫ-ḫe-eš-ki-nu-un* "When I roamed the [. . .]" KUB 31.4 obv. 17 (legend), ed. Otten, ZA 55 (1963) 160f.

d. in figura etymologica: (Ḫattuša will become as before, Ḫattuša will again take its place) LUGAL-*uš karuiliu*[*š*] *la-a-aḫ-ḫu-u-uš la-aḫ-ḫi-iš-ki-u-wa-an* "Then the king (will begin) to conduct campaigns as before" KBo 16.86 i 7-10 (omen apod.?, OH/NS); □end of paragraph; only one sign expected at end of line: either inf. in -*wa-an*[-*zi*] with auxillary verb or [ME-*i*] as the auxillary after supine, cf. Riemschneider, StBoT 9:13 n. 8; *namma kuitman* [*ABUYA apūš*(?) *la-aḫ-ḫ*]*u-u-uš la-aḫ-ḫe-eš-ki-it* "While [my father] conducted [those cam]paigns" (such and such cities rose up) KBo 14.4 i 4 (DŠ frag. 18; rest. after preceding quote).

2. trans. make war on, attack — **a.** finite forms: (Whoever is an enemy for me shall be an enemy for you) *nan la-aḫ-ḫi-ia-a*[*t-ten*] "Make war upon him!" KUB 21.47:14 + KUB 23.82 obv.! 19 (instr., MH); *apaššašmaš mān UL* [LÚ]KÚR *nan la-aḫ*[-*ḫi-i*]*a-at-te-ni UL* "but if he is not an enemy for you, and you do not make war upon him, (that shall be put under oath)" KUB 21.47: 21f. + KUB 23.82 obv.! 26; [[m]NIR(.GÁ)]L *kuit* LUGAL KUR *Mizrī* [LUGAL KUR (*A-mur-r*)]*i-ia la-aḫ-ḫi-ia-it* "Because Muwatalli made war upon the King of Egypt and [the King of] Amurru" KUB 21.17 i 14f. with dupl. KUB 31.27 i 2f. (Ḫatt. III); (in military oracles of Ḫatt. III:) [d]UTU-*ŠI* [URU]*Tanizilan la-ḫi-ia-iz-zi* "Shall His Majesty attack T.?" KUB 5.1 i 5; [URU]*Talmaliankan* TA [ḪUR.SAG]*Ḫaḫarwa* GAM *la-ḫi-ia-iz-zi* . . . *nankan* GAM UGU-*ma la-ḫi-ia-iz-zi* "Shall he attack T. downward from Mt. Ḫ.? . . . Or shall he attack it upwards from below? i 65, 68; *naš* [URU!]*Liḫayama kuwapi la-ḫi-ia-am-mi* "Or, when I attack them (i.e., the Gašga, ii 14) in Liḫaya, (will the oracle for Nerik become favorable as a result?)" ii 17f.; *nu* [URU]*Tanizilan* RA-*zi nu* [URU]*Ḫurnan* [URU]*Tašmaḫan la-ḫi-ia-iz-zi* i 10; ERÍN.MEŠ *ŠA* [ḪUR.SAG]*Ḫaḫarwa* as direct object i 1, 55, 60, 86, ii 61, 74f., iii 24, 29f., ed. (differently) THeth 4 (1974) 32-35, 40-47, 54f., 60-63, 68-71.

b. in inf. construction (in oracles of Ḫatt. III): [*nan*] DINGIR-*LUM-ma la-ḫi-ia-u-an-zi UL pešti* "Or do you, oh god, not allow [it] to be attacked?" KUB 5.1 iii 10; *nu* DINGIR. MEŠ-*za kīma malān* [URU]*Neriqa*<*n*>*zakan karpmi nu la-ḫi-ia-u-an-zi* [URU]*Tanizilan pi*(*r*)*an arnumi nu ŠA* [ḪUR.SAG]*Ḫaḫarwa* ERÍN.MEŠ *QATAMMA la-ḫi-ia-iz-zi* "Or has the following been agreed to by the gods? I shall 'lift' Nerik (cf. acc. ii 66, above sub usage 1b) and mobilize (the town/people of) T. for attack (so that) it will attack the troops of Mt. Ḫ. in the same way'" iii 28-30, cf. DINGIR.MEŠ-*zapat ANA* [ḪUR.SAG]*Ḫaḫarwa la-ḫi-ia-u-an-zi arān* iv 80.

arḫa KUB 5.1 i 55 and *kattan* KBo 4.4 iii 50, KUB 21.5 iii 21, 23 (= Alakš. iii 7, 9) are not preverbs, but postpositions, EGIR-*pa* KUB 5.1 ii 66, GAM ibid. i 65 and GAM UGU ibid. i 68 are adverbs.

The forms with single *ḫ*, attested only in KUB 5.1, have here been taken as a spelling variant of *laḫḫiyai-*, contra HW; Kammenhuber, MIO 2 (1954) 52; Ünal, THeth 4 (1974) 94; against the equation of *laḫiyai-* with RA (Akk. *maḫāṣu*, Hitt. *walḫ-*) "to hit = attack" are the facts that *laḫiyai-* is used with abl. and loc. and with direct object, but RA with direct object only, and that the two verbs occur side by side in KUB 5.1 apparently in contrast.

Götze, Ḫatt. (1925) 87; Friedrich, HW 124.

Cf. *laḫḫa-*.

[(LÚ)]**laḫḫiyala-** n.; traveler(?); from OH.†

sg. nom. *la-aḫ-ḫi-ia-la-aš* KUB 12.63 rev. 3, 6 (OH/MS); [LÚ]*la-aḫ-ḫi-ia-la-aš* KUB 13.9 i 6 (MH/NS); **acc.** *la-aḫ-ḫi-ia-la-an* KUB 12.63 rev. 2 (OH/MS); [LÚ]*la-aḫ-ḫi-ia-la-an* KBo 18.14 rev. 5, 6 (sg. with numerals; MS?); **d.-l.** [LÚ]*la-aḫ-ḫi-ia-l*[*i*] KUB 36.85:11 (MS?).

pl. nom. [[LÚ].MEŠ]*la-aḫ-ḫi-ia-le-eš* KBo 20.16 obv.? 9 (OH/OS).

[. . . LÚ].[MEŠ] *la-aḫ-ḫi-ia-le-eš dan*[*zi*] (in a list of persons who receive sacrificial animals, preceded by [LÚ]GUDÚ, [S]AL *šiunzannaš*, [[LÚ]]*arzanalaš*, followed by the elders of Zip-landa, etc.) KBo 20.16 obv.? 9 (OH/OS); cf. KBo 25.24:6; "(The Temple of the Stormgod said to the men: ...)" *nuwašmaš piḫḫi ma-u-wa gimri la-aḫ-ḫi-ia-la-an maḫḫa[n ...]* [*UMMA* LÚ.MEŠ *A*]*NA* É.[d]IM *la-aḫ-ḫi-ia-la-aš-wa nuwaratšikan dauwani* [... *š*]*uppizzi* "'I shall give (it) to you, if in the open country [you rob him(?)] like a traveler (acc.).' [The men said] to the Temple of the Stormgod: 'He is a traveler! We shall take it from him, [while(?) ...] he sleeps!'" KUB 12.63 rev. 2-4 (myth, OH/MS), cf. ibid. 6; (When I, Tudḫaliya, came home from Aššuwa, the Hittites said to me:) [d]UTU-*ŠI-wa anzel BELINI* [LÚ]*la-aḫ-ḫi-ia-la-aš* [*z*]*ik nuwašša*[*n*] *ḫannešnanni* [*ḫa*]*nnauwanzi UL tarratta* "You, Your Majesty (Tudḫaliya), our lord, are a traveler, and (therefore) you were unable(?) to give judgment on litigation" KUB 13.9 + 40.62 i 6-8 (edict, MH/NS); 10 [LÚ]*la-aḫ-ḫi-ia-la-an ú*[*watezzi*(?)] 20 [LÚ]*la-aḫ-ḫi-ia-la-an-ma UL uwatez*[*zi*] "He will bring 10 travelers but not 20 travelers" KBo 18.14 rev. 5-7 (letter, MS?); [LÚ]*la-aḫ-ḫi-ia-l*[*i ... k*]*arp*[*a*]*n ḫarzi* "he has removed [...] from the traveler" KUB 36.85:11f. (letter frag.?, MS?).

While Tudḫaliya upon his return from a major campaign may have been called "a leader of campaigns," the other occurrences rather favor the nonmilitary sense of "traveler."

Laroche, RHA IX/49 (1948-49) 14, RA 48 (1954) 46.

Cf. *laḫḫa-*, [LÚ]KASKAL-*la-aš*.

laḫḫiyatar n.; military expedition, campaign, military obligation; NH.†

sg. nom.-acc. *la-aḫ-ḫi-ia-tar* KBo 22.264 i 1, 14; **d.-l.** *la-aḫ-ḫi-ia-an-ni* KBo 4.10 obv. 44 and dupl. ABoT 57 obv. 17.

pl. (?) nom.-acc. *la-aḫ-ḫi-ia-tar* KUB 21.5 iii 24 with dupl.

ANA [d]UTU-*ŠI la-aḫ-ḫi-ia-tar* DINGIR-*LUM kedani* MU-*ti* ZAG KUR *Durmitta malān ḫarti* "Have you, O god, approved of the frontier of Durmitta as (the goal of) a military campaign for His Majesty?" KBo 22.264 i 1f. (oracle), cf. ibid. 14-16; [URU]*Ḫattušazmawatta ke la-aḫ-ḫi-ia-tar* "But from Ḫattuša these are your military obligations" (i.e., with the capital as base, in contrast to those based in the vassal's own country) KUB 21.5 iii 24 with dupl. (Alakš. §14, cf. SV 2, p. 69 n. 5, and p. 95, where Friedrich argues for sg.); *nušši ziladuwa ŠA* [URU]*Ḫatti la-aḫ-ḫi-ia-an-ni* 200 *iyattaru* "In the future let (only) 200 men of his go on a military expedition of Ḫatti" KBo 4.10 obv. 43f. and dupl. ABoT 57 obv. 16-18 (Ulmi-Tešub treaty).

Sommer, Heth. 2 (1922) 48; Götze, Ḫatt. (1925) 87; Friedrich, SV 2 (1930) 95.

Cf. *laḫḫa-*.

laḫḫilaḫḫeškinu- see *laḫlaḫḫeškinu-*.

laḫḫema- n. com.; errand(?); OH/NS.†

"The king took Išpudašinara — Šuppiuman and Maraššan were ... -grooms — but he made him their *urallaš*" *išpanti la-aḫ-ḫé-mu-uš ḫueškizzi* "(and so) he always runs errands(?) by night" KBo 3.34 ii 21-23 ('Palace Chron.', OH/NS); *laḫḫemuš* is in broken portion of dupl. KBo 3.36:27.

Laroche, RA 52 (1958) 187: "marche, mouvement."

Cf. *laḫḫa-*.

[*laḫlaḫḫi-*] for *la-aḫ-la-aḫ-ḫi-aš* (KUB 5.22:35) and *la-aḫ-la-aḫ-ḫi-mu-uš* (KUB 18.12 obv. 15) listed in HW 121 under this stem see *laḫlaḫḫima-*, n. com.

laḫlaḫḫiya- v.; **1.** to be agitated, to be anxious, to worry, **2.** to mill(?); from OH(?).†

pres. sg. 2 [*l*]*a-aḫ-la-aḫ-ḫi-ia-ši* KBo 12.17:3; **pl. 1** *la-aḫ-la-aḫ-ḫi-ia-u-e-ni* KUB 5.11 iv 24 (NH); **act. pret. or mid. pres. sg. 3** *la-aḫ-la-aḫ-ḫi-ia-at-ta* KBo 22.6 i 15; **iter. pres. pl. 1** *la-aḫ-la-aḫ-ḫe-eš-ga-u-e-ni* KBo 2.2 i 44, ii (8) (NH); **mid. pres. 3** [*la-a*]*ḫ-*⌈*la*⌉*-aḫ-ḫi-iš-ki-it-ta-ri* KBo 3.21 ii 27 (coll.) (OH?/NS).

1. to be agitated, to be anxious, to worry, with *-kan*: *mān*(?) *aši*(?) *iš*[*ḫiu*]*l* DÙ-*ri* [*U*]*L*[*k*]*án*! *kuitki la-aḫ-la-aḫ-ḫi-ia-u-e-ni nu* I[GI-*zi*] *TE*[MEŠ] SIG_5-*ru* "If that treaty is concluded(?) (and) we will have nothing to worry about, then may the first exta be favorable" KUB 5.11 iv 23f. (readings uncertain), cf. *UL-kán kuitki la-aḫ-la-aḫ-ḫi-i*[*a-u-e-ni*] KUB 16.62 rev. 6 (oracle); *pirankan kuedani memiyani la-aḫ-la-aḫ-ḫe-eš-ga-u-e-ni nankan :tapaššaš apiya kuiški anda wemiyazi* "The matter about which we constantly worry in advance: (if) some fever(?) will find him (the king) there (let the MUŠEN

ḪURRI oracle be unfavorable)" KBo 2.2 i 43-47; *mānkan piranm[a] la-aḫ-la-aḫ-ḫe-eš-ga-u[-e]-ni nu eni uttar apiy[a :tap]ašani(!) nammama* DINGIR-*LUM ANA* ᵈUTU-*ŠI dammain :tapaššan UL kuinki uškiši kuitmanaškan INA* ᵁᴿᵁ*Ḫatti še[r]* KBo 2.2 ii 1-13; *[l]a-aḫ-la-aḫ-ḫi-ia-ši* KBo 12.17:3 (in broken context, probably a letter); cf. the fragmentary letter KBo 18.11 obv. 10 *la-aḫ-l[a? . . .]* or *-t[a? . . .]*, cf. *laḫ-* B; restored: *našta tandukiš* DUMU-*aš [. . . la-a]ḫ-⌈la⌉-aḫ-ḫi-iš-ki-it-ta-ri* KBo 3.21 (BoTU 6) ii 26f. (hymn to Stormgod, OH). □The fragmentary context has *ḫatuga* (24) and *ḫeunma ḫinganaš* [. . . -*š*]*i*(?) (25f.) "[Yo]u[. . .]the rain [as a . . . (?)] of death", so 26f. could mean "The mortal man is constantly agitated/anxious."

2. to mill about(?): *Šarrukinaš* ᵁᴿᵁ*Puruš-ḫanda iyanneš tazkan tu-uz-z[i-o]-mi-iš araḫ-zanda la-aḫ-la-aḫ-ḫi-ia-at-ta* "Sargon set out for Purušḫanda, and his(!?) army milled (lit. mills) about. (Then he sacrificed one bull and seven sheep to the holy river Aranzaḫ)" KBo 22.6 i 14-16 (King of Battle), ed. MDOG 101:19, 22; □restoration and interpretation uncertain, cf. ibid. 24. Alternatives would be: "His(!) army (*tuzz[iš]*) around him was worried," (but he answered them by making the sacrifice), or "He was worrying about the army around him" (*tuzz[iaš]miš*?, in any case disregarding the pronoun -(*š*)*miš*).

Götze, KlF 1 (1930) 185f.; Güterbock, Oriens 10 (1957) 351; MDOG 101 (1969) 24.

Cf. *laḫlaḫḫima-*, *laḫlaḫḫinu-* with *laḫlaḫḫinuški-*, *laḫlaḫ-ḫiškinu-*.

laḫlaḫ(ḫ)ima- n. com.; agitation: mental agitation, worry, agony, (also physical agitation, commotion, movement?); NH.†

sg. acc. *la-aḫ-la-aḫ-ḫi-ma-an* KUB 14.14 obv. (40), KUB 14.10 i (16), with dupl. KUB 14.11 i (10), KUB 14.12 rev. 4, KBo 14.75 i 12; *la-aḫ-la-ḫi-ma-an* KUB 14.14 rev. 38; **gen.** *la-aḫ-la-aḫ-ḫi-ma-aš* KUB 18.15 obv. 17, KBo 16.98 ii 23; **d.-l.** *la-aḫ-la-ḫi-mi* KUB 22.38 i 8; *la-aḫ-la-aḫ-ḫi-mi* 354/z i 15; **abl.** *la!-aḫ-la!-aḫ-ḫi-ma-za* IBoT 1.33:46, 62; *la-aḫ-la!-ḫi-ma-za* IBoT 1.33:15; *la!-aḫ<-la-aḫ>-ḫi-ma-za* IBoT 1.33:110.

pl. acc.(?) *la-aḫ-la-aḫ-ḫi-mu-uš* KUB 18.12 obv. 15.

a. in the Plague Prayers Götze, KlF 1 (1930) 186 and related usage: *ammukmaz* ŠÀ-*az la-aḫ-la-aḫ-ḫi-ma-an UL tarḫmi* NÍ.TE-*asmaza pittuliyan namma UL tarḫmi* "But I cannot overcome the worry of (lit. from) (my) heart, and I can no longer overcome the anguish of (lit. from) (my) self" KUB 14.10 i 16-18, with dupl. KUB 14.11 i 10-12 (Second Plague Prayer), ed. Götze KlF 1:206f. §1.6, cf. KBo 14.75 i 12; cf. also KUB 14.14 + KUB 19.2 obv. 39f., KUB 14.14 rev. 38f. + KUB 19.1 rev. 51f. (First Plague Prayer), ed. Götze, KlF 1:168-71, 176f.; *nuwa kel antuḫšaš idalu inan idal[un] uriteman naḫšaratta<n> la-aḫ-la-aḫ-ḫ[i-ma-an] tupran nuwarankan anda ANA* [URU.DIDLI.ḪI.A ᴸᵁ́KÚR(?)] *pedatten* Bo 2490 ii 9-12; cf. Götze, KlF 1 (1930) 185f.

b. a location at the pool used for snake oracles Laroche, RA 52 (1958) 162: 2 *la-aḫ-la!-ḫi-ma-za uit n[aškan] ANA* EZEN.MEŠ DINGIR.MEŠ *munnait* 3 *dušgaranaza uit* [o] É.ŠÀ . . . *mun<na>it* "Second: it (the snake) came from 'agitation' and hid at 'the festivals of the gods'; third it came from 'joy' and hid at 'the inner chamber of . . .'" IBoT 1.33:15f., ed. Laroche, RA 52:152, 156; cf. 2 *la!-aḫ-la!-aḫ-ḫi-ma!-za ḫadandaza* GAM-*anda uit* ibid. 62; 2 *la!-aḫ<-la-aḫ>-ḫi-ma-za* UGU-*za* DAB-*za uit* ibid. 110; *tama[i]šmakan* MUŠ.GUNNI-*iš IŠTU* É.LUGAL *parā uit naškan la-aḫ-la-ḫi-mi pa[it]* "But another hearth-snake came out of 'the king's palace' and went to the 'agitation' (and from there to the 'prison', etc.)" KUB 22.38 i 7-8, ed. Laroche, RA 52 (1958) 150f.

c. in bird oracles preceding the word "birds": *nu* IGI-*anda la-aḫ-la-aḫ-ḫi-ma-aš* MUŠEN.ḪI.A *NĪ[MUR]* "In front of us we saw the birds of *l.*" KUB 18.15 obv. 17, KBo 16.98 ii 23. □Unclear whether the birds themselves are agitated or only presage agitation; *nu* IGI-*anda la-aḫ-la-aḫ-ḫi-mu-uš* MUŠEN.ḪI.A *NĪMUR* (KUB 18.2 obv. 15) either contains a scribal mistake for *-ma-aš*, or could be translated "in front of us we saw movements, namely birds." Since *-ima-* forms nouns, interpretation of *laḫlaḫḫimuš* as an adjective is unlikely. *kī kuit ŠA* ᵈUTU-*ŠI* MUŠEN.ḪI.A *la-aḫ-la-aḫ-ḫi<-ma>-aš* MUŠEN.ḪI.A *gallareš-ki[r]* "Since the birds of His Majesty, as birds of *l.*, were unfavorable, (if some deity is angry because of the word of a god, . . .)" KUB 5.22:35f. (oracle). □This emendation is preferable to positing a noun or adjective **laḫlaḫḫi-*.

Götze, KlF 1 (1930) 185f.; Laroche, BSL 52 (1956) 76f.

Cf. *laḫlaḫḫiya-*.

laḫlaḫḫinu- v.; to cause to be agitated, or worried; with *-kan*; NH.†

pret. pl. 3 *la-aḫ-la-aḫ-ḫi-nu-e-<<nu-e->>er* KUB 9.34 iii 31; **iter. pret. pl. 3** *la-aḫ-la-aḫ-ḫi-nu-uš-ki-ir* KUB 35.146 ii 16.

kuiš⸗an weritenuer kueš⸗an⸗kan la-aḫ-la-aḫ-ḫi-nu-e<<-nu-e>>-er "those who caused him fear, those who caused him worry" KUB 9.34 iii 30f. (rit.); *la-aḫ-la-aḫ-ḫi-nu-uš-ki-ir-ra-an-kán kuieš* "those who constantly caused him worry" KUB 35.146 ii 16 (rit.), cf. the parallel *[ka]rdimiyaḫḫan⸗ziankan kuieš* "those who make him angry" ibid. 13.

Götze, KlF 1 (1930) 186.

Cf. *laḫlaḫḫiya-*.

laḫlaḫḫeškinu-, laḫḫilaḫḫeškinu- v.; to agitate (horses), cause (the horses) to run; NH.†

pres. sg. 3 *la-aḫ-la-aḫ-ḫe-eš-ki-nu-zi* KUB 1.13 + KBo 8.53 iv 8; *[la-aḫ-l]a-aḫ-ḫe-eš-ki-nu-zi* KUB 1.13 i 16; *la-aḫ-ḫi-la-aḫ-ḫe-eš-k[i-nu-zi]* ibid. iv 42 (for spelling without *-ḫi-* in the first two instances see Otten, ZA 55 (1963) 282 n. 3).

To date occurs only in tablet I of Kikkuli: *[na]š tūriyanzi naš* 1 DANNA *pennai [la-aḫ-l]a-aḫ-ḫe-eš-ki-nu-zi-ma-aš ANA* 7 IKU.ḪI.A "They harness them and he drives them (at a moderate gait) one DANNA, but he makes them run over seven IKU's" KUB 1.13 i 15f., ed. Hipp.heth. 54f., cf. ibid. iv 6-8 (p. 70f.), 41-43 (p. 72f.). Cf. *naš* 3 DANNA *pennai parḫzimaš ANA* 7 IKU.ḪI.A KUB 1.13 i 4f. and passim. For synonymous use of *parḫ-*, literally "to chase", referring to the fast gait of horses, and *laḫ(ḫi)laḫḫeškinu-* see Kammenhuber, MSS 2 (1957) 103, OLZ 1954:231.

The irregular formation with *-nu-* added after *-šk-* may be explicable on semantic grounds: "cause to be continuously agitated, cause to keep running."

Hrozný, ArOr 3 (1931) 441, 457; Kammenhuber, Hipp.heth. (1961) 336 (ref.); Güterbock, Oriens 10 (1957) 351, MDOG 101 (1969) 24, for "agitate" as semantic basis of "cause to run" and "worry".

Cf. *laḫlaḫḫiya-*.

laḫma- n.; (mng. unkn.); from OH.†

In a festival: *periš uizzi* [. . .] *peran* SÌR(coll.)-*RU la-aḫ-ma-aš paizzi* UGULA $^{\text{LÚ.MEŠ}}$AL[AN.ZU$_{x}$ . . . (-)]*iešzi* KBo 17.43 iv 5-6 (OH/MS?).

In a list of offerings: [. . . ^{GIŠ}G]A.ZUM.ḪI.A *la-aḫ-ma*(coll.)-*aš* ^{TUG}*kišuda*[- . . . 1-(*NU-TUM*)] ^{GIŠ}*urala*[- . . .]x *la-aḫ-ma*!(coll.)-*aš* KÙ.GI-*ya anda*[. . .] KBo 21.87 obv. 4-5 + KBo 20.29 obv. 3 with dupl. KBo 21.30 i 6-8 which has *la-aḫ-ma*(coll.)-*aš* in i 8.

It is possible that *laḫpa-* "ivory" and *laḫma-* are two spellings of the same word.

Cf. *laḫmant-*.

laḫmant- n. or adj.; (mng. unkn.); OH?/NS.†

In the monthly festival: UGULA $^{\text{LÚ.MEŠ}}$MUḪALDIM SAG.DU.MEŠ GÌ[R.MEŠ o o o o] *la-aḫ-ma-an-du-uš udai* KUB 2.13 ii 34-35.

Cf. *laḫma-*.

laḫni- n. com.; (a substance mixed in water and drunk); from pre-NH.†

1 ^{DUG}ḪAB.ḪAB *ME-E la-aḫ-ni-iš anda immeyanza* ^{GIŠ}*alanzanan* ^{GIŠ}*ḫatalkišnaš galaktar ANA* ^{DUG}ḪAB.ḪAB *anda dai nat* UD-*at* UD-*at akuwanna pešk[i]zz[i]* "one vessel of water with *laḫni-* mixed in . . . and she gives it daily (to the person for whom the ritual is performed) to drink" KUB 28.102 iii! 11-17 (rit. of Ḫutuši, pre-NH/NS).

In the literary text describing the siege of the city of Uršu, which is written in Akkadian, a section occurs which contains some Hittite words: KI.UD *la-aḫ-ni-it še-ḫu-wa-en* UR.TUR *kur-zi-wa-ni-eš* GUD SAG KI UD KBo 1.11 rev.! 15; ed. Güterbock, ZA 44:122f., 129f.

(:)laḫpa- n. com.; ivory(?); NH.†

a. in a lyric description: (Akk.) *[m]akūt šinni quttûtu [š]a ulṣa malât* "(she is) a finished(?) pillar(?) of ivory (lit. tooth); she is full of rejoicing" = (Hitt.) *la-aḫ-pa-aš-ma-aš kurakkiš mān zinnanza naš* ME.LÁM-*az šu[w]anza* "she is like a finished pillar(?) of *laḫpa-*; she is full of radiance" RŠ 25.421, 28-29, ed. Laroche, Ugar. 5:773, 775, 777.

b. unclear: [. . .] *:la-aḫ-pa-aš unuwandu* KUB 36.25 i 4 (frag. of Kumarbi myth).

The translation is based on the trilingual RŠ 25.421. The Hitt. and Akk. versions, however, do not agree in all respects. The employment of the gloss wedge (usage b) may indicate the word is Luwian. Because of the uncertainty of the translation "ivory" the logographic representations of ivory (KA×UD AM.SI, etc.) will be treated in the section of the dictionary devoted to logograms.

Laroche, Revue de Philologie 39 (1965) 56ff., Ugar. 5 (1968) 777; Güterbock, Anatolia 15 (1971) 1 n. 2.

Cf. *laḫma-*.

laḫšanili adv.; in the manner of the city of Laḫšan (= Liḫšina); NH.†

Dancers (LÚ.MEŠHÚB.BÍ) dance in various modes, each successively introduced by EGIR-*ŠÚ-ma*. In the list of modes: EGIR-*ŠÚ-ma la-aḫ-ša-ni-li* EGIR-*ŠÚ-ma ḫuppiššanili* "next (they danced) in the mode of the city of Laḫšan, next in the mode of the city of Ḫupišna" KUB 4.1 iv left side 39-40. Cf. *lapat(a/i)-*.

Laroche apud Kammenhuber, RHA XX/70 (1962) 8; RGTC 6:247.

laḫu- see *laḫ(ḫ)uwai-*.

laḫḫu- n. com.; (a vessel); NH.†

DAG.KISIM$_5$×LA (+ sign name and pronunciation) = (Akk.) *la-aḫ-ta-nu* = (Hitt.) *a-⌈ar⌉-ru-ma-aš la-aḫ-ḫu-uš* "an *l.*-container of (i.e., for) washing" KUB 3.94 ii 16f.

Friedrich, ZA 35 (1924) 11; Forrer, BoTU 1 (1922f.) 23, cf. MSL 2:117, CAD L 44 (Akk. *laḫtanu* "beer vat").

Cf. *laḫ(ḫ)uwai-*.

laḫ(ḫ)uwai-, laḫ(ḫ)u- v.; **1.** to pour (liquids, salt, intangibles), **2.** to empty (a container), **3.** to (over)flow (intrans.); from OH.

pres. sg. 1 *la-ḫu-a/uḫ-ḫi* KUB 7.1 i 30 (pre-NH/NS); **sg. 2** *la-aḫ-ḫu-ut-ti* KUB 30.34 iv 14 (MH/NS); **sg. 3** *la-a-ḫu-i* KBo 17.1 i 16, 17 (OH/OS), KBo 15.33 ii 4 (OH/MS), KUB 15.31 i 26, KBo 21.33 i 22, 26, 2Mašt. iii 23 (all MH/MS); *la-a-ḫu-u-i* KBo 11.51 iv 11 (thoroughly modernized OH/NS), KUB 13.4 i 62, KBo 5.1 iv 14, 16 (both NH); *la-ḫu-i* KBo 20.128:6 (MH/NS), KUB 9.22 ii 26, KUB 46.48 obv. 5, KBo 17.103 rev. 14 (same tablet as KUB 46.48) (all NH); *la-a-ḫu-u-wa-i* KUB 24.11 iii 14, KUB 27.29 iii 10 (both MH/NS), KBo 11.17 i 4, (5) (NH); *la-a-ḫu-u-wa-<i>* KUB 28.89 i 14; *la-a-ḫu-wa-i* KUB 10.18 i 11 (OH/NS), KBo 2.3 ii 31, KBo 15.37 iv 50 (both MH/NS), KUB 8.2 obv. 8 (NH); *la-a-ḫu-wa-a-i* KUB 8.38 iii! 15, KBo 17.94 iii 25, KUB 44.55 rev. (10) (all NH); *la-a-ḫu-u-wa-a-i* KUB 28.82 ii 9, HT 23 obv. 6 (both OH/NS), KUB 9.28 iv 8 (MH/NS); *la-ḫu-u-wa-a-i* KUB 41.40 i 20, 41.26 iv 13 (both OH/NS); *la-ḫu-wa-a-i* KBo 21.59:11 (NH?); *la-ḫu-u-wa-i* KUB 33.67 i 23 (OH/NS), KUB 6.45 iv 51, 54 (Muw.); *la-ḫu-wa-i* KUB 15.35 i 7, KBo 10.45 iv (7) (both MH/NS); *la-aḫ-ḫu-u-wa-i* KUB 13.3 i 12, KUB 9.31 ii 9 (both MH/NS); *la-ḫu-uz-zi* KUB 24.7 ii 13 (NH), *la-a-ḫu-u-wa-a-iz[-zi]* 1373/u 11.

pres. pl. 1 (see also *lāḫ-* A) *la-ḫu-e-ni* KBo 19.156 ii 15 (OH/MS), KUB 35.93 obv.! 5 (same tablet), KBo 17.25 obv. 9; *la-a-ḫ[u]?-⌈e-ni⌉* KUB 39.56 iv 2; **pres. pl. 3** *la-ḫu-an-zi* KBo 20.33 obv. 10, 14 (OH/OS), KBo 21.70 i 14, 24 (OH?/MS), *la-ḫu-u-an-zi* KUB 20.11 ii 18 (OH), 45.59 rev. 19; 43.38 rev. 8; *la-a-ḫu-u-an-zi* KUB 25.37 i 45 (NS), KBo 23.70 ii 11; IBoT 3.26:(10); KUB 46.61:(8); *la-a-ḫu-an[-zi]* KUB 25.48 iii 24 (MH/NS) w. dupl. *la-a-ḫu-wa-an⌈-zi⌉* KBo 20.116 "rev." 2; *la-ḫu-u-wa-an-zi* KBo 20.34 obv. 9 (OH/MS), KUB 15.34 iii 27 (MH/MS?), KUB 30.33 iv 2 (MH/NS); *la-ḫu-wa-an-zi* KBo 2.3 iv 5, (7) (MH/NS), KBo 23.10 iv (17); *la-ḫu-wa-a-an-zi* KUB 30.56 iii 8 (NH); *la-a-ḫu-wa-an-zi* 2Mašt. ii 42; *la-a-ḫu-u-wa-an-zi* KUB 29.4 iii 25; *la-a-ḫu-wa-a-an-zi* KUB 15.31 iii (53) (MH/NS).

pret. sg. 1 *la-a-ḫu-wa-nu-un* IBoT 3.106 rev. 3′ (NH?), [for *la-a-ḫu-un* see under *lāḫ-* A.]; **sg. 3** *la-a-aḫ-ḫu-uš* KUB 33.24 ii 8 (OH/NS), *la-a-ḫu-wa-aš* FHG 2:19 (OH/NS), *la*(coll.)*-a-ḫu-u-wa-iš* VBoT 30 rev.!(coll.) 13 (NS); **pl. 3** *la-ḫu-wa-a-ir* KBo 23.26 iv 3.

imp. sg. 2 [*la-a-aḫ* see *lāḫ-* A.]; **pl. 2** *la-aḫ-ḫu-ten* KUB 13.3 ii 28 (NS), *la-a-aḫ-ḫu-wa-ten* ibid. iii 2; **pl. 3** (all NS) *la-ḫu-wa-[a]n-du* KUB 41.33 obv. 15, *la-ḫu-wa-a-an-du* ibid. obv. 14, *la-a-ḫu-wa-an-du* ibid. obv. 14, *la-a-ḫu-u-wa-an-du* KUB 41.32 obv. 15.

iter. sg. 3 *la-ḫu-uš-ki-iz-zi* 2Mašt. iii 32 (MH/MS), *la-ḫu-iš-ki-iz-zi* (KUB 33.84 +) Bo 6404 iv 23 (StBoT 14 p. 60) (MH/NS); **pl. 3** [*l*]*a-a-ḫu-wa-iš-kán-zi* KBo 26.129 iv? 4.

mid. pres. sg. 3 *la-ḫu-wa-a-ri* KBo 3.29:11 (OH/NS), *la-ḫu-ut?-ta-ri* KUB 13.8 obv. 8 (MH/NS), *la-a-ḫu-ut-ta-ri* 829/z: 1 (cf. ibid. 3), *la-ḫu-u-wa-a-ri* KUB 25.37 i 26, 27, (28) (OH?/NS); **sg. 3** *la-ḫu-ut-ta-at* KBo 13.106 i 15 (OH/NS); **pl. 3** [*la*]*-a-ḫu-u-wa-an-da-at* Bo 3090 obv. 17 (StBoT 5 p. 104); **imp. sg. 3** *la-ḫu-u-wa-ru* KBo 10.45 i 26 (MH/NS).

part. neut. sg. *la-a-ḫu-an* KBo 17.40 iv 11 (OH/MS?), KUB 45.47 i 16 (MS?), [*l*]*a-a-ḫu-u-wa-a-an* KUB 35.54 iii 13; *la-a-ḫu-u-wa-an* KBo 21.34 ii 34 (MH/MS?), *la-a-ḫu-wa-an* KUB 24.9 iii (27) (OH/NS), KBo 15.10 ii 3 (MH/

MS), *la-ḫu-a-an* KBo 17.15 obv.? 17 (OH/OS); *la-ḫu-u-wa-an* KBo 21.8 iii 9 (OH/NS), *la-ḫu-u-wa-a-an* KUB 15.34 i 9 (MH/MS?).

nom. com. sg. *la-a-ḫu-wa-an-za* KUB 41.8 iv (23) (MH/MS), KUB 11.34 v 56 (OH/NS), *la-a-ḫu-u-wa-an-za* KUB 7.46:3.

verbal subst. nom.-acc. *la-a-ḫu-u-wa-ar* KBo 1.42 iii 50, *la-a-ḫu-wa-ar* ibid. iv 10; **gen.** *la-ḫu-aš* KBo 18.181 rev. 33, *la-a-ḫu-wa-aš* FHG 2:19 (gen. or finite verb form?); **inf.(?)** *la-a-ḫu-wa-an-⌈na⌉* 495/w right col. 9.

1. to pour, pour out — **a.** objects: contents of vessel, liquids and salt. The following are the direct objects of active forms or subjects of mid. forms: *watar* "water" KUB 30.34 iv 14, KUB 32.128 i 30-34, KUB 9.28 iv 5-8; *waḫešnaš watar* KUB 7.1 i 28-32, KUB 33.24 ii 7-8; *šiḫelliyaš watar* KBo 5.2 iii 55f., KBo 11.5 vi 27-29; *kueluwanaš watar* KUB 9.1 iii 21f.; ŠU.MEŠ-*aš watar* "water of the hands" HT 5:14; oils: Ì-*an* KBo 2.3 ii 31, 2Mašt. iii 22f., KBo 11.32 obv. 9, KUB 13.8 obv. 8; Ì.DÙG.GA KUB 33.67 i 23, KUB 6.45 iv 51, 54, 58; Ì.NUN KBo 15.24 ii 33f., KBo 23.10 iv 16f.; Ì.GIŠ KUB 9.6 i 6-8, KUB 44.49 rev.? 10; Ì ^{GIŠ}*ZERTUM* 2Mašt. ii 42; LÀL "honey" KUB 6.45+ iv 51, 54, 58, KBo 15.10 i 29; GEŠTIN "wine" KUB 8.38 iii! 14-15 + KUB 44.63 iii 6-7; KUB 10.18 i 11, KBo 15.37 iv 45f., 49f., v 17-21; KAŠ(-*eššar*) "beer" KUB 30.15 obv. 25, KBo 10.16 iv 7f.; *marnuwan* (beverage) KUB 2.3 ii 26f., VBoT 3 v 21; *tawal* (beverage) KUB 15.34 iii 26f.; *walḫi* (beverage) KUB 15.34 iii 26f., KUB 20.11 ii 3, KBo 21.70 i 24; KA.DÙ.NAG KBo 10.45 iv 7, 24; *šeḫur* "urine" KUB 9.28 iii 17; MUN "salt" KBo 15.24 ii 34.

b. to pour out something intangible as though it were a liquid (metaphorical use): "Just as water flows down from the roof and doesn't go back into the bucket," [(*kella parnaš*)] ... [*par*]*ā la-ḫu-u-wa-ru na*[(*t namm*)]*a* EGIR-*pa le uizzi* "(so also) may ... (the various evils) ... of this house be poured out and not come back again!" KBo 10.45 i 24-27 w. dupls. KUB 7.41 i 29-32 and KUB 41.8 i 8-11 (rit., MH/NS), ed. Otten, ZA 54:118f., i 30-33; "Whoever does an impure act and gives defiled water to the king" *nuwakan apēl* ZI-*an* DINGIR.MEŠ *uwitenaš iwar arḫa la-a-aḫ-ḫu-wa-ten* "pour out, O gods, his soul like water!" KUB 13.3 ii 29-30, iii 1-2 (instr., MH/NS), ed. Friedrich, MAOG 4:47, 49 and tr. ANET 207.

2. to empty a container (acc.) by pouring its contents out: *nammakan ANA PANI* ^{d}IM 2 GAL *IŠTU* GESTIN *šuwanduš la-a-ḫu-u-wa-an-zi* "next they empty out two goblets filled with wine before the Stormgod" KBo 21.34 i 24f., cf. 40f. (fest., MH/NS); *nukan* SAL ŠU.GI ^{DUG}*ḫu-p*[(*uw*)]*aya ḫašši anda la-ḫu-uš-ki-iz-zi* "The Old Woman repeatedly empties the *ḫ*.-vessels onto the hearth" 2Mašt. iii 31f., ed. Rost, MIO 1:360f. [EGI]R-*andama wardulin la-ḫu-u-w*[*a-i*?] "Afterwards [he?] empties the *w*.-vessel" KUB 24.10 iii 29 (^{f}Alli rit., MH/NS), ed. THeth 2:48f., cf. also ibid. 15-20; *nukkan apun* [^{DUG}*ḫ*]*ūpurnin parā la-ḫu-u-wa-an-zi* "They empty that *ḫ*.-vessel (and smash it)" KBo 20.34 obv. 8-10 (Ḫantitaššu rit., OH/MS); cf. KUB 13.3 ii 26-28.

3. Intrans.: to flow, overflow (OH): [*arun*]*an tarmāmi nu appa natta la-a-ḫu-i* "I will fix [the se]a, so that it may not flow back" KUB 31.4:14 + KBo 3.41 (BoTU 14) 13 (OH/NS), ed. Otten, ZA 55:160f., 165; *arunašša la-a-ḫu-wa-i* "and the sea will flow (away)" KBo 2.19 obv. 9 (lunar omen, OH?/NS), cf. Otten, ibid. 165; *karaiz la-a-ḫ*[*u-i*] "the flood will flow, (will dislodge the house and carry it off to the sea)" KUB 36.110:19-21 (benedictions for Labarna, OH/OS), ed. Forrer, MAOG 4:32, and Laroche, RHA XI/53:69, Hoffner, AlHeth. 20 with different restor. of verb ending.

Associated preverbs, postpositions, or adverbs: **1′** *anda* following loc. case in KUB 24.9 iv 18 + KBo 12.126 iv 4, KBo 2.3 iv 7, 2Mašt. iii 32, KUB 9.1 iii 22, but without loc. in KBo 2.3 ii 31, KUB 30.22:11, KUB 15.34 i 8f., iii 26f.; **2′** *appa* in KUB 31.4:14 + KBo 3.41:13, KUB 30.34 iv 14; **3′** *appan* in KUB 30.33 iv 2, KUB 30.34 iv 15, KUB 46.38 i 13; **4′** *appanda* in KUB 9.19:14 (broken context); **5′** *arḫa* in KUB 13.3 ii 27f., iii 1f.; (KUB 33.84 +) Bo 6404 iv 23 (StBoT 14:60); KUB 41.8 ii 23 and dupl. KBo 10.45 ii 58 (ZA 54:126), KUB 43.38 rev. 8, 13; **6′** *katta* in KUB 10.11 v 4, KUB 11.21 v 23-24, KBo 16.100:10; **7′** *kattan* in KUB 47.89 iii 17, KBo 21.34 ii 35-36, 56; **8′** *menaḫḫanda* in KBo 21.33 ii 29, KUB 32.49b iii 7, 8, KBo 20.128:21, KUB 32.43 i 6, etc.; **9′** *parā* in KUB 17.28 iv 37, KUB 39.71 ii 10, HT 5:14; **10′** *piran* in KBo 13.217 iv 10; **11′** *piran arḫa* in KBo 4.13

vi 23; **12′** *šarā* in 2Mašt. A iv 24; **13′** *šer* in KUB 39.57 i 10, KBo 23.20 i 7, KBo 23.70 ii 6, (11); **14′** *šer arḫa* in KUB 13.5 ii 1 w. dupl. 13.4 i 62.

Hrozný, SH (1917) 34, 79; BoSt 3 (1919) 76 n. 6; Sommer & Ehelolf, Pap. (1924) 74; Otten, BiOr 8 (1951) 227 n. 27.

Cf. *laḫ-* A, *laḫḫu-* n., *lalḫuwant-*, *lilḫuwa-*, *lilḫuwai-*, *lelḫuwartima-*, ^{DUG}*lelḫundai-*, *lelḫunda(i)-* v., ^{DUG}*lel-ḫuntalli-*.

^{GIŠ}**laḫḫuwarnuzzi-** see $^{\text{(GIŠ)}}$*laḫḫurnuzzi-*.

$^{\text{(GIŠ)}}$**laḫḫura-** n. com.; offering table(?) or stand (for pots and offerings); wr. syll. and with logogram ^{GIŠ}GAN.KAL; from OH.

sg. nom. ^{GIŠ}*la-aḫ-ḫu-ra-aš* VBoT 58 iv 18 (OH/NS), KUB 42.81:(2) (NH); ^{GIŠ}*la-aḫ-ḫu-u-ra-aš* KBo 5.2 i 23 (MH/NS); **without det.** KUB 29.5 i 12 (NH); **sg. acc.** ^{GIŠ}*la-aḫ-ḫu-ra-an* KUB 45.12 ii 17 (MH/NS), KBo 4.13 iv 35 (NH); **without det.** KUB 34.49 rev. 2; ^{GIŠ}*la-aḫ-ḫu-u-ra-an* KBo 5.2 ii 34 (MH/NS); **loc.** ^{GIŠ}*la-aḫ-ḫu-ri* KBo 15.33 iii 3 (OH/MS), KBo 20.72 iv! 9; ^{GIŠ}*la-aḫ-ḫu-u-ri* KBo 5.2 ii 53, KBo 23.67 iii 4 (MH/NS); [...]*la-a-ḫu-ri-ia* KBo 11.18 v 12; **all.** ^{GIŠ}*la-aḫ-ḫu-u-ra* KBo 23.67 ii 21; **without det.** ibid. 19, KUB 32.84 i? 5, 10.

stem form ^{GIŠ}*la-aḫ-ḫu-u-ra* KBo 5.2 ii 35, 45, 46 (MH/NS), KBo 17.83 i (17) (NH).

laḫḫūraš KUB 29.5 i 12 corr. to ^{GIŠ}GAN.KAL in parallel 29.4 i 28 (NH).

a. object made at least partly of wood, occasionally plated with precious metals: [*la-a*]*ḫ-ḫu-ra-aš* GIŠ-*ṢÍ* KÙ.GI GAR.RA KUB 42.81:2; made of *šunilaš* wood (a conifer) VBoT 58 iv 18.

b. can be small (TUR VBoT 58 iv 18) or large enough to have under it 32 containers (KBo 5.2 ii 35f.; cf. Pap. 25).

c. usually occurs singly, although attested in following numbers: two KUB 29.4 i 28, seven KBo 5.2 ii 46.

d. grouped with other furniture such as: ^{GIŠ}ŠÚ.A KBo 5.2 ii 52, ^{GIŠ}BANŠUR KUB 29.4 i 28; 20.1 iii 4, KBo 14.88 iii 8, ^{GIŠ}BANŠUR.AD.KID and ^{GIŠ}*KANNUM* KBo 5.2 i 23f., KUB 29.4 i 28.

e. set up before the ^{GIŠ}ZAG.GAR.RA KBo 4.13 iv 35f.; can be lifted up together with bread and meat KBo 19.142 iii 12f.

f. two ox heads placed on each side of it KUB 30.41 iii 13f.; fragmented breads placed (KBo 23.67 ii 18f., iii 2-5) or scattered (KUB 9.31 ii 8) on it; ^{UZU}NÍG.GIG and ŠÀ (KUB 12.11 iii 10f.) set on it; cedar resin or shavings put on it ibid. iv 9f.; a *ḫalwani*-vessel placed on it KBo 23.67 ii 20-22, cf. KBo 19.142 iii 14f., KUB 45.3 i 15, KUB 12.11 iii 26.

Sommer & Ehelolf, Pap. (1924) 25 (a rather large vessel), Friedrich, HE 1st ed., 2. Teil (1946) 92 ("Opfergerät"), HW (1952) 125 (offering table?).

$^{\text{(GIŠ)}}$**laḫ(ḫ)urnuz(z)i-**, ^{GIŠ}**laḫḫuwarnuzzi-** n. neut. and com.; foliage, leafy branches, greenery (of trees or shrubs); from OH.

sg./pl. nom. neut. ^{GIŠ}*la-aḫ-ḫur-nu-uz-zi* RS 25.421:43 (Ugar. 5:445, 774); **sg./pl. acc. neut.** *la-aḫ-ḫu-ur-nu-zi* KBo 15.10 ii (17), 28, (30), etc. (MH/MS); *la-aḫ-ḫu-ur-nu-uz-zi* KBo 15.25 obv. 15 (MH/MS); ^{GIŠ}*la-aḫ-ḫur-nu-uz-zi* KBo 10.37 iii 27, 35 (OH/NS), KUB 27.67 iii 64 (MH/NS), KUB 9.32 obv. 38, rev. 27 (NH), KBo 19.142 ii 16; **without det.** KUB 9.32 rev. 13 (NH), KBo 13.212:(8); ^{GIŠ}*la-ḫur-nu-zi* KUB 27.67 ii 43 (MH/NS); ^{GIŠ}*la-aḫ-ḫur-nu-zi* KBo 17.105 iii 25 (NH); **sg. loc.** ^{GIŠ}*la-aḫ-ḫur-nu-uz-zi* KUB 9.31 iv 9, HT 1 iv 15, KBo 10.37 iv (30) (OH/NS); **without det.** KUB 9.32 rev. 7 (NH); ^{GIŠ}*la-ḫur-nu-zi* KBo 4.2 iii 34 (pre-NH/NS).

pl. nom. com. [^{GIŠ}*l*]*a-*[*ḫ*]*ur-nu-uz-zi-e-eš* KBo 14.142 ii 17 (NH); *la-aḫ-ḫur-nu-uz-zi-uš* KUB 25.23 i 23, (48), ii (27), HT 71:6 + IBoT 3.100:11, KUB 17.36:(11) (all NH); **pl. ergative** *la-aḫ-ḫu-ur-nu-uz-zi-ia-an-t*[*e-eš*] KBo 17.22 iii 12 (OH/OS); **pl. loc.** ^{GIŠ}*la-ḫur-nu-zi-aš* KUB 9.32 rev. 28 (NH); ^{GIŠ}*la-ḫur-nu-uz-zi-ia-aš* KUB 27.67 ii 46 (MH/NS); **without det.** KUB 38.25 i 7 (NH); ^{GIŠ}*la-aḫ-ḫur-nu-uz-zi-aš* KUB 43.62 iii 5, KBo 10.37 iii 52 (OH/NS) could be gen. sg. before *piran* in OH; ^{GIŠ}*la-aḫ-ḫur-nu-uz-zi-aš* VBoT 24 ii 35 (MH/NS); ^{GIŠ}*la-aḫ-ḫur-nu-zi-ia-aš* KBo 20.107 + 23.50 iii 17 (MH/MS), KUB 7.38 obv. 7 (MH).

acc. by context, but ending lost: *la-aḫ-ḫur-nu-z*[*i-* ...] KUB 33.86 iii 4 (NH), ^{GIŠ}*la-aḫ-ḫ*[*u-* ...] KBo 17.83 ii 6; ^{GIŠ}*la-ḫur*[*-* ...] KUB 27.67 iii 48 (MH/NS); **broken** ^{GIŠ}*la-aḫ-ḫu-wa-an-nu-u*[*z-zi-* ...] KBo 22.216:4 (NS).

Sum.: GIŠ.Ú.SAR (var. nì-tu-ḫu-um) [itu b]ara$_2$-zag-gar (var. nisag-gá) = Akk.: *mu-ut-ḫu-mi* (var. *-ḫu-mu*) *ni-is-sà-ni* (var. *-sà-a-n*[*i*]) = Hitt.: IGI-*ziyašmaš* IT[U.]KAM-*a*[*š*] ^{GIŠ}*la-aḫ-ḫur-nu-uz-zi* "She (is) the foliage of the first month" (tr. of Hitt.), RS 25.421:43 (Ugar. 5:445) with dupl. KUB 4.97:8; on Sum. cf. Civil, JNES 23:8f.; on Akk. cf. Nougayrol in Ugar. 5 (1968) 314f., 318; on Hitt. cf. Laroche in Ugar. 5:774f., 778f., Goetze, JCS 22:115.

a. foliage of trees and shrubs growing in the mountains: *it laḫḫiya*<<*ya*>> ḪUR.SAG.ḪI.A ^{GIŠ}*la-aḫ-ḫur-nu-uz-zi* "Go and roam the mountains (and their) dense growth!" KUB 27.67 iii 64 (rit., MH/NS), different tr. by Carruba, StBoT 2:22 and Goetze, JCS 22:115; "O noble deity! Eat! [Before you] let [the rivers] be bridged! [Before you] let the valleys be [fi]lled in!" ḪUR.SAG.ḪI.A-*mawa la-aḫ-ḫu-ur-nu-uz-zi katta appandu* "Let them hold down the mountains (and) the dense foliage (like a carpet for you)!" KBo 15.25 obv. 13-15 (rit., MH/MS), ed. Carruba, StBoT 2 (1966) 2f., 21f., comments by Goetze, JCS 22:114-16; on *katta ep-* cf. Sommer, HAB 114; "I am an ... girl" *numu šarawar* GIM-*an* ḪUR.SAG.MEŠ-*uš la-aḫ-ḫur-nu-z[i- ...]* KUB 33.86 iii 3-4 + 8.66 iii 4-5 (myth of Ḫedammu), ed. Siegelová, StBoT 14 (1971) 56f.

b. in description of tree: GIŠ*la-aḫ-ḫur-nu-uz-zi-aš-ša-an šer* ÁMUŠEN *tiya[t] kattamanzan* GIŠ*gapanušši* MUŠ-*aš neyat ištarna pedimakan* NIM.LÀL *ney[at?]* "Above an eagle perched on the branches, below a snake coiled about its trunk(?), in the midst a bee ... [...]" KUB 43.62 rev. iii? 5-7 (myth); *Labarnaš šurkišš[eš] tēgaššit wemiya[nzi Labarnaš] la-aḫ-ḫu-ur-nu-uz-zi-ia-an-t[e-eš-še-eš (nepiš)šit wemiyanzi]* KBo 17.22 iii 10-12 (Ḫattic-Hitt. praise for Labarna, OH/OS), with dupl. KUB 28.8 rev. right 7-9.

c. in the time expression "when the leafy branches seize the sun of heaven" = sunset: *maḫḫanma* dUTU AN![-*E* GIŠ*l]a-[ḫ]ur-nu-uz-zi-e-eš appanz[i]* KBo 14.142 ii 17; GIM-*an* dUTU <AN>-*E la-aḫ-ḫur-nu-uz-zi-uš appanzi* KUB 25.23 i 23, 48, ii 27; HT 71:6 + IBoT 3.100:11; KUB 17.36:11 (all cult inv., NH); further, unpublished refs. given in Szabó, FsSalonen 339 n. 1. Correct tr. first by Goetze, JCS 22:116; different tr. by Laroche, Ugar. 5 (1968) 779 "on cueille les fruits," and C. Carter, JAOS 94:139.

d. foliage of specified trees or shrubs: *nu* GIŠ-*ruwaš* GIŠ*la-ḫur-nu-zi dai* "(s)he takes the greenery of the trees (breaks breads, and places them on the greenery/mats)" KUB 27.67 ii 43-46 (rit.); *ŠA* GIŠḪAŠḪUR.KUR.RA GIŠ*la-aḫ-ḫur-nu-zi išparanzi* "they spread out mats/greenery of the 'mountain-apple' tree" VBoT 24 ii 31-32, Sturtevant, Chrest. 110f. (resumed in line 35 by a plural); GIŠ*a-la-an-za-na-aš* GIŠ*ḫa-t[al-ki-iš-na-aš-ša ...]* GIŠ*la-aḫ-ḫur-nu-zi* "foliage/greenery of the *a.* and *ḫ.* trees" KUB 7.23:7-8 (rit.); GIŠ*karšaniyašša* GIŠ*la-aḫ-ḫur-nu-u[z-zi ...]* KUB 7.22 obv. 10 (rit.); *[Š]A* GIŠPÈŠ *la-aḫ-ḫur-nu-uz-z[i- ...]* KBo 12.111:6 (rit.); [GIŠo-]x-*an-za-aš* GIŠ*la-aḫ-ḫur-nu-uz-zi* GIŠ*ḫarauwaš* GIŠ*la-aḫ-ḫur-nu-z[i]* KBo 19.142 ii 16-17 (fest.).

e. used to make wreaths: 6 *KILILU-ya* GIŠ*alanzanaš la-aḫ-ḫur-nu-uz-z[i ...] iyanda* "six wreaths (are) made [from] the foliage of *a.*-trees" KUB 32.123 ii 12f., Carruba, StBoT 2 (1966) 54f.

f. spread out on the ground like a carpet or mat and items are placed upon it (Goetze, JCS 22:116, and Szabó, FsSalonen (1975) 333-41, esp. 338; always neuter in this usage): *nu* GIŠ*la-aḫ-ḫur-nu-uz-zi* (var. KUB 9.31 iii 62: *-nu-zi*) *kattan* (var. KUB 41.17 iii 11: *katta*) *išparranzi* "they spread out foliage below (i.e., on the ground, and lay out meat and bread thereon)" KUB 9.32 obv. 38f. (dupls. KUB 9.31 iii 62f.; KBo 13.212:8f.; KUB 41.17 iii 11f.) (rit. of Ašḫella); *nu arḫayan* [o o o o-]*adi* GIŠ*la-aḫ-ḫur-nu-uz-zi dagan iš-p[ár!-ra-an-zi]* "separately [they] sp[read] out foliage on the ground [...]" KBo 10.37 iii 27f. (rit.); *namma* [GIŠ*la-a]ḫ-ḫur-nu-uz-zi* [NINDA.KUR$_4$.R]A.ḪI.A KA×[U] EME 12 KA×UD.M[EŠ *A-NA ḫu-u]r-li paršiya* "on the foliage he breaks breads for the mouth, the tongue, the 12 teeth and for the *ḫurli* (uvula?, larynx?)" KBo 10.37 iv 30f. (rit., OH/NS); for the construing of all body-parts as datives compare ibid. iii 35-37 where KA×U-*i* is explicitly "for the mouth"; *nammanšan* GIŠ*la-aḫ-ḫur-nu-zi-aš šara ḫukanzi* "they slaughter it (a goat) on top of the mats" VBoT 24 ii 35-36 (rit.); cf. also KBo 17.105 iii 24f.; KBo 4.2 ii 54 (with dupl. KBo 9.126:9); *n[u l]a-aḫ-ḫu-ur-nu-zi tagan dai* "he places the foliage on the ground (and breaks three loaves to the Sungod)" KBo 15.10 ii 17 (rit.); Szabó, THeth 1:22f.; "This is how they offer to dLAMMA *innarawanza*:" *ŠA* GIŠḪAŠ-ḪUR.KUR.RA GIŠ*la-aḫ-ḫur-nu-zi išparanzi šeraššan* 3 NINDA.KUR$_4$.RA *paršianduš tianzi našta* MÁŠ.GAL dLAMMA *innarauwanti šipanti nammanšan* GIŠ*la-aḫ-ḫur-nu-zi-aš šara ḫukanzi* "They spread out the mats/beds of greenery of 'mountain-apple.' Thereon they place fragments of 3 breads, and offer a goat to dLAMMA *i.* They slaughter it (the goat) over the mats/beds of greenery" VBoT 24 ii 30-36 (Anniwiyanni rit.); cited also under d, because of specification of tree from which *l.* is taken; *nu* GIŠ*la-aḫ-ḫur-*

nu-zi waḫnume[*n* . . .] "we waved the mat/ foliage"   KUB 18.15 obv. l5 (bird oracle, NH); cf. also KBo 15.25 obv. 13-15 tr. above under a.

Since one never reads that *l.* is eaten, it may be doubted (with Szabó, FsSalonen 338) that the translation "fruit" is proper. The context points to fibers, leaves and stalks of trees or bushes. Perhaps the choice of *l.* to translate Sum. and Akk. was inexact. For "fruit" a word *šeša-* is known; for "branch" *alkišta(na)-*. Writings with -*ḫu-ur-* KBo 15.25 obv. 15, etc. and -*ḫu-wa-ar-* KBo 22.216:4 determine quality of second vowel. Mostly the word is written with ḪAR sign. The neuter form *laḫḫurnuzzi* is also modified by a neuter adjective *tamai* KBo 15.10 ii 30, Goetze, JCS 22:115 n. 11 and is resumed by the enclitic pronoun -*at* KBo 15.10 ii 36. Common gender forms are all plural. The alleged com. gender sg. nom. form *laḫḫurnuzziaš* cited by Szabó, FsSalonen 339 n. 1 without reference cannot be verified.

J. Friedrich, ZA 37 (1927) 187; A. Götze, KlF 1 (1930) 201; F. Sommer, AU (1932) 396 (all the foregoing understand *laḫḫurnuzzi-* as a kind of offering table); E. Laroche in J. Friedrich, HW 3. Erg. (1966) 22 (announcing Ugar. 5 evidence); O. Carruba, StBoT 2 (1966) 21f., 54f. (reevaluation stimulated by Laroche); E. Laroche in Ugaritica 5 (1968) 774f., 778f. (presentation of evidence cited above in lex. section); A. Goetze, JCS 22 (1968/9) 115f.; H. Hoffner, AlHeth (1974) 38 with n. 178, 116; G. Szabó, FsSalonen 333-41 adds "woven mat."

lai- see *la-*.

lak- v.; act.: **1.** to knock out (a tooth), **2.** to turn (one's ear or eyes toward), **3.** to train (a grapevine branch), mid.: **4.** to fall; from OH.

act. pres. sg. 3 *la-a-ki* KBo 6.2 i 9, 11 (OH/OS), KBo 6.4 i 18, 19 (OH/NS).
mid. pres. sg. 3 *la-ga-a-ri* KBo 2.3 iii 19, KUB 10.76:7 (both MH/NS), KUB 19.23 rev. 18, 19, KUB 8.36 iii 9, KUB 29.9 i 28 (all NH); *la-qa-a-ri* KUB 34.79:9 (MH?/ NS); *la-ga-a-it-ta-ri* KUB 5.7 obv. 18 (NH).
part. sg. neut. *la-ga-an* KUB 36.110:10 (OH/OS), IBoT 3.113 rev.? 4 (NH); *la-ga-a-an* KUB 33.68 ii 4 (OH/MS), KUB 12.65:19 (MH or NH/NS), etc.
imp. act. sg. 2 *la-a-ak* KBo 7.28:11, 12, KBo 21.22 rev. 46 (both OH/MS), KUB 43.61 i? 5 (OH), 43.63 obv. 7, 12, 18 (OH/NS); **mid. sg. 3** *la-ga-a-ru* KBo 2.3 iii 22 (MH/NS), *la-a-ga-a-ru* KBo 9.106 iii 18 (MH/NS).

1. to knock out (a tooth): *takku* LÚ.U₁₈.LU-*an ELLAM kuiški* . . . KAxUD-*ŠU la-a-ki* "If

someone . . . knocks out a free man's tooth" KBo 6.2 i 9 (Law §7, OH/TOS), ed. Friedrich, HG 16f., cf. §8 and par. §VII; *mān* 2 KAxUD *našma* 3 KAxUD *la-a-ki* "If he knocks out two or three teeth" KBo 6.4 i 18-19 (NH); □ Friedrich's "schief schlägt" (HG 17) seems unnecessarily literal; Walther's "knock out" in J. M. Powis Smith, The Origin and History of Hebrew Law (1931) 248, and Goetze's (ANET 189) "knocks out" is much better, cf. Forrer, Forsch. 1 183 "einschlägt".

2. to turn (one's ears or eyes toward): *aššū* IGI.ḪI.A-*KA la-a-ak* LĪM *laplippuš karp* [. . .] [LU]GAL-*un anda aššu šakuwaya* GEŠTU. ḪI.A-*KA la-a-ak nu aššu uttar* [*i*]*štamaš* "Turn (hither) your benevolent eyes! Lift (your) thousand eye-lashes! Look kindly at the king! Turn your ears and hear a good word!"   KBo 7.28 obv. 11-13 (prayer, OH/MS); cf. also KUB 43.61 i 3-6 with par. 43.63 obv. 6-14 (OH/NS); "The offerer is (now) giving sacrifice to you. Accept, O god, the sacrifice! Turn toward him with benevolence!" *nutta kuit memiškizzi nušši* GEŠTU-*an parā la-ga-a-an ḫark* "Turn (your) ear toward what he says to you!"   KBo 12.96 iv 10-14 (rit.); "I am attracting you with sacrificial breads and libations! So be soothed/pacified." *nutta kuit memiškimi numu* DINGIR *ištamanan la-ga-a-an ḫark* "and turn (your) ear, O god, toward what I say to you!"   KUB 24.1 i 13-17 with dupl. KUB 24.2 obv. 12-14 (royal prayer of Murš. II to Tel.); "O Mukišanu, my vizier!" *uddārt*[*a (kue tem)i numu ut(tanaš* GEŠTU-*an parā)*] *la-ga-a-an ḫark* "Turn (your) ear to the words which I speak to you!"   KUB 12.65 + KBo 26.71:18f. with dupls. KBo 26.72 ii 4 and KBo 26.73:2 (Ḫedammu), ed. StBoT 14:52f. lines 23-24; cf. also KUB 36.7a iii 37-39 + KUB 17.7 iii 8-10 (song of Ullik.), ed. Güterbock, JCS 5:20f.; *nu* GEŠTU-*an la-ga-a-an ḫark nutta kuit* LUGAL [SAL.LUGAL] *memiškanzi nuš ištamaški* "Turn (your) ear! Listen to what the king (and) [queen] are saying to you!"   KUB 33.68 ii 4-5 (rit. and prayer of OH tradition), ed. Laroche Myth. 68; [*iš*]*tamaššantan* GEŠTU-*an parā* [*la-a-ak* . . .] *anda* SIG₅-*antet* IGI.ḪI.A-*it* [*ša-ku-wa-ia*] "[Bend] down a listening ear! [Look] with good (= keen) eyes at [. . .]!"   KBo 11.72 iii 30-32 (rit. for infernal powers, MH?/NS); "May Labarna, King of Ḫatti, be your/our fortress!" *nuzapa utniyanza ḫumanza iškišmet anda* URU*Ḫattuša* *la-ga-an ḫar-d*[*u*?] (or -*z*[*i*?]) "May the entire land bend down their backs (or: the entire land will bend down their backs) toward Ḫatti!" KUB 36.110 rev. 8-12 (Labarna "blessings", OS), ed. Forrer, MAOG 4:30f.

3. to train (a grapevine): [. . . *š*]*aliki* GIŠ*maḫli napa iškišitti appa la-a-ak* [. . . *š*]*aliki akuki nuza parkunumar dā* [. . . *šal*]*iki ANA* GEŠTIN.KU₇ *nuza milidduššit* [. . .] "Approach the grapevine and train it on your back! Approach the *a.* (part of vine?) and take purification! Approach the sweet wine and [imbibe?] its sweetness!" KBo 21.22 rev. 46-49 (incant., OH/MS), ed. Kellerman, Tel Aviv 5 (1978) 200, 202.

4. (mid.) to fall down, fall over, be toppled — **a.** of a person: *mānkan antuḫšaš la-ga-a-ri našmaškan* GIŠGIGIR-*az katta maušzi* "If a person falls down (Neu, StBoT 5:105 "(sch)wankt") or if he falls out of a chariot" KUB 8.36 iii 9-10 (catalogue entry, NH); ed. StBoT 19:38-40 and Laroche, CTH p. 189-190; it is not clear what kind of text this is the catalogue entry for, but perhaps a ritual.

b. of upright stones or stelas (opp. of *wete-* "build, erect"): [(*kui*)]*šwarat weteškit* [(N)]A₄*ḫuwaši*ḪI.A *šanita* (var. *tanita*) *kinunna*[(*waratkan*)] *kāša la-ga-a-ri* ... *nuwakan apēya udd*[(*ār*)] *QATAMMA la-ga-a-ru* "Who erected the(se) solitary(?) stelas? Now they have fallen over.... In the same way, let those (hostile) words (which estranged the two clients) fall over!" KBo 2.3 iii 17-22, with dupl. KUB 10.76:5-10 + KUB 12.59 iii 7-12 (1Mašt); cf. sub *lala-* 1 b.

c. of a country falling to an invader; contra Forrer, Forsch I, 184 ("sich neigt"): *nukan mān* KUR URU*Lala*[*nda d*]*apianpat la-ga-a-ri* ... [*m*]*anmakan* KUR.ḪI.A *ŠAPLI*<*TI*>-*ma la-ga-a-ri* "If the entire country of Lala[nda] falls ... if the Lower Lands fall" KUB 19.23 rev. 17-19 (letter to Hittite queen); *natkan la-ga-a-ri* KUR-*e ḫarkzi* "It will fall (and) the land will perish" 932/u iv 8 with dupl. IBoT 3.139:6 (apodosis of astron. omen); cited in StBoT 5:105.

d. of person falling out of bed: *takkukan* UN-*an* GIŠNÁ-*anteš kattan šarā šiyanzi naššan* [GÙB-*l*]*a la-ga-a-ri* "If a bed shoves a person completely (out) so that he falls (out) on [the lef]t side" KUB 29.9 i 26-29 (tr. of Akk. *šumma ālu* omen); cf. Güterbock, AfO 18 (1957) 79f.

parā often accompanies the *lagan ḫar-* construction when the object is "ear" (*parā* is absent in KUB 24.1 i 16f. and dupl. KUB 24.2 obv. 14 and in KUB 33.68 ii 4) but not with "back". It is probably an adverb rather than a preverb and does not alter the meaning of *lak-*. If *parā* means "forth", the image may be of ear extended. If it means "forward", the image may be drawn from canine or equid ear movement, i.e. "prick up (or cock) the ears." The fundamental conception is inclining, as Forrer noted (Forsch. I/2 pp. 183f.), but not just at a 45° angle (Forrer, p. 184)!

Forrer, Forsch. I/2 (1929) 183-85; Sommer, AU (1932) 170f.

Cf. *laknu-*, *lagan*, *lilakk-*.

lagan n. neut.; bent, inclination, disposition(?); from MH.†

sg. (or pl.?) acc. *la-ga-a*(*š-mi-it*) KUB 41.8 iv 1 (MH/NS); **gen.** *la-ga-na-aš* KUB 12.26 ii 11 (NH).

(The Sungod and Kamrušepa treat the mortal's twelve body parts), *nuwaran* EGIR-*pa aliyaš la-ga-na-aš eššanzi nuwaran* EGIR-*pa* AMA-*ni* TUR-*an eššanzi* "they make him again one of an *a.*'s disposition, they make him again a child to (its) mother" KUB 12.26 ii 11-13 (myth, NH). [(*nu*) ... -]*aš* KI-*paš* (var. GE₆-*iš* KI-*aš*) *la-ga-aš-mi-it ēp* (var. *arḫa ēp*) "O dark earth, restrain their (the evil deities') inclination!" KUB 41.8 iv 1 with dupl. KBo 10.45 iv 1-2 (purif. rit., MH/NS), ed. Otten, ZA 54 (1961) 134f.

The parallelism in KUB 12.26 suggests that the *aliyaš* is something young or gentle like the child. Cf. the animal *aliyaš* in KUB 14.1 rev. 91, 92 (Madd.), which contra HW^2 is probably not the *alliyaš* bird, cf. Otten, ZA 66:97f. The translation "inclination", etc. is based on assumed derivation from the verb *lak-* (cf. *naḫ-* "to fear", *naḫḫan* "fear", etc. and H. Berman, Diss. 133f.).

Cf. *lak-*.

^{GIŠ}**lakarwa** n. neut.; (a tree or its fruit).†

In a rit. frag.: ^{GIŠ}*šaḫiš e*[- . . .] § ^{GIŠ}*la-kar-wa ki-i*[*t*- . . .] *galaktar k*[*i*- . . .] KBo 12.90:8-10. Cf. [^{URU}*L*]*a-kar-wa* (var. ^{URU}*La-ak-kar*[-*wa*]) KBo 18.156:2 with dupl. 18.157:3.

This word is to be distinguished from *lakkar-wan*$^{(SAR)}$ (a garden plant), because the GIŠ and SAR determinatives do not usually interchange.

lakkarwan$^{(SAR)}$ n. neut.; (a garden plant); from MH.†

sg. nom.-acc. *la-ak-kar-wa-an* KBo 10.45 iii 53 (MH/NS), KBo 19.142 ii 17 (NH), KUB 7.1 i 21, 37 (pre-NH/NS); *la-ak-kar-wa-an*^{SAR} KBo 5.2 i 15 (NH).

a. used in an ointment: EGIR-*antama šāna kukkullan la-ak-kar-wa-an* Ì.UDU *anda tarnai* "Afterwards she combines (crushed, see i 26) *š.*, *k.*, *l.*, (and) tallow" (this preparation is then rubbed on the body of a sick child) KUB 7.1 i 37-38 (pre-NH/NS).

b. in lists of ingredients: *ŠA* ^{GIŠ}KIRI₆ SAR.ḪI.A *ḫūman* . . . *la-ak-kar-wa-an* KUB 7.1 i 19-21 (rit. of Ayatarša, pre-NH/NS), cf. also KBo 10.45 iii 53 (Otten, ZA 54:132-33), KBo 5.2 i 15 (rit. of Ammiḫatna, NH), and KBo 19.142 ii 17 (rit., NH). Cf. [^{URU}*L*]*a-kar-wa* (var. ^{URU}*La-ak-kar*-[*wa*]) KBo 18.156:2 with dupl. KBo 18.157:3.

The stem of this word may be *lakkarwa-* or *lakkarwan-*.

Cf. *lakarwa-*.

^{KUŠ}**laggašduš** n. com. pl. acc.; (a leather bag).†

In a rit. frag.: *nu kī ḫūman anda arnuwanzi našta* ^{KUŠ}*la-ag-ga-aš-du-uš šunnanz*[*i*] "They bring all these (types of flour) in and they fill (leather) *l.*'s" KBo 13.248:20-21; prob. to be restored ibid. 3: *nu* ^{KUŠ}*la-a*[*k*- . . .].

To be compared and perhaps equated with ^{KUŠ}DÙG.GAN in 1328/z (Hoffner, AlHeth 63, Ertem, Flora 136f.) and Bo 3367 (Ertem, Flora 22).

laknu- v.; **1.** to knock over, overturn (stelas, thrones, tables), **2.** to fell (a tree), **3.** (a wrestling maneuver:) to throw, make (an opponent) fall, **4.** to train, bend (a vine), **5.** to make (someone) fall out of favor, **6.** to bend (someone) to one's own viewpoint, persuade, **7.** to pass (the day or night) sleepless; from MS.

pres. sg. 2 *la-ak-nu-ši* KUB 26.1 iii (41), 43 (Tudḫ. IV); **sg. 3** *la-ak-nu-uz-zi* KUB 29.9 iv 11 (NH); *la-ak-nu-zi* KBo 23.55 i 22; **pl. 3** *la-ak-nu-an-zi* KUB 44.32:14 (NH), Bo 2646 ii 16 (cited in StBoT 18:80); *la-ak-nu-wa-an-zi* KUB 43.55 iv 8 (pre-NH/NS); *la-ak-nu-u-wa-an-zi* KUB 39.7 i 14 (NH/NS), KUB 39.1 ii (13) (NS).

pret. sg. 3 *la-ak-nu-ut* KUB 14.3 iv (9) (NH), KBo 26.102:4, KUB 5.7 obv. 24 (NH?), KBo 11.1 obv. 40 (NH), KUB 16.29 obv. 25 (MH/MS).

imp. sg. 2 *la-ak-nu-ut* KUB 26.1 iii 40 (Tudḫ. IV).

iter. pres. sg. 1 *la-ak-nu-u*[*š-ki-*]*mi* KUB 36.75 iii 8 (OH/MS).

1. to knock over, overturn (stelas, thrones, tables); cf. *lak-* mng. 4 b: ^{NA_4}ZI.KIN.ḪI.A-*maššan la-ak-nu-wa-an-zi* KUB 43.55 iv 7-8 (rit., pre-NH/NS); *ma-a-an* ^{GIŠ}GU.ZA ^{d}U ^{NA_4}ZI.KIN *kuiški katta la-ak-nu-ut* "If someone has overturned the throne of the Stormgod (or) a stela (or if he has clogged a sacred spring)" KBo 11.1 obv. 40 (Muw. prayer), ed. RHA XXV/81:108, 117; UR.GI₇-*wakan* ŠÀ É.DINGIR-*LIM pait nukan* ^{GIŠ}BANŠUR *la-ak-nu-ut* "A dog entered the temple and overturned a table (and scattered the sacrificial loaves)" KUB 5.7 obv. 24-25 (oracle question); cf. ANET 497; UDU.ŠIR knocks something over in KUB 16.29 obv. 24-26 (oracle report).

2. to fell (a tree); cf. also *lilak-*: [. . .] GIŠ-*ru la-*[*ak-* . . . GIŠ-*r*]*u la-ak-nu-ut* "He felled the [tre]e" KBo 26.102:3-4 (Gilg. myth).

3. to throw, make (opponent) fall, (a wrestling move, accomplishment of which constitutes victory), with *-kan*: "They bow three times to the deity and co[mmence] wrestling" *nankan maḫḫan anzel la-ak-nu-zi* "When our (man) throws him, (they bow again: he bows to the deity, and our man crouches)" KBo 23.55 i 20-23 (fest. or cult inv.); cf. Hoffner, BiOr 35:247.

4. to train, bend (a vine), with *-šan*; cf. *lak-*, mng. 3: "They wrap the stem of a grapevine with cl[oth] and decorate it with clusters of grapes and grape clusters of ^{SÍG}*iyatnaš*. Then they take it up, and a *taptara*-woman brings it into the tent" *nanšan ANA* ^{GIŠ}BANŠUR *akkantaš anda la-ak-nu-u-wa-an-zi* "They bend (i.e. train) it in and around the table of the deceased" KUB 30.19 i 4-8 + 39.7 i 10-14, ed. HTR 32f.

5. to make (someone) fall out of favor, with *-kan*: "If someone has established himself in His Majesty's favor, and an enemy of His Majesty solicits(?) you (saying)" *ašiwakan PAN* ^{d}UTU-*ŠI la-ak-nu-ut* "Make that one fall from His Majesty's favor!" *zikma[t iy]aši nankan la-ak-nu-š[i]* "and you do it, you cause him to fall out of favor," (or if someone is disagreeable to you, but well-liked by the king,) *zikmankan innarā la-ak-nu-ši* "and on your own initiative you cause him to fall out of favor" KUB 26.1 iii 37-43 (instr. to eunuchs), ed. von Schuler, Dienstanw. 13f.

6. to bend (someone) to one's own viewpoint, persuade; without *-kan*/*-šan*: "The king of Ḫatti and I were at odds over the matter of the city of Wiluša," *nu[wam]u ap[ed]ani* INIM-*ni la-ak-nu-ut* "but he persuaded me in that matter (and we became reconciled, and now hostility between us is not permitted)" KUB 14.3 iv 7-10 (Taw. letter), ed. AU 16f.

7. to pass (the day or night) sleepless; cf. Otten, ZA 46 (1940) 210f., Neu, StBoT 18 (1974) 79f. (discusses alternation with *lukkanu-*): *pittuli[ya]š piran* UD.ḪI.A-*uš* GE$_6$.ḪI[.A-*uš*] *la-ak-nu-u[š-ki-]mi* "From anxiety I go sleepless days (and) nights" KUB 36.75 iii 7-8 (prayer, MS); "If he (the king) prefers, he can sleep there. He sits before Ištar of the Field," $^{\text{LÚ.MEŠ}}$NAR $^{\text{LÚ.MEŠ}}$AZU-*ya* GE$_6$-*an la-ak-nu-wa-an-z[i]* "(But) the singers and incantation priests keep active through the night" KUB 27.1 iv 48-50 (fest., NH); cf. Bo 2646 ii 15f. cited in StBoT 18:80; "If in the fourth month the moon undergoes eclipse at the time of its descent," GE$_6$-*an la-ak-nu-uz-zi* "(and thus) passes (the rest of) the night," (the Hurrian will die) KUB 29.9 iv 9-12 (lunar eclipse omen); cf. also KUB 39.7 iii 53-55 *lak[nuwanzi]* with dupl. 39.8 iii 14-17 *lu[kkanuwanzi]* (HTR 44, lines numbered 52-54), KUB 39.1 ii 12-14 (HTR 20f.), KBo 20.94:6. The equivalent Akk. expression in lunar eclipse omens is EN.NU.UN-*šu igmur* "(if the moon is eclipsed in the ... watch,) and it finishes (thus) its watch" KUB 4.64A obv. 7ff.; cf. CAD M/1 338 sub mng. 3d.

Not yet attested in OS. In mngs. 1-6 MH/NH *laknu-* replaces OH active *lak-*; mid. *lak-* continues from OH through NH.

Forrer, Forsch. I/2 (1929) 183-85; Sommer, AU (1932) 170f. (principally on mng. 6); Otten, ZA 46 (1940) 210f. with n. 1 (on mng. 7); Friedrich, HW (1952) 125f., HW 2. Erg. (1961) 17; Neu, StBoT 18 (1974) 79f. (on mng. 7); Hoffner, BiOr 35:247 (on mng. 3).

Cf. *lak-*.

lakšaiš n.; (an object of silver), MH?.†

In a birth ritual: *la-ak-ša-iš* KÙ.BABBAR TUR KI.LÁ-*ŠU* 1 *tarnaš* "a small silver *lakšaiš*, its weight 1 *tarna-*" KBo 17.65 rev. 55, ed. Beckman, Diss. (1977) 170, 178.

lakšeniš n. com.; (mng. unkn.); OH?/MS.†

nu kuišša ^{LÚ}ALAN.Z[U$_x$ 1 ^{GIŠ}*išḫā]ur ḫarzi* ^{GIŠ}*išḫāurra*[(-) ... K]Ù.BABBAR-*it ḫališšian* 1 GÍN.GÍN [KI.LÁ Á^{M}]^{UŠEN}-*ŠUNU la-ak-še-ni-iš-mi-ša* Z[ABA]R? "Each performer holds [one] *i.*, and the *i.*'s are plated with silver. Their 'eagle-weight' is one shekel, and their *l.* is/are of b[ronz]e(?)" KBo 23.52 iii 3-6 (fest.).

$^{\text{GAD/TÚG}}$**lakkušanzani-** n. com.; (linen article, perhaps a bedsheet; NH.†

sg. nom. ^{TÚG}*la-ku-ša-an-za-ni-iš* KBo 18.181 rev. 23; **pl. nom.** ^{GAD}*la-ak-ku-ša-an-za-ni-eš* KBo 18.170a rev. 10; **Luw. inflection** *la-ak-ku-ša-an-za-ni-en-zi* KBo 18.175 v 15; **pl. acc.** ^{GAD}*la-ak-ku-ša-an-za-ni-uš* KBo 18.154:9; **broken** ^{GAD}*la-ak-ku-ša-an-za-ni*[-...] KBo 18.170 obv. 8; ^{TÚG}*la!-ku-ša-a[n-...]* KUB 42.57:8; ^{GAD}*la!-ak*[-...] KUB 42.43 obv. 12; [... *l*]*a-ku-š[a-a]n!-za-ni*[-...] KBo 18.181 rev. 1.

Only in inventories — **a.** listed with beds: 1 ^{GIŠ}NÁ KA×UD AM.SI 4 GÌR UR.MAḪ KÙ.GI GAR.RA 1-*NUTUM la-ak-ku-ša-an-za-ni-en-zi* BABBAR? GAD-*ya MAYALU* ^{d}IM ^{URU}*Nerik* ⸢*ŠA* KASKAL⸣-*NI* "One bed of ivory (with) four lion's feet plated with gold, and one set of white linen *l.*'s, the bed of the Stormgod of Nerik; of the campaign" KBo 18.175 v 13-16; [1-*NUT*]*UM* ^{GIŠ}NÁ ^{GIŠ}TÚG 1-*NUTUM* ^{GAD}*la-ak-ku-ša-an-za-ni*[-...] "One bed of boxwood, one set of linen *l.*'s" KBo 18.170 obv. 8;

cf. KUB 42.43 obv. 12; 1 ^{TÚG}*la-ku-ša-an-za-ni-iš* 1 ^{GIŠ}NÁ KBo 18.181 rev. 23; [. . . *la-ku*]-*ša-an-za-ni-iš MAYA*[*LI*? . . .] ibid. rev. 9.

b. listed with other items: 15 TÚG.GUZ.ZA 6[. . .] 6 ^{TÚG}*la*!-*ku-ša-a*[*n-za-ni-* . . .] 2 *šašan-na*[*š* . . .] KUB 42.57:7-9; also [. . .]x *TAPAL* ^{KUŠ}E.SIR LÚ-*LIM* 11 ^{KUŠ}E.SIR.ḪI.A SAL-*TI* SA₅[o o o] *TAPAL* ^{GAD}*la-ak-ku-ša-an-za-ni-eš* KBo 18.170a rev. 9-11.

lala- n. com. and neut.; **1.** tongue (body part), **2.** model of tongue; **3.** (true or correct) speech, **4.** harmful speech, slander, defamation, blasphemy, **5.** (blend of mngs. 1, 2, and 4), **6.** *lalaš išḫaš*, **7.** blade (of knife), ingot (of metal), **8.** *lalan karp-*; from OH/TOS; written syllabically and ^(UZU)EME.

sg. nom. com. *la-a-la-aš* 2Mašt. iii 7 (MH/MS), KUB 9.34 iii 30 (NH); *la-la-aš* KBo 11.72 iii 5 (MH?/NS); EME-*aš* KUB 33.8 iii 12 (OH/NS), KBo 15.10 ii 8, iii 50 (MH/MS), KUB 12.44 iii 7 (NH); **sg. acc. com.** *la-a-la-an* KBo 17.1 i 18 (OH/TOS); EME-*an* KBo 10.37 ii (4) (OH/NS); KUB 24.10 iii (25) (OH/NS), 2Mašt. iii 11, 13 (MH/MS), IBoT 2.109 ii 26, (28) (MH/NS), KUB 41.8 ii 14 (MH/NS).

sg. neut. EME-*an* KBo 2.3 i 50 (MH/NS), KBo 23.72 rev. 24 (OH or MH/MS); **sg. neut.** or **sg. acc. com.** *la-a-la-an* KUB 36.49 i (6), (7), (8) (OH/OS), KUB 17.28 ii 33, 40 (MH/MS); *la-la-a-an* KBo 11.11 i 9 (NH); EME-*an* KBo 20.73 iv 15 (OH or MH/MS), KBo 10.37 iv 54 (OH/NS), KBo 11.11 i 9, KUB 21.42 iii 9 (both NH), KUB 21.19 ii 3′ (i.e., Bo 4222:3′); **sg. gen.** *la-la-aš* KUB 30.35 i 2, iv 7 (MH/NS) (dupl. has EME-*za* KUB 39.102 i 2), KUB 30.51 iv 11 (NH); *la-la-a-aš* KBo 11.11 i 1 (NH); EME-*aš* 2Mašt. iv 20 (MH/MS), KBo 2.3 iii 44 (MH/NS), KUB 12.62 obv. 10 (NH?/NS), KBo 2.8 i 22 (NH); **sg. loc.** *la-a-li* KBo 20.59:16, (18) (OH or MH/MS); EME-*i* 2Mašt. ii 29, iii 53 (MH/MS), KBo 2.3 i 49, iii 9 (MH/NS); **inst.** *la-a-li-it* KUB 1.16 iii 8 (OH/NS); EME-*it* KBo 2.3 i 37, ii 43, 51! (MH/NS), KBo 16.57:12, KBo 20.111:16; **abl.** EME-*za* KUB 30.33 i 10 (MH/NS), KUB 46.38 ii (9) (NH); EME-*az* KUB 12.59 iii 10 (MH/NS), KUB 18.67 obv.? 11, 12 (NH); *IŠTU* EME KBo 2.11 obv. 13 (NH), KUB 21.33 iv? 20 (NH), ^{UZU}EME KUB 7.1 iii 23.

pl. nom. *la-a-le-eš* KBo 17.2:4 (OH/TOS); EME.ḪI.A-*eš* 2Mašt. i 23 (MH/MS); EME.MEŠ KBo 10.37 ii 37 (OH/NS); EME.ḪI.A KUB 30.48:12; **pl. acc.** *la-a-lu-uš* KBo 17.4 ii 6, KBo 17.1 i 11 (both OH/TOS); EME.MEŠ-*uš* KBo 10.37 iii 24 (OH/NS); EME-*uš* KBo 17.5 ii (11) (OH/TOS, cf. StBoT 8:24 n. 1), KUB 44.56 iii 12 (OH?/NS); EME.MEŠ KBo 10.37 i 33 (OH/NS); EME.ḪI.A KBo 15.10 iii 30 (MH/MS); **pl. neut.** EME.ḪI.A KUB 12.34 + KUB 15.39 i 10, 12, 17, 21, resumed by *ku-e* ibid. i 21 and *na-at-* . . . ibid. i 14, 18, KBo 2.3 i 28 with KUB 15.39+ i 26; *la-la-na-aš* KBo 11.72 iii 5, cited by Friedrich, HW 3. Erg. (1966) 22 is to be read *la-la-aš-wa* Laroche, RA 62:88; ⸢EME⸣-*ul-še-et* in KUB 17.10 iii 10, discussed by Sommer, HAB, 220, Güterbock apud Laroche, Myth. 34 reads *uš-*[*d*]*u*?-*ul-še-et*; *la-a-* writings all OH or MH.

1. tongue (body part) — **a.** OH — **1′** *mān ištam*[*aššun nuwakan* DUMU].MEŠ ^{URU}*Ḫatti UŠM*[*IT*] *išḫaḫrušm*[*itšišta ša*]*nḫun tak-kumana*<*š*>*ta UL-ma šan*[*ḫun* GAM-*an šarām*]*āmmu la-a-li-it epten* "When [I] hear[d]: 'She ki[lled son]s of Ḫatti', I [so]ught [from her] their/your tears. Had I not sou[ght] (them) from (her), you (pl.) would have [sl]andered me with the tongue" KUB 40.65 iii 6-9 + 1.16 iii 6-8 (Ḫatt. I edict, OH/NS), cf. *-ma* sub usage f 2′ b″; □restoration and translation "slander" based on vocabulary: ŠÀ.GAR.RA = *A-KÍL KAR-ṢÍ* = GAM-*an ša-ra-a ku-iš ap-pé-eš-ki-zi* KBo 13.1 iv 19.

2′ Cutting off of the tongue, ears and tails of livestock slaughtered for sacrifice: KBo 11.45 ii 6, 10, 17 (fest., OH/NS).

3′ passages from incantation rit., in which various parts of the body, which have been bound magically (*ḫamikta*), are enchanted (*ḫuekdu*), and loosed from the evil spell (*lau*): *naš* ^{UZU}EME-*ŠU ḫamikta* KBo 3.8 iii 35, *nan* EME-*ŠU ḫuekdu* KUB 7.1 iii 14 (= KBo 3.8 + KUB 7.1 iii 48), *nan* ^{UZU}EME-*ŠU* KI.MIN (= *lau*) KUB 7.1 iii 23 (NH), ed. Kronasser, Die Sprache 7 (1961) 158-60, translit. in Laroche, Myth (1965) 110f.

4′ in enumeration of body parts: [EME-*Š*]*U ANA* EME *dakki* "his tongue is similar to (his) tongue" KUB 43.53 i 5; EME-*ŠU ANA* EME-*ŠU* GAL-*li* "his tongue is larger (note neut.) than his tongue" ibid. i 21 (Zuwi rit., OH/NS), discussed as unpublished Bo 3263+ by Sommer in HAB 219; dupl. KBo 17.17 shows OS.

5′ ^{GIŠ}*laḫḫurnuzzi dagān d*[*ai* . . .] 1 NINDA.KUR₄.RA KA×U-*i* 1 NINDA.KUR₄.RA EME 1 NINDA.KUR₄.R[A 12 KA×UD.MEŠ 1 NINDA.KUR₄.RA] *ANA ḫurli dai* "he places foliage on the ground and places (thereon) one loaf each for the mouth, the tongue, [the twelve teeth], and the *ḫurli* (uvula? or larynx?)" KBo 10.37 iii 35-37 (rit., OH/NS), cf. also same text ibid. iv 5, 30-32, 46, 48, colophon:

"If any person constantly speaks [evil] against the gods . . . ," *nu* EME-*an kišan aniy[ami]* "I treat (his) tongue this way." ibid. iv 51-54; the body parts enumerated in ibid. iii 35-37 were all considered speech organs.

b. MH passages: *kattawara(t?)šm[aškan] waršan eštu idalauwa uddā[r]* KA×U-*aš* EME-*aš* "Let the evil words of the mouth (and) tongue be wiped off of them!" KBo 2.3 iii 42-44 (1Mašt., MH/NS); "Now (these stelas) have fallen down" *nuwakan ANA* 2 E[N.SISKUR *k]uit apedani* UD-*ti* KA×U-*az* E[ME-*az*] *uit nuwakan apeya uddā[r] QATAMMA lagaru* "so also let those words which on that day came forth from the mouths [and tongues] of the two clients fall down!" ibid. iii 18-22 (1Mašt. rit., MH/NS), with dupl. KUB 10.76:7-10 + 12.59 iii 8-12; cf. *lak-* mng. 4 b; SAG.D[U.MEŠ-*ašw]ašmaš* NÍ.TE-*aš ḫumand[aš] tarpalliš* UDU.GE$_6$ K[A×U-*i*] EME-*i ḫurtiyašša* EME-*an* "Let the black sheep be the substitute for your persons (and) for all (their) members! For the mo[uth], tongue, and curses, the tongue (is the substitute)." KBo 2.3 i 48-50 (1Mašt. rit., MH/NS), slightly different in 2Mašt. ii 27-29, cf. Drohla cited in HAB 220 n. 1; KA×U-*it* EME-*it* [(*kuit*)] *memiškitte[n]* "What you used to say with (your) mouth (and) tongue" 2Mašt. i 44-45 (MH/MS); the Old Woman says: *parkuwaešwašmaš namma ešten* KA×U-*it* EME-*it* "Be pure (pl.) again in mouth (and) tongue!" 2Mašt. ii 24-25 (MH/MS); *aiš* EME-*aš gagaš qāšašmaškan parkuin mišriwantan ḫarkin* ^{GIŠ}PA *UL walḫantan* UDU-*un šipantaḫḫun* "Mouth, tongue, tooth! I have offered to you a pure, faultless(?), white sheep not beaten with the rod" KBo 15.10 ii 8-10 (rit., MH/MS), ed. THeth 1 p. 20f.; *aiš* EME-*aš gagaš šumeš azzikiten* "Mouth, tongue, tooth! Eat!" ibid. iii 50; *la-la-aš-wa armizzi* "the tongue is a bridge" KBo 11.72 iii 5 (saying quoted in rit., MH?/NS) with dupl. EME-*aš-wa* ^{GIŠ}*armizzi* KBo 11.10 iii 17 with § line following immediately.

c. NH passages — [BE-*a]nkan* UN-*ši* EME-*aš* ZAG-*na ne!-an-za* "If a man's tongue is turned to the right" KUB 43.8 iii 9a (physiognomic omen protasis, NH); *ida[luš* ..] EME-*aš apel ḫuḫḫurti*[. . .] KBo 21.6 rev. 8-9 (rit., NH); KA×U-*az* EME-*az* in KUB 18.67 obv.? 12 (MUŠEN *ḪURRI* oracle, NH) and KA×U-*za* EME-*za* in KUB 46.38 ii 9 (Kizz. rit., NH); *nu* DINGIR.MEŠ *kuieš* (dupl. adds *kuš*) *kedani* UD-*ti kuedani arkuešni IŠTU* EME-*IA ḫalziḫḫun* (O Sungod, call) "these gods whom I invoked on this day, in whatever prayer, with (my) tongue" KUB 6.45 iii 21-22 with dupl. KUB 6.46 iii 60-62 (Muw. prayer), cf. ibid. iii 34, 36f.

2. model of the tongue — **a.** OH: practitioner takes from the king and queen the *utniyandan laluš* (tongues of the lands), the royal couple wash their mouths out three times, then: [DU(MU)].É.GAL LUGAL-*aš* SAL.LUGAL-*ašša iššazmit la-a-la-an* AN.BAR-*aš* [*d*]*ai* "the courtier takes from the mouths of king and queen a tongue (made) of iron" KBo 17.1 i 18-19 with dupl. KBo 17.3 i 13-14 (rit., OS), ed. StBoT 8:20f.; cf. also *ḫatugauš la-a-lu-uš* AN.B[AR-...] KBo 17.4 ii 6; 5 ALAM IM ŠÀ.BA 2 LÚ.MEŠ *nu kuršuš karpan ḫarkanzi našta anda* EME.ḪI.A IM (var. A3: EME.MEŠ) (var. A3, B3 add *kiantari*) 3 SAL.MEŠ *nat* ^{TÚG}*kurešnanteš* § 1 *kurtali* IM EME.ḪI.A IM *šū* (var. A4: *nat IŠTU* EME IM [*šū*]) 1 ANŠE IM *nu apāt karpan ḫarzi* "five clay figurines: among them two men — and they hold shields lifted, and clay tongues are lying on them — three women — and they wear women's headwear — one clay model of a basket filled with clay tongues, one clay donkey (which) holds that lifted" KBo 11.12 i 3-6 (^{f}Alli rit., OH/NS) with dupls. KBo 12.126 i 2-5 (A), IBoT 2.123:2-5 (B) and 861/z:3-5 (C) (Otten, ZA 63:81), ed. THeth 2:20f.; cf. 3 SAL.MEŠ *aranda* ^{KUŠ}*kur[š]u[š karpan ḫarkanzi] našta anda* [E]ME.ḪI.A GAB.LÀ[(L *ki*)*tta*??] *nušmaš piran katta* EME.MEŠ (var. EME.Ḫ[I.A]) [. . . *š*(*u?-u-wa-an kitta*)] "(figurines of) three women are standing; [they hold] shields [lifted], and thereon tongues made of wax are lying; and down in front of them lie tongues (and) a filled [. . .]" KUB 24.10 ii 17-19 (MH/NS) with dupl. KUB 41.1 iii 1-3 (MH/NS); different restorations and interpretation in Rost, THeth 2 (1972) 40f. EME.ḪI.A IM "clay tongues" in broken context KBo 13.146 i 11 (Zuwi rit., OH/NS).

b. MH: materials for ritual include: 2 *kurdali*

išnaš nuššan k[e]dani! 7 EME *išnaš išḫuwan kedaniyaššan* 7 EME *išnaš išḫuwanteš* "two baskets (made) of dough — in this one seven tongues of dough have been dropped, and in this one seven tongues of dough have been dropped" KBo 15.10 i 2-4 (rit., MH/MS), ed. THeth 1:12f., 52f. (on gender change); "he cooks the intestines and shoulder of the mouse" *kuin ANA DÙ EME šipantaš* "which he sacrificed in order to make the tongue" KBo 15.10 iii 58-59 (rit., MH/MS) differently translated by Szabó, THeth 1 (1971) 44f. and 71; cf. 7 EM[E] in KBo 22.109 i 6 (Mašt. rit., MH?).

c. NH: *nukan EN.SISKUR kuieš alwan‑ zaḫḫeški[r] nukan ḫumandaš EME-an ANA KÙ.BABBAR [k]uwannanaš andan gulšanzi naškan ANA GÌR?.ḪI.A anda neyanzi* "They depict in silver and jewels the tongue of all those who have been bewitching the client, and they wind them about his feet" KUB 24.12 ii 5-8 (rit., NH); *EGIR-ŠÚ-kán EME.ḪI.A alwanzaḫ‑ ḫanteš ḫumanteš ANA GU₄.MAḪ UDU!.ŠIR GÚ-ŠÚ anda neyanzi* "Afterwards they wind all the enchanted tongues about the neck(s) of the bull (and) the ram" ibid. ii 12-14; cf. iii 12-15; in the list of equipment required for Tunnawi ritual (NH): 12 EME IM EGIR-*an ḫalupanteš* "twelve clay tongues bent(?) back" KUB 7.53 + 12.58 i 44; used in the ritual: EGIR-*andamaššiššan* EME IM *šer ep[z]i nu ŠA EME ḫukmain ḫukzi* "Afterwards she holds over him the clay tongue and pronounces the charm of the tongue" ibid. 63-64; spells to remove ill effects of malicious verbal abuse from the client in ii 39, iii 41; *nu ALAM.ḪI.A KA×U EME.ḪI.A DÙ-mi* KUB 43.59 i 6 (incant. rit., NH); GIM-*anmakan ḫantez‑ ziyaš ḫuprušḫiyaš* 1 EME[A.GAR₅?] 1 *lingainna URUDU ḫašš‑kan anda peššiezzi* "Just as (s)he throws into the first/former *ḫ.*-vessels one tongue [of lead] and one 'oath' of copper, (in the same way he/she will keep on throwing into these)" KBo 24.47 iii 16-18 (ceremonies performed for Hurrian gods); compare broken context of KBo 9.117 rev. iv? 1 (Kizzuwatna rit.); EME's made of metal could be models of real tongues or blades of knives (cf. below under 7); for the models cf. 1 EME KÙ.BABBAR 1 EME KÙ.GI 1 ᵁᶻᵁGEŠTU KÙ.BABBAR 1 ᵁᶻᵁGEŠTU KÙ.GI KUB 43.49:33 (substitute king rit., NH).

3. (true or correct) speech: *tepu pedan EME‑ aš ḫandanza annariš tarpiš* ZI-BU *šarrumar* ᵈUD.SIG₅-*ia* KUB 2.8 ii 12-14 (ANTAḪŠUM fest., OH/NS), cf. also *[t]epu pedan EME-an ḫan‑ d[a]ntan lammar tartan* ᵈUD.SIG₅ KBo 19.128 vi 22-24 (ANTAḪŠUM festival? OH/NS), ed. Otten, StBoT 13 (1971) 16f., 47; *[tepu] pedan EME-an ḫandan* (neut. sg.) *annarin tarpin QATAMMA [ekuz]i* KBo 23.72 + KUB 32.87 rev. 24-25 (festival OH/NS), cf. rev. 4, 34-36. □ The implication of *ḫandant-* could either be that the words spoken were true, or that the person's manner of speech was correct, as opposed to slurring, stuttering (*tapuša pai-*).

4. harmful speech, slander, defamation, blas‑ phemy (in magical rituals or incantations often quite indistinguishable from a physical repre‑ sentation of the harmful speech or tongue, which may have been manipulated during the utterance); cf. also mng. 5 — a. OH — 1' (with qualification *idalu-*): "Let Telepinu's evil wrath, anger (and) irritation, sin," *idaluš EME-aš* "harmful speech (and evil fetter go in! And let it not come up out again! Let it perish in there)!" KUB 33.8 iii 10 (2nd vers. Tel. myth, OH/NS), ed. Laroche, Myth., p. 44; cf. KUB 33.1:12; *nu* ᵈUTU ᵈU ᵈLAMMA ḪUL-*lun* EME *ANA* TUR-*RU a[wan] arḫa parḫten* "Oh Sungod, Stormgod, Patron god! Expel the blasphemy from (this) child!" KBo 10.37 ii 18-19 (rit. performed on blasphemer, OH/NS), cf. ibid. i 33, 41, ii 7-9, iii 23-26, 45.

2' (without *idalu-*): sequence of clauses in which *ka-ra-ap-ta* "he devoured" takes various evils as object — *ḫazzīšar, ḫutkišnaš, [ḫ]ūrna‑ pištan, lappiyan, dammišḫantan [la-a-l]a-an* ("oppressing tongue"?), [… *l]a-a-la-an, ŠA DINGIR-LIM la-a-la-an* KUB 36.49 i 3-8 (myth and rit., OH/OS), cf. below under mng. 8.

b. MH and NH — 1' with qualification "evil" (*idalu*) — a' in lists of evils being removed magically: *parkunuddu šuppiš A-anza* ḪUL-*lu-un* EME-*an papratar ešḫar waštul ḫurtain* (var. adds *kurkurain pan[g]auwa<š>* EME-*an*) "Let the holy water purify the evil tongue, impurity, bloodshed, sin, curse, damage(?), tongue of the multitude!" KUB 41.8 ii 14-15 (rit., MH/NS) with dupl. KBo 10.45 ii 49-51, ed. Otten, ZA 54:124f.; cf. KUB 24.10 iii 25-27 (rit., MH/NS), ed. THeth 2 (1972) 46f.; *idalunna* ⌈EME⌉-*an idalun* MUŠEN-*in* [*Q*]*ATAMMA warnuandu* "let them likewise burn the evil tongue (and) evil bird!" KBo 11.72 iii 14-15 (MH?/NS); *idālušа* UD-*az manikuwa*[*n* . . .] *idāluš* EME-*aš alwanz*[*enaš* . . .] KUB 34.79:6-7 (MH?/NS); □in these passages it is not clear whether the evil tongue is another's, directed against the client, or the client's own tongue which is being purified or removed.

b′ object of *parkunu-* "purify" in KUB 41.8 ii 14 (cited above), KBo 10.45 iv 40-41 (same ritual), obj. of *kartai-* "remove" in KUB 24.10 iii 25-27, obj. of sequence *warnuandu* . . . *para pedau* . . . *arḫa ḫarnikdu* "burn . . . carry off . . . destroy" in KBo 11.72 iii 15-17.

2′ with qualification "of the multitude" (*pangawaš*) — in lists of evils with *ešḫar*, *linkaiš*, *inan*, *ḫurtaiš*, *waštul*, *papratar*: KUB 30.35 + KUB 39.104 i 1f., iv 6f., 17f. (rit., MH/NS), KUB 30.36 ii 14 (rit., MH/NS), KUB 30.34 iv 17f., 28f. (rit., MH/NS), KUB 30.33 i 9-11, 18, iv 9 (rit., MH/NS), KBo 13.131 iii 9 (rit., MH/NS), KBo 10.45 ii 34f., iv 2f. (rit., MH/NS), ed. Otten, ZA 54:124f., 134f.; in Luw. rits. with *maninkuwantan* MU-*an* DINGIR.MEŠ-*aš karpin* "short year (short life?), anger of the gods" KUB 9.4 ii 7-8 (rit. with Luwian, MH?/NS), KUB 9.34 i 29-30 (rit. with Luwian, NH).

3′ making the *pangawaš* explicit through the enumeration of persons who might pose a threat (Old Woman rituals with Luwian influence): DINGIR.MEŠ-*aš karpin pangauwaš* EME-*an* KI.MIN (= *mutaiddu*) KUB 9.34 i 30, ii 2(!), iv 8 is followed by a list of officials or occupations in KUB 9.34 i 31ff., ii 3ff., iv 9ff. (MH?/NS), KUB 34.85:7-10 (rit., MH/MS).

4′ in plural EME.ḪI.A denoting magic spells, whether malicious or salutary: EME.ḪI.A EME.ḪI.A *kuwapiwa pa*[*i*]*tte*[*ni*] "tongues, tongues, where are you going?" KUB 44.4 + KBo 13.241 rev. 22 (birth rit., NH), cf. below under mng. 6; *mānkan* EME.ḪI.A *kuedani uwanzi* "If tongues come upon someone (the Old Woman will treat him as follows)" KUB 7.1 iv 13-14 (colophon to rit., NH) and KUB 30.49 iv 26-28 (shelf list, NH), ed. Laroche, CTH p. 166.

5′ "Thus speaks [f]Uruwanda:" *mān la-la-a-aš aniyami* "whenever I treat (someone for ill effects) of slander/blasphemy" KBo 11.11 i 1 (rit., NH), cf. shelf list entry for an [f]Allaituraḫi ritual (MH): *nan la-la-aš kiššan ani*[*yami*] "I treat him/her thus (for ills) of slander/blasphemy" KUB 30.51 iv 11.

5. (blend of mngs. 1, 2, and 4): all exx. from MH Maštigga rit., where it is often impossible to determine whether "tongue" refers to (1) the tongue of the client, (2) a model of these tongues used by the sorceress, or (3) the malicious words spoken by the client(s): *kuit-wazakan kuit ištarna ḫurzakitten kinunawa apuš ḫurdauš* EME.ḪI.A [d]UTU-*uš* GÙB-*la waḫnuddu* "Whatever you (pl.) cursed between yourselves — now let the Sungod turn to the left (i.e., undo/reverse) those curses (and) tongues!" KUB 12.34 + 15.39 i 16-18 (= 1Mašt. B), cf. 2Mašt. ii 1-3; KA×U-*it* EME-*it kuit memiškitte*[*n*] (var. *memiškeš*) *kinunawa kāša tiššatwa nuš-maškan* (var. *nu-wa-a*[*š-m*]*a*<-*aš*>-*kán*) *tuḫ-šan ēštu tueggaš* (var. NÍ.TE-*aš*) *apedaš* UD.KAM-*aš* EME.ḪI.A *natkan ḫašši* (var. [GUN]NI-*i*) *peššiyazzi* "'That which you spoke with mouth and tongue — here are *tiššatwa* (pieces of fat wrapped in colored wool) — let the tongues of those days, (those) of the body, be detached from you!' And she throws them (the *tiššatwa*) onto the hearth." 2Mašt. i 44-47 with variants from KUB 12.34 i 7-10 (1Mašt., MH/NS); "The Old Woman takes a fish, waves it over the two clients together, and speaks thus: 'This fish (is) the bull of the sea. As this fish has been removed from the sea,'" *kinuna tuḫšandu* [*ap*]*edaš* UD-*aš* EME.[ḪI.]A *ḫurtauš* "'now let the tongues (and) curses of those days be removed!" (And she throws the fish onto the hearth.) 2Mašt. i 36-41 (MH/MS); "The Old Woman takes a lizard, makes for it red and blue wool, waves it over the two clients, and speaks thus:" *karp pittiyališ* GÌR-*aš id*[*ālun*] EME-*an nuwaran iškišaz karpdu* [*IŠT*]*U* EME.ḪI.A-*ŠU-yawaran* (2Mašt. *-yawarat*) *karpdu* [*idāl*]*u* KA×U-*iš idālun* [E]ME-*an* "O fleet-foot! Lift off the evil tongue! Let him lift it from the back; let him lift it [f]rom their(!) tongues (namely) the [evi]l mouth (and) evil tongue!" IBoT 2.109 ii 21-28 (1Mašt.), cf. 2Mašt. iii 8-13 (MH/MS).

6. *lalaš išḫaš* — **a.** "lord of the tongue", the client, whose tongue/speech is being magically treated: The Old Woman breaks bread and cheese for the Sungod, pours out wine, and says: *k[āšawatta parā tittanunun] BĒL* EME "I have herewith handed over to you the lord of the tongue" KUB 32.113 ii 9-10 (3Mašt., MH/MS) with restoration based on the parallel with 2Mašt. i 16-23, which (lines 22-23) has *mantallīeš* EME.ḪI.A-*eš* (acc. pl., referring to the two clients) instead of *BĒL* EME (referring to the sole client in KUB 32.113).

b. perhaps not genitive construction, but "lord tongue" in: EME-*aš* EN-*aš kuwapi pāši* "lord tongue, where are you going?" KUB 12.62 obv. 10 and EME EN-*aš kuwapi pāši* ibid. rev. 3 (rit. with dialogue sections, MH?/NS); compare EME.ḪI.A EME.ḪI.A *kuwapiwa paitte[ni]* "tongues, tongues, where are you going?" KUB 44.4 + KBo 13.241 rev. 22 (birth rit., NH), cf. mng. 4 b 4′. SAL.EME-*aš* "woman (who is called) tongue(?)" KBo 2.8 i (22), 32 may belong here.

7. blade (of knife), ingot (of metal): in Akkadian texts metal objects designated EME, to be read *lišānu* ("tongue"), have been described as either blades or ingots (CAD L 214-15). On the basis of this parallel use of the word "tongue" we include metal EME's under Hitt. *lala-*. There is, however, no evidence that the Hitt. syllabic reading of EME in the meanings "ingot" or "blade" was *lala-*. It is possible that a few passages which mention metal EME's could refer to models of the tongue, on which compare mng. 2; 56 EME.GÍR AN.BAR[. . .] 8 EME. GÍR ^{LÚ}MUḪALDIM "fifty-six knife blades of iron [. . .] eight knife blades of the cook (sixteen weapons of black iron, etc.)" KBo 18.158:3-5 (inventory, NH), cf. KUB 42.11 rev. 4-6; probably blades or ingots are meant also in enumeration of EME's of black iron KUB 42.76 obv. 3, KUB 12.1 iii 8, KUB 42.42 iv 5, gold KUB 38.38 obv. 3, bronze KUB 12.1 iii 9, 10, lead KUB 42.97:10, bronze, gold, and iron together (?) KBo 18.172 obv. 14.

8. *lalan karp-* (MH): [*m*]*ān antuḫši* ^{LÚ}*TAPPUŠU la-a-la-an karpzi* "If against a man his companion 'lifts the tongue', (or invokes the gods against him)" KUB 17.28 ii 33-34 (rit., MH/NS) beginning of new text after double rule; and in same text: *kuiš* DUMU.L[Ú.U$_{18}$.LU-*i*]*a*? *la-a-la-an* DINGIR.MEŠ-*naš piran karpta* "whatever person at all has 'lifted the tongue' before the gods, (whoever invoked the gods against me)" ii 40-42. □Keep apart *la-a-la-an ka-ra-ap-ta* in KUB 36.49 i 6-8 (OH/OS), since the syllabification and lines 3-5 favor the interpretation *karap-/karip-* "devour", cf. mng. 4 a 1′.

Sommer, HAB (1938) 136-38, OLZ 1939:684, Friedrich, HW (1952) 126, Laroche, RA 48 (1954) 46.

Cf. *lala-* B v.

lala- A v.; (mng. uncertain); always in texts with Luwianisms; NH.†

inf. *la-la-u-wa-an-zi* KUB 12.62 obv. 12 (NH), *la-la-u-na* KBo 13.241 rev. 12 (NH).

EME-*aš* EN-*aš kuwapi pāši* KASKAL-*ši karipuwa*[*nzi pāimi*] UR.MAḪ *tarwauwanzi pāimi alili waršuwanzi pāimi* DUMU.<LÚ.> U$_{18}$.LU *la-la-u-wa-an-zi pāimi* KASKAL-*ašza karipuwanzi UL memmai* UR.MAḪ-*ašza tarwauwanzi UL memmai alilašza waršuwanzi UL memmai* ^{d}UTU-*ušza* ḪUL-*muš* EME.ḪI.A *UL memai* KUB 12.62 obv. 10-15 (dialogue in rit., NH), cf. Sommer, HAB 136; EME.ḪI.A EME.ḪI.A *kuwapiwa pa*[*i*]*tte*[*ni*] ^{NA_4}*peruni :palḫuna pāiueni . . . ANA* ^{NA_4}KA *:duwarnuma*[*nzi p*]*āiueni* UR.MAḪ GIŠ-*ruanzi* KI.MIN UR. BAR.RA *:patalḫauna* KI.MIN *:za*[*mm*]*anti* DUMU.NITA *la-la-u-na* KI.MIN KUB 44.4 rev. 22-24 + KBo 13.241 rev. 10-12 (birth rit. with Luwian, NH), ed. G. Beckman, Diss. 226, 228.

In Luwian text: ^{GIŠ}NÍG.GUL-*in la-a-la-an-du nu* [. . .] *tarmiššandu* "Let them take(?)/release(?) the hammer and drive in/affix [the . . .]!" KBo 9.145:7-8 (NH).

Since the KUB 12.62 and KUB 44.4 + KBo 13.241 passages contain many Luwianisms, the presumption is that *lala-* is Luwian. If so, since the verb *lala-* in Luwian passages hardly fits "artikuliert reden" suggested by Sommer, only Laroche's "prendre" (reduplicated form of Luw. v. *la-*) or Rosenkranz's "lösen" (reduplicated form of Hitt. *la*(*i*)- "to loose") are possible. The crucial Hittite passages, however, are obscure.

Sommer, HAB (1938) 136; Laroche, DLL (1959) 61; Rosenkranz, OrNS 33 (1964) 241, 247; van Brock, RHA XXII/75 (1964) 124, 141-42.

Cf. (:)*lalami-*.

lala- B v. mid.; (verb of speech?); from MH.†

[*mā*]*n ŠA* URU*Lalanda memai nu la-la-at-ta-ru* [*mā*]*n ŠA* URU*Wattarwa memai nu wattarittaru* "If someone from Lalanda speaks, let it/him . . . ! If someone from Wattarwa speaks, let it/him . . . !" KBo 12.96 i 14-15 (MH/NS), ed. Rosenkranz, OrNS 33:239, 241, 247, cf. Neu, StBoT 5 (1968) 105f.

The city names are chosen to match the two verbs, not vice versa.

Cf. *lala-* n.

GIŠ**lallaḫḫa-** (tree or its fruit, or wooden object).†

GIŠ*la-al-la-aḫ-ḫa* 330/e i 6 and GIŠ*la-la-ḫ*[*u-* . . .] 4/p 2 cited by Ertem, Flora 160.

lalakueša- see *lalaweš*(*š*)*a-*.

lalakueššar see *lalawiššar*.

(:)lalami- n. com.; list, accounting receipt; NH.

sg. nom. *la-la-me-eš* KBo 9.91 obv. 1, 5, 11, (19), KBo 18.153 obv. (4), 14, 15, 16; :*la-la-mi-eš* KUB 13.35 i 5, iv 40; *la-la-mi-iš* KUB 31.53 (StBoT 1, text G) obv. 8; the word :*la-la-a-ma* in KUB 36.89 obv. 23 (cf. Haas, KN, 164) is problematic.

"(For) the objects which [the queen] had periodically given to G., the son of U., the commander of ten, (namely) [cha]riot(s), bronze and copper object(s), etc., he (G.) never sealed (a document about) which object he had issued to whom" *nušši* :*dušdumiš UL ešta* :*la-la-mi-eš-ši UL ešta* "He did not have a *d.*; he did not have an itemized list." KUB 13.35 i 1-6, ed. StBoT 4:4f.; "Thus (says) U., . . . : 'When they sent me to Babylonia, I sealed the (waxed) writing boards which I had concerning horses and mules. But during the time I was going to Babylonia and coming back I did not seal them again.'" :*la-la-mi-eš-ša UL šiyanza* "And the itemized list was not sealed." KUB 13.35 iv 35-40, ed. StBoT 4:14f.; "(Concerning) 287 ewes, 100 rams, 11 male goats which they issued from the palace," *la-la-mi-iš* "(there is) an itemized list" KUB 31.53 obv. 7-8 (vow of Puduḫ.), ed. StBoT 1:20-21, lines 47-48; as heading for paragraphs listing objects (garments, weapons, containers) issued to men of Araunna in the Nerik garrison KBo 9.91 obv. 1, 5, 11, 15, (19); list of weighed amounts of gold and copper issued: [. . . M]A.NA KÙ.GI *MANDATT*[*U* . . .]KÙ.GI GIŠ*tuppaza la-la-me-eš* N[U.GÁL . . . *ANA* m*Pa*]*lla* m*Zuzuli zanum*[*anzi pier*(?)] "[So many] minas of gold, trib[ute . . .] gold from the *t.*-chest, (for which) there [is] no list, [. . . they gave(?) to P.] and Z. [for] melting down" KBo 18.153 obv. 3-5; cf. also 14-16; cf. Otten, StBoT 17:17 and note 8.

Güterbock, Symb.Koschaker (1939) 31-32 with n. 18; Laroche, RA 43 (1949) 69: "liste, inventaire"; Rosenkranz, ZA 57 (1966) 246: "Empfangsbescheinigung" from Luw. *la-* "to take, receive(?)".

Cf. *lala-* A v.

NINDA**lallamuri(ya)-, lalla(m)puri(ya)-** n. com. and neut.?; (a dish made from cereal, pudding); from MH.

sg. nom. NINDA*la-al-la-am-mu-ri-iš-š*(*a*) KUB 32.128 i 8; NINDA *la-la-mu-ú-ri-iš* Bo 5593 ii 24 (dupl. of preceding); NINDA*la-al-la-am-pu-ri-iš* KBo 21.34 ii 24 (preceded by the number 5; may be plural); NINDA *la-la-mu-ri-ia-aš* KBo 21.38:4; NINDA*la-al-la-am-pu-u-ri-ia-aš* KBo 21.34 iii 52, iv 5; NINDA*la-al-la-pu-u-ri-ia-aš* ibid. iii 35; **loc. or nom.-acc. neut.** NINDA*la-la-mu-ri* KUB 45.58 iv 10; [NINDA*la-la-a*]*m-mu-u-ri* KUB 27.19 iii 5.

Occurs only in Kizzuwatnean rituals and festivals.

a. numbered: one KBo 21.39:7, KBo 21.38:4; two KBo 21.37 rev.? 11; five KBo 21.34 ii 24.

b. usually paired with NINDA*ḫaršupani-*: KBo 17.98 v 3, 21.34 iii 35f., 52f., 21.37 rev.? 11f., 21.38:3f., KUB 32.128 i 7f.

c. grouped with other types of NINDA: KBo 21.34 ii 21-24, KUB 25.46 ii 11-12.

Always made from BA.BA.ZA (Akk. *pappašu* "(barley) mash").

Hoffner, AlHeth (1974) 170.

(:)lalatta- n. com.; (mng. unkn.; a plant?); Luw. in Hitt.; NH.†

sg. gen. (Hitt.) *la-la-ta-aš* KBo 26.168 ii 2; *la-la-at-ta-[aš]* KUB 16.16 obv. 9; **(Luw. genitival adj.) neut. sing. nom.** *:la-la-at-ta-aš-ši* KUB 8.75 iv 52.
Luw. pl. acc. *la-la-at-ta-an-za* KUB 22.67:(2), 5, 8, (14). **broken** *:la-la-at-ta-*x 305/f:6 (Rosenkranz, JKF 1:193).

3 EZEN.MEŠ EZEN *parā [tarnummaš(?)]* EZEN *la-la-ta-aš* EZEN [. . .] KBo 26.168 ii 1-2, cf. KBo 19.126:2 and KUB 46.33 obv. 12 (cult invs.); 1 DUG.KA.DÙ.A *ANA* EZEN *la-la-at-ta[-aš]* KUB 16.16 obv. 9 (ext.; cf. *parā tarnummaššaya* EZEN ibid. 14); *nu ANA* DINGIR-*LIM la-la-at-ta-an-za-ma* [. . .] *nušši* SISKUR *piḫḫi* "Or shall I [perform/prepare?] *l.*s for the god and give him an offering?" KUB 22.67:8-9, cf. ibid. 2-3, 5-6, 14-15 (ext.); [1 A].ŠÀ *:la-la-at-ta-aš-ši* 5 *PA* NUMUN-*ŠU ŠA* [m]*Ḫimmuili* "[One fi]eld of *l.*, 5 *parīsu*-measures (are) its seed grain, belonging to Ḫimmuili" KUB 8.75 iv 52, ed. Souček, ArOr 27:24-25, 390.

Cf. [URU]*La-la-at-ta* KUB 31.55:6.

:lalattašši- (Luwian genitival) adj.; (mng. unkn.); NH.†

neut. sg. nom. *:la-la-at-ta-aš-ši* KUB 8.75 iv 52.

For semantic analysis see *(:)lalatta-*.

lalaweš(š)a-, lalakueša- n. com.; ant; from MH.†

sg. nom. *la-la-ú-e-ša-aš* KUB 8.63 iv 12 (NH); **acc.** *la-la-ku-e-ša-an* KUB 33.93 iii 22 (NH); *la-la-ú-e-ša-an* KBo 26.91 ii 4 (NH); *[la-la]-ú-e-ša-an* KUB 8.63 iv 8 (NH); **pl. gen.** *la-la-ú-i-iš-ša-aš* KBo 13.29 ii 5 (NH); **unclear** *la-la-ú-[e-ša-aš?]* KUB 17.27 ii 5 (MH/NS).

For the vocabulary entry KUB 3.94 ii 26 (NH) cf. *lalawiššar*.

a. in similes: *la-la-ku-e-ša-an-ma-wa-ra-an-[kán?* GIM-*an?*] GÌR-*it anda pašiḫaiddu* "Let him crush him with (his) foot like an ant" KUB 33.93 iii 22 (Ullik. I A), ed. Güterbock, JCS 5:152f., cf. KBo 26.91 ii 4.

b. as an insect pest: *la-la-ú-e-ša-aš garapi* "An ant is eating" (grain? cf. *ḫalkin* in iv 16) KUB 8.63 iv 12 (Atramḫaši).

c. in the phrase *lalawiššaš* É.ḪI.A "ant hills" (lit. "houses of ants"): *mānzan* NIM.LÀL *la-la-ú-i-iš-ša-aš* É.Ḫ[I.A . . .] KBo 13.29 ii 5 (omen), cf. É.ḪI.A NIM.LÀL "bee hives" ibid. 6.

Güterbock, JCS 6 (1952) 37.

Cf. *lalawiššar*.

lalawiššar, lalakueššar n.; a swarm or colony of ants(?).†

sg. nom. *la-la-ku-e-eš-šar* ABoT 38 left col. 3 (NH); **sg. gen.(?)** *la-la-ú-i-iš-na-aš* KUB 43.59 i 3 (NH); ⌈*la*⌉*-la-wi₅-iš-n[a-aš]* KUB 3.94 ii 26 (NH); *la-la-ú-e-eš-na-aš* Bo 2499 (ZA 66:94) i 3.

(Sum.) DAG.KISIM₅×GÍR! = (Sum. pron.) ki-ši-ib = (Akk.) *kúl-bá-ab!-tù* = (Hitt.) ⌈*la*⌉*-la-wi₅-iš-n[a-aš]* KUB 3.94 ii 26. The reading of the Hittite column is not certain. ⌈*la*⌉*-la-wi₅-iš-aš* is possible but less likely because of the sequence of two VC signs. *lalawišnaš*, the genitive of *lalawiššar*, would mean "a member of a swarm of ants", hence "an ant".

a. as an insect pest: *la-la-ku-e-eš-šar uizzi* "[If] a swarm of ants comes (I conjure [as follows])" ABoT 38 left col. 3f.

b. in a magic spell: *la-la-ú-eš-na-aš* AMA-*aš* GUD-*uš* "cow mother of *l.*" Bo 2499 i 3 (par. with *a-<aš->ku-wa-aš* AMA-*aš* GUD-*uš* Bo 2738 i 17, ZA 66:94f.).

Güterbock, JCS 6 (1952) 37; Hoffner, AlHeth (1974) 91.

Cf. *lalawišša-*.

lalḫuwant- part.; poured(?); NH.†

[. . . *IŠTU* K]AŠ GEŠTIN *aršer ḫāriuš* [. . .]x *la-al-ḫu-u-wa-an-ti-it* [*aršer*(?)] "[the . . . -s] flowed [with b]eer (and) wine, the valleys [flowed] with poured [. . .]" KUB 36.2b ii 19-20 (kingship of [d]LAMMA myth, NH) translit. Laroche, Myth. 147.

Possibly this is a participle of the verb *lelḫuwai-* with *-a-* rather than *-i/e-* in the reduplicated syllable.

Cf. *laḫ(ḫ)uwai-*.

(:)lali(n)naimi- Luw. part.; (mng. unkn.); NH.†

sg. or **pl. nom. com.** *la-*⌈*li*⌉*-in-na-i-me-eš* KUB 42.69

obv. 23; *la-li-i-na-i-me-iš* KUB 42.78 ii? 21; **pl. nom. com. Luw.** *la-li-na-i-me-en-zi* KUB 12.1 iv 44.

Modifies various objects in inventories: 4 SAG.DU.KI KÙ.GI NA_4 ŠÀ.BA 3 *la-li-na-i-me-en-zi* KUB 12.1 iv 44; 5 *kaluppaššiš la-li-i-na-i-me-iš* KÙ.[. . .] KUB 42.78 ii? 21; [. . .]-x-*eš* ZA.GÌN *la-li-in-na-i-me-eš* KUB 42.69 obv. 23; [o^{TÚ}]^{G} *galupaššiš* KÙ.GI 1-*ŠU* :*la*!-*li*[-*na-i-me-iš*] KUB 42.84 obv. 6.

Laroche, DLL 62 under *lalina*(*i*)-.

Cf. *lalini-*.

lalini- n. neut.; (mng. unkn.); NH.†

1 *kalupaššiš* KÙ.GI NA_4 1 *la-li-ni* (erasure) [o *t*]*a*(*ša*!?)-*ri-an-z*[*a* . . .] KUB 42.64 rev. 6 (inv.).

Cf. (:)*lalin*(*n*)*aimi-*.

lalu- n. neut.; penis; from pre-NH; written syll. and ^{UZU}*IŠARU*.†

sg. nom.-acc. *la-a-lu* KBo 1.51 rev. (19), 20; with neut. poss. pron. *la-a-lu-u*(*š-še-e*[*t*]) KUB 34.19 iv 5 (pre-NH/NS).

Akk. ^{UZU}*I-ŠA-RI* KUB 44.61 rev. 21 (NH); *I-ŠA-RI* 125/r ii 12 (MDOG 93:76 n. 2).

(Akk.) *i-ša-a-ru* = (Hitt.) *la-a-*[*lu*] KBo 1.51 rev. 19; (Akk.) *mu-ša-a-ru* = (Hitt.) *la-a-lu*[-*pát*] ibid. 20.

a. in an omen: *takku IZBU la-a-lu-uš-še-e*[*t*] "If the penis of a malformed fetus [. . .]" KUB 34.19 iv 5 (pre-NH/NS), ed. StBoT 9:56-57.

b. in a medical rit.: [*mā*]*nkan antuḫše IŠTU* ^{UZU}*I-ŠA-RI-ŠU z*[*a-* . . .] . . . *nu tappin enuz*[*i* . . . *na*]*n* ^{UZU}*I-ŠA-RI-ŠU anda zikkizzi* "If from a man's penis (it) d[rips(?)] ... then one heats a *t*. [. . .] and places it on/in his penis" KUB 44.61 rev. 19-21 (NH), ed. StBoT 19:20-21.

c. in an offering list: 1 AMAR 1 MUŠEN.GAL ŠA ^{d}U *PU-UQ-QA*(var. *GA*)-*TI ANA I-ŠA-RI-ŠU-ia* "one calf (and) one 'large bird' for the buttocks and penis of the Stormgod" 125/r ii 11-12 (cult of Tešub, NH), with dupl. IBoT 3.109:6; cited by Otten MDOG 93:76 n. 2.

^{GAD}*la-a-lu-wa-az* KUB 46.48 obv. 16 should be read ^{GAD}*a*!-*la*!-*lu-wa-az*, cf. *alalu-*.

For ^{UZU}ÚR in the sense of penis, see the Sumerogram.

Friedrich, Glotta 23 (1935) 210-13.

[*lalukki-*] adj.; luminous, shining, resplendent, Friedrich, HW 126, is not attested.

lalukki- v.; to be or become luminous; OH/MS.†

pret. sg. 3 *la-lu-uk-ki-it* KUB 33.66 ii 17.

ANA DUMU.LÚ.U_{18}.LU-*ma tuekkišši* [*ḫumanti*?] *la-lu-uk-ki-it ḫaršaniš*<*ši*?> K[I.] MIN *šakuw*[*aš* KI.MIN] *wālulaššaš* KI.MIN IGI.ḪI.A-*aš ḫarki*[*yaš*] KI.MIN *ḫanti*[*š*]*ši* KI.MIN *ene*[*raš*] KI.MIN *laplipašša* [KI.MIN] "It became luminous on the mortal's [entire?] body: on his head ditto, on the eyes, on his *w*., on the white[s] of the eyes, on his forehead, [on] the eyebro[ws], and on the eyelashes [ditto]" KUB 33.66 ii 16-20 (missing deity myth), Laroche, Myth, 70.

Athematic stative *lalukke-* (cf. Watkins, IESt 178, where the adj. *lalukki-*, not the verb *lalukke-*, should be starred) or thematic *lalukki-*/**lalukka-* (analogous to *lukki-*/*lukka-*, on which cf. Neu, StBoT 18:79).

Cf. *luk-*.

lalukkima- n. com.; **1.** source of light, luminary, radiance, rays of sunshine, **2.** (object in a lot oracle); from OH; written syll. and ZALAG.GA(?).

sg. nom. *la-lu-u*[*k-ki-ma-aš*] KBo 25.112 ii 12 (OH/OS); *la-lu-uk-k*[*i-m*]*a-aš* KUB 24.3 i 44 (Murš. II); [*la*]-⌈*a*⌉-*lu-ki-ma-aš* KUB 31.127 i 15 (OH/NS); *l*[*a-lu-u*]*k-ki-ma-aš* KUB 30.11:2 + 31.135:9 (OH/NS).

sg. acc. *la-a-lu-k*[*i-ma-an*?] KBo 18.95 rev. 3 (NH); *la-lu-ki-uk-ma-an* (with sign interchange) KUB 34.56:13 (NH); *la-lu-uk-ki-ma-an* KUB 16.37 ii 9 (NH); KUB 15.32 i (57) (MH/NS); KBo 22.77 obv. (11) (NH), KUB 24.1 iii (7), KUB 31.144:(7), (9) (both Murš. II).

sg. d.-l. [*la-lu-u*]*k-ki-mi* KUB 48.88 obv. 4 (NH).

pl. nom. *la-lu-uk-ki-mi-iš* KUB 36.19 rev. iv 14 (MH/NS).

1. source of light, luminary, radiance, rays of sunshine: *nepiš*[*aš t*]*agnašša ḫulalešni zikpat* ^{d}UTU-*uš* [*la-*]⌈*a*⌉-*lu-ki-ma-aš* "In the circumference of sky and earth you, Sungod, are the source of light" KUB 31.127 i 14-15 (solar hymn, OH/NS), Güterbock, JAOS 78:239; with no employment of *-za*, Hoffner, JNES 28:227; *manašt*[*a* ^{d}UTU-*uš karuwariwar n*]*ēpišaz šara up*[*zi nuššan*] *š*[*arazzi*]*yaš katteršša* KUR.KUR-*aš* [*ḫuman*-

daš ^{d}]UTU-*waš* *l*[*a-lu-u*]*k-ki-ma-aš* *tiya*[*ri*] "In the morning when the Sun(god) rises through the sky, the radiance of the Sun(god) appears on all the upper and lower lands" KUB 30.11:1-2 + 31.135 obv. 6-9 (text sim. to solar hymn, OH/MS), cf. KUB 31.127 + i 39-42 which lacks *lalukkimaš*, Güterbock, JAOS 78:240; "The sun and moon say to 'Silver':" [*l*]*ēwannaškan kueši wešawa* [AN-*aš* KI-*ašš*]*a la-lu-uk-ki-mi-iš* (var. [ZALAG.G]A-*aš-mi-iš*, coll.) ... *wešauwaz* (var. [*ú*-]⌈*e*⌉-*ša-wa*) ^{GIŠ}*zuppari* "Don't kill us! We are the luminaries [of sky] and [earth] (var. we are their light) ... we are torches" KUB 36.19 rev. iv 13-15 (myth of Silver, MH/NS) with dupl. 33.91:7-9 (MH/NS), ed. Laroche, Myth 181; *nepišaššaz tagnašša ḫūlalēšni zikpat* ^{d}UTU ^{URU}*Arinna la-lu-uk-k*[*i-m*]*a-aš* "In the circumference of sky and earth you alone, Sungoddess of Arinna, are the light-source" KUB 24.3 i 43-44 (prayer of Murš. II); [*ŠA* ^{d}UTU *la-lu-u*]*k-ki-mi ŠA* ^{d}U *kalmešni* [... *ŠA* ^{d}U ^{URU}*N*]*erik* ^{GIŠ}*ḫinzi* (or ^{GIŠ}*ḪINZI*) "For the [radia]nce [of the Sungod], for the lightning of the Stormgod, [...] for the *ḫ*. [of the Stormgod of N]erik" KUB 48.88 obv. 4-5 (prayer(?) of Puduḫepa, NH); *nušši pišk*[*itten*] *ḫaddulatar* ... *dušgarattan* DINGIR.MEŠ-*aš miumar* ZI-*aš la-lu-uk*[-*ki-ma-an*] ... *piškatt*[*en*] "Give to him! Health ... joy, the gentleness of the gods, brightness of spirit ... give to him!" KUB 15.32 i 55-58 (evocatio rit., MH/NS); *nu AN*[(*A* ^{m})*Muršili*] ÌR-*KA* TI-*tar ḫattul*[(*atar*) *inna*]*rauwātar ŠA* EGIR.UD-*MI* [(ZI-*aš*) *la-lu*]-*uk-ki-ma-an* [MU.KAM.G]ÍD.DA-*ia* [(*pešk*)*i*] "Give to Muršili your servant, life, health, vigor, brightness of spirit for (lit. of) the future, and longevity!" KUB 24.3 iii 17-20 (+) 31.144:5-7, dupl. 1229/u:6-9 (prayer of Murš. II); (May the gods give you) ... *ḫaddulātar* ZI-*aš la-a-lu-k*[*i-ma-an* ...] "health, brightness of spirit ..." KBo 18.95 rev. 3 (letter, NH); *nušmaškan ANA* ZI-*ŠUNU anda* [... *la-lu-u*]*k-ki-ma-an dušgaradanna* [*peški*] "Give to them in their spirits [gentleness(?), rad]iance, and joy!" KUB 24.1 iii 6-8 (prayer of Murš. II).

2. (object in a lot oracle): *IŠTU* SAL.ŠU.GI I[R-*TUM QATAMMA-pat* ...] *la-lu-uk-ki-ma-an* [...] *nan pangaui* [*paiš*] "The oracle (taken) by the Old Woman [is the same; ... took] light [and gave] it (*-an*) to the congregation" KUB 16.37 ii 8-10 (NH); Archi, OA 13 (1974) 135, 142 suggests that *lalukkima-* is the reading of ZALAG.GA in the lot oracles.

Güterbock, OrNS 12 (1943) 356; Laroche, RHA IX/49 (1948-49) 19f.; on ZALAG.GA first Laroche, Myth (1968) 182 n. 9.

Cf. *luk*(*k*)-.

lalukkeš- v.; **1.** to become bright (impers. subj.), **2.** to become bright, shine, glow, gleam, beam, blaze (subj.: celestial phenomenon), **3.** to glisten, reflect light (subj.: moist or oily surface); from OH.

pres. sg. 3 *la-lu-uk-kiš-zi* KUB 33.11 iii 11 (OH/NS); *la-lu-uk-ki-iš-zi* KUB 33.51:7 (OH/NS); *la-lu-ki-iš-zi* KUB 43.2 ii 2 (NH); *la-lu-ke-eš-zi* KUB 8.16:9 (NH).

imp. sg. 3 *la*[*-lu-uk-ki-i*]*š-du* KUB 33.51:9 (OH/NS); *la-lu-kiš-du* KUB 41.20 rev. 2 (NH); *la-lu-ke-eš-du* KUB 15.34 ii 28 (MH/MS); *la-lu-uk-ki-iš-du* IBoT 3.108:3 (NH); [*la-lu-u*]*k-ki-iš-du* KBo 7.29 ii 14 (NH).

participle [*la-l*]*u-uk-ki-iš-ša-an* KUB 15.34 ii 27 (MH/MS).

1. to become bright (impers. subj.): [*n*]*u* ^{GIŠ}*waršama*[*n*] *maḫḫan lukkanz*[(*i n*)]*ašta anda* 4-*taš ḫalḫaltūmar*[(*iya*)*š*] *la-lu-uk-ki-iš-zi* ⌈DINGIR.MAḪ-*niya*⌉*kan AN*[*A* ZI-*K*]*A karatešteš*[(*a an*)*da QATAM*(*MA*)] *la*[*-lu-uk-ki-i*]*š-du* "As they ignite the kindling, and it becomes bright in the four corners, in the same way let it become bright in your soul and in(!) your *karateš*, O Mothergoddess!" KUB 33.51:5-9 with dupl. KUB 33.45:9 + FHG 2 iii? 4-7 + KUB 33.53:5 (myth, OH/NS); translit. Laroche, Myth 80-81; cf. also KUB 33.11 iii 10-11 in Myth 49 (OH/NS).

2. to become bright, shine, glow, gleam, beam, blaze (subj.: celestial phenomenon): *takkukan* ^{MUL}*leššallaš uizzi nuššikan ḫapparnuwataršet parā mekki la-lu-ke-eš-zi* "If the *leššallaš*-star comes, and its *ḫ*. shines very brightly, (it will happen that the king of the world will die)" KUB 8.16:7-10 + 24 rev. 8-10; cf. also KUB 8:24 obv. 10 + KUB 43.2 ii 1-4 (star omens, NH).

3. to glisten, reflect light (subj.: moist or oily surface): "He/she sprinkles oil with the red wool and says:" *ke!-da-ni-kán ANA* SÍG.SA$_5$

maḫḫan and[a la-l]u-uk-ki-iš-ša-an ANA DINGIR.MEŠ LÚ.MEŠ GIŠERIN *tueggaš=*[*maš a*]*nda QATAMMA la-lu-uk-ke-eš-du* "Just as in/on this red wool (there is something) glistening, so also let it glisten on your body parts, O male deities of the cedar (lands)!" KUB 15.34 ii 26-28 (evocatio rit., MH/MS); [*ANA*] SAG.KI-*ma-pa la-lu-kiš-du* "Let it glisten [on] the forehead!" KUB 41.20 rev. 2 (rit., NS).

Güterbock, OrNS 12 (1943) 356; Laroche, RHA IX/49 (1948-49) 19f.

Cf. *luk*(*k*)-.

lalukkešnu- v.; to give light, illuminate; from OH or MH/NS.†

imp. 3 sg. *la-lu-uk-k*[*i-iš-nu-ud-du*] KUB 34.77 obv.? 6 (OH or MH/NS); *la-lu-uk-ke-eš-nu-uš-ki-id-du* KBo 18.133:20′ (NH); **part.** *la-lu-ki-iš-nu-wa-an* KUB 34.77 obv.? 5.

nu dUTU-*uš maḫḫan še*[*r* . . .] *nepišza ḫuyanza našta utniy*[*aš ḫumandaš*] *la-lu-ki-iš-nu-wa-an ḫarzi U* DINGIR.MAḪ *A*[*NA* SAL.LUGAL DUMU.MEŠ-*ŠU*] *INA* ZI-*ŠU andan QATAMMA la-lu-uk-k*[*i-iš-nu-ud-du*] "Just as the sun ab[ove] runs across(?) the sky and has given light in [all] the lan[ds], so also [may] the Mothergoddess give light in the soul t[o the queen (and) her children]" KUB 34.77 obv.? 3-6 (rit., OH or MH/NS), *A*[*NA* SAL.LUGAL DUMU.MEŠ-*ŠU*] restored from line 11 of continuing context; for the other restorations cf. Laroche, RHA IX/49 (1948-49) 19; cf. [*nu*?] DINGIR.MAḪ Z[I? . . .] *la-lu-uk-ki-i*[*š*?-*nu-ud-du* . . .] KUB 30.30 obv. 2-3, ed. Beckman, Diss. 257f.; [o o o o]x-*kan* ZI-*ni anda la-lu-uk-ke-eš-nu-uš-ki-id-du* "May (the deity) ever give light in [your] soul!" KBo 18.133:20 (letter, NH), reporting favorable oracles to the king.

Contra Laroche this verb in KUB 34.77 should not be translated "réchauffe", since it is light, not heat, which is denoted.

Laroche, RHA IX/49 (1948-49) 19.

Cf. *luk*(*k*)-.

lalukkiwant- adj.; luminous, radiant, shining, resplendent; from OH.†

sg. nom. *la-lu-uk-ki-u-wa-an-za* KUB 31.71 iv 33 (NH); **neut. nom.-acc.** *la-lu-uk-ki-u-wa-an* KUB 39.17 iii 4 (MH/NS); *la-lu-ki-u-wa-an* KBo 13.101 rev. 17 (NS); **broken** *la-lu-ki-wa-an*[- . . .] KBo 7.29 ii 12 (NH).

a. *tuwāttu* d[UT]U-*i d*[*andukešni*] dUTU-*uš zīk* DINGIR.MEŠ-*naša ištarna la-lu-u*[*k-ki-u-wa-an-za*] DINGIR-*uš* SAL.LUGAL *zīk* "Mercy, O [Sungodde]ss! [Among] m[ortals] you are the Sungoddess but among the gods you are a resplen[dent] deity, a queen" KBo 25.112 ii 11-13 (invoc. of Ḫattic deities, OS), par. Laroche, JCS 1:197, lines 21-22 where the Ḫattic equivalent to Hitt. *lalu*[*kkiwanza*] is *kašbaruyaḫ*.

b. *nuwašši uk*[*turi*] *la-lu-uk-ki-u-wa-an ešdu* "Let it be to him ete[rnally] resplendent (or endu[ring] and resplendent)!" KUB 39.17 iii 3-4 (rit., MN/NS), HTR 86-87.

c. [*n*]*anakuššiyan ešdu* [. . .] *piran la-lu-ki-u-wa-an e*[*šdu*] "Let it be *n.*; before [. . .] let it be resplendent!" KBo 13.101 rev. 16-17 (rit., NS).

d. [. . .]-*mawakan maḫḫan anda la-lu-ki-wa-an*[(-) . . . (x-*ia-an ANA* Z)]I-*TI* d*IŠTAR-yawakan U ANA* EN.SISKUR *an*[*da QATAMMA lalu*]*kkišdu* "Just as in [. . .] it is resplendent . . . , so also in the soul of Ištar and within the one who commissions the ritual let it become resplendent!" KBo 7.29 ii 12-14 with dupl. KUB 39.74 + 75 rev. 1ff. (*pabilili* rit., NH).

Cf. *luk*(*k*)-.

[*lam-*] mid. "to be mixed together" HW 126 is probably to be read (*anda*) *kulam-*.

[DUG*lammaya-*] n. (copper container) HW 126 is to be read *galamma-*.

lammami- n. com.; (an object made of precious metal); NH.†

sg. nom. *lam-ma-am-mi-iš* KUB 42.69 rev. 21; *lam-ma-mi-iš* KUB 12.1 iv 26. **Luw. pl. nom.** *lam-ma-me-en-zi* KUB 42.69 rev. 26.

Only in inventories: [o o] KÙ.GI ŠÀ.BA 1 *lam-ma-mi-iš* KÙ.GI NA4 "[. . .] of gold: among them one *l.* of gold and jewel(s)" KUB 12.1 iv 26; [. . .] KÙ.GI NA4 *lam-ma-am-mi-iš* [. . .] *ḫašḫašanteš* [. . .] KUB 42.69 rev. 21-23;

[. . . *šupp*]*išduwaranteš lam-ma-me-en-zi* ibid. 26.

Laroche, DLL 62 (Luw. part.?).

laman n. neut.; name; written syll. and with Akkadogram *ŠUMU* (usually without Akk. inflection, employing the single sign *ŠUM*); from OH.

Syll. spellings and Akkadogram with Hitt. compl.:

Sg. nom.-acc. *la-a-ma-an* KBo 19.152 i 20 (OH/MS?), KBo 3.21 iii 19, KUB 34.16 iii 9 (both OH/NS); KUB 31.124 ii 23 (MH/MS); *la-a-am-ma-a-mi-it* (= *lamman* + *mit*) KUB 1.16 iii 13 (OH/NS); *la-ma-an* FHG 1 ii 17 (OH?/NS); *lam-an* KUB 24.8 iii 7 (pre-NH/NS); *ŠUM-an* ibid. 10, 14, 16 and passim, KUB 31.141:4 (NH).

gen. *la-am-na-aš* Bo 5698:5 (HHT 81) (cf. sub h.); *lam-na-aš* ibid. 8, KBo 13.34 iv 2 (NH).

d.-l. *la-am-ni* KUB 30.41 iv 5, 18 (OH/NS); *lam-ni* 30.11 rev. 16 (OH/MS?); *ŠUM-ni* KUB 21.38 obv. 52 (NH); **endingless loc.?** *lam-ma-an* KUB 31.127 iii 6 (OH?/NS) with *lam-ni(-mi)* in parallel 30.11 rev. 16.

inst. *lam-ni-it* KBo 5.11 i 7 (MH/NS), KBo 24.93 iii 12; *ŠUM-it* KBo 11.32 obv. 30 (OH/NS), KUB 10.72 ii 20 (pre-NH/NS).

abl. *ŠUM-za* KUB 17.9 i 8 (NH); *ŠUM-az* KUB 39.97 obv. 12.

pl. gen. *ŠUM*$^{HI.A}$*-aš* KUB 2.1 iii 27 (NH); **pl. d.-l.** *lam-na-aš* KUB 24.3 i 30 (Murš. II based on an older prototype); *ŠUM*$^{HI.A}$*-aš* 24.1 ii 21 (Murš. II).

Akkadogram without Hitt. compl.:

Not construed with a genitive: **sg.** *ŠUM*^{UM} KBo 3.6 ii 14 (Ḫatt. III); *ŠU-UM* KUB 30.15 obv. 30 (MH/NS); **pl.** *ŠUM*^{MEŠ} KUB 31.61 ii 2 (Ḫatt. III).

Construed with a genitive: *ŠUM* KUB 13.4 ii 46 (MH?/NS); *ŠUM* with pron. suff. is common; *ŠUM* + *ŠA* + gen. KUB 38.3 ii 8 (NH); *ŠUM-MI* KBo 7.28:19, 29, 34 (OH/MS), KBo 14.68:19 (NS); *ANA ŠUM-MU*(sic) KUB 42.100 iv 34; *ŠUM*$^{HI.A}$ KUB 2.1 i 42, iii 25.

pl. acc. *ŠUM-MA-TE-ŠU-NU* KUB 32.124 obv. 4.

a. "name of . . . ": MUŠ *ŠUM* LUGAL "the snake of (= representing?) the name of the king" KUB 18.6 iv 9; [MUŠ] *ŠUM* LUGAL-*UT-TI* "the [snake] of the name of kingship" ibid. i 5, (17) (snake oracle, NH), cf. StBoT 3:29; 3 NINDA.SIG *paršiya* KI.MIN *nu ANA ŠUM-MI* LUGAL SAL.LUGAL *dāi* "He breaks three thin breads; ditto (the passage thus repeated is lost); and he puts (them) on/at (= deposits them for?) the names of the king and queen" KBo 13.245 rev. 17-18 (ANTAḪŠUM fest., OH/NS); (after libations to GUNNI, *ḫattalwaš* GIŠ, and GUNNI *tapušza*) *namma* ^{DUG}*išpantuz*[*i* 1-*ŠU*] LUGAL-*aš la-am-ni* 1-*ŠU* [*šipanti*] KUB 30.41 iv 4-5, cf. 17-8 (fest., OH/?); cf. *ḫa-aš-*⌈*šu*⌉*-w*[*a-aš lamni*(?)] 1-*ŠU šipanti* KBo 13.165 ii 6-7 (OH/MS); in the rituals for all the tutelary deities, the many different kinds of ^{d}LAMMA and ^{d}Aala are referred to as "all the names of DN": ⌈2 GU₄.GAL⌉ *ANA ŠUM*$^{HI.A}$ ^{d}LAMMA *ḫūmandaš* KUB 2.1 i 42; ŠU.NIGÍN 1 ME 12 *ŠUM*$^{HI.A}$ ^{d}LAMMA 1 ^{GIŠ}BANŠUR ibid. iii 25; 1 ^{GUD}ÁB *gimmaraš* 3 MÁŠ.GAL ^{d}*A-a-la-aš ŠUM*$^{HI.A}$*-aš ḫūmandaš* ibid. 26-27; cf. KUB 40.107 i 3-4 + IBoT 2.18 i! 4-5, ii! 6.

b. in adducing a name — **1′** in the phrase "his/her/its name is . . . ," usually with the name in the stem form: **a′** applied to humans: ^{m}*Ḫuzziya ŠUM-ŠU* KBo 8.42 rev.? 8 (OH/OS); cf. KUB 26.20:13 (MH treaty); [U]RU-*aš ŠUM-an-še-et* ^{UR}[^{U}*Š*]*udul . . . nukan šer* LÚ-*aš* ^{m}*Appu ŠUM-an-še-et* "There is a town, its name is Šudul . . . and up there (in the town of Šudul) is a man, his name is Appu" KUB 24.8 i 7-10 (Appu, NH), ed. StBoT 14:4f.; contrast nom. [^{m}*A*]*ppuš* ibid. i 21 etc.; "Keššì took the sister of U. as wife" SAL-*aš ŠUM-še-et* ^{f}*Šintalimeni* "The woman's name was Š." KUB 33.121 ii 4-5 (Keššì story, NH), ed. Friedrich, ZA 49 (1950) 234f.; frequent in the Vow of Puduḫepa, StBoT 1 (1965), quoted by lines of composite text as given there in the translation: ^{f}*Ābbāš* 1 DUMU.SAL-*ŠÚ* [(^{f}*Niwa ŠU*)*M-Š*(*U* 1 TUR.SAL-*m*)]*a* BA.ÚŠ (var. adds 1) TUR.NITA ^{m}*Dudu*(?) *ŠUM-ŠU* "A., one daughter of hers, Niwa is her name; one girl died; one boy, Dudu is his name" i 10-11; the same construction also in i and ii *passim*; contrast 1 TUR.NITA ^{m}*Tatiliš* i 52 without *ŠUM-ŠU*; 2 DUMU.MEŠ-*ŠU* ^{m}*Ḫappanuš* ^{m}*Šarraduwašša ŠUM*^{MEŠ} "two sons of his, Ḫ. and Š. are the names" ii 1-2, note the nom. form of the names and the lack of possessive suffix with *ŠUM*^{MEŠ}; *ŠUM-ŠU mertat* "his/her name got lost" (i.e., could not be ascertained) iv 15 (KUB 31.56:6).

b′ applied to objects — **1″** *ŠUM-ŠU* "its name" precedes the name: 1 AŠ.ME KÙ.GI *ŠA* 1 GÍN *ŠUM-ŠU* ^{d}*Pirinkir* "one sun disk of gold of one shekel (weight), its name is P." KUB 29.4 i 13 (rit., NH), ed. Kronasser, Schw.Gotth. 6-7; cf. KUB 42.78 ii? 11-12 (inv., NH); Á^{MUŠEN} KÙ.GI

ŠUM-ŠU Eribuškiš "the gold eagle, E. by name" KBo 15.37 i 21 (EZEN *ḫišuwaš*, MH/NS); **2″** *ŠUM-ŠU* or *ŠUM-anšet* follows the name: [(*kezza k*)]*ezziya wašši ḫuwallarī ŠUM-ŠU* (var. *ŠUM*) [(*ḫar*)]*ezzi* (var. *ḫariyaz*[*zi*]) "On either side he buries the drug called *ḫ*." HT 1 i 16-17 with dupl. KUB 9.31 i 23f. (rit. of Zarpiya, MH/NS), parallel KUB 35.10:9 has [*ḫuw*]*allarin* and omits *ŠUM-ŠU*; *nušš*[*iš*]*šan* ^{d}*Ušš*[*a* ...] *ŠUM-ŠU* (name of an image) KUB 30.54 ii 19-20 (shelf list), ed. CTH p. 179.

c′ applied to a city: URU-*aš ŠUM-an-še-et* ^{URU}[^{U}*Š*]*udul* KUB 24.8 i 7 (Appu), cf. above sub b 1′ a′.

2′ in the phrase "your name is ..." (attestations are all with names of gods): [... ^{LÚ}N]AR-*ša memai* [*tandukešni* ...] *ŠUM-KA* DINGIR. MEŠ-*nana ištarna gimraš* [^{d}IM-*aš zik*] "And the singer says: '[Among mortals, ...] is your name, but among the gods [you are the Storm-god] of the steppe'" KUB 31.143a ii 3-5 (OH/OS), ed. Laroche, JCS 1:203, D; [... ^{LÚ}N]AR *memai tanduki*[*šni*... DINGIR.MEŠ-*naša*(?) *i*]*štarna ŠUM-an iš-*⌈*ḫar*⌉*-wa-an-za* SAL.LUGAL-*aš* "The singer says; 'Among mortals [you are/ your name is ..., but] among [gods] the name is The Blood-red Queen.'" 259/s rev. 7-9 (OH/NS). □ In these OH lists of Ḫattic deities and their double names (Laroche, JCS 1:187-216) the usual wording is with *zik* "you are" rather than with *laman* "name".

3′ "what's-his-name" is expressed by *UMMA ŠU-UM*, for which see below under d 2′ a′ 3″.

c. In name-giving cf. Hoffner, JNES 27 (1968) 198ff. — **1′** name-giving described — **a′** with *dai-* and *-šan*/*-kan* cf. Kümmel, StBoT 3:29: ^{URU}KÁ.DINGIR.RA-*maššan kuedani* URU-*ri* ^{d}*Anuš la-a-ma-an daiš* "Babylon, the city to which Anu gave (its) name" KBo 3.21 iv 18-19 (hymn to Adad, OH/NS), translit. BoTU 6; ^{d}UTU ^{URU}TÚL-*na* ... *nuzakan INA* KUR ^{URU}*Ḫatti* ^{d}UTU ^{URU}TÚL-*na ŠUM-an daišt*[*a*] *nammamaza kuit* KUR-*e* ^{GIŠ}ERIN-*aš iyat nuzakan* ^{d}*Ḫebat ŠUM-an daišta* "O Sungoddess of Arinna! ... In Ḫatti you gave yourself the name of S. of A., but (in) the land which you made that of the cedar (forest) you gave yourself the name Ḫebat" KUB 21.27 i 3-6 (prayer of Puduḫepa); *nuššiššan šanizzi lam-an* ^{LÚ}ḪUL-*lu daiš* "and he gave him the fitting name Bad" KUB 24.8 iii 7 + 36.60 iii 8 (Appu story, pre-NH/NS), ed. StBoT 14:10:13; *nuššikan* NÍG.SI.SÁ-*an ŠUM-an daiš* "and he gave him the name Just" ibid. 13 (19), note different word order; the epithet of brother Bad later in the text (e.g., ^{LÚ}ḪUL-*aš* iv 21, 28, [^{LÚ}ḪU]L-*pa-aš* iv 24 var.) is *Ḫuwappaš, not *Idaluš (cf. Siegelová, StBoT 14:23), but this is never called his *laman*, nor is the PN wedge used for either of the brothers' epithets in this story; where the adj. precedes *laman*, an attributive construction "a bad name", "a just name" (**ḫandan laman*) is possible, but it is impossible in the case of *šanezzi laman* ^{LÚ}ḪUL-*lu*, contra E. A. Hahn, Naming 35f. n. 124; ^{d}*Kumarbišza PANI* Z[I-*ŠU memi*]*škiuwan daiš kuitwaššikan ŠUM-an* [*teḫḫi*(?)] "K. spoke to himself: 'What name [shall I give] him?'" KUB 33.93 iii 15-16 (Ullik. myth, NH), ed. JCS 5:152; cf. frag.: *ŠUM-an teḫḫi* KUB 21.37 obv. 11 (hist., Ḫatt. III); [*Š*]*UM-an dait*[*ti*] KBo 9.101:3 (prayer).

b′ with *pai-*: *nu šanezzi ŠUM-an* [TUR-*li*(?) *p*]*é-eš-ki-u-wa-an* (coll.) *daiš* "And he (Kumarbi) undertook to bestow [on the child] a fitting name" KUB 33.93 iii 14 (Ullik.).

2′ name-giving formulas — **a′** with *eš-*: *nušši*[*ššan* ^{LÚ}ḪUL-*l*]*u ŠUM-an ešdu* "Let Idalu be his name!" KUB 24.8+ iii 10 (16); *paiddu* NÍG.SI.SÁ-*an ŠUM-an ešdu* ibid. 16 (22); *paid*-*d*[*uwaššišša*]*n* ^{d}*Ullikummi ŠUM-an ešdu* "Henceforth, let Ullikummi be his name!" KUB 33.93 iii 18 (Ullik.), ed. JCS 5:152.

b′ with *ḫalzišša-*: [(*paid*)*duwara*]*nšan* NÍG. SI.SÁ-*an ŠUM-an ḫalzeššandu* "Henceforth, let them call him by the name Just." KUB 24.8 iii 14 (Appu, pre-NH/NS), StBoT 14:10:20.

3′ bestowing of royal title: *nu kišan* [(*tezzi kāš*)]*awa kāš* LUGAL-*uš ŠUM* LUGAL-*UT-TI-yaw*[*a*]*kan kedani* [*teḫḫun*] "Then he speaks as follows: 'Behold, this one is king. I have [given] the name of kingship (the royal title) to this one" KUB 24.5 + 9.13 obv. 20-22 (rit. of substitute king, NH), with dupl. KUB 36.93 obv. 15; ed. StBoT 3:10f:28-29.

d. Pronouncing, saying someone's name — **1′** genitive of named: *takku* LÚ *ELLAM* MUŠ-

an kuenzi damella ŠU[(*M-an*)] *tezzi* 1 MA.NA KÙ.BABBAR *pai* "If a free man kills a snake and (while doing so) says another one's name, he shall give one mina of silver." Law §170 (KBo 6.26 ii 1-2 rest. by KBo 6.13 i 10-11, both OH/NS); *URRAM ŠĒRAM* ᶠ*Tawanannaš* [*ŠUM-ŠU*] *lē kuiški tezzi ŠA* DUMU.MEŠ-*ŠU* [DUMU. DUMU.MEŠ-*ŠU*] *ŠUM-ŠUNU lē kuiški tezzi* KBo 3.27 i 6-8 (edict of Ḫatt. I, OH/NS), translit. BoTU 10β; *nu taknaš* ᵈUTU-*i piran* LUGAL-*un aššu memiški našta ŠUM-MI* LUGAL *taknaš* ᵈUTU-*i piran aššu tarški* KBo 7.28:18-19, 33-34, etc. (prayer, OH/MS); *nu* LUGAL-*waš ŠUM-ŠU aššu m*[*emiš*≁*kitten*] "And speak well of the king's name!" ibid. 47 (the trace is *m*[*e*], not *t*[*ar*]); "When your father died, I did not reject you," *ABUKA-mu kuit* [*tu*]*el* [*Š*]*UM-an :ḫuiduwaluwara piran memiškit* "Since your father during (his) lifetime(?) had often mentioned your name before me, (therefore I took care of you)" KBo 5.9 i 11-14 (Dupp.), ed. SV 1:10f.; "Then it will happen that ᶠKaššulawiya will always come to praise you, O god," *ŠUM-anna t*[*uelpat*] *ŠA* DINGIR-*LIM memiškizzi* "and to pronounce yo[ur] name [only], O god" KBo 4.6 rev. 24-26 rest. from obv. 18-20 (prayer, Murš. II); *maḫḫanmakan* ᴸᵁNAR *ŠUM-MI* LUGAL *weriyazi* ᴸᵁALAN. ZUₓ *memai* "When the singer calls the name of the king, the actor recites" KUB 1.17 vi 17-19 (monthly fest., OH/NS) followed by Ḫattic text; cf. also with dat. pl. sub 3′ below; 1 *ṬUPPU QATI nuššan* UN-*aš ŠUM-ŠU ḫalziyauwa*[*r* . . .] GUD-*aš* GISKIM-*aš* . . . *aniyan* (entry in shelf list:) "One tablet, complete. On it is written (compositions regarding) the calling of a person's name, . . . an omen of an ox, and . . . " KUB 30.55:10-11 (NH), ed. CTH p. 174; name of a river: [SAL ŠU.GI *mema*]*i wappuwaš* DINGIR. MAḪ-*aš* ÍD-*aš ŠUM-ŠU tezzi* ÍD-*aš* [*welwilaš*(?) DINGIR].MEŠ *šumeš azzikkiten akkuškitten* "[The Old Woman sa]ys: 'O Ḫannaḫanna of the river bank!' She pronounces the name of the river. 'You [gods of the *w.*] of the river, eat and drink!'" KUB 24.9 iv 15-16 (rit., MH/NS); cf. Jakob-Rost, THeth 2 (1972) 52:27; p. 75.

2′ acc. of named — **a′** with "name" in acc. — **1″** [(*UL-makan u*)]*k* ᵈÉ[.A-*a*]*n ŠUM-an daranzi* "Do they not call me (*uk*), Ea, by name?" KUB 33.100 + KUB 36.16 iii 23 (Ḫedammu myth, MH/NS), ed. StBoT 14:46-47, restored by KUB 33.103 ii 14; "The king pours a libation on a bull." *nu* GAL *MEŠEDI* GU₄.MAḪ *ŠUM-an tezzi* "The chief of the bodyguard pronounces the name of the bull" KUB 20.87 i 5-9 (fest.); "(Whatever gods are listed on the first tablet,)" *nuškan šippanduwanzi ŠUM*ᴴᴵ·ᴬ-*ŠUNU ḫumandušpat ḫalzai* "he calls them all by their names for making libations" KBo 19.128 iii 8-12 (ANTAḪŠUM fest., OH?/NS), ed. StBoT 13:6-9; cf. *nuzakan ABUŠU ŠUM-an ḫalzaiš* KUB 23.72 obv. 38 (Mita, MH/MS); *ABUŠU* could be either subj. or obj.; cf. [. . . *ŠU*]*M-an U*[*L k*]*uiški ḫalzai* KUB 17.14 rev.! 24 (rit. for subst. king, NH), ed. StBoT 3:60f., 89. **2″** in figura etymologica with *lamniya-*: see passages cited in *lamniya-*, 1 a. **3″** in parenthetic direction to the reciting person for insertion into the wording of the incantation: — **a″** name of the patient: "I speak as follows" (followed by 5 lines of spells) *nu anniškimi kuin* [*nankan*] *ŠUM-ŠU ḫalziḫḫi* "And I call the one whom I am treating by name (and say 'Let him go to battle!')" KUB 35.148 iii 37-43 (Zuwi rit., OH/NS); other exx. from the Zuwi rit. are: *nu anniškimi kuin nankan ŠUM-ŠU ḫalziḫḫi* KUB 12.63 obv. 28; ibid. 12-13 (restored); ibid. 34 (with *nukan*); KUB 7.57 i 1; KUB 35.148 ii 4; cf. ibid. iii 16, KBo 13.94:7, KBo 21.24:6, 7, 14; *našta/nukan* EN.SISKUR.SISKUR *ŠUM-an ḫalzai* KUB 29.8 iv 18 (Hitt. inserted into Hurr. text., MH/MS); ibid. 10, 23-24 with *ŠUM-ŠU*, cf. KBo 4.1 i 11, with dupl. KUB 2.2 i 10 (rit., NH); KUB 30.36 iii 9 (rit., MH/MS); in the royal funeral rit.: *akkanza kuiš nankan ŠUM-ŠU ḫalzeššāi* "He keeps calling the name of him who died" KUB 30.28 rev. 2, ed. HTR 96f.; [*naš*]*ta akkandan ŠUM-an* (var. *ŠUM-ŠU*) *ḫalzai* "Then he calls the deceased by name" KUB 30.25 + 39.4 rev. 20, with dupl. KUB 39.5 rev. 21, ed. HTR 28f.; "The Old Woman speaks thus in front of her colleague" GIDIM-*makan ŠUM-an ḫalzai* [*w*]*edaizziwaran UMMA ŠU-UM nuwaran kuiš wedaizzi* "and she calls the deceased by name: '(Someone) will bring him, what's-his-name. Who will bring him?'" KUB 30.15 + 39.19 obv. 29-30, ed. HTR 68f.; *nu* TUR-*an kuin ḫukkiškimi nankan ŠUM-ŠU temi* "I pronounce the name of the child whom I am treating" (inserted in prayer) KUB 7.1 i 7 (rit., pre-NH/NS); cf. *nu ḫukkiškizzi kuin nankan ŠUM-ŠU tezzi* KUB 9.34 iii 32 (rit. with Luw., NH); *[nu a]nniški[zzi] kuin* UN-*an nankan [(ŠUM-Š)]U tezzi* ibid. iv 19, (with dupl. KUB 7.42:5 and par. KUB 9.4 iv 17-18); cf. ibid. i 20, ii 12-13; HT 6 + KBo 9.125 obv. 24, KBo 17.54 i 6-7; KBo 21.6 obv. 12; *nukan* EN.SISKUR *ŠUM-ŠU tezzi* VBoT 120 iii 10 (MH/NS) (all rit.). **b″** name of a deity: "'Behold, this(!) temple which we have built for you, O god,'" DINGIR-*LIM-yakan ŠUM-an* (var. *ŠUM-ŠU*) *ḫalzai wedanziyat kuedani* "and he calls out the name of the god for whom they built it, ('It wasn't we who built it, all the gods built it!')" KUB 2.2 i 33-37, with dupl. KBo 4.1 obv. 28-30 (rit., NH); another example of the parenthetic direction but employing the gen. of the named cited above under d 1′.

b′ with "name" in inst., obj. in pl. (all exx. pre-NH): *našta* DINGIR.MEŠ *ḫumandu[š] lam-ni-it ḫalzai* "Then he calls all the gods by name" KBo 19.128 iv 4-5 (fest., OH?/NS), ed. StBoT 13:10f.; cf. p. 39 contrasting ibid. iii 10-12, above 2′ a′ 1″; DINGIR.MEŠ-*ma* GAL $^{LÚ.MEŠ}$SAGI *lam-ni-it ḫalziššai* KBo 21.85 i 11 + KBo 8.109 i 6 (fest., OH/MS) followed by a list of DNs; *našta kī kue* ḪUR.SAG.MEŠ ÍD.MEŠ *nepiš tekan ŠUM-it ḫalzišai* "Then these mountains, rivers, sky (and) earth which he calls by name" KUB 10.72 ii 19-20 (evocatio, pre-NH/NS); *našta* ḪUR.SAG.ME[Š] *lam-ni-it ḫalzai* KUB 15.34 iii 49-50 (evocatio, MH/MS), ed. Zuntz, Scongiuri 38f.; [(*našta* ÍD).MEŠ *ḫumandu*]*š*(?) *lam-ni-it ḫalzai* ibid. iii 9, with dupl. KUB 15.33a iii 5, followed by a list of rivers (Zuntz, p. 32f.; Haas-Wilhelm, AOATS 3:200f. and 194f.); *nu INA* É.GAL-*LIM kuieš šer šešanzi nat parā tianzi* ^{LÚ}Ì.DU$_8$-*maškan ḫa[tti]li lam-ni-it ḫalziššai* "Those who sleep up in the palace step forward, and the gatekeeper calls them by (their occupational) titles in Ḫattic" KBo 5.11 i 5-7 (instr., MH/NS), followed by a bilingual list of professions; cf. LÚ.DUGUD-*yakan ŠUM-ŠU ḫalzai* KUB 26.23 ii 15 (same text).

3′ dat. of the named: [(*šu-ma*)]-⸢*a-aš*⸣ DINGIR.MEŠ-*aš* (var. *ANA* D[INGIR.MEŠ]) *apedaš ANA* KUR.KUR.ḪI.A *l*[(*a-a-ma-a*)]*n-na UL kuiški werizzi* "No one in those countries even invokes your names, O gods" KUB 17.21 iii 12-13 (MH/MS), with dupl. KUB 13.124 ii 22-23 (prayer of Arn. and Ašm.), ed. von Schuler, Kaškäer 158f.

e. inscribing of name: *zikmu* DUB.SAR-*aš aššuli ḫatrai nammaza* [*Š*]*UM-an* EGIR-*an iya* "You, scribe, write me in friendship and put (lit. make) (your) name after (it)!" VS 12:202 = VBoT 2:21-23 (scribe's P.S. to letter from the king of Arzawa to the Egyptian pharaoh, MH), ed. Hrozný, JA 218 (1931) 310f., Rost, MIO 3 (1956) 229f.; "But whoever does not sell a gift of the king" *ŠUM* LUGAL-*kan kuedani gulšan* "on which the name of the king is inscribed" KUB 13.4 ii 46-47 (instr., MH/NS), ed. Sturtevant Chrest. 154 ii 53-54; *ŠUM ŠA* LUGAL-*kan kimrašša ḫuitar andan gulšan* "the name of the king and the animals of the steppe engraved on it" KUB 38.3 ii 7-9 (descr. of cult image, NH), ed. von Brandenstein, HG 18f., Rost, MIO 8:183f.; 1 *KILĪLU* KÙ.BABBAR *ŠUM ŠA* ^{d}U *GAŠRU-kan andan gul*(*a*)*ššan* KUB 38.1 i 32-33 (cult inv., NH); see further refs. under verb *gulš-*; *ŠAṬRU ŠUM* ^{m}*Muršili*/^{m}*Dudḫaliya* KUB 38.9:8, 10 (descr. of animal figures, NH); cf. KUB 38.8:4, 6, 8; KUB 38.20 obv. 5; *ŠUM-ŠU* PN DÙ-*an* (said of bronze blade) KUB 42.42 iv 4 (inv., NH); *nuššan ANA* GUD IM *kue*[*dani*] *ŠA* KUR ^{LÚ}KÚR *ŠUM-an kitta* "the clay bull on which the name of the enemy country is put" KUB 20.77:4-5 (fest.); *nuw*[*akan ANA* ALAM] ^{GIŠ}ERIN *ŠUM* ^{LÚ}KÚR ^{d}UTU-*ŠI tiy*[*awen*] *ANA* ALAM IM-*mawakan ŠUM* ^{m}PU[-*šarrumma tiyawen*] "and [on the] cedar [image] we put the name of the enemy of His Majesty, but on the clay image [we put] the name of P." KUB 7.61:4-7 (incant., NH); "They made three images of wax and tallow [and ...] coated [them w]ith clay" *nuwa ANA* 1 ALAM [*ŠUM* PN *tier ANA*] 1 ALAM-*mawakan ŠUM* ^{m}GAL.UR.MAḪ ME-*er* [*ANA* 1 ALAM-*mawakan ŠUM* ^{m}LUGAL-^{d}]*SIN-uḫ tier nuwarat patter* "And on one image [they put the name of ...], on another image they put the name of G., [and on the third image] they put [the name of] Šarrikušuḫ, and they buried them" KUB 40.83 obv. 14-17 (depos., NH), ed. StBoT 4:64; cf. frag.: *ŠUM-ŠU tianzi* KBo 13.152 obv. 12 (fest.). □The verb "put" (*dai-*) and its passive equivalent *ki-* (mid.) in the passages cited above might mean either name-giving, as sub 1 c 1′, or physical inscribing of the figures. Favoring the latter is *andan gulša[n]* in KBo 15.17:4f., which is parallel to KUB 7.61 cited above, and indicates that the names of the king's enemies were inscribed on the figures; indicating that a name is missing or not inscribed: [*Š*]*UM* NU.GÁL KBo 18.184 rev. 5 (in list of garments), 1 *ṬUPPU ŠUM-MI* S[AL ŠU.GI? N]U.GÁL KBo 14.68:19 + KUB 30.58 i 5 (cat., NH), Laroche, CTH p. 159 as var. to p. 158:20; [ALA]M SAL-*TI* KÙ.GI *ŠUM-an UL ḫandān* KUB 42.42 i 12 (inv., NH). Cf. *ŠUMŠU mertat* above in b 1′a′.

f. qualities of a name: *ŠUM-antit daššu* "your name is important" KUB 31.141:4 (hymn to Ištar, NH), corr. to Akk. *šu-um-ki ṣi-ra* KUB 37.36 ii 8, *šu-mu-ki ṣi-ru* "excellent" STC 2 pl. 75:4, ed. Reiner-Güterbock, JCS 21 (1967 [1969]) 258; "You, Sungoddess of Arinna, are a weighty deity," *nuttakkan ŠUM-an lam-na-aš ištarna nakki* DINGIR-*LIM-yatarmatakkan* DINGIR.MEŠ-*aš ištarna nakki* "and your name is weighty among names, and your godhead is weighty among the gods" KUB 24.3 i 29-31 (prayer of Murš. II), ed. Gurney, AAA 27 (1940) 22f.; [*nuttakkan ŠUM-a*]*n ŠUM*ḪI.A*-aš ištarna*<<*š*>> *nakki* KUB 24.1 ii 21 (par. prayer to Telibinu, Murš. II), ed. Gurney, ibid. p. 20f. Cf. c 1′b′ and c 2′.

g. in the fixed Akkadographic phrase *MIM-MA ŠUMŠU* (read **kuit imma kuit lamanšet*?) "whatever its name," meaning "all this," "of all kinds": *MI-IM-MA ŠUM-ŠU* L[UGAL.GAL *I*]*ŠŠ*[*IMA* . . .] "All this the Great King 'lifted' (i.e., took from its previous owner)" SBo 1 text 4 rev. 11 (land deed, OH/OS), ed. Riemschneider, MIO 6 (1958) 364f.; [. . .] NA_4 *MIM-MA ŠUM-ŠU* "[objects of/with] precious stones of all kinds" KUB 42.40 rev.? rt. 7, cf. 67.13(?); [. . . N]A_4? *ME-MA ŠUM-ŠU* KBo 18.161 obv. 12 (all inv.).

h. "name" in the sense of renown, reputation: "Do you, my brother, want to get rich at my expense?" *UL-at ŠUM-an išḫaššarwatarra* "That is neither (good) reputation nor lordly behaviour!" KUB 21.38 obv. 16 (letter of Puduḫepa), ed. Sommer, AU 258, Helck, JCS 17 (1963) 88; *UL-at ŠUM-ni ḫandaš iyanun* "Did I not do it for the sake of reputation?" ibid. 52, ed. Helck, loc. cit. 91; *nušši ŠUM-an katta lē tarnatti* "and do not debase his (viz., your father's) name!" KUB 23.92 obv. 11 (letter to Tukulti-Ninurta), ed. Otten, AfO 19 (1959-60) 40; (The young Assyrian king says:) *ma-* (var. *+a-*)*an-wa-za ŠUM-an kuitki iyami* "I would like to make a certain name for myself" KUB 23.103 rev. 14 with dupl. 23.92 rev. 13 (Hittite draft for Akk. letter to Baba-aḫa-iddina of Assyria), ed. Otten, AfO 19:42f., cf. Güterbock, OrNS 12 (1943) 154; *lamnaš* LUGAL-*uš* (in omen apodoses) "a king of renown" (possibly rendering Akk. *šarru dannu* "mighty king" or *šar kiššati* "king of the world", see Riemschneider, StBoT 9:33-35); *la-am-na-aš* [LUGAL-*uš utnī an*]*dan* [*kiša*] Bo 5698:5-6; *lam-na-a*[*š* LUGAL-*uš utnī and*]*an kiša utne*[*kan ḫarkzi*] "[a king of] renown will appear and the land [will perish]" ibid. 8-9 (after Riemschneider, Omentexte, and photo) with Akk. par. KUB 4.63 i 24-27 with dupl. KUB 37.154:7-10 (Leibovici, RA 50 (1956) 12) [*šar*] *kiššati ina mātim ibašši* and *ibaššima mātum iḫalliq*, resp.; another Hitt. translation, KUB 8.23:5′, 7′, has [*šar*]*-ku*!*-uš* LUGAL-*uš* and *šar*[*-ku-uš* LUGAL-*uš*] instead; cf. *lam-na-aš* LUGAL-*uš*[. . .] KBo 13.34 iv 2 (birth omen), ed. StBoT 9:28f., coll. For possible restoration in KBo 6.25 + 13.35 iii 10 see Riemschneider, StBoT 9:35; "If the moon is eclipsed on the 16th day, [. . .] will surround the city," *lam-n*[*a-aš-ma*(?) (LUGA)L-*uš* . . . *-n*(*u*!*-zi* BÀD.ḪI.A-*ŠU*)] *pippanzi* "(a king of renown will [. . .], and they will knock down its walls" KUB 34.7 iii 5-6. Dupl. KBo 13.15:8-9 has KUR.ZU-*na-aš-ma* LUGA[L . . .] (coll.). KUR.ZU (mistake for *lam*?) also in KUB 8.1 ii 18-19: KUR.ZU-*na-aš* [LUGA]L-*uš aki*; see Riemschneider, StBoT 9:33-34; "Now all the neighboring countries began to attack the lands of Ḫatti. That shall forthwith become a cause of revenge for the Sungoddess of Arinna," *nuza* DINGIR-*LUM tuel ŠUM-KA lē tepšanuši* "O goddess, do not debase your name!" KUB 24.3 ii 49-53 (prayer of Murš. II), ed. Gurney, AAA 27 (1940) 30f.; the MH prayer KUB 24.4 + 30.12 rev. 9 writes *nuza tu-e*!*-el*! *ŠUM-KA tepnuškiši* "(in allowing this to happen) you are debasing your name" cf. Hoffner, JCS 29 (1977) 154; otherwise Gurney, AAA 27:107, who considered it an accidental omission of *lē* by the scribe or a rhetorical question; [. . . *a*]*mmela la-a-am-ma-a-mi-it* [*tepnut*/*tepšanut*?] "she [debased my . . .] and my name" KUB 1.16

iii 13 (OH/NS) with restoration based on Sommer, HAB 12-13, 141; cf. Hoffner, JCS 29:154, note 16; ^d^*IŠTAR-mukan* GAŠAN-*YA* IGI-*zi palši ŠUM^UM^* (var. *ŠUM-an*) *kedani* KASKAL-*ši ḫalzaiš* "(This was my first manly deed,) and my lady Ištar called my name (i.e., gave me fame) for the first time on this campaign" KBo 3.6 ii 13-14 with dupl. KUB 1.2 ii 17 (Ḫatt. ii 29-30); *nuza kuedani(ya?) aššuš apāš aššu ŠUM-an UL dāi* "Who(ever) I am dear to does not 'take a good name'" (does not acquire a good reputation through association with me, or through acts of kindness toward me?) KUB 31.127 iii 17-18 (prayer to Sungod, OH/NS).

i. "name" in the sense of memory: "Let the divine oaths destroy you together with your wives and children" [. . . *dag*]*anzipaz ŠUM*^MEŠ^*-KUNU* NUMUN-*K*[*UN*]*U-ya arḫa ḫar*[*ninkandu*(?)] "[and] from the [dark e]arth [let them] dest[roy(?)] your names and your offspring!" KBo 19.58:8-10 (treaty; MH?/MS?); "Just as salt has no seed," *apedaniyakan* UN-*ši ŠUM-ŠU* NUMUN.ḪI.A-*ŠU* É-*ŠU* GUD.ḪI.A-*ŠU* UDU.ḪI.A-*ŠU QATAMMA ḫarkdu* "so let this person's name, his offspring (lit. seeds), his house, his cattle (and) his sheep likewise perish!" KBo 6.34 ii 16-18 (Soldiers' Oath, MH), ed. StBoT 22:10f.; [*ap*]*el ŠUM-an* NUMUN-*an pankurš*[*et* . . . *ḫarni*]*nkan*[*du*] KUB 23.76:17-18 (instr./treaty); cf. KUB 26.30:7 (treaty fragment); KUB 26.41 obv. 15-18 (treaty, MH), ed. Kempinski-Košak, WO 5 (1970) 192f. [*takku* . . . . *ḫul*]*alizzi la-a-ma-an* [. . . . .] *ḫarkzi* "[If . . . .] surrounds [the moon(?)], (this means:) the name [. . . .] will perish." KUB 34.16 iii 9-10 (omen).

B. Hrozný, VSpr (1920) 27 n. 5; Friedrich, SV 2 (1930) 92; Hrozný, JA 218:316f.

Cf. *lamniya-*.

lammaniya- see *lamniya-*.

lammar n. neut.; **1.** a small unit of time, moment, instant, **2.** (used adverbially:) instantly, immediately; from MH.

sg. nom.-acc. *lam-mar*(!) KBo 19.128 vi 23; **gen.** *lam-na-aš* KBo 9.106 ii 1; **d.-l.** *lam-ni-i* KBo 5.3 ii 35 (MH/NS), *lam-n*[*i-i*] KUB 21.47:19 (MH), *la-am-ni-i* KUB 35.145 rev. 4; *la-am-ni* KUB 17.15 iii 15; **endingless d.-l.** *lam-mar*! 453/d ii 4 (see under mng. 1), *lam-mar lam-mar* KUB 21.27 iii 46-47 (Puduḫ.); **endingless d.-l. used adverbially** *lam-mar* KBo 5.3 ii 28 (MH/NS), and passim in vassal treaties.

1. (a small unit of time) moment, instant: [*kedani* M]U.KAM-*ti kedani* ITU.KAM-*mi* (var. ITU-*mi*) *kedani* UD[.KAM-*ti k*(*ed*)]*ani* GE_6.KAM-*anti la-am-ni-i* (var. [*k*]*edani la-am-ni*) *ḫaltatti* "He will call in [this] year, in this month, on this day, in this night, at this moment" KUB 35.145 rev. 3-4 with dupl. KUB 17.15 iii 14-15 (rit. with Luw.); *zigan* GIM-*an ištamašti nan-mu mān apedani lam-ni-i UL ematti* "if you do not indicate him to me the very moment you hear of him" (then these oaths shall destroy you) KBo 5.3 ii 34-35 (Ḫuqq.); in a list of deities provided with libations: *tepu pedan* EME-*an ḫandantan lam-mar*! *tar-ta-an* ^d^UD.SIG_5 "the 'little place', true speech, the . . . moment, the propitious day" KBo 19.128 vi 22-24 (fest.), ed. StBoT 13:16, 46-47; ^d^LAMMA(-*aš*) DINGIR[(.LÚ.MEŠ)-*aš*] *ḫūmantaš* ^d^*Innari* ^d^*Tarpi lam-mar*! *tar-t*[*a-* . . .] *tepu pedi* EME *ḫanta*[(*nti*)] ^d^UD.SIG_5-*ia dāi* "He deposits (offerings) for all the male gods of ^d^LAMMA . . . " (DNs in the dat. with *dāi*, hence *lammar* should also be dat.; the part. could be restored as *tar-t*[*a-an-ti*]) 453/d (+) 660/c ii 3-6, rest. by parallel iv 3-6 (coll., cf. Otten, StBoT 7:29, with corrections StBoT 13:47 with n. 97); (The Old Woman makes model tongues) [*naškan ANA* 2 *BĒL* SISKUR.SISKUR *šer arḫ*]*a waḫnuzi apelwa lam-na-aš* [EME.ḪI.A *k*]*āša attaš* ^d^UTU-*uš tarmāit* "[and] moves [them around over the two patients] (saying): 'Behold! Father Sungod has fixed the [tongues] of that moment!'" KBo 9.106 ii 1-2 and end of lost col. i (2Mašt. B), cf. 2Mašt. A ii 19 (Rost, MIO 1:354) which has *apel* UD-*aš* EME.ḪI.A-*eš* "the tongues of that day" instead; "O Zintuḫi, . . . to the Stormgod and the Sungoddess of Arinna you are an ornament of the breast" *nudduza lam-mar lam-mar katta uškanzi* "and they look at you constantly" KUB 21.27 iii 43-47 (prayer of Puduḫepa).

2. (used adverbially:) instantly, immediately: (passim in vassal treaties) — **a.** with *ar-* "to arrive, come": (If . . . I write to you) *numuššan mān warri lam-n*[*i-i*] *UL erteni* "and if you do not instantly come to my aid" KUB 21.47 obv. 19

+ KUB 23.82 obv.! 24 (instr., MH), trace *n*[*i*] rather than *m*[*ar*], coll.; cf. *nat mān ANA* ᵈUTU-*ŠI ḫu*[*d*]*āk UL mematteni* "If you do not tell it to My Majesty right away" ibid. obv. 20 + 25; *numuššan mān* ERÍN.MEŠ-*it* ANŠE.KUR.RA[.ḪI].A-*it lam-mar UL ārti . . . numuššan mān apiyaya lam-mar UL ārti* KBo 5.3 ii 28-31 (Ḫuqq.); cf. KUB 26.37 obv. 7, 9, 11 (Ḫuqq.), ed. SV 2:172-74; *mā*[*n w*]*arri lam-mar UL erteni* "If you do not instantly come to (my) aid" KBo 5.3 iv 23 (Ḫuqq.), ed. SV 2:134f.

b. with *ar-* (mid.) "to stand": "If I write to you" ERÍN.MEŠ-*waz* ANŠE.KUR.RA.MEŠ *piran ḫūinut nuwakan ANA* ᵈUTU-*ŠI warri lam-mar* [*ārḫut*] "'Take command of the troops and chariotry and instantly stand by My Majesty for help!' (Then take command of the troops and chariotry)" *nuššan ANA* ᵈUTU[-*ŠI w*]*arri lam-mar ārḫut* "and instantly stand by My Majesty for help!" KBo 5.4 obv. 19f., cf. ibid. 11 (Targ.), KBo 5.9 ii 18 (Dupp.); for *arḫut* as a mistake for *ar-nu-ut* in KBo 5.13 iii 10 (Kup. C) see Friedrich, SV 1:126 n. 5.

c. with *arnu-* "cause to arrive, bring": "If I, His Majesty, write you:" ERÍN.MEŠ-*waz* ANŠE.KUR.RA.MEŠ *piran ḫūinut nuwaratmukan warri lam-mar arnut nuza* ERÍN.MEŠ ANŠE.KUR.RA.MEŠ *piran ḫuinut natkan ANA* ᵈUTU-*ŠI lam-mar ārnut* KBo 5.13 ii 34-iii 3 (Kup.), ed. SV 1:124f., cf. ibid. iii 15, KBo 4.3 iii 6, KBo 19.67:6 + KUB 6.41 iv 3, KUB 6.41 iv 5, 6 (for var. *ḫuenut* in KBo 4.3 iii 10 see mng. 2 d) (all Kup.); *nuššan* ANŠE. KUR.RA.MEŠ *wa*[(*rri lam-mar arnut*)] KBo 19.73a + KUB 21.1 iii 15, with dupl. KUB 21.5 iii 29f. (Alakš.), ed. SV 2:68f., cf. also note to mng. 2 b.

d. with *ḫuenu-* "cause to run": "If it is not feasible for you, and [you] write My Majesty: 'Put an officer in command of the troops and chariotry!'" *natka*[(*n ANA* ᵈUTU-*ŠI*)] *war*[(*ri lam*)]-*mar ḫu-u-e*[-*nu*]-⌜*ut-ma*?⌝ (var. *ar-n*[*u-ut*]) "then nevertheless dispatch them (lit. make them run) instantly to the help of My Majesty!" KBo 4.3 iii 8-10 with dupl. KUB 6.41 iv 3-5 + KBo 19.67:7 (Kup.), ed. SV 1:132f.

Hrozný, BoSt 5 (1920) 27-28 n. 5; Friedrich, SV 2 (1930) 92-93 ("Stunde" or "sofort"); Otten, StBoT 13 (1971) 47.

Cf. *lamarḫandatt-*, *lamarḫandattašši-*.

lamarḫandatt- n. com.; the setting or fixing of an hour or moment; NH.†

pl. nom.(?) *la-mar-ḫa-an-da-at-ti-eš* KUB 2.1 ii 40.

In a Luwian-influenced cult text of Tudḫ. IV for all tutelary deities, in listings: *meḫunaš* ᵈLAMMA-*aš ŠA Labarna* [ᵈLAMM]A *tepauwaš pē*<*d*>*aš la-mar-ḫa-an-da-at-ti-eš ŠA Labarna lapattaliyaš* ᵈLAMMA-*ri ŠA* [*L*]*abarna arauwaš* ᵈLAMMA-*i* KUB 2.1 ii 39-42; *lamarḫandatteš*, formally nom. pl. com., hardly fits the context; possibly a mistake; not preserved in dupl. KUB 44.16 iii 19 or in the parallel text KBo 2.38 ii 4-6.

Otten, StBoT 13 (1971) 47 with n. 98, 99; Laroche, DLL 40, sub *ḫanda*(*i*)-, posits *lamar ḫandatt-* (two words): "décision immediate"

Cf. *ḫandai-* v., *lammar*, *lamarḫandattašši-*.

lamarḫandattašši- (Luw. gen.) adj.; pertaining to the setting or fixing of an hour or moment; NH.†

ᵈ*Aalaš walipattaššiš* ᵈ*Aalaš la-mar*(!)-*ḫa-an-da-at-ta-aš*[(-*ši-iš*)] "(the goddess) A. of *w*., (the goddess) A. of 'setting a time'" KUB 2.1 iii 45-46 with dupl. KUB 44.16 iv 1.

Cf. *lamarḫandatt-*.

lamniya- (lammaniya-) v.; **1.** to name, call (by name), **2.** to mention (by name), enumerate, **3.** to specify (a number), **4.** to assign, appoint; from MH; written syll. and *ŠUM*.

pres. sg. 2 *lam-ni-ya-ši* KUB 31.112:17 (MH/NS); **sg. 3** *lam-ni-iz-zi* IBoT 1.36 i 30 (MH/MS); *lam-ni-e-ez-zi* KUB 34.98:8 (NH); *lam-ni-az-zi* KUB 32.124 obv. 6; *lam-ni-ya-zi* KBo 4.13 iv 34, KBo 8.123:6, KBo 13.177 i 14 (NH?), KUB 29.4 i 15 (NH), KUB 41.35 ii 9; *lam-ni-ia-az-zi* KBo 10.37 iii 55 (OH/NS), KUB 43.58 iv 6 (MH/MS); **pl. 1** *lam-ma-ni-i-e-u-e-ni* KBo 16.50:17 (MH/MS); **pl. 3** *lam-ni-ia-an-zi* KUB 17.35 iii 9, KUB 25.27 i 11, 15.

pret. sg. 1 *lam-ni-ia-nu-un* KUB 23.11 ii 29 (MH/NS); **sg. 3** *lam-ni-ia-at* KBo 3.6 i 31 (Ḫatt. III), KUB 38.12 ii 21 (NH); **pl. 1** *ŠUM-u-en* IBoT 1.33:5 and passim; *ŠUM-en* IBoT 1.33:9!, 13 and passim; **pl. 3** *lam-ma-ni-ir* 354/z i 11; *lam-ni-ir* KUB 36.109:6 (MH/MS); *lam-ni-e-er* KBo 4.2 ii 22 (pre-NH/NS).

part. com. *lam-ni-an-za* KUB 32.137 ii 5 (NH); **neut.** *lam-ni-ia-an* KBo 4.2 ii 12, KUB 13.4 ii 33 (both pre-NH/NS?), KBo 21.37 rev.? 6; *ŠUM-an* KUB 22.56 rev. 9 (NH).

iter.-dur. *lam-ni-iš-kán-zi* Bo 6111 obv. 4.

1. to name, call (by name) — **a.** in figura etymologica: "He [of]fers one *gaparta-* (a rodent) to the Sungod, one *g.* to the Stormgod, and one *g.* to [^{d}LAMMA]" *nukan* DINGIR.MEŠ *ŠUM-an lam-ni-ya-az-z[i]* "and calls the gods by name" KBo 10.37 iii 54-55 (rit., OH/NS), Del Monte, OA 12 (1973) 176-77, cf. also KUB 32.124 i 4, 6? (rit., NH?).

b. beside *ḫalzai-*: *nu* $^{\text{LÚ.MEŠ}}$GURUŠ *takšan arḫa šarranzi naš lam-ni-ia-an-zi nušmaš takšan šarran* LÚ.MEŠ ^{URU}*Ḫatti ḫalzeššanzi takšan šarramašmaš* LÚ.MEŠ ^{URU}*Maša ḫalzišanzi* "They divide the (group of) young men in half and name them: one half of them they call Men of Ḫatti, the other half of them they call Men of Maša" KUB 17.35 iii 9-11 (fest./cult inv.), ed. Ehelolf, SPAW 1925:269-72.

2. to mention (by name), enumerate: — **a.** a single item: "We shall promptly inform the border commander of any impending enemy attack. § We shall not deceive him (to wit:)" *nuzakan* ^{LÚ}KÚR*-aš uwalḫuwanzi damēte pēti dāi wēššašši damai pēdan lam-ma-ni-i-e-u-e-ni nu damai pēdan paḫḫašnuanzi* ^{LÚ}KÚR*-ašša damai pēdan uwalḫzi* "(If) the enemy prepares to attack at one (lit. another) place, and we mention to him (still) another place (so that) they secure (that) other place and (then) the enemy attacks the other (i.e., the first) place (that shall be forbidden under oath)." KBo 16.50:9-21 (14-20) (instr., MH/MS), cf. Otten, RHA XVIII/67 (1960) 121-27.

b. several items: *nu kī kue* KUR.KUR.ḪI.A *lam-ni-ia-nu-un [kur]ur kuiēš ēppir natmu* DINGIR.MEŠ *parā piēr* "The gods delivered to me those countries which I have enumerated (above) which engaged in hostilities" KUB 23.11 ii 29-30 (ann. of Tudḫ., MH/NS) referring to the names listed ibid. 14-19; (A temple official shall not own silver or gold, etc.) *mānmašši IŠTU* É.GAL*-LIM AŠŠUM* NÍG.BA*-ŠU* KÙ.BABBAR KÙ.GI TÚG*-TUM UNŪT* ZABAR *pianzi nat lam-ni-ya-an ēšdu kāšwaratši* LUGAL*-uš paiš* "But if they give him silver, gold, garments (or) bronze utensils as a gift from the palace, let them be enumerated (in a document saying): 'This king gave it to him'!" KUB 13.4 ii 32-34 (instr., pre-NH/NS), ed. Chrest. 154:39-41; "The Old Woman ties unspun red wool to the hand, foot, and neck of the patient" 3 LÚ.MEŠ *kuiēš imma antuḫšuš UL-kan kuiēšqa tukkanta[ri?] kuiuš antuḫšuš* EN.SISKUR.SISKUR *lam-ni-ia-zi* "(representing?) three men, whatever persons — it does not matter what persons the patient names" KBo 13.177 i 10-14 (rit., NH?).

3. to specify (a number): NINDA.KUR$_4$.RA *paršiyanzi mašiwan* LUGAL*-uš lam-ni-ia-zi* "They break thick loaves, as many as the king specifies" KBo 4.13 iv 33-34 (fest.), cf. KUB 41.35 ii 8-9, KUB 25.27 i 11, 15, KBo 21.37 rev.? 6.

4. to assign, appoint — **a.** to a place: *nuwakan idālu k[allar? uttar] pēdāu nuwarat kuwapi* DINGIR.MEŠ *lam-ni-ia-an ḫarkanzi nuwarat apiya arnuddu* "Let (the live puppy) carry the evil (and) [portentous word] there where the gods have assigned it!" KBo 4.2 ii 11-13 (rit., pre-NH/NS); *nuwašmaš kuwapi* DINGIR.MEŠ *kuedani lam-ni-e-er nuwa kē kallar uttar apiya paiddu* "Let these portentous words(!) go to whatever (place) the gods have assigned each of them!" ibid. 22-23.

b. to assign to persons: 1 AŠ.ME KÙ.GI *ŠA* 1 GÍN *ŠUM-ŠU* ^{d}*Pirinkir* 1 LI.DUR KÙ.GI 1*-NUTIM purkiš* KÙ.GI *nat IŠTU* NA$_4$.KÁ.DINGIR.RA *tiyanteš naš ANA* $^{\text{LÚ.MEŠ}}$SIMUG+A *aniūršet* ^{LÚ}SANGA *lam-ni-ia-zi* "One gold disk of one shekel (weight) — its name is *P.* — one gold navel, one set of gold *p.* — they are set with Babylon stone — these the priest assigns to the smiths as their work (pensum)" KUB 29.4 i 13-15 (rit., NH); cf. *nušši kuit lam-ni-ia-ši* [. . .] *nutta apāt UNŪT* x[. . .] KUB 31.112:17-18 (instr. for *ḫazannu*); KUR.KUR ^{URU}*Ḫatti* AN*-za* (? DINGIR*-za*?) *ŠUM-an edanipat* ^{LÚ}KÚR 1 x x NU.ŠE*-du* (possibly:) "Are the lands of Ḫatti assigned(?) by Heaven (or: by a god) to this same enemy? (If so) let one (oracle) be unfavorable" KUB 22.56 rev. 9-10 (oracle), cf. *ŠUM* in oracle under mng. 4 d; *[k]īma* SISKUR.SISKUR EN.SISKUR.SISKUR *[kuedaš]* DINGIR.MEŠ*-aš lam-ni-ia-az-zi nat apēdaš ḫandanzi* "For whatever gods the patron assigns/designates this ritual, for those they prepare it" KUB 43.58 iv 6-7 (Kizz. rit.,

MH/MS); *nuza* DINGIR-*LIM-ni kuēdani lam-ni-an-zi našta menaḫḫanda apūnpat* DINGIR-*LAM uški* "Look upon that god for whom you are assigned/designated!" (addressed to a part of a building) KUB 32.137 ii 5-6 (rit., MH/NS); cf. [*nu*]*ddušan* [*ḫalz*]*iḫḫun kuēdani* DINGIR-*LIM-ni* [*našt*]*a menaḫḫa*[*nda a*]*pūnpat* DINGIR-*LAM uški* ibid. 24-25 + KBo 15.24 ii 3-4.

c. to an office or function: [*kinu*]*na kāša ANA* DUMU.MEŠ.LUGAL *ištarna* x[. . . LUGA]L-*uizni lam-ni-ir nanza* ŠEŠ.MEŠ-*ŠU* ⌜NIN⌝.ḪI.A-*Š*[*U* . . . *p*]*ankušša* LÚ.MEŠ URU*Ḫatti šekkandu* "Now, among the princes, they have appointed [PN] to [king]ship. Let his brothers, sisters, [. . .] and all the Hittites recognize him!" KUB 36.109:5-7 (protocol, MH/MS), ed. Carruba, SMEA 14:89; [*mānan*] LUGAL-*ušma lam-ni-iz-zi nanza parā piez*[*zi*] "But if the king appoints him, then he (an official) may dispatch him" IBoT 1.36 i 30-31 (instr., MH); LUGAL-*uš* LÚ*parāuwandan kuin* [*ANA*] EZEN *wurulli lam-ni-ia-zi* "The high-ranking (man) whom the king appoints [for] (performing) the *purulli* festival" Bo 4962 i 3-4 (fest.), Haas, KN 252; 6 LÚ.MEŠ*ḫilam*[*madduš*(?)] LÚSANGA LÚḪAL LÚDUB.SAR LÚNAR LÚNINDA.DÙ.DÙ LÚKURÚN.NA! GAL LÚDUB.SAR.MEŠ *lam-ni-ia-at* "The chief of scribes named/appointed six cult functionaries: priest, diviner, scribe, singer, baker, (and) brewer" KUB 38.12 ii 19-21 (cult inv.).

d. (in snake oracles): MUŠ SAG.DU-*kan ANA* dU *ḫaršanaš ŠUM-u-en* "We named/called/assigned(?) the 'snake of the head' for/to(?) the 'Stormgod of the Head'" IBoT 1.33 i 17 (snake oracle); MUŠ SAG.DU-*kan* dU *ŠUM!-en* ibid. 9; □similar statements with different destinations passim in this text, see Laroche, RA 52 (1958) 150-62. All nouns and names used in this position must be in the d.-l. even where the form is not expressed in the spelling. That *ŠUM-*(*u*)*en* is indeed *lamniyawen* is shown by 354/z i 11: MUŠ SAG.DU-*kan ANA* dU *lam-ma-ni-ir*. The snakes never go to the place mentioned with *ŠUM-*(*u*)*en*, hence "called to . . . " would seem pointless.

e. to the GIŠ/dUMBIN: [*num*]*u* ŠEŠ-*IA* mNIR.GÁL-*iš ANA* dUM[BI]N (var. GIŠUMBIN) *lam-ni-ia-at* "My brother Muwatalli assigned me to the (divine) 'wheel'" KBo 3.6 + ABoT 62 i 30-31 with dupl. KUB 1.1 i 35-36, ed. Götze, Ḫatt. 10-11; □just what is meant by the Sumerogram GIŠ/dUMBIN is not clear. But despite the uncertainties the translation "to assign to" seems appropriate as a rendering of *ANA* . . . *lamniya-*.

Götze, Ḫatt. (1925) 68f.; Friedrich, SV 2 (1930) 92f. n. 2.

Cf. *laman*.

lamnišan (mng. unkn.); (Luw.?); OH/NS.†

[. . .]x-*in* KI.MIN UR.MAḪ *lam-ni-ša-an* KI.MIN [. . . K]I.MIN DUGÚTÚL-*in mar-ruwammin* KI.MIN [. . . -*i*]*mmin* KI.MIN *ḫurkilaššinza* LÚ.MEŠ-*inza* [. . .] KUB 35.148 iv 11-13 (rit. of Zuwi).

Either acc. sg. of adj. modifying "lion" or d.-l. *lamni* + *šan*. No other loc.'s occur in this context but cf. *ulipanan pargauei ḫamikta* UR.MAḪ *za-am-ni-ša-an ḫamikta šāšan ḫūrattišan ḫamikta* KBo 3.8 iii 10-12, and UR.MAḪ *za-am-na-aš lāttat* [*šā*]*šaš ḫūrattišan lāttat* ibid. 29-30.

lankunni (Hurrian offering term); MH.†

In the *ḫišuwaš* fest.: EGIR-*ŠÚ-ma alanni la-an-ku-un-ni* [*š*]*ipanti* "Next he sacrifices to *alanni lankunni*" KUB 45.53 iii 13-iv 1.

Laroche, Gl.Hourrite 159.

lap- v.; to glow(?); from OH.†

pres. sg. 3 *la-ap-zi* KUB 19.23 rev. 3 (NH); **pret. sg. 3** *la-ap-ta* KUB 17.8 iv 25, 26 (NH), KUB 46.54 obv. 14, 16, KBo 23.108 i 6; *la-a-ap-ta* 398/w 6 (OH/OS?) (photo).

In a mythological section of a ritual (following *lappiyaš merta*, iv 14): *nu* ÍD-*aš la-ap-ta natkan parā* x[. . . -*a*]*š la-ap-ta* KUB 17.8 iv 25-26, cf. (after §) [. . .] *wellu pē ḫarkanzi nu* Ú.SAL *wara*[*ni* . . . Ḫ]UR.SAG.MEŠ *pē ḫarkanzi nu* ḪUR.SAG.MEŠ *wara*[*ndari*] "They hold onto the meadow, and the meadow burn[s . . .] They hold onto the mountains, and the mountains burn" ibid. 27-28, also ḪUR.SAG-*aš la-ap-ta* . . . [. . .] *la-ap-ta* § [. . . *w*]*arāni* KUB 46.54 obv. 14-17 (rit., NS); in broken context: [. . .]x *ša-at la-a-ap-ta* "and it glowed" 398/w 6 (OH/OS?, photo).

The other passages are fragmentary and the subjects of *lap-* are not well preserved. The definition of *lap-* is based on the meaning of the causative *lapnu-* "to kindle" and is supported by the passages cited above in which *lap-* is followed by *war-* "to burn" (intrans.).

Friedrich, ZA 39 (1930) 70-72.

Cf. *lappanu-*, *lappiya-*, ^{GIŠ}*lappiya-*, *lappinai-*, *lapnu.*

lappa- n.; (a metal implement) tongs(?); from MH.†

abl. *la-ap-pa-za* KUB 8.35 obv. 5 (NH); **inst.** *la-a-ap-pí-it* 1961/c obv. 6 (HTR 142); stem used with Akk. prep. *IŠ-TU la-ap-pa* KUB 30.15 obv. 4 (MH/NS); context not cited ^{URUDU}*la-a-ap-pa* Bo 2861 iii 10 (HTR 145); unclear *la-ap-pa-a*[*š* . . .] KUB 16.42 obv. 20 (NH).

In the royal funeral rit.: *nu ḫaštai IŠTU la-ap-pa* KÙ.BABBAR *daškanz*[*i n*]*atkan ANA* Ì.DÙG.GA *ḫūpar* KÙ.BABBAR *anda zikkanzi* "They take the bones (from the extinguished fire) with a silver *l.* and they put them into perfumed oil in a silver *ḫ.*-vessel" KUB 30.15 obv. 3-5 (MH/NS), ed. HTR 66f. *apaškan* TUR-*aš* ÍD!-*az* x-x-*an-ta-za* IZI-*za la-ap-pa-za iyattari* "That child will pass through river, . . . , fire, and tongs(?)" KUB 8.35 obv. 4-5 (omen, NH).

In KUB 9.19:5 (rit.) read *ŠA* IGI.ḪI.A-*ŠU* *la-ap*<-*li*>-*pu-uš.*

Sommer, OLZ 1939:681; Otten, HTR (1958) 142, 145.

:lapana- n. com.; summer pasture; NH.†

sg. acc. *:la-pa-na-an* KBo 4.10 obv. 35.

ZAG KUR $^{\text{URU.d}}$U-*ašša kuiš našta* LÚ.MÁŠ.GAL ŠÀ KUR-*TI lē paizzi mānna IŠTU* KUR $^{\text{URU.ÍD}}$*Ḫulaya šalli :la-pa-nu-u-wa-ni-ya pennanzi nuššikan :la-pa-na-li-ya-an-za lē danzi ANA* LUGAL KUR $^{\text{URU.d}}$U-*taššat piyan* MUN(coll.)-*ma daškiddu* ^{URU}*Šarmananna* URU-*an IŠTU* A.ŠÀ A.GÀR ⸢Ú.SAL⸣ *Ù IŠTU RE-E-ET* UDU *:la-pa-na-an-na ḫumantan* LUGAL.GAL *ANA* LUGAL KUR $^{\text{URU.d}}$U-*tašša piḫḫun ANA* MUN ^{URU}*Šarmanakan tamaiš* URU-*aš anda lē*[. . .]x-*du* "As for the territory of the country of Tarḫuntašša, let no goatherd enter the country! And if they drive to the great summer grazing from the country of the Ḫ. river, let them not take the summer pastures away from him: it has been given to the King of T. And let him take the salt lick! The town of Š. with its fields, grounds, and meadow(s), and with sheep pasture and the whole summer pasture I, the great King, have given to the King of T. Let no other town [encroach] upon the salt lick of Š.!" KBo 4.10 obv. 33-35 (treaty).

That this section may be dealing with transhumance rights is suggested (1) by the verb *pennanzi* "they drive (animals)"; (2) by the listing of *:lapanan* beside (therefore distinct from) "meadow and sheep pasture"; (3) by the mention of MUN "salt", in this connection apparently a place where the animals may find it. The morphology of some of these Luw. terms is difficult to explain. *:lapanaliyanza* must be obj., hence Luw. pl. acc. com., although the next clause (-*at piyan*) refers to a neut. sg. Although ^{LÚ}*lapanalli-* is a profession, this meaning does not fit *:lapanaliyanza* here, especially with "given by the king". For the possibility that a noun in -*ali-* may be synonymous with the basic noun cf. van Brock, RHA XX/71 (1962) 110 sub no. 193. *:lapanuwani-* may contain the formative -*wanni-* "the area devoted to summer pasture."

Güterbock, OrNS 25 (1956) 122; Laroche, DLL 62f. (for hierogl. Luw. verb *lapana/i-* see Meriggi, HHGl. s.v. and Manuale II/2, 13 frase 4); Laroche, NH p. 260.

Cf. *lapanašši-*, *lapanali-*, *lapanallaḫit-*.

lapanallaḫit- n. neut. (Luw.); summer pasturing; NH.†

sg. d.-l. *la-pa-*⸢*na*⸣*-al-*⸢*la*⸣*-ḫi-ti* KUB 40.69 rev. 9 (treaty) in broken context.

Cf. *:lapana-*.

:lapanali- n. com.; summer pasture; NH.†

pl. acc. Luw. *:la-pa-na-li-ia-an-za* KBo 4.10 obv. 34.

For discussion of this passage see *:lapana-*.

^{LÚ}**(:)lapanalli-** n. com.; herdsman (on summer pasture); Luw. in NH.†

pl. nom. $^{\text{LÚ.MEŠ}}$⸢*la-pa*⸣*-na-al-li-e*[-*eš*(?)] IBoT 2.131 rev. 10; $^{\text{LÚ.MEŠ}}$*la-pa-na-al-li*$^{\text{ḪI.A}}$-*uš* ibid. obv. 42, rev. 22; $^{\text{LÚ.MEŠ}}$*:la-pa-na-al-li*$^{\text{ḪI.A}}$-*uš* ibid. rev. 17.

3 UDU $^{\text{LÚ.MEŠ}}$*la-pa-na-al-li*$^{\text{ḪI.A}}$-*uš ŠA* x.GAL *peškir* "Three sheep the herdsmen of

the ... used to give" IBoT 2.131 obv. 42 (cult inv.); *nu* LÚ.MEŠ*:la-pa-na-al-li*ḪI.A*-uš* 300 NINDA. KUR4.RA *ŠA* MUN 100 NINDA.ḪI.A 2 DUG KAŠ 20 UDU 10 *EMṢU* 10 GA.KIN.AG 3 *PA* NAGA-*ya* MU.KAM-*tili peškir* "The herdsmen used to deliver every year 300 cakes of salt, 100 loaves of bread, 2 vessels of beer, 20 sheep, 10 pieces of rennet, 10 cheeses, 3 *parīsu*-measures of alkaline plants" ibid. rev. 17-19; cf. 10-11, 22. For rev. 10-12 cf. sub *luššanu-*.

On NINDA.KUR4.RA as shapes of material other than bread cf. Hoffner, AlHeth (1974) 121f.

Cf. *:lapana-*.

lapanašši- (Luw. gen.) adj.; belonging to summer pastures; NH.†

[d*Aalaš*] *la*[*-pa*]*-na-aš-ši-*⌈*iš*⌉ "The tutelary deities of the summer pastures" KUB 2.1 iv 16 (cult, Tudḫ. IV), with var. [... *-n*]*a-aš-ši-eš*, in dupl. KUB 44.16 iv 15.

Cf. *:lapana-*.

lappanu- see *lapnu-*.

:lapanuwani- n. neut.; summer grazing (area); Luw. in NH.†

sg. loc. *:la-pa-nu-u-wa-ni-ia* KBo 4.10 obv. 33.

For semantic discussion of this passage see *:lapana-*.

:lappanziḫini probably n., d.-l.; (mng. unkn.).†

[LÚ.É.DINGI]R?-*LIM-yašmaškan :la-ap-pa-an-zi-i-ḫi-ni ti-ia-zi* KBo 13.72 rev. 7 (vow).

labarna-, tabarna- n. com.; (PN which became title of Hittite kings); from OH/TOS; written syll. and once LUGAL-*na*.

spelled with *la-*:

sg. nom. *la-ba-ar-na-aš* KBo 17.22 iii 5, 9, 10, 18 (OH/OS), KUB 36.110 rev. 8, 11, 13 (OH/OS), KUB 1.16 iii 46! (see HAB 168), 55!, 64, KUB 29.1 i 49, KUB 2.2 ii 44, 48 (all OH/NS), KUB 28.4 ii 33; *la-pa-ar-na-aš* KUB 11.23 vi 4 (OH/NS), cf. KUB 35.4 iii 16 (case?); m*la-ba-ar-na-aš* KBo 3.67 i 2 (OH/NS), KUB 21.2 + KUB 48.95 i 3 (Muw.), KUB 21.29 ii 4 (Ḫatt. III); m*la-bar-na-aš* KUB 36.89 rev. 42 (OH?/NS).

sg. acc. *la-ba-ar-na-an* (all OH/NS) KUB 1.16 ii 3, iii (42), KUB 29.1 i 25, KUB 41.23 ii 10, KUB 43.61 i 5′, KUB 20.92 vi 11; *la-bar-na-an* KUB 36.89 rev. 50 (OH?/NS); m*la-bar-na-an* ibid. 49; LÚ*la-ba-ar-na-an* IBoT 1.30 obv. 3.

sg. gen. *la-ba-ar-na-aš* KUB 41.23 ii (20), 24, KUB 43. 63 obv. (11), KUB 20.92 vi 10 (all OH/NS), KBo 2.38 rt. 5, KUB 2.1 ii 31 and passim (both pre-NH/NS), KUB 13.4 iii 33 (pre-NH/NS); *la-bar-na-aš* KUB 36.89 rev. 43 (OH?/NS).

sg. old dat. in *-ai*: *la-bar-na-i* KUB 2.2 iii 9 (OH/NS); *la-bar-na-i*(*a*) KUB 36.89 rev. 61 (OH?/NS); cf. *tabarnai*.

sg. dat. *la-ba-ar-ni* KBo 21.22:(45) (OH/MS?), KUB 1.16 ii 31 (OH/NS); *la-bar-ni* KUB 31.136 iii 4; [*l*]*a-pa-ar-ni* Bo 5156 obv. 9 (StBoT 15:28).

pl. acc. [*l*]*a-bar-nu-uš* KUB 24.5 obv. 6.

Akk. *la-ba-ar-na* KUB 20.92 vi? 1, KUB 2.1 iv 5, 6, 9 (both OH/NS), KBo 13.241 obv. 12 + KUB 44.4 obv. 28, KBo 13.253 rev. 7, KUB 46.17 iv 5, KUB 11.9 iv 24 (all NH); m*la-ba-ar-na* KBo 13.238 ii 10, KUB 21.1 iv 39, KUB 44.4 obv. 21; *la-bar-na* KBo 16.58 ii 3, 6; LUGAL-*na* Ugar. 3:108 on the seal RS 18.03.

spelled with *ta-*:

sg. nom. *ta-ba-ar-na-aš* KBo 10.2 i 27, iii 37, KUB 41.29 iii 3, KBo 3.38 obv. 11 (all OH/NS), KUB 28.4 obv. 32b; *ta-ba-ar*<*-na*>*-aš* KBo 17.22 iii 14 (OH/OS); *ta-ba-ar-na-š*(*a-aš-ši*) KUB 44.60 ii 18; *ta-bar-na-aš* KBo 12.38 ii 22 (Šupp. II).

sg. acc. m*ta-ba-ar-na-an* KBo 22.2 rev. 11 (OH/OS) perhaps PN.

sg. old dat. in *-ai*: *ta-ba-ar-na-i* KUB 44.60 iii 15.

sg. dat. *ta-ba-ar-ni* KBo 20.59:5 (OH/MS); KUB 44.33 ii 4 (possibly with det. m after a break).

Akk. *ta-ba-ar-na* LS 2 = SBo I 2 obv. 1; LS 3 = SBo I 3 obv. (1) (both OH/OS), KBo 10.1 obv. 1, 13 (OH/NS), KBo 3.67 i 1 (OH/NS), KBo 5.7 rev. 49 (MH/MS), KUB 23.64 i 1, KUB 40.62 i 1 (both MH/NS), KUB 6.45 i 1 (Muw.), KBo 6.28 i 1 (Ḫatt. III); *ta-bar-na* KBo 12.38 i 11, KUB 26.32 i 1 (both Šupp. II).

in Ḫattic contexts *ta-ba-ar-na* KBo 21.90 obv. 34, rev. 40, KBo 21.109 ii 20, 21, iii 3, 4; KBo 23.103 i 9, 10, KUB 2.2 ii 42; *ta-ba-ar-na-an* KBo 21.109 iii 6, 7.

a. as PN — **1′** written *la-* **a′** *la-ba-ar-na-an* KUB 1.16 ii 3 (OH/NS), ed. HAB (1938) 2ff., 31f. (name of a prince, corr. to Akk. *la-ba-ar-na* ibid. i 2), *la-ba-ar-na-aš* (nom.) ibid. iii 64, (gen.) 46, *la-ba-ar-na* (Akkadogram) iii 55 (ref. to author of text); contrast *ta-ba-ar-na* ibid. ii 1 and in Akk. vers. below sub usage b 1; [*ka*]*rū* m*la-ba-ar-na-aš* LUGAL.GAL *ēšta* KBo 3.67 i 2 (Tel.pr., OH/NS), ed. Chrest. 182 (corr. to m*la-ba-ar-na* in Akk. vers., KUB 3.85 i 2); m*la-b*[*a*]*-ar-na-aš ABI* [(*ABBĀYA*)] KUB 21.2 + KUB 48.95 i 3 (Alakš.)

dupl. KUB 21.5 i 2; *ḫantezziyaš⸗ma⸗aš⸗kan* ^{m}*la-ba-ar-na-aš* ^{m}*Ḫattušiliš* ^{ÍD}*Kumešmaḫan parian UL tarneškir* "But the first Labarna (and) Ḫattušili did not let them cross the K. River" KUB 21.29 ii 4-5 (Ḫatt. III), cf. Kaškäer 146; in offering lists: *ANA* ^{m}*la-ba-ar-n[a]* KUB 11.4:4, ed. Otten, MDOG 83:64; *ŠA la-ba-ar-na* LUGAL-⌈*RI*⌉ KBo 11.36 iii 10.

b′ buildings or places either named after L. or meaning "the (present) king's . . . ": É ^{m}*la-ba-ar-na* KBo 13.238 ii 10, KUB 44.4 obv. 21; ⌈LÚ.MEŠ É⌉.GAL *la-ba-ar-na* KBo 13.241 obv. 12 + KUB 44.4 obv. 28 (followed by LÚ.MEŠ É.GAL ^{d}UTU-*ŠI* in next line); É *la-ba-ar-na* KUB 46.17 iv 5; É *la-bar-na* KBo 16.58 ii 6; *la-ba-ar-na-aš luliyaza* KUB 13.4 iii 33 (instr.), ed. Chrest. 158.

2′ written *ta-*: ^{m}*ta-ba-ar-na-an* ^{m}*Ḫappinna* "T. and Ḫ." KBo 22.2 rev. 11 (Zalpa story, OH/OS), ed. StBoT 17:12, 50; □ Ḫattušili I is called *tabarna* in the Akk. vers. incl. colophon of KUB 1.16 (HAB) and in both versions of his bil. "annals," KBo 10.1 and 2, with dupl. KUB 23.20 (all NS). In KUB 1.16 ii 1 *ta-ba-ar-na* (Akkadogram) occurs at the beginning of the Hitt. vers. (contrast *labarna-* above sub a 1′a′); for KBo 10.2 i 1 see below sub usage b 1′a′2″.

b. as royal title — **1′** as part of titulary — **a′** in seal inscr. and introductions (Akkadographic and always with *ta-*) — **1″** alone in the ^{NA_4}KIŠIB *ta-ba-ar-na* and *AWĀT ta-ba-ar-na* formulas passim in land deeds and their seals, from OH/OS, e.g. SBo 1.3 obv. (1), İnandık obv. 1, to NH, e.g. KBo 1.28 rev. 5 (Murš. II?), PRU IV p. 107:1 (Ḫatt. III), KUB 26.43 rev. 15 (Tudḫ. IV). — **2″** preceding RN in introduction: [o o *ta-ba-ar-n*]*a* ^{m}*Ḫattušili* KBo 10.2 i 1 (Ḫatt. I, NS); KBo 3.67 i 1 (Tel.pr., OH/NS), rest. from Akk. vers.: *umma* ^{m}*ta-ba-ar-[na . . .]* KUB 3.85 obv. 1, KUB 23.64 i 1 (Arn. I), KBo 1.6 obv. 1, KUB 6.45 i 1 (Muw.), ^{m}*ta-ba-ar-na* Ḫatt. i 1 (in A, B, and C), PRU IV p. 103:1; without det. KBo 6.28 i 1, KUB 21.17 i 1, KUB 21.29 i 1, KUB 26.58 i 1 (all Ḫatt. III), KUB 26.43 i (1) (Tudḫ. IV); INIM *ta-ba-ar-na* LUGAL.GAL KBo 2.4 iv 27 (fest., NH — Ḫatt. III?); in seal inscr. ^{NA_4}KIŠIB *ta-ba-ar-na* LUGAL.GAL *Ḫuzziya* WVDOG 76, no. 147 (p. 32); ^{NA_4}KIŠIB LUGAL.GAL *ta-ba-ar-na Allu⸗wamana* ibid. no. 146; ibid. no. 162 (Arn. I); ibid. no. 186, no. 230, Ugar. III, pp. 108ff. (all Ḫatt. III).

b′ in Hitt. context: *ta-ba-ar-na-aš-š(a)* KBo 3.38 obv. 11, rev. (13), 28 (Zalpa story, OH/NS), ed. StBoT 17; *ukza* ^{d}UTU-*ŠI ta-bar-na-aš* ^{m}KÙ.GA.TÚL-*aš* KBo 12.38 ii 22-23 (Šupp. II); ^{d}UTU-*ŠI* ^{m}*la-ba-ar-na* ^{m}NIR.GÁL KUB 21.1 iv 38-39 (Alakš.) ^{m}*l.* omitted in dupl. KUB 21.4 iv 9, ed. SV 2:82; [^{m}*ta*/*la-ba-a*]*r-na-aš* LUGAL.GAL HT 8:6 (Alakš.), cf. Sommer HAB 29 to SV 2:76:80f.; [(*mānza*) ^{m}*ta*/*la-ba*]-*ar-na-aš* ^{m}*Tudḫaliyaš* KUB 20.42 i 1 (AN.TAḪ.ŠUM fest.), with dupl. KUB 20.63 i 1 which omits the title; [*ANA* ^{m}*Šup*]*piluliyama ta-bar-na* LUGAL.GAL KUB 26.32 i 1 (Šupp. II); [*ITT*]*I*(?) ^{d}UTU ^{URU}TÚL-*na U ta-bar-na* LUGAL.GAL KBo 12.38 i 11 (Šupp. II).

2′ neither PN nor part of titulary but referring to either the present or former Hitt. kings — **a′** with *la-* (majority): *la-ba-ar-na-aš* KUB 36.110 rev. 8, 11, 13 (OH/OS); normal in Hitt. versions of Ḫattic-Hitt. bil. corresponding to Ḫattic *tabarna* (rarely *ta-* in Hitt. vers., see c 2′) KUB 2.2 passim; frequent in rits., e.g. KUB 2.1 passim (cult of protective deities); [*karuil*]*iuš la-bar-nu-uš* KUB 24.5 obv. 6 (subst. king rit., NH), ed. StBoT 3:8, 15.

b′ with *ta-* (rare): *ta-ba-ar-na-aš* LUGAL-*uš* KUB 41.29 iii 3; *ta-ba-ar-ni* KUB 44.33 ii 4 (both fest. at Zippalanda, Ḫatt. III); *ta-ba-ar-ni* LUGAL-*i* KBo 20.59:5 (myth, OH/MS), KUB 44.56 iii 2 (myth, pre-NH/NS); KBo 19.155:6, 21 (Hitt. followed by Pal.), ed. StBoT 10:25f.; in Hitt. versions of Ḫattic-Hitt. bil. (cf. with *la-*, above sub c 1′): KUB 28.4 obv. (32b) (contrast 33b with *la-*), KUB 28.6 rev. 5b, KUB 28.8 rev. 10b with dupl. KBo 17.22 iii 14 (contrast with *la-* in preceding §§), KUB 44.60 ii 18, iii 15, KUB 28.9 rev. 13b, KBo 22.133:4, 5.

c′ illustrating how different spellings and determinatives can occur in the same narrow context compare: "When the king bows to the gods, the 'anointed' (priest) recites as follows:" *ta-ba-ar-na-aš-kán* (var. A: *la-ba*[-. . .]) LUGAL-*uš* DINGIR.MEŠ-*aš aššuš ēšdu* "May the *t*/*l*., the king, be dear to the gods! (The land belongs only to the Stormgod, heaven and earth with the people belong only to the Stormgod)" *nuza* ^{LÚ}*la-ba-ar-na-an* (var. B without det.) LUGAL-*un* ^{LÚ}*maniyaḫḫatallan iyat* "And he made the *l*., the king, his deputy (and gave him the whole land of Ḫattuša. Now let the *la-ba-ar-na-aš* govern the whole land with his hand!)" IBoT 1.30:1-6, with dupl. A HT 67 rev. 1-5 and dupl. B KUB 48.13 rev. 9-14, ed. (without dupls.) Goetze, JCS 1:90f.; cf. [*ši*]*uniyašmaza* KUR-*eaš* ᵐ*la-bar-na-an* LUGAL-*un piran* ᴸᵁ́*maniyaḫḫatallan* DÙ-*at* KUB 36.89 rev. 49 (Ḫatt. III).

The distribution seems to confirm the theory that *labarna* or *tabarna* was first a PN. Because it was borne by an early king (and one or two princes) it became the traditional designation for the king which linked him with the early king, whose personal name was Labarna. The title was predominantly spelled with *la-* in Hittite rituals; Ḫattic and Palaic ritual texts use only the form with *ta-*, which was taken over in a few of the Hittite rituals. This traditional designation was used by many kings of the Old and New Kingdoms in their own texts. Conspicuous examples of kings who did not employ it in titulary are Šuppiluliuma I and Muršili II, although in KBo 1.28 rev. either Muršili II or Arnuwanda used *AWĀT tabarna* "word of the T." to describe his own edict (cf. b 1′ a′ 1″). The title occurs mostly in Akkadographic formulas, where it is always written with *ta-*. Outside these formulas it occurs spelled with *la-* only once (Alakš.) cf. above b 2′ a′.

The bilingual inscriptions of Ḫattušili I, preserved only in late copies, are exceptional: HAB follows the pattern in that it spells the name of the king with *la-* in the Hittite version (except the first line) but with *ta-* in the Akkadian. In the 'deeds', however, it is spelled with *ta-* in both versions. Possibly the scribe of this late manuscript generalized this form because he considered it as the title of the king otherwise known as Ḫattušili.

For an instance of the reinterpretation of the PN *Tabarna* by later scribes as a royal title see Otten, StBoT 17 (1973) 50.

If the hieroglyphic sign-combination Laroche no. 277 = Meriggi no. 289 represents the title, the bottom sign, *la*, would point to a reading **labarna*.

Hrozný, VSpr (1920) 49f., JSOR 6 (1922) 63ff. (considered *Tabarna* and *Labarna* the same word, explained as different renderings of /tl/); Götze, Madd. (1922) 138 n. 3 (wondered if *Tabarna* was connected with *tapar-* "Gewalt ausüben"); Sommer, OLZ 1921:316f. (distinguished "Appellativum" *tabarna-* from the name *Labarna*, while admitting that they might eventually derive from a common source); Sturtevant, Chrest. (1935) 85, 172, 194f. (followed Sommer, but derived the "Luwian(?)" title *tabarna-* "ruler" from the verb *tapar-* "to rule"); Sommer, HAB (1938) 20-29 (extremely thorough and fundamental analysis which is even today valid in almost all points; attempts to determine criteria by which texts in different languages [Hitt., Ḫattic, Akk.] and from different periods preferred the writings with *la-* and *ta-*; argued for an ultimate common source for the two differently spelled words and the priority of its use as a personal name, although [p. 25 and 26 n. 2] he considered the possibility of a Ḫattic common noun; Bo 2327 [pub. as KUB 41.17] ii 3-13, however, which he adduced for an equating of UDU.NITÁ with UDU *taparnant-*, does not in our opinion establish *taparnant-* "male"); Laroche, Ugar. III (1956) 109f. (considered the writing LUGAL-*na* to be based on a word play on Luw. *tapar-*) and 150 (opposed M. Riemschneider's connection with hieroglyphic Luw. *tap*(*a*)*r*(*a*)- "hare"); Kronasser, EHS I.1 (1962) 61-69 (assumed a "Cappadocian" root **labar-* "to rule" and defended the connection with both Luw. *tapar-* "to rule" and hieroglyphic Luw. *tap*(*a*)*r*(*a*)- "hare"); Kammenhuber, HbOr (1969) 432, 486, HbOr Ind 113 (claimed Ḫattic *tabarna* was originally a common noun "ruler"); Schuster, HHB (1974) 66 and passim (wrote "der Tabarna", as a common noun; his reasons will be published in a later part of the work); H. Gonnet, "La titulature royale hittite au IIᵉ millénaire avant J.-C.," Hethitica 3 (1979) passim (esp. pp. 21-22 on use and non-use of the title by various kings).

laparša- n.; (a garden herb or vegetable).†

la-a-pa-ar-ša in a long list introduced by *ŠA* ᴳᴵᆺKIRI₆ SAR.ḪI.A *ḫuman* "all the vegetables of the garden" KUB 7.1 i 24 (rit. of Ayataršа, pre-NH/NS).

Friedrich, HW 1. Erg. (1957) 127; on the other vegetable names in this context cf. Hoffner, AlHeth (1974) 112; on the Cappodocian PN *Labarša* see Laroche, NH p. 339.

ᴺᴵᴺᴰᴬ**lapaššī-** Luw. gen. adj.; (a kind of bread or cake); from MH.†

In enumerations of breads or cakes in Kizzuwatnean religious texts: [...] *ŠA* 2 *UPNI* 1 ᴺᴵᴺᴰᴬ*allinaššiš* [... *l*]*a-a-pa-aš-ši-iš ŠA* ⸢1⸣ *UPNI* [... -*i*]*š ŠA* [o *UPN*]*I* KBo 13.167 i 3-5 (*ḫišuwaš* fest., MH/NS); 3 NINDA ⸢*a-a*⸣-*an* BA.BA. <ZA> *UPNI* [...]x 1 ᴺᴵᴺᴰᴬ*la-ba-aš-ši-iš*

BA.BA.ZA *UPNI* [. . . B]A.BA.ZA *UPNI* 1 NINDA*allinaššiš* BA.BA.ZA *UPNI* 163/x iv 13-15.

Hoffner, AlHeth (1973) 170.

lapat(a/i)- n. com.; (a kind of dance or music?); OH/MS.†

sg. nom. (or **pl. nom.**?) *la-pa-ti-iš* KUB 4.1 iv b 32, 33; **sg. d.-l.** *la-pa-ti* KUB 4.1 iv b 38.

The last section of the Sammeltafel KUB 4.1, col. iv 32ff., contains a list in two subcolumns (iv a, iv b). It begins: LÚ.MEŠḪÚB.BÍ *tarkuer* "The dancers danced" KUB 4.1 iv a 32. There follows a series of 17 entries, each beginning with EGIR-*ŠU*/*ŠÚ-ma* "But thereafter". Among these: EGIR-*ŠÚ-ma tūwaz la-pa-ti-iš* 1-*ŠU* "thereafter *lapatiš* (nom.) once from afar" KUB 4.1 iv b 32; EGIR-*ŠÚ-ma la-pa*(eras.)-*ti-iš* SAL*ku*(or *šal-ku*?)-*pa-re-eš* ibid. iv b 33; EGIR-*ŠÚ-ma la-pa-ti pideššan* "Thereafter on/at *lapati* (d.-l.) on the spot" ibid. iv b 38, followed by EGIR-*ŠU-ma* EGIR-*pa parā tarkuwar* "Thereafter again dancing forward (or dancing back and forth)" ibid. iv b 39-40 (last entry).

lapattali(ya)- n.; (mng. unkn.); NH.†

sg. gen. *la-pa-at-ta-li-ia-aš* KUB 2.1 ii 41.

Š[*A*] *Labarna la-pa-at-ta-li-ia-aš* dLAMMA-*ri ŠA* [*L*]*abarna arauwaš* dLAMMA-*i* "to the tutelary deity of the Labarna's *l*., to the tutelary deity of the Labarna's getting up" KUB 2.1 ii 41-42 (cult of all tutelary deities, Tudḫ. IV). □The preceding entries in KUB 2.1 concern various aspects of time, cf. *lamarḫandatt-*.

lapati- see *lapat*(*a*/*i*)-.

lappiya- n. com.; fever; from OH.†

sg. nom. *la-ap-pí-ia-aš* KBo 13.2 rev. (3), KUB 17.8 iv 14, etc. (OH/NS); *la-ap-pí-aš* KBo 16.63 obv. 12 (NH); **acc.** *la-ap-pí-ia-an* KBo 24.51 obv. (8) (OH/MS?), KUB 36.49 i (5) (OH/OS).

KBo 13.2 rev. 1-11 (lex. series Ugumu) contains a sequence of entries closely resembling Izi Q in MSL 13 p. 221f. lines 272-300. In KBo 13.2 rev. 2-3 the entries probably were [nam-tar = *šīmta šâmu*] = *gulšaš gulšuw*[*ar*], [nam-tar = *murṣu* or *diḫu*] = [*l*]*a-ap-pí-ia-aš*. On the Akk. *di*ʾ*u* disease cf. CAD D 166.

a. in a deposition: *la-ap-pí-aš uwanza ešta numu* m*Ḫutupiš* m*Akiyašš*‹*a*›*a* LÚ.MEŠA.ZU-*TIM* SIG₅-*aḫḫiški*[*r*] "the fever was raging(?), and the physicians Ḫ. and A. healed me" KBo 16.63 obv. 12 (depos., NH), ed. StBoT 4:50f.; □on *uwanza* cf. KBo 16.36 + Bo 5768 + KUB 31.20 iii 1, 4 and KUB 19.8 iv 7, 10 + KBo 12.44:3, 6 both describing flooded rivers "raging".

b. "Incantation of the 'fire'" (title pertaining to preceding or following context?) § "They sent off from him" . . . (maladies of the eyes, feet, hand, and head) *nušši la-ap-pí-ia-aš merta* "and the fever disappeared from him" KUB 17.8 iv 10-14; [*nuwamukan*] *la-ap-pí-ia-aš genupi merta* ibid. iv 20-21, cf. 16, 23, 30; translit. in Laroche, Myth. 106-108; in sequence of evils and diseases all obj. of *karapta* "he ate" KUB 36.49 i 5 (OH/OS); sim. list of obj. of *lipir* "they licked" KBo 24.51 obv. 8 (OH/MS?); cf. also KUB 8.36 ii 4, KUB 30.43 ii 5.

Friedrich, ZA 39 (1930) 70-72 "Glut, (Fieber)hitze"; Werner, StBoT 4 (1967) 51; V. Haas, OrNS 40 (1971) 411.

Cf. *lap-* v.

GIŠ**lappiya-** n. com.; embers(?), or perhaps resinous wood(?), kindling(?).†

In Kizzuwatna rituals: *nukan maḫḫan* GIŠ*la-ap-pí-ia-aš* [. . .] *ḫalziyanpat nukan* DINGIR?.MEŠ? *ašnū*[*wanzi*] "When [the . . .] of (or 'in') the embers(?) is called for, [they] provide for the gods" KBo 8.91 obv. 10f.; [. . . GI]Š*la-ap-pí-ia-aš anda arnuanz*[*i*] "They bring in the embers (acc. pl.?)" or "They bring in [. . .] in/on the embers (loc. pl.?)" KBo 21.37 obv.? 6; [. . . GIŠ*l*]*a*?-*ap-pí-ia-aš piran* xḪI.A [. . .] ibid. 18; the gram. case represented by *-aš* is not completely clear in any example because of broken contexts; the *-kan* in KBo 8.91 obv. 10 requires a local postpos. or adverb in the lacuna.

Translation based entirely on the apparent connection with *lap-* "to glow", *lapnu-* "to kindle (a fire)". If "embers", then it may underlie Akk. *PÍ-IN-DU* KUB 44.4 obv. 10, cf.

pēmtu/pēndu in Akk. dictionaries. If "kindling", then it is a synonym of ^{GIŠ}*waršama-*.

J. Friedrich, HW 1. Erg., p. 12.

Cf. *lap-*.

[*lāppiya-*] v.; *la-a-ap-pí-ya-an*[*-zi*?] KUB 27.16 i 9 is probably a scribal error for *kar*!*-ap-pí-ya-an*[*-zi*?]; cf. *karp-*.

lappina-$^{(SAR)}$ n.; **1.** (a plant); **2.** wick(?); from OH/NS.†

sg. acc. *la-ap-pí-na-an* KUB 39.7 ii 20 (MH?/NS), KBo 20.79:14 (OH/NS); [*la-ap*]*-pí-na-an* Tel Aviv 2:92:17; *la-ap-pí-na-an*^{SAR} KBo 21.106 obv. 6 (OH/NS); *la-pí-na-a-an* KUB 39.8 i 17 (MH?/NS); **pl. inst.** [ ]*la-ap-pí-ni-*⌈*it*⌉ KBo 10.47g iii 14 (NH); **uncertain** *la-ap-pí-na-aš* Tel Aviv 2:92:20; KBo 23.9 i 11.

1. (a plant): ḪUR.SAG.MEŠ-[*u*]*š war⸗ḫunuškizzi* [...] *la-ap-pí-ni-*⌈*it*⌉ *aršanteš*[... DUMU.LÚ].U₁₈.LU *parran*[*t*]*a pauwanzi*[...] "He covers the mountains with forests, [the ...s] are planted with *l.*-plants [... (so that) a mor]tal [cannot(?)] go over" KBo 10.47g iii 13-15 (Ḫuwawa and the cedar mountain), ed. Otten, IM 8:108f.

2. wick(?) in funeral rit.: ^{SÍG}*iyatna la-ap-pí-na-an* (var. *la-pí-na-a-an*) *i*[(*yan*)*zi*] "They make the *i*-wool into a *l.*" KUB 39.7 ii 20 (with dupl. 39.8 i 17), ed. HTR 36f. This passage might refer to a wick rather than to a woollen model of a *l.*-plant.

Cf. the GN: ^{URU}*la-ap-pí-na-a*[*š-š*]*i* KBo 13.237 rev. 5.

If our interpretation "wick" sub 2 is correct, this plant might be flax. GADA "flax" takes det. SAR (CAD K 473). In Hitt. texts GAD seems always to be the textile, not the flax plant.

Otten, HTR (1958) 37 n. 3 ("Gartengewächs").

lappina(i)- v.; to light(?), to insert a wick (in a lamp)(?); NH.†

pres. pl. 3 *la-ap-pí-na-an-zi* Bo 5230:12, KUB 46.21 obv. (3).

^{DUG}*ša-ša-nu-uš* [...]x *la-ap-pí-na-an-zi* "They light(?)/insert wicks in(?) the lamps" Bo 5230:11-12; [... *šaš*]*anuš tianzi* [... *la*]*-ap-pí-na-an-zi* KUB 46.21 obv. 2f. (cult inv., end of a section).

von Brandenstein, OrNS 8 (1939) 71f.

Cf. *lap-*.

$^{(KUŠ)}$**laplai-** n. com.; (an internal[?] body part); from OH.†

sg. nom. ^{KUŠ}*la-ap-la-iš* KUB 28.102 iii! 7 (OH/NS), [^{KUŠ}]*la-a*[*p-l*]*a-a-iš* KUB 41.7 ii 3 + KUB 28.102 ii! 8 (perhaps both are pl. nom., preceded by numeral "2"); **inst.** [$^{KUŠ?}$]*la-ap-li-t*(*a-at-*[*ká*]*n*) KBo 17.17 i? 8 (OH/OS).

pl. nom. *la-ap-li-eš* IBoT 2.134:17 (NS). All attested forms are possible plurals.

a. enumerated in an incantation along with internal body parts: [$^{KUŠ?}$]*la-ap-li-ta-at*[*-ká*]*n da*[*-a-ú* ... *ta*]*gganit⸗at⸗kan* [*d*]*āu* [... *ḫaḫr*]*išnit⸗at⸗kan* [*d*]*āu* [... *š*]*arḫuwantit⸗at⸗kan* [*dāu* ...] "Let him/her take it with the *laplaiš*, [...] let him take it with the thorax(?), ... the lung(?), ... the stomach!" KBo 17.17 i? 8-11 (OH/OS); compare HAB 219f.

b. with materials for rituals: 3 ^{GIŠ}B[ANŠUR 2? ZAG-*az*] 1 GÙB-*laz* 2 *la-ap-li-eš* 1 ZAG-*a*[*z* 1 GÙB-*laz*] GA.KIN.AG ZAG-*az EMṢU* GÙB-*la*[*z*] "three tables: two on the right, one on the left; two *l.*'s: one on the right, one on the left; a cheese on the right, a rennet on the left" IBoT 2.134:16-18 (rit., NS); cf. [2] ^{KUŠ}*la-a*[*p-li-eš* ...] ibid. 2; "One cheese, one rennet, one red nanny goat skin, one black nanny goat skin, one white fleece (SÍG), one black fleece" 2 ^{KUŠ}*la-ap-la-iš* 1 ^{UZU}SA 3 ^{GIŠ}*šāḫiš* 3 GI.DÙG.GA (she puts on the right, and subsequently the same things on the left) KUB 28.102 iii! 5-9; cf. KUB 41.7 ii 3 + KUB 28.102 ii! 8.

As a material for the rituals (usage b) it is not clear whether the *laplai-* is eaten or used (for example) as a container. In the latter instance it could be a hollow internal organ (stomach, urinary bladder, gall bladder, colons, caecum, etc.). All attested forms could be plurals. When numbered, it is always "two". Perhaps it is a paired body part.

laplapa- see *laplipa-*.

laplipa-, laplapa- n. com.; **laplapi-** n. neut.; eyelash; from OH.†

sg. acc. *la-ap-la-ap≪-pí≫-pa-an* KUB 24.12 ii 32 (NH?/NS); *la-ap-le-e[-pa-an?]* KUB 32.8 iii 7 (MH?/NS).
sg. neut. nom.-acc. *la-ap-la-pí* KUB 24.12 ii 21, iii (34) (NH?/NS); *la-ap-li-pí* KUB 24.12 iii 6 (NH?/NS).
sg. inst. *la-ap-li-pí-it* KUB 48.13 obv. 15.
pl. acc. ⌈*la*⌉*-ap-li-ip-pu-uš* KBo 7.28 obv. 11 (OH/MS); *la-ap-li-pu-uš* KUB 15.34 ii 11 (MH/MS), KUB 9.19:5(!) (NH), FHG 4:5; *la-ap-l[i-p]a-aš* KBo 22.120:4.
pl. d.-l. *la-ap-li-pa-aš* KUB 33.66 ii 20 (OH/MS?).
Luw. pl. acc.? *la-ap-li-pa-an-za(-an)* KUB 9.34 iii 40 (NH/NS).
pl. abl. *l[a-a]p-la-pa-za* KUB 9.34 iii 46 (NH/NS); *la-ap-li-pa-az-z(a-aš)* KUB 9.4 iii 11 (NH/NS); *[la-ap-l]i-pa-az* HT 55:7.
uncertain *la-ap-l[i- . . .]* KBo 20.49:11 (NH?); *la-a-ap[- . . .]* KUB 9.4 iii 2 (MH?/NS).

a. in rits.: *kuitmanmazan BĒL* SISKUR. SISKUR *IŠTU* SAG.DU-*ŠU te-e-ta-*<*na-*>*an la-ap-le-e[-pa-an?] eneranna ḫuittiyannai* SAL ŠU.GI-*ma lūili kiššan ḫūkkiškizzi* "While the patient pulls out from his head a hair, an eyelash, and an eyebrow (hair), the Old Woman conjures as follows in Luwian" KUB 32.8 iii 6-10 (rit., MH/NS), ed. LTU 21; following *enira-* KUB 9.34 iii 40, 46, HT 55:6-7, KUB 24.12 ii 21, 32, iii 6.

b. with the verb *karp-*: *aššū* IGI.ḪI.A-*KA lak LĪM la-ap-li-ip-pu-uš kar-ap* "Turn (hither) your benevolent eyes! Lift (your) thousand eyelashes!" KBo 7.28 obv. 11 (prayer, OH/MS), cf. KUB 15.34 ii 11, FHG 4:5.

c. in a list of body parts which under enchantment become luminous KUB 33.66 ii 20, cf. sub *lalukki-* v.

Laroche, RHA IX/49 (1948-49) 16f.

laplipanza- see *laplipa-*.

lapnu-, lappanu- v.; to kindle, make to glow; NH.†

iter. supine *la-ap-nu-uš-ki-u-wa-an* KUB 17.1 ii 8; **part. neut. sg.** *la-ap-pa-nu-wa-an* KUB 42.69 obv. 14; *la-ap-pa-nu-an* KUB 32.76:20.

a. kindling a fire: *n[u]* ᵐ*Kiššiyaš attaš* DINGIR.ME[Š] *paḫḫur la-ap-nu-uš-ki-u-wa-an dāir* "The father gods of K. began to kindle a fire" KUB 17.1 ii 7-8 (Kešši myth, NH), with dupl. KUB 33.121 iii 9-10, ed. Friedrich, ZA 39:66f.

b. describing a glowing jewel or metal: GURUN KÙ.GI NA₄ *la-ap-pa-nu-wa-an anda* [. . .] KUB 42.69 obv. 14; [. . .] KÙ.GI *la-ap-pa-nu-an l[i- . . .]* KUB 32.76:20; on GURUN as an ornament cf. CAD I/J sub *inbu* 1 c p. 146.

Friedrich, ZA 39 (1930) 70-72.

Cf. *lap-*.

ᵁᶻᵁ**lapruwa** n. neut.; (part of goat's body); NS.†

(The ritual practitioner opens up a pit, and they cut up a he-goat down in the pit) *našta ANA* MÁŠ.GAL ZAG-*n[a-an? . . .]* ᵁᶻᵁGEŠTU-*NI* ᵁᶻᵁ*la-ap-ru-wa* ᵁᶻᵁGÌR ᵁᶻᵁELLAG[. . .] *kur(a)škizzi* "he cuts off from the he-goat the right [. . .], ear, *lapruwa*, foot, kidney [. . .] (and [they put] them down into the pit)" 933/u i 11-13 (rit. with Hurr.-Kizzuwatnean setting, NS).

If the ZAG "righthand" carries on through the next line, the ear, *lapruwa*, foot and kidney would also be "righthand".

lari(ya)- n.?; (mng. unkn.); OH.†

In the KI.LAM festival: *mān tieštes la-ri-i-e-eš* (var. *la-a-r[i- . . .]*) *arunaš tuḫḫandat* KBo 10.24 iii 11-12 (NS), with dupl. 462/t 1-2; cf. Neu, StBoT 5:174.

t. and *l.* could both be nouns or *t.* an adj. and *l.* a noun.

Cf. the PN *Lariya* in Laroche, NH 106.

lariya- v.?; (mng. unkn.); OH.†

In a festival for ᵈTetešḫapi: *nuwaššan mān pāimi na-*⌈*a*⌉*-[(ḫi-mu)]* (var. *na-ḫi-mu*) *pár-aš-ni* (var. *pár-ni*) UR.BAR.RA-*ni la-ri-ia-wa* (var. *la-a-r[i-ia-wa]*) *wātar* "When I go there, be afraid for me of the panther and the wolf! *lariya* the water!" KBo 21.90:51-52 (OH/MS), with dupl. KBo 21.103 rev. 28 (sim. phrase repeated in following lines; *la-ri-ia-wa* ibid. 54 with var. *la-a-ri-ia-wa* KBo 25.155 + 21.103 rev. 31).

lariya might be the sg. 2 imp. of a verb, used in a construction parallel with *naḫi* "fear!"

Cf. *lari(ya)-*.

:larella n.; (mng. unkn.); Luwian word, NH.†

In an inventory for the cult of Pirwa: *nu* ᵈ*Pirwan :la-re-el-la* ᴸᵁ́*ḪATANIŠU peda*[*n*]*zi nu* ᵈ*Pirwan :la-re-el-la ANA* ᵈUT[U.LU]GAL *kattan* ᴳᴵŠZAG.GAR.RA-*ni daninuwanzi* IBoT 2.131 rev. 7-10.

Laroche, DLL 63 (Luw. pl. acc. neut.).

larpu- v. mid.; (mng. unkn.); OH.†

takku PA₅-*an* EGIR-*an arḫa kuiški nāi* 1 GÍN KÙ.BABBAR *pāi takku* PA₅-*an* EGIR-*izziaz kuiški šarā nāi* (var. *šer dāi*) *ta la-ar-pu-ut-ta takku kattanna dāi naš apēl* (dupl. adds -*pat*) Law § 162 KBo 6.26 i 18-21 with dupl. KBo 6.15:6-8 and unpub. 684/c ii 1′-2′, which confirms the reading *la-* and the space before it, against Friedrich HW 32 and HG p. 109. [*la*]-*ar-pu-ut-ta* KBo 19.104:5 (Appu myth, pre-NH/NS), ed. StBoT 14, p. 14f. in broken context.

The definition of *l.* depends on the interpretation of the protasis of Law § 162, in which *appizziyaz* and *šarā nāi* (var. *šer dāi*) are open to different interpretations. Cf. discussions in Friedrich, HG 108-9 and Imparati, Leggi 286f., Güterbock, WO (forthcoming) and Melchert, JCS 31 (1979) 59-62.

laršiya (Hurrian offering term); NH.†

In the *ḫišuwaš* fest.: *šarraššiya la-a-ar-ši-ya* KBo 24.40 rev.? 7 (MH/NS).

Perhaps to be restored in KUB 15.20 iii 5: *šarraššiya l*[*a-* . . .] (vow).

ᴳᴵ?**laššumi(ya)-** n.; (a plant which produces a seed); NH.†

[. . .] *ēpzi nu kē* / [. . . ᴳ]ᴵ*la-aš-šu-mi-ia-aš* NUMUN-*an* / [. . .] NU.ÚR.MA *ūnḫazi* KUB 35.79 i 3-5 (rit. with Luw.); form is sg. gen.

Reading [ᴳᴵ]ˢ*ḫilaššumi*(*ya*)- cannot be excluded.

Hoffner, EHGl (1967) 43 with n. 59.

ᴳᴬᴰ**latagga[. . .]** n.; (something made of linen); NH.†

[. . .]x 1 GÌR KA×UD.AM.SI 1 ᴳᴬᴰ*la-tág-ga*[- . . .] "one foot of ivory, one *l.* [. . .]" KBo 18.186 left edge 7 (inv.) in context with five other named objects of GAD (linen).

lātar n. neut.; loosing, dispelling; from pre-NH.†

sg. nom./acc. *la-a-tar* Tel Aviv 2 (1975), 91f., line 10 (pre-NH/NS); **loc.** *la-a-an-ni* KBo 11.1 i 8 (NH).

"The Sun(god) of heaven who then stood in the sky, that [same Sun(god) is] also now [standing in the sky]" *naš ANA ŠA* ᵈU *šāuwarri* EGIR-*pa la-a-an-ni kutruwanni artar*[*i*] "And he stands to witness the dispelling of the Storm-god's wrath" KBo 11.1 i 7-8 (prayer of Muw.), ed. Houwink ten Cate, RHA XXV/81 (1967) 105, 114 (note the use of the verb *lā-* in the preceding and following lines); *la-a-tar-ša-me-et-ta* "and their/our *l.*" Tel Aviv 2 (1975) 91f., line 10 (rit. of Zuwi, pre-NH/NS) in broken context.

Friedrich, HW 3. Erg., 22; Josephson, RHA XXV/81 (1967) 129f.

Cf. *la*(*i*)- v., mng. 8.

ᴺᴵᴺᴰᴬ**lattari-** see ᴺᴵᴺᴰᴬ*alattari-*.

latti- n. com.; **1.** tribal troop(s), tribe(?), **2.** (a feature of the exta); from MH; written syllabically and (ERÍN.MEŠ) *ŠUTU.*

sg. nom. *la-at-ti-iš* Maşat 75/113 obv. 5, 6 (MH) (Alp, FsLaroche 29f.), KBo 16.97 rev. 11 (NH), AT 454 i (18), 49 (NH); **sg. acc.** *la-at-ti-en* KUB 17.18 iii 14 (NH); **pl.?** ⌈*la*⌉-*at-ti-uš* (or read: -*iš*!) KBo 16.97 rev. 22 (NH); **unclear case** *la-ti* 388/i ii 10 (Lebrun, Samuha 202); **broken** *la-at-t*[*i-* . . .] 1550/u:3, 4.

Akkadogram *ŠU-TI* KBo 14.3 iii 16, 54, iv 9, (11) (DŠ); KUB 23.22:(7); KUB 22.70 obv. 5, 27, etc., KUB 16.16 obv. 11 and l. e. 2; *ŠU-TUM* KUB 5.11 i 27 (NH); ERÍN.MEŠ *ŠU-TI* KUB 19.11 i 6, KBo 14.3 iii 18 (DŠ); KBo 18.39:9 and KBo 18.88 rev. (12); KUB 5.1 ii 47, KUB 22.51 obv. 12, 13, KUB 6.17 ii 4, KUB 49.7 i 8 (all NH); ERÍN.MEŠ *ŠU-TI* ᴴᴵ·ᴬ KUB 19.11 iv 6 (DŠ), KUB 31.10:8 (AM 78), KBo 16.16 iii (19), KUB 19.37 iii 27 (AM); KUB 22.25 rev. 21, 22 (NH); ERÍN.MEŠ *ŠU-TE*ᴹᴱŠ KBo 5.6 ii 5 (DŠ); ERÍN.MEŠ *SU-TE-I* ibid. ii 4; ERÍN.MEŠ *ZU-TE-E* KUB 19.12 iii 8 (DŠ); ERÍN.MEŠ *ŠU-TUM* KUB 49.11 ii 21, Bo 6987 obv. 1 (StBoT 5:183).

la-at-t[*i-* . . .] in 1550/u:3, 4 = *ŠU-TUM* in dupl. Bo 4171:2, 3 according to Otten apud Alp, ZA 68:271 with n. 3.

1. tribal troop(s), tribe(?) — **a.** of the enemy (Kaška, Arzawa): "The enemy has just crossed (our border) en masse in two places" *nukan* 1-*iš la-at-ti-iš INA* URU*Išteruwa zāiš* 1-*išmakan la-at-ti-iš INA* URU*Zišpa zaiš* "one tribal troop crossed at I., and the other tribal troop crossed at Z." Maşat 75/113:3-7 (letter, MH), ed. Alp, Belleten 41:638f. and FsLaroche 29f.; "The Kaškaean enemy which my father encountered in the midst of the land" *naš* 12 *ŠU-TI kišat* "turned out to be (lit. became) twelve tribal troops" KBo 14.3 iii 15f. (DŠ), ed. Güterbock, JCS 10:67; cf., also in DŠ, "three tribes" ibid. iii 49; "nine tribes" KUB 19.11 iv 6; "six tribes" KUB 19.18 i 7; "seven tribes" ibid. 9; *nu* LÚKÚR URU*Gašga pankun* ERÍN.MEŠ *ŠU-TI IN*[*A* ŠÀ KUR-*TI*] *IKŠUD* "(my father) encountered all of the enemy Kaškaean tribe(s) in the midst of the land" KUB 19.11 i 6; 9 ERÍN.MEŠ *ŠU-TI* ḪI.A *taruppi*[*r*] "They gathered nine tribes" KUB 19.11 iv 6; *nukan uni* LÚKÚR URU*Gašgan* ERÍN.MEŠ *ŠU-TI kuin kuwapi damaškit* [*n*]*ankan kuwaškit kuitma pē ḫarta* [*n*]*atšikan ABUYA arḫa daškit* "Wherever my father caught that enemy Kaškaean tribe, he slew it and took from it what it was holding" KBo 14.3 iii 17-20 (DŠ); cf. also KBo 14.3 iii 49f., KUB 19.18 i 7-10 (both DŠ); □note that, though the numbers show that several tribes are in view, the adjectives, pronouns, and verbs in agreement indicate that the underlying noun *latti-* is always singular; *nuza* GIM-*an* ERÍN.MEŠ *SU-TE*MEŠ *tar(a)ḫta* "When (my brother) had defeated the tribal troops, (and the enemy land saw it, they became afraid)" KBo 5.6 ii 5f.

b. in the employ of the Hittite king: (furthermore up in Timmuḫala I tarried) *nukan* ERÍN.MEŠ *ŠU-TI*ḪI.A *parā neḫḫun* "and I sent out tribal troops" KUB 19.37 iii 26f. with dupl. KBo 16.16 iii 18f. (AM 174f.); "(Assuming that) His Majesty (will go) to the fortified [camp of the father] of His Majesty, in the morning the chariot[ry] shall attack [. . .]," ERÍN.MEŠ *ŠU-TI*ḪI.A-*ia-aš-ši parā t*[*i*]*yanzi* . . . *nuššikan* ANŠE.KUR.RA.MEŠ ERÍN.MEŠ *ŠU-TI*ḪI.A-*ia* EGIR *panza* "the tribal troops shall advance before (the chariotry) . . . the chariotry and tribal troops having gone back to him (His Majesty)" KUB 22.25 rev. 21-23 (statement leading up to question in an oracle on campaigns of the king, NH), ed. Kaškäer 182f.; note *parā tiyanzi* here and *piran tianzi* in Bo 4171 cited in 1 c; "when (the king) comes down from Mt. Ḫaḫarwa" *nu ANA* m*Temeti* ERÍN.MEŠ *ŠU-TI* [SU]M-*zi* "will he give tribal troops to T.?" KUB 5.1 ii 47 (oracle question on campaigns of king, NH); m*Maniya*-LÚ-*ma* TA ERÍN.MEŠ *ŠU-TI tieššanzi* "will they set M. on the road together with tribal troops?" KUB 22.51 obv. 13 (oracle question, NH); [. . .]INIM ERÍN.MEŠ *ŠU-TI TAŠPUR* "You wrote about the matter of the tribal troops" KBo 18.39:9 (letter, NH).

c. in non-military context: GIM-*anma zen*⸗*nanzi namma la-at-ti-en-š*[*i*?-*in*? . . . *gu*]*lšanzi* "But when they finish, they write down h[is?] tribe" KUB 17.18 iii 14f. (rit. for *taknaš* dUTU, NH), note mention of GIŠ.ḪUR "document, list" at the end of line 15, and compare [. . . *a*]*pel la-at-t*[*i*- . . .]x *apel la-at-t*[*i*- . . .] "his tribe . . . his tribe" also in 1550/u:3f. with *ŠU-TUM piran tianzi* "they put his tribe in front" in dupl. Bo 4171:2, 3 (Otten apud Alp, Belleten 41 (1977) 639 with n. 3a, FsLaroche 30 n. 4, and ZA 68 (1978) 271 with n. 3).

2. (a name given to a feature of the exta), in NH extispicy oracles — **a.** looks/faces in a certain direction (Hitt. *uškizzi*, corr. to *iṭṭul* in Akk. extispicy): *ni ši la-at-ti-iš* ZAG-*aš iškiša* GAM *uškizz*[*i* . . .] 10 ŠÀ.DIR SIG$_5$ AT 454 i 18f., cf. ibid. i 49; [. . . -*a*]*š šalliš ši ta ŠU-TI* ZAG-*naš* [. . . *u*]*škizzi* 10 ŠÀ.DIR SIG$_5$ KUB 16.77 ii 29f.

b. (identified as either "left" or "right", but never a pair together) — **1′** lefthand: *ŠU-TI* GÙB-(*l*)*aš* KUB 22.70 obv. 5, 27, 64; KUB 16.16 obv. 11, l. e. 2; KUB 5.20 i 18, etc.; *ŠU-TUM* GÙB-*aš* KUB 5.11 i 27; *la-ti* GÙB[. . .] 388/i ii 10, ed. Lebrun, Samuha 202.

2′ righthand: cf. above mng. 2 a; KASKAL *ANA urnirnimaššan* ZAG-*aš la-at-ti-iš* GÙB-*lazziya walḫan* KBo 16.97 rev. 10-11; [*š*]*i ta ŠU-TI* ZAG-*aš* GÙB-*za* RA-*IṢ* KUB 18.2 ii? 14 (cf. preceding ref.); *ŠU-TI* ZAG-*aš* KUB 22.70 rev. 50; KUB 22.69:13; KUB 5.6 i 14!; *ŠU-TUM* ZAG-*aš* KUB 49.11 ii 27; *ni ši la-at-ti-iš* ZAG-*aš* AT 454 i 18, also 49′.

In military contexts *latti-* and its log. denote groups of fighting men characteristic of the Kaška. The log. through its relationship to the name Sutaeans suggests that these bands were made up of nomads cf. Kupper, Nomades (1957) 83-145. It is probable that *latti-* or the log. denoted not just troops, but also the tribe itself. This cannot be established from our limited evidence. As a kind of shorthand, however, we have used the term "tribe" in our translations.

As a feature of the exta which "looks" (*aušzi/ uškizzi*) the *latti-/ŠUTI* "tribe" belongs in the group which includes KASKAL-*NU* (KUB 18.11 rev. 6), *TE*^{MEŠ}/SU.MEŠ   (KUB 18.2 ii 15, KUB 5.10 obv. 18), ZÉ *ḫi-li*$_x$ (GIBIL) (KUB 46.37 obv. 30), *ke(ldiš)* (KUB 5.1 iv 49), and *ta(naniš)* (KUB 46.37 obv. 38f.). Like KASKAL, ^{GIŠ}ŠÚ.A and *keldiš*, it is a non-anatomical term employed in extispicies to designate a feature of the exta. Although *Š/SUTU* itself has not yet been identified in Mesopotamian extispicy texts, support for the interpretation given above can be found in the analogous Akk. *kiṣru(m)* and *kiṣirtu(m)*, which occur as terms for a feature of the exta and in the meaning "troop, gang" cf. Nougayrol, JCS 21 (1967) 227 note 59, 234; and CAD K s.v.

Since many of the technical terms in Hittite extispicy texts are of Hurrian origin, *latti-* might also be. Yet Hurrian words beginning with *l* or *r* are quite rare Speiser, Intr. 27.

Götze, AM (1933) 242 and Güterbock, JCS 10 (1956) 62 with note c (both on the logogram); Alp, Belleten 41 (1977) 639 with note 3a (on *latti-*, written in Turkish, translating it "kol", and in FsLaroche (1979) 30, with n. 4 ("colonne/contingent d'armée"); Hoffner, FsMeriggi 2 (1980) 261-66 (combining *latti-* = ŠU-*TUM/TI* with ERÍN. MEŠ *ŠU-TUM/TI* and proposing "tribal troops, tribe").

ŠU-*TUM* in rituals and festivals occasionally represents Hitt. *aniyatt-* (Laroche, BiOr 21 (1964) 321; Otten, ZA 68 (1978) 271 with note 3). Note also ŠU-*TI* in this usage KUB 32.133 i 17. Other ŠU-*TUM* and ŠU-*TI* writings represent Hitt. *keššar(a)*- "hand".

(:)lawarr- Luw. v.; to despoil, strip; from MH.†

act. pret. sg. 3 :*la-wa-ar-ri-it-ta* KUB 13.35 ii 32 (NH); **pl. neut. pass. part.** [:*la*]-*wa-ar-ri-ma* ibid. 29; **inf.** *la-u-wa-ar-ru-na* KUB 24.3+ ii 30′ (Murš. II with MH par. *la*[-...] KUB 30.12 obv. 19′). All forms are Luwian.

"They transgr[essed] the oaths" ⌈É.ḪI⌉.A.

DINGIR.MEŠ-*ma* (par. É.DINGIR.MEŠ-*ma*) *la-u-wa-ar-ru-na šanḫiškanzi* "and seek to despoil the temples of the gods" KUB 24.3 ii 29-30 (prayer of Murš.); MH par. KUB 30.12 obv. 19′; ed. Gurney, AAA 27:28f.; "The gold-covered bows which the queen had counted" *nuwarat ḫēš*[*anda* :*la*]-*wa-ar-ri-ma wemiyanun* "I found them open[ed (and) s]tripped. (I [did not] take the gold.)" ... *apaddayawa UL IDI* [*kuiš*]*warat* :*la-wa-ar-ri-it-ta* "Nor do I know who stripped them (... I took the gold of my mother and covered them with that)" KUB 13.35 ii 29-32 (deposition in court, NH), ed. StBoT 4:8f.

Gurney, AAA 27 (1940) 96-98 ("despoil"); Werner, StBoT 4 (1967) 9 ("der Einlage berauben"); cf. DLL 63.

lāwatt(a)- n.; (mng. unkn.); OH.†

In a ration list for a festival: [... *ḫam*]*ešḫi* ⌈*la*⌉-*a-wa-at-ta-aš meḫ*[*uni* ...] "in the spring at the time of *l.*" KBo 20.21 rev.? 1′ (OH/OS).

$^{(GIŠ)}$lazzai-, ^{GIŠ}**lazi-** n. com.; (a kind of tree or wood); from OH.†

sg. nom. *la-az-za-iš* KUB 17.10 ii 31 (OH/MS); ^{GIŠ}*la-az-za-iš* 950/c iv 2 (NS), KBo 13.86 rev. (3) (OH/NS); **case uncertain** ^{GIŠ}*la-az*[- ...] KBo 17.75 i 35; ^{GIŠ}*la-z*[*i*-...] KBo 2.12 ii 19.

In a list of offering material: ^{GIŠ}*ḫa-ši-ik al-la-ia-ni-iš ḫa-ap-pu-ri-ia-aš* ^{GIŠ}*la-az-za-iš* ^{GIŠ}*ša-a-ḫi-iš* GÚ.TUR GÚ.GAL 950/c iv 1-3 (rit. with Ḫattic); ZI(or GI?)-*az la-az-za-iš māḫḫan ḫandānza zi-ga*(coll.) ^{d}*Telepinuš QATAMMA ḫandaḫḫut* KUB 17.10 ii 31-32 (Tel., 1st vers., OH/ MS), translit. Laroche, Myth 33; cf. ^{GIŠ}*la-az*[-*za-iš* ...] *ēšdu* KBo 13.86 rev. 3-4 (missing god, OH/NS); *našta* LUGAL-*uš* ^{GIŠ}*la-az*[- ... *š*]*ipanti* KBo 17.75 i 35-36 (fest., OH/NS).

The identification of ^{GIŠ}*lazzai-* with GI. DÙG.GA in HW 128 based on a comparison of KUB 17.10 ii 31f. (above) with GI.DÙG.GA! (text TA) *maḫḫan ḫandanza* KUB 33.8 iii 19f. (Tel., 2nd vers.) is uncertain cf. Goetze, JCS 17 (1963) 62. The interpretation of ZI/GI-*az* remains unclear, and *l.*'s det. GIŠ is inappropriate for a kind of reed, although ^{GIŠ}GI. DÙG.GA is attested once (KUB 7.9:5), and GI. DÙG.GA occurs in lists similar to 950/c above:

VBoT 58 iv 23-24, KUB 41.13 ii 21-23, KBo 12.106 + KBo 13.146 i 16, KBo 20.129 i 32-33, KUB 28.102 iii(!) 8-9, ABoT 1 i 22.

Cf. *lazzi-*?

lazzandati- n. com.; (an animate being); MH/MS.†

In the cult of ^{d}Ḫuwaššanna: [. . .] *ḫāwēš la-az-za-an-da-ti-in ḫašta* [o o *la-az*]*-za-an-da-ti-iš* ^{d}*Aindupinzu ḫašta* "*ḫāwēš* (cf. Luw. *ḫawi-* "sheep"?) bore/begot *lazzandati-*; *lazzandati-* bore/begot (the deity) A." KBo 24.26 iii 3-4.

^{GIŠ}lazi- see ^{GIŠ}*lazzai-*.

lazzi- adj.; good, pleasant; from OH.†

(Sum.) [o o]x = Akk. *ṭub-bu-tù* = (Hitt.) *la-az-z*[*i-* . . .] KBo 1.42 iv 50, ed. MSL 13, p. 142:277 (coll.).

[*t*]*andukišni* [*Ḫalkiš zik* DINGIR.MEŠ-*n*]*aša ištarna* [. . .]x *la-az-zi-iš* [*zik*] "Among mortals [you are Ḫalki,] but among [the gods you are] a pleasant(?) [. . .]" KUB 31.143a iii 1-2 + VBoT 124 rev.(!) 12 (invocation of Ḫattic gods, OH/OS), ed. Laroche, JCS 1:204 (without VBoT 124), restored after KUB 8.41 iii 8, ed. ibid. p. 190. *la-az-z*[*i* . . .] KBo 1.42 iv 50 collated, cf. Otten, AfO 16 (1952-53) 70 n. 6; Akk. *ṭubbūtu* (if this is meant) could be either abstract noun in *-ūtu* or masc. pl. adj.

The Hitt. adj. is so far attested only in the one OH text. The Hitt. reading of SIG$_5$-*in* (adv.) is not known; see under logogram.

Cf. ^{GIŠ}*lazzai-*(?), *lazziya-*, *lazziyaḫḫ-*, SIG$_5$.

lazziya- v.; (act.:) **1.** to set straight, rectify, **2.** to prosper(?); (mid.:) **3.** to be good, flourish, thrive, **4.** to recover, get well, **5.** to abate, subside (of ills), **6.** to be favorable (of oracles); **7.** (with preverb *appa*:) to become normal again (sim. to mng. 4); from OH. Written syllabically, SIG$_5$ and (in oracle texts) ŠE.

act. pres. sg. 1 SIG$_5$-*zi-ia-mi* KUB 33.24 i 44, 45 (OH/NS); **sg. 3?** (see mng. 2) SIG$_5$-*iz-zi* KUB 43.8 ii 9b (NH?); **pl. 2** SIG$_5$-*at-te-ni* KUB 39.99 obv. 17 (NH?); **pl. 3** SIG$_5$-*an*!-*zi* VBoT 108 i 15 (NH?).

mid. pres. sg. 3 *la-a-az-zi-at-ta* KBo 6.2 i 18 (OS); *la-az-zi-at-ta* ibid.; SIG$_5$-*at-ta* KBo 3.7 iii 21 (OH/NS); SIG$_5$-*ta* Bo 6993:9 (StBoT 5:106, 108 n. 3); SIG$_5$-*ad-da* KUB 7.1 ii 38 + KBo 3.8 ii 4 (NS); SIG$_5$-*at-ta-ri* KBo 6.3 i 27 (OH/MS), KUB 17.24 ii 13; SIG$_5$-*ta-ri* KBo 6.4 i 24 (2x) (NS); SIG$_5$-*ri* KBo 5.11 iv 18 (MH?/NS), KBo 6.5 i 7 (OH/NS).

mid. pres. pl. 3 SIG$_5$-*an-ta* KUB 8.1 iii 9 (NH); SIG$_5$-*an-da* 1560/c:6 (StBoT 5:107), KUB 34.16 ii 12 (OH/NS); SIG$_5$-*ia-an-ta-r*[*i*] KBo 10.7 ii 29 (OH/NS); SIG$_5$-*an-ta-r*[*i*] KUB 43.4 i 6 (OH/NS).

mid. pret. sg. 1 *la-az-zi-aḫ-ḫa-at* KUB 30.10 obv. 17 (MH?/MS); SIG$_5$-*aḫ-ḫa-at* ibid. 18.

mid. pret. sg. 3 ⌈SIG$_5$⌉-*ta-ti* KUB 23.103 obv. 4 (NH), KUB 34.50:4 (NH?); SIG$_5$-*ia-at-ta-at* KBo 4.8 ii 21 (NH); SIG$_5$-*at-ta-a*[*t*] KBo 13.87:2 (NH?); SIG$_5$-*ta-at* 142/r iv 11 (StBoT 5:107) ("alt"); SIG$_5$-*at* KUB 5.6 iv 26 (NH), KUB 5.8:8 (NH).

mid. pret. pl. 3 SIG$_5$-*ia-an-ta-at* KUB 33.36 iii 6, (8) (OH).

imp. mid. sg. 3 (all exx. NH) *la-az-z*[*i-ia-a*]*t-ta-ru* KUB 14.8 rev. 9 (Murš. II); SIG$_5$-*ia-at-ta-ru* KUB 14.11 iii 24; SIG$_5$-*ta-ru* KBo 8.55:18; SIG$_5$-*ru* KUB 22.25 obv. 22 and passim in oracle texts; SIG$_5$-*rù* KUB 22.52 obv. 9, 13 etc.; ŠE-*ru* KBo 13.68 obv. 1, 24 and passim; ŠE-*rù* KUB 6.2 obv. 1, 3, etc.

iter. mid. pres. sg. 3 SIG$_5$-*iš-kat-ta-ri* KBo 6.29 i 11 (NH); **verbal noun** *la-az-zi-ia-u-wa-ar* KUB 17.27 ii 3 (MH/NS).

Bilingual corr. in Hitt. translations of Akk. omen texts: SIG$_5$-*ta-ri* "he will prosper" KBo 13.35 iv 7, ed. StBoT 9:22f. = SIG$_5$ GAR-*šú* "(the child) is endowed with prosperity" Leichty, Izbu III 36 (StBoT 9:24); [*arm*]*alaš* SIG$_5$-*at-ta-ri* "the sick man will get well" KUB 8.19:14 = GI[G].GA T[I.L]A KUB 4.63 iii 24; BURU$_{14}$.ḪI.A SIG$_5$ KI.LAM-*tar-ra* SIG$_5$-*a*[*t-ta-ri*?] (traces on photo not *-t*[*a-ri*]) "the crops will be good and business will be good" KUB 34.14 rev. 4 = BURU$_{14}$ *i-iš-še-er* KI.LAM SIG$_5$ GAR-*an* "the harvest will prosper, and business will be good" KUB 4.63 iii 21; *uttar* SIG$_5$-*ta-ri* "the word will be favorable" KUB 34.14 rev. 7 = ⌈INIM DÙG⌉.GA! "the word will be good" KUB 4.63 iii 24.

In other genres: the use of SIG$_5$-*ri* "he will recover" in med. texts (mng. 4b) corr. to that of Akk. *iballuṭ* in omen apod. and in diagnostic omens; see CAD B p. 54; *maršanza* GUD-*uš ḫamešḫipat* SIG$_5$-*ri* KUB 4.3 obv. rt. 13-14 (wisdom text), ed. Laroche, Ugar. V:781, all that is preserved of the Akk. vers. ibid. 14 is [. . .]⌈*i*⌉-*da-me-e*[*q* . . .], Nougayrol, Ugar. V:289; which corr. to SIG$_5$-*ri*, cf. the dupl. Ugar. V:279, 282, 437 iii 11.

1. (act.:) to set straight, rectify (from OH): *UMMA* ^{d}NIN.TU *lēwatta nāḫi tuē*[(*lku wa*)*šta-iš*] *ugat* SIG$_5$-*zi-ia-mi UL-akku* (var. C [*na*]*t-takku*) *tu*[(*el w*)*aštaiš*] *ugat* SIG$_5$-*zi-ia-mi* "Ḫannaḫanna said: 'Fear not! (If) it is your fault, I will set it straight, and (if) it is not your fault, I will (also) set it straight'" KUB 33.24 i 43-45 (myth, OH/NS), with dupls. B=KUB 33.22 ii 7 and

C=33.27 obv. 7-8, translit. Laroche, Myth. 55, translation Güterbock in MAW (1961) 146; *šumenzanat uttar šumešat* SIG$_5$-*at-te-ni* "It is your affair; you will set it straight" KUB 39.99 obv. 16-17 + KBo 14.100 obv. 11 (rit. for infernal deities, MH?/NS with some old sign forms); □a gloss wedge before SIG$_5$-*atteni* indicates that it is the first word in an indented line; in VBoT 108 i 15 (inv., NH) SIG$_5$-*an*!-*zi* might be for **lazziyaḫḫanzi* (cf. KUB 5.6 i 7-8, 38) or **lazziyanzi* and probably takes *waškuš* (i 14) as its object.

2. (act.:) to prosper(?): [. . K]A×KAK GÙB-*la pān* SIG$_5$-*iz-zi* "[If a man's] nose goes to the left, he will prosper(?)" KUB 43.8 ii 9 (omen); it is possible that SIG$_5$ here stands for some other verb.

3. (mid.:) to be good, flourish, thrive — **a.** people: [DU]MU.MEŠ-*ya* SIG$_5$-*an-ta-r*[*i*] "and the children will thrive" KUB 43.4 i 6 (omen), ed. StBoT 9:18f.; cf. KBo 6.25 + KBo 13.35 iv 7 (omen, NH), ed. ibid. 22f.; *nuwa* DUMU LÚ.MEŠ-*LUTTI* SIG$_5$-*ru* "'Let the son of mankind thrive'" KUB 36.89 rev. 55 (prayer to the Stormgod, NH), ed. Haas, KN 156f.

b. cattle: *maršanza* GUD-*uš ḫamešḫipat* SIG$_5$-*ri* "In the spring (even) a poor(?) cow may look good" KUB 4.3 obv. rt. 13-14 (wisdom text, NH), Hoffner, AlHeth 17; also GUD-*uš* ⸢*mekki*⸣ *marri* SIG$_5$-*t*[*a-at*] KUB 24.7 ii 52 (cow and fisherman story); and [. . . G]UD.ÁB SIG$_5$-*ru* KUB 24.8 iv 32 (Appu), StBoT 14:12f.

c. crops: [(KUR-*e*)-*aš* BU]RU$_{14}$.ḪI.A SIG$_5$-*an-d*[*a*] "The crops of the land will be good" KUB 8.4:2 (omen), with dupl. 76/g obv. 9, ed. Riemschneider, Omentexte 271f.; BURU$_{14}$.ḪI.A SIG$_5$-*an-ta* KUB 8.1 iii 9 (omen, NH); BURU$_{14}$.ḪI.A SIG$_5$ KUB 34.14 rev. 4 (omen); also [*mā*]*n* GAŠAN-*YA* GE$_6$-*in* KI-*an lāši ḫalkiš* SIG$_5$-*ri* "If, my lady, you release the dark earth and the crop flourishes" KUB 15.11 ii 7 (vow, NH).

d. spring: MU.2.KAM *ḫamešḫanza* SIG$_5$-*at-ta* "For two years the spring will be good" KUB 29.11 ii 6, 8 (omen), with dupl. KUB 8.6 ii 6, 8, ed. Riemschneider, Omentexte 177, 179.

e. business: KI.LAM-*tarra* SIG$_5$-*a*[*t-ta-ri*?] "and business will be good" KUB 34.14 rev. 4 (omen).

See the bilingual section above for the Akk. corr. to these texts in mng. 3.

4. (mid.:) to recover, get well (opp. of *ištark*-, *irmaliya*-, and *armaniya*-) — **a.** laws: *takku* LÚ.U$_{18}$.LU-*an kuiški ḫūnikzi tan ištarnikzi nu apūn šaktāizzi pēdiššima* LÚ.U$_{18}$.LU-*an pāi nu* É-*rišši anniškizzi kuitmānaš la-a-az-zi-at-ta* (vars. KBo 6.3 i 27: SIG$_5$-*at-ta-ri*, KBo 6.5 i 7: SIG$_5$-*ri*, KUB 29.13 obv. 2: SIG$_5$-*ta*[-. . .]) *mānaš la-az-zi-at-ta-ma* (var. KBo 6.3 i 27: SIG$_5$-*at*[-. . .]) *nušše* 6 GÍN KÙ.BABBAR *pāi* ^{LÚ}A.ZU-*ya kuššan apāšpat pāi* "If someone injures a man and he becomes sick, he will take care of him. He will give a man in his place, who will work in his house until he recovers. When he recovers, he will give him six shekels of silver and will give the doctor (his) fee" KBo 6.2 i 16-19 (Law §10, OS), cf. KBo 6.4 i 24 (par. §IX).

b. medical texts: *naš* SIG$_5$-*ri* "he (the patient) recovers" KUB 44.61 rev. 18, KBo 21.76 rt. 19; *mānmaš apez UL* SIG$_5$-*ri* "But if he (the patient) doesn't recover by means of that (remedy)" KUB 44.61 obv. 10; cf. *mān apez UL* SIG$_5$-*ri* ibid. obv. 17; *kuitmanaš* SIG$_5$-*ri* "until he (the patient) recovers" KUB 8.38 iii 7, KUB 44.64 rev. iii 6-7; cf. StBoT 19, passim.

c. rituals: *mānaš* SIG$_5$-*ad-da-ma* "But if he (the sick child) recovers" KUB 7.1 ii 38 + KBo 3.8 ii 4.

d. omens: LÚ-*aš witti meyani armaniyatta naš* SIG$_5$-*at-ta* "The man will become sick every year and will recover" KUB 4.72 rev. 2-3 (liver model); [*arm*]*alaš* SIG$_5$-*at-ta-ri* "The sick man will recover" KUB 8.19:14 (solar omens); cf. in broken context: [*tui*]*kkiši* SIG$_5$-*ri* KBo 13.24:9.

e. oracles: *maḫḫanma* ^{d}UTU-*ŠI* SIG$_5$-*ri* "If His Majesty recovers" KUB 5.6 i 32; cf. GIG ^{d}UTU-*ŠI* ibid. i 42; *kuitmanwa irmalanza* SIG$_5$-*ri* "Until the sick man recovers" ibid. i 47-48.

f. prayers: *kinunaman mān la-az-zi-iḫ-ḫa-at nu tuel šiunaš uddanta natta* SIG$_5$-*aḫ-ḫa-at* "If I were to recover now, would I not have recovered at your divine word?" KUB 30.10 obv. 17-18 (prayer of Kantuzzili, MH?/MS).

5. (mid.:) to abate, subside (of ills): *mānwa ANA* ^{d}UTU-*ŠI eni* IZI *ŠA* GÌR.MEŠ-*ŠU nu-un-tar-aš* SIG$_5$-*ri* "If the inflammation of His Majesty's feet subsides soon" KUB 15.3 i 18-19 (vow) translation, Güterbock apud Oppenheim, Dreams 255; ŠÀ KUR.KUR.ḪI.A-*kan* ŠÀ KARAŠ Š[À . . .] ÚŠ-*an* SIG$_5$-*ri* "(If) in the lands, in the army, in [. . .] the plague subsides" KUB 15.1 i 23-24 (vow); *nukan INA* [(ŠÀ KUR ^{URU}*Ḫatti*)] *ḫingan la-az-z*[*i-ia-a*]*t-ta-ru* (var. SIG$_5$-*ia-at-ta-ru*) "Let the plague subside in Ḫattuša" KUB 14.8 rev. 9 (plague prayer of Murš.), with dupl. KUB 14.11 iii 23-24, ed. Götze, KlF 1:214f.; *akkiškittari kuedaš ANA* URU.DIDLI.ḪI.A *nu* SIG$_5$-*ru ANA* URU.DIDLI.ḪI.A-*ma kuedaš* SIG$_5$[-*ri*? *n*]*ukan ḫinkan* EGIR-*pa lē paiz*[*zi*] "In the cities where there is dying, let (the plague) subside, and in the cities where it subsides, let the plague not return" KUB 14.13 iv 19-21 (plague prayer of Murš.), ed. ibid., 248-49; cf. KUB 14.14 rev. 37 (plague prayer of Murš.), ed. ibid. 176.

6. (mid.:) to be favorable (of oracles) (opposite of *kallareš-*) — **a.** in festivals: *kuedani pēdi IŠTU* DINGIR-*LIM* SIG$_5$-*at-ta-ri nu apēdani pēdi ḫūkanzi* "They slaughter in that place which (the oracle) from the deity (indicates) is favorable" KUB 17.24 ii 12-13 (*wittaššiyaš* fest.); cf. *k*[*uedani pedi IŠTU* DI]NGIR-*LIM ḫandāittari* [*nu apedani ped*]*i ḫuēkzi* KUB 32.105:10-12 (par. to preceding text).

b. in oracle texts — **1′** in extispicy: *nu* SU.MEŠ SIG$_5$-*ru* "Let the exta be favorable" KBo 2.6 i 42, iii 23, iv 3, KUB 5.3 i 4, 18, KUB 22.70 obv. 28 and passim; *nu TE*^{MEŠ} SIG$_5$-*ru* "Let the exta be favorable" KUB 5.6 i 37, ii 55, 64, iii 28, KUB 22.70 obv. 50, rev. 37; [^{UZU}NÍG.GI]G.ḪI.A SIG$_5$-*ta-ru* "Let the exta be favorable" KBo 8.55:18 (restored following ^{UZU}NÍG.GIG.ḪI.A *kallarišdu* "Let the exta be unfavorable" ibid. 17); *nu* IGI-*zi* SU.MEŠ SIG$_5$-*ru* EGIR-*ma* NU.SIG$_5$-*du* "Let the first exta be favorable and the following be unfavorable" KBo 2.6 i 16-17, ii 26-27, KUB 16.31 iv 14 and passim; *nu* IGI-*zi TE*^{MEŠ} SIG$_5$-*ru* EGIR-*ma* NU.SIG$_5$-*du* "Let the first exta be favorable and the following unfavorable" KBo 22.264 i 8-9, KUB 16.71:9; *nu* IGI-*zi TE*^{MEŠ} NU.SIG$_5$-*du* EGIR-*ma* SIG$_5$-*ru* "Let the first exta be unfavorable and the following be favorable" KUB 5.11 i 10-11, KUB 5.20 + KUB 18.56 ii 16, (26); *zilaš* SIG$_5$-*at* "the *z.*-oracle was favorable" KUB 5.6 iv 26.

2′ in lot oracles: *nu* KIN SIG$_5$-*ru* "Let the lots be favorable" KUB 5.1 iv 44 and passim, KUB 22.25 obv. 22 and passim; *IŠTU* SAL ŠU.GI KIN SIG$_5$-*ru* "Let the lot oracle (performed) by the Old Woman be favorable" IBoT 2.129 obv. 37.

3′ in MUŠEN *ḪURRI* oracles: *nu* MUŠEN *ḪURRI* SIG$_5$-*ru* "Let the shelduck (oracle) be favorable" KBo 2.6 ii 45, 54, KBo 13.64 obv. 16 and passim; *nu* IGI-*zi* MUŠEN *ḪURRI* SIG$_5$-*ru* EGIR-*ma* NU.SIG$_5$-*du* "Let the first shelduck (oracle) be favorable and the following one unfavorable" KBo 2.2 i 15-16, KUB 18.63 i 24, iv (22); with IGI-*iš* for IGI-*zi* KUB 16.34 i 2-3, (11)-12, 17; [*nu* IGI-*iš* M]UŠEN *ḪURRI* NU.SIG$_5$-*du* EGIR-*ma* SIG$_5$-*r*[*u*] KUB 16.34 i 23.

4′ in bird oracles: □in the bird oracles other than those of the MUŠEN *ḪURRI* type, the verb *lazziya-* is not used. The corresponding verb is *ḫandai-*, often written SI×SÁ, q.v.; Archi, SMEA 16 (1975) 144ff. A possible exception is *IŠTU* ^{LÚ}IGI.MUŠEN IR-*TAM QATAMMA-pat nu* MUŠEN!.ḪI.A SIG$_5$-*r*[*u*] "Let the oracle (taken) by the augur be the same. Let the birds be favorable" KUB 5.11 i 62; the reading of MUŠEN! "bird", however, is uncertain.

5′ in snake oracles: *nu* ^{TÚL}*aldannieš* SIG$_5$-*ru* "Let the pool (oracle) be favorable" KUB 22.38 i 5, (15); *INA* 2 KASKAL-*NI* 4(?) SIG$_5$-*ru* KBo 23.117 rev. 5; cf. rev. 7, 9, 17, 18, 19; 4(?) SIG$_5$-*ru* ibid. rev. 15.

6′ in sheep oracles: IGI-*ziš* UDU-*iš*(sic) SIG$_5$-*ru* EGIR-*ma* NU.SIG$_5$-*du* "Let the first sheep be favorable and the following one be unfavorable" KUB 18.11 obv. (13), rev. 3, 12, KUB 6.9 + KUB 18.59 ii 5-(6), (18), KUB 6.14 rev. (18)-(19); cf. 2!-*uš* UDU-*uš* SIG$_5$-*ru*[. . .] KUB 18.49:7 (cf. line 11); *nu* IGI-*ziš* UDU.ŠIR-*iš* SIG$_5$-*ru* EGIR-*ma* NU.SIG$_5$-*du* "Let the first ram be favorable and the following one be unfavorable" KUB 16.29 obv. 8, 14, 19, 24.

In all types of oracles, the sequence "let the first be favorable, let the following be unfavorable" is much more frequent than "let the first be unfavorable, let the following be favorable."

7. (sometimes with preverb *appa*:) to become normal again — **a.** in myth. texts: "The Stormgod took back (his) heart and his eyes" §*mān ešrešši appa karūiliatta* SIG$_5$*-at-ta* "When he had recovered his former physical well-being (hist. pres.), (he went again to the sea to battle)" KBo 3.7 iii 18-22 (Illuyanka, OH/NS), Laroche, Myth. 10; (without *appa*:) *ištananiššan* [DINGIR.MEŠ (SIG$_5$*-ia-an-ta-at*)] *ANA* GU[NNI*-išš*]*a*[(*n* ^{GIŠ}*kalmišani*)*š* SIG$_5$(*-ia-an-ta-at*)] § TÙR*-kan* UDU.ḪI.A SIG$_5$*-an-t*[*a-at INA* É.GUD*-kan* GUD.ḪI.A SIG$_5$*-antat*] AMA*-ŠU* DUMU*-ŠU-ya* SIG$_5$*-an-ta*[*-at* DAM*-SÚ-kan* ^{LÚ}*MUDIŠU-ya*?] SIG$_5$*-an-ta*[*-at*] "[The gods] recuperated at the altar, the logs recuperated on the hearth, the sheep recuperated in the fold, [the cattle recuperated in the corral,] mother and child recuperated, [wife and husband] recuperated" KUB 33.67 iv 10-14 (OH/NS), with dupl. KUB 33.36 iii 6-8 (OH/MS?); translit. Laroche, Myth. 77; □in this passage *lazziya-* expresses the opposite of *wišuriya-* (mid.) in KUB 33.36 ii 6ff. In most versions of the missing god myth, the verb which corresponds to *lazziya-* is *ḫandai-* (mid.), e.g. KUB 33.24 iv 12ff. (dupl. KUB 33.29 iv 5ff. + KUB 30 iv 4ff.), KUB 33.32 ii 7ff., KUB 33.40 iv 6ff.; ed. Laroche, Myth., passim.

b. in lunar eclipse omens, translating Akkadian *nawāru* "to clear up": . . . [*ki-š*]*a-*⸢*ri*⸣ *naš* [*INA* IM.MAR.TU EGIR*-pa*] SIG$_5$*-ta-ri ŠA* L[UGAL KUR ^{URU}*Agade*] ⸢*U*⸣ LUGAL KUR ^{URU}MAR.TU [*šagaiš*] ". . . [occ]urs and [in the west] it clears up, [it is the omen] of the k[ing of Akkad] and the king of Amurru" KUB 43.3:3-5, ed. Riemschneider, Omentexte 240; □Riemschneider (ibid. 239) suggested that this omen corresponds to the Akk. omen UD AN.TA.LÙ ^{d}UTU.È.A *iḫmuṭma ana* IM.MAR.TU *iwwer* AN.TA.LÙ LUGAL URI *u* LUGAL MAR.TU "If an eclipse begins in the east and clears up towards the west, it is the eclipse of the king of Akkad and the king of Amurru" KUB 4.63 ii 25-26, ed. Riemschneider, ibid. 75, 81; cf. CAD Ḫ, p. 63. The Hitt. text is restored following this Akk. omen; cf. [. . . -]*az ḫuwandaz* DÙ*-r*[*i* . . .]x EGIR*-pa* SIG$_5$*-ta-r*[*i* . . .] KUB 8.21:11-12, ed. Riemschneider, Omentexte 143f.

In MH mng. 1 began to be assumed by *lazziyaḫḫ-*, q.v.

Zimmern, OLZ 1922:298; Sommer, Heth. II (1922) 39; Laroche, RHA XII/54 (1952) 24 (liver oracles).

Cf. *lazzi-*.

***lazziyaḫḫ-, SIG$_5$-yaḫḫ-** v.; **1.** to make right (again), repair, correct, redress, cure, alleviate, **2.** to show favor to (someone), **3.** to give a favorable sign or portent, **4.** to sweeten(?) (a substance); from MH.

pres. sg. 1 SIG$_5$*-aḫ-mi* KUB 9.39 i 1, KUB 24.13 iv 4, KUB 26.12 iii 21, KBo 11.1 obv. 33, 41 (all NH); **sg. 2** SIG$_5$*-aḫ-ti* KUB 48.119 obv.? 3 (NH); **sg. 3** SIG$_5$*-aḫ-zi* KUB 14.8 rev. 25, KUB 44.64 ii 13, KBo 21.74 iii 9, KUB 6.10:8 (all NH); SIG$_5$*-aḫ-ḫi* KUB 26.1 iii 63, KUB 22.61 i 7 (all NH).

pl. 1 SIG$_5$*-aḫ-ḫu-e-ni* KUB 18.18 rev. 23 (NH); SIG$_5$*-aḫ-ḫu-ni* 1691/u ii 18 (MH/MS); **pl. 2** SIG$_5$*-aḫ-te-ni* KBo 20.75 rev. 9 (NH); **pl. 3** SIG$_5$*-aḫ-ḫa-an-zi* VBoT 24 ii 25, KUB 6.45 iii 47, KUB 18.25 iv 2, KBo 11.1 rev. 5, 6 (all NH).

pret. pl. 1 SIG$_5$*-aḫ-ḫu-u-en* KUB 28.1 iv 7; **pl. 3** SIG$_5$*-ia-aḫ-ḫi-ir* KUB 5.6 i 8, 38 (NH); SIG$_5$*-aḫ-ḫi-ir* ibid. iv 24, KUB 16.51 obv. 1.

imp. pl. 3 SIG$_5$*-aḫ-ḫa-an-du* KUB 13.2 ii 39 (MH/NS); **part. neut. sg.** SIG$_5$*-ia-aḫ-ḫa-an* KUB 40.56 iv! 8 (MH/MS), KUB 13.2 iv 25 (MH/NS); SIG$_5$*-aḫ-ḫa-an* KUB 13.24:14, KUB 38.12 i 2 (NH).

iter. pres. sg. 1 SIG$_5$*-aḫ-ḫi-iš-ki-mi* KUB 14.8 rev. 39; SIG$_5$*-aḫ-ḫe-eš-ki-mi* KBo 11.1 obv. 43 (NH); **pl. 1** SIG$_5$*-aḫ-ḫe-eš-ki-u-w*[*a-ni*] 1691/u ii 10 (MH/MS); **pret. pl. 3** SIG$_5$*-aḫ-ḫi-iš-ki-ir* KBo 16.63 obv. 12 (NH).

1. to make right (again), repair, correct, redress, cure, alleviate — **a.** to repair, maintain in good condition (buildings, equipment): É.DINGIR*-LIM-ši* [(*and*)]*urza IŠTU* ^{LÚ}KÙ.DIM ^{LÚ}BUR.GUL SIG$_5$*-aḫ-ḫa-an* "the temple interior has been put in order for him (the god) by the goldsmith and the stonecutter" KUB 38.12 i 1-2 (cult inv., NH), dupl. KUB 38.15 obv. 2; "If someone has knocked over the throne of the Stormgod (namely) the stela, or has blocked a sacred spring, [. . .]" *nat* EGIR*-pa* SIG$_5$*-aḫ-mi* "I will repair/correct it" KBo 11.1 obv. 40-41 (Muw. prayer), ed. Houwink ten Cate, RHA XXV/81:108, 117, cf. ibid. 33; É*-ŠU* SIG$_5$*-aḫ-ḫi-iš*[*-kán-zi/du*?] KUB 31.112:3 (*ḪAZANNU* instr.), ed. Daddi Pecchioli, OA 14:106-7, 125; *kuitašmaššan waqqāriya . . . nat* SIG$_5$*-aḫ-ḫe-eš-ki-u-w*[*a-ni*] "W[e] will set right ... that which is missing to you (gods)" 1691/u ii 8-10 (prayer of Arn. and Ašmunikal), unpublished portion of KUB 17.21 not available for ed. in Kaškäer 152ff.; "If any temple develops a leak," *nat auriyaš* EN-*aš* LÚMAŠKIM.URUKI-*ya* EGIR-*pa* SIG5-*aḫ-ḫa-an-du* "the commander of the border forts and the 'mayor' must repair it" KUB 13.2 ii 37-39 (instr., MH/NS), ed. Dienstanw. 46; *ŠA* TU7.ḪI.A (or <DUG>UTÚL.ḪI.A?) *AŠRI*ḪI.A SIG5-*ia-aḫ-ḫa-an ēštu* "Let the places of the cooked food offerings (or of the pots?) be kept in good order!" KUB 13.2 iv 25, ed. ibid. 51, cf. Hoffner, JCS 24 (1971) 31f.; cf. KUB 40.56 iv! 6-9 (instr., MH/MS), ed. Dienstanw. 50; "the bird ponds which are in your domain" *nat* SIG5-*an-te-eš* (**lazziyaḫḫanteš*?) *ašandu* "let them be kept in good condition" KUB 13.2 ii 25, ed. Dienstanw. 45; cf. article SIG5-*ant-*.

b. to cure, heal (someone): *lappiaš uwanza ēšta numu* m*Ḫūtupiš* m*Akiyašša* LÚ.MEŠA.ZU-*TIM* SIG5-*aḫ-ḫi-iš-ki-ir* "The fever was raging, and Ḫ. and A., the physicians, healed me" KUB 34.45 + KBo 16.63 i 12 (depos., NH), ed. StBoT 4:50f.; *mān alwanzaḫḫandan* UN-*an* EGIR-*pa* SIG5-*aḫ-mi* "when I cure a bewitched person" KUB 24.13 iv 3-4 (rit., MH/NS); cf. also KUB 44.54 iv 5-6 + KUB 41.5 iv 3; KUB 41.22 iii 11-12; KUB 7.33 obv. 2; KUB 9.39 i 1; *nu mān* DINGIR.MEŠ [...]x SIG5-*aḫ-te-ni* "If you gods will heal [...], (His Majesty will do these things)" KBo 20.75 rev. 8-9 (rit.); *nan* SIG5-*aḫ-ḫu-u-en* "and we healed him" KUB 28.1 iv 7 (Ḫattic-Hittite incant.).

c. to alleviate, relieve (disease, suffering, sorrow): [*mān*]*na-mu* DINGIR-*LUM kī UL šekkan* GIG SIG5-*aḫ-ti* "[If] you, oh god, will cure this unknown disease of mine" KUB 48.119 obv. 3 (vow); "When the gods hear my words" *numukan kuiš idaluš memiaš* ZI-*ni anda nanmu* DINGIR.MEŠ EGIR-*pa* SIG5-*aḫ-ḫa-an-zi* "the gods will relieve the unpleasant thing which is in my mind" KUB 6.45 iii 45-47 (Muw. prayer).

d. to rectify, redress (a wrong, misdeed): "If some people are giving (away?) orphaned children, [...] and he appealed to Šarruma, and Š. ap[pealed] to the Stormgod, [...]" *nat* [EG]IR-*pa* SIG5-*aḫ-ḫa-an-zi* "they will make it right again" KBo 11.1 rev. 3-5 (Muw. prayer), ed. Houwink ten Cate, RHA XXV/81:109, 118, 126; [*nu mā*]*n kēzza kuwatqa uddānaz akkiškittari nat kuitman* [EGIR-*p*]*a* SIG5-*aḫ-ḫi-iš-ki-mi* "[I]f it is because of this matter that people are dying, then while I am in the process of rectifying it (let them not die any more)" KUB 14.8 rev. 38-39 (2nd plague prayer of Murš. II §11), ed. Götze, KlF 1:218f.; "If something is troubling a slave, he makes an appeal to his master, and his master hears him and has p[ity] on him" *kuit nakkiyaḫḫan natši* SIG5-*aḫ-zi* "and rectifies whatever was troubling him" KUB 14.8 rev. 23-25 (2nd plague prayer of Murš. II), ed. ibid. 216f.; "[Let] that deity [reveal] to us tha[t sin(?)] by means of a prophet or a [...], and we will begin to [...]" *nat* SIG5-*aḫ-ḫu-ni* "and we will redress it (the wrong)" 1691/u ii 16-18 (prayer of Arnuwanda and Ašmunikal, MH); *ANA* DINGIR-*LIM kuiēš waškuiēš* SI×SÁ-*antat naš* EGIR-*pa* SIG5-*ia-aḫ-ḫi-ir* "They rectified whatever wrongs against the deity were indicated by oracle" KUB 5.6 i 38 (extispicy, NH); cf. i 8; KUB 6.10:7f.; KUB 18.18 rev. 22f.

2. to show favor to (someone): *nuza parā kuinki kuedanikki wiyami apāšman* SIG5-*aḫ-ḫi apāšma* KA×U-*iš duwarnāi nušši* INIM.MEŠ LUGAL *parā memai* "(If) I send A to B, and B shows favor to A, so that A breaks confidence and blurts out to him the words of the king" KUB 26.1 iii 62-65 (instr., NH), ed. Dienstanw. 14; *n*[*ašm*]*a* dUTU-*ŠI kuinki* SIG5-*aḫ-mi* "Or (if) I, His Majesty, show favor to someone" KUB 26.12 iii 21 (instr., NH), ed. Dienstanw. 26 with discussion on p. 31.

3. to give a favorable sign or portent: "Next they go into the city; but they take observations by means of bird(s)," *nu kuwapi* MUŠEN.ḪI.A SIG5-*aḫ-ḫa-an-zi* "and when the birds give a favorable sign, (they go into the city)" VBoT 24 ii 23-26 (rit. of Anniwiyani, NH), ed. Chrest. 110ff.

4. to perfume or scent(?) (a substance): "On the second day (s)he takes these [ingred]ients: ..." *nat anda tarnāi nammat kīnaizzi pūwāizzi* SIG5-*aḫ-zi* "(s)he combines them, *k.*'s them, grinds them, and perfumes(?) (them) (and pours them into a leather container)" KUB 44.64 ii 5-15 (med. rit.), cf. i 4-14, ed. StBoT 19:49 (no translation);

"these herbs (s)he takes: ..." *nat anda* [*tarnai nammat*?] *kināizzi* SIG₅-*aḫ-zi nu* UN-*an kuit* [*AŠRA*?] *auliš ḫarzi nan apat AŠRA* [...] *anda ḫanišezzi* "... she makes (the salve) aromatic and plasters it on the place where the *a.*-ailment was afflicting (lit. 'holding') the man" KBo 21.74 iii 7-9 (med. rit.), ed. StBoT 19:26f., here with translation "macht es gut", although in index on p. 81 "in Ordnung bringen" is given for both passages; SIG₅-*an-ta-an* (**lazziyaḫḫantan*?) GEŠTIN-*an* "scented/perfumed/resinated(?) wine" KBo 3.34 (BoTU 12A) ii 3.

One cannot be sure about the attribution of the above passages to *lazziyaḫḫ-*, but the spellings SIG₅-*yaḫḫir* and SIG₅-*yaḫḫan* (cf. morphology) indicate that the stem ended in *-yaḫḫ-*, and the semantic similarities with *lazziya-* are sufficient to make our attribution probable.

Friedrich, HW (1952) 292 sub SIG₅-*aḫḫ-*.

Cf. *lazzi-*.

laznaššakit (mng. unkn.); MH/NS.†

nukan GEŠTIN [...] BAL-*ti natkan la*!(coll.)-*az-na-aš-*⌜*ša-ki*⌝*-it* [... *-p*]*í*(?)*-ia aranšzi* VBoT 16 rev.? 4-6 (rit.).

lē adv.; (strong negative, usually expressing negative wish or command); from OH/OS.

Akk. ⌜*la*⌝[*-a te*]*pperekkianni la-a inūma* LUGAL *kīam iqab*[*bišum*] KUB 1.16 iii 64-67 = Hitt. *le-e-ma-mu-uš-ša-an paškuitta le-e-ma-an-še* [LUG]AL-*uš kiššan tezzi* "Don't reject me! May the King not have to speak thus about her!" KUB 1.16 iv 65-68 (Ḫatt. I edict, OH/NS), ed. Sommer, HAB 16-17, 189-91, cf. below usage b; Akk. *ē tašām* [*alp*]*a* [*ina pān šatt*]*i* (var. *-n*]*a*?*-ti-i ša-a-t*[*i*]) *ē tāḫuz a*[*r*]*d*[*a*]*ta ina i*[*sinni*] (var. *i-na i-*[*si*]*-in₄-ni*) RŠ 22.439 iii 10-11 with dupl. KUB 4.3 obv. 12a-13a = Hitt. *ḫamešḫiza* (coll., AU 391) GUD-*un le-e wašti karšantinmaza gallištarwanili* <*le*>*-e* <<*da*>> *da-at-ti* "Don't buy a cow in the spring! Don't take (in marriage) a young woman in festal attire!" KUB 4.3 obv. 12b-13b (NH); one LI was omitted (haplography) and one DA added (dittography) in the Hittite; Akk. ed. Nougayrol, Ugar. V:279, 282, 289, Hitt. ed. Laroche, ibid. 781, 783.

a. with pres.-fut. — **1′** sg. 1: ⌜*eḫ*⌝*uwa it kuwapiwa paiši ammukmawatta* ⌜*l*⌝*e-e šaggaḫḫi* "Go! And I don't want to know where you go!" KBo 5.9 ii 43-45 (Dupp.), ed. SV 1:18f., cf. sim. KUB 6.50 iii? 4-5 (Kup.), ed. SV 1:148, KUB 21.1 iii 54-55 (Alakš.), ed. SV 2:74f.; [...] *iyandu* DINGIR.MEŠ *nu le-e-pát zaluganumi* "Let the gods make [...]; I don't want to cause delay!" KUB 21.38 i 37 (letter of Puduḫepa), ed. Helck, JCS 17:90.

2′ sg. 2 — **a′** in OH: *ANA* É.EN.NU.UN *le-e daitti idaluman le-e iyaši ḫenkanše le-e takkišši* "Don't put him in prison, harm him, or execute him!" KBo 3.28(= BoTU 10γ):14-15 (OH/NS).

b′ in MH: [UR.G]I₇-*aš wappiyazi* ŠAḪ-*aš ḫuntarnuzzi* [*nu* DIN]GIR-*LAM le-e kuēlqa ištamašti* "[The do]g barks, the pig grunts. [O g]od, don't listen to (the sound) of either!" KBo 12.96 i 12-13 (rit., MH/NS), cf. StBoT 5:105 for restorations.

c′ in NH: *dannamanza* (var. *dannamaza*) *le-e ilaliyaši UL-at a-a-ra* "Don't desire to take her (sexually)! It is not permitted." KBo 19.44 rev. 26 with dupl. KBo 5.3 iii 38 (Ḫuqq.), ed. SV 2:126f.; "The lords said to me: The year has become too short for you" *nuwa BĒLINI INA* ᵁᴿᵁ*Ḫayaša le-e pāiši* "Our lord, don't go to the city of Ḫayaša!" KBo 4.4 iii 24-25, ed. AM 124-27; "Regarding the land which I gave you, Ulmi-Tešub: the boundaries which I set" *našza paḫši le-e-aš-kán šaratti* "guard them, do not transgress them!" KBo 4.10 obv. 15 (treaty of Ḫatt. III/Tudḫ. IV with Ulmi-Tešub).

3′ sg. 3 — **a′** in OH: *nu* ᴸᵁ*ḫippari ḫāp⸗par le-e* [*k*]*uiški izzi* DUMU-*ŠU* A.ŠÀ-*ŠU* ᴳᴵˢKIRI₆.GEŠTIN-*ŠU le-e kuiški wāši* "No one may do business with a *ḫ.*- person; no one may buy his child, his field (or) his vineyard!" KBo 6.2 ii 49-50 (Laws §48, OH/OS); "If (the cuckolded husband) brings (his wife and her lover) to the palace gate and says," DAM-*TI le-e aki* "Let my wife not be executed!" KBo 6.26 iv 10-11 (Laws §198, OH/NS); also in missing god myths of OH tradition, but not OS, e.g. KUB 33.8 iii (2), 5, (13), KUB 33.54 ii 12, KUB 33.49 ii 5; also in KBo 17.1 iii 13, iv 3 (rit., OH/OS), ed. StBoT 8:30f., 34f.

b′ in MH: *parāmaškan le-e kuiški tarnai* GUD.ḪI.A-*yašmaš* UDU.ḪI.A *le-e kuiški appatriyazi natkan ḫumantaza arawēš ašandu* "Let no one sell them (as slaves)! Let no one commandeer their livestock! Let them be exempted from all (these duties)!" KUB 13.8:9-11 (decree regarding stone-house personnel, MH/NS), ed. HTR 106f.; "As from ancient times in the lands the procedure for cases of *ḫurkil* was followed: in whatever town they killed them, let them kill them, in whatever town they banished them, let them banish them! Afterwards the town should bathe, and it should be proclaimed" *naššan* EGIR-*pa le-e kuiški tarnai* "(that) no one should let them back (into the town)" KUB 13.2 iii 15-16 (Bel Madg. instr., MH?/NS), ed. Dienstanw. 47, cf. also Hoffner, AOAT 22 (1973) 85; cf. also KBo 6.34 + KUB 48.76 iii 42-45 (Soldiers' Oath, MH?/NS), ed. StBoT 22:14f.; KUB 15.34 i 42-43 (evocatio, MH/NS); note word order in: *našta š[uḫḫa warḫ]ui zappiyattari le-*⌈*e*⌉ "A roof (which is) weed-grown will leak. Let it not be (so)!" KUB 31.86 ii 17-18 (Bel Madg. instr., MH/NS), ed. Dienstanw. 43, 54, cf. parallel KUB 31.89 ii 7: *šuḫḫa le-e warḫūi zappiya[ttari]* "Let the roof not be weed-grown! It will leak." Hoffner, JCS 29:152 with notes 3 and 6; cf. usage d (nominal sentence).

c′ in NH: "Whoever in the future takes the descendants of Ḫattušili and Puduḫepa from the service of Ištar . . . , let him be the opponent-at-law to Ištar of Šamuḫa!" *šaḫḫaniyaš luzzi le-e kuiški epz[(i)]* "Let no one seize them for *š*.- and *l*.-obligations!" KUB 1.1 iv 81-85 with dupl. KUB 1.3:1-7 (Ḫatt. III); cf. also KUB 23.1 iv 12-17 (treaty of Tudḫ. IV); KUB 26.58 obv. 12-13 (Ḫatt. III decree); "The man in whose watch the desecration occurs" *naš aku le-e-ia-aš-kán weḫtari* "he must die! He may not be pardoned" KUB 13.4 iii 19-20 (instr., pre-NH/NS).

4′ pl. 1: [. . .] *le-e ú-me-e-ni na[mma . . .] le-e ištamaš[šueni?]* "we must not see [. . . we?] must not hear [. . .]" KUB 40.28:4-5 (treaty, MH/NS?), ed. Kühne, ZA 62:252f.

5′ pl. 2: — **a′** in OH: "The king said to his wife and sisters," *itten azzikatten akkuškatten* LUGAL-*waša šākuwamet le-e ušteni* "Go. Eat (and) drink. But you must not see my, (i.e.) the king's, eyes." KBo 3.28(=BoTU 10γ):7-9 (edict, OH/NS).

b′ in MH — **1″** with *-tani* form: KUB 23.72 rev. 53-55a (Mita, MH/MS); KBo 8.37 rev. 4, 6 (treaty); **2″** with *-teni* form: KUB 23.77:49 (treaty), ed. von Schuler, Kašk. 120; KUB 23.77a rev. 12 (treaty); 1684/u (JCS 28:61) + KUB 23.72 obv. 42, rev. 62 (Mita).

6′ pl. 3: *našta* (var. *napa*) *l[(e-e)] āššawēš idālauwaš anda ḫarkanzi* "Let not the good people perish together with the bad!" KUB 24.3 ii 55-56 (prayer of Murš. II), with older dupl. KUB 24.4 + KUB 30.12 rev. 11, note the unusual position of *lē* in the word order.

b. *lē* and potential *ma-an* with pres.-fut., conveying the sense of an optative (cf. Lat. *utinam ne*): *le-e-ma-an-še* [LUG]AL-*uš kiššan tezzi* KUB 1.16 iv 65-66 (OH/NS), cited fully with translation above in bil. sec.; *A-BU-IA-ma-an-wa-kán* SAL. LUGAL-*ya le-e ḫannetalwaneš am-mu-uq-qa-ma-an-wa le-e kuitki* ḪUL-*uešzi . . . le-e-ma-an-wa-mu kuitki* ḪUL-*uešzi* "I wish that my father and the queen would not be opponents-at-law. O that it would not do me any harm! . . . O that it would not do me any harm!" KUB 31.66 iii 5-8, 19 (NH); discussion of usage by Sommer, HAB 189, cf. Friedrich, HE 2 §280b, and Güterbock, OrNS 12:154.

c. with imp. (all exx. OH): *le-e-wa-at-ta naḫi* "Don't be afraid!" KUB 33.24 i 43 (myth, OH/NS), ed. Laroche, Myth 55; cf. also KUB 30.36 ii 8, KUB 30.33 obv. 15; *le-e ḫandānpat ēšdu* KUB 1.16 ii 50, 55; *nutta* LÚ.MEŠ ŠU.GI ^{URU}KÙ.BABBAR-*ti le-e memiškandu* "Let not the elders of Ḫatti keep on speaking to you" ibid. 60 (testament of Ḫatt. I, OH/NS), both discussed by Sommer, HAB 91f., also Sommer, OLZ 1939:683f.

d. in nominal sentences (from OH): "If among my subjects someone mentions th[eir] name(s)" ÌR-*miš le-e* "let him not be my subject!" KBo 3.27 obv. 10-11 (edict of Ḫatt. I, OH/NS); possibly in KUB 31.127 + ABoT 44 iv 7 (prayer, OH/NS); *ANA* LÚ.MEŠ ^{URU}*Mirāmawaza [anda le]-*⌈*e*⌉ *weriyanza* "Don't let yourself be involved with(?) the men of Mira!" KUB 14.15 iv 48-49, ed. AM 74f.; *[nuwaza] ANA* LUGAL KUR *Ḫatti [k]uwapi kurur nuwaza damedaza* KUR-*eza kurur ēš ammetazamawazakan* KUR-*eza arḫa le-e kurur* "When you make war against the Hittite king, make war from some other country! But don't make war from my country!" KUB 14.3 iv 3-5 (Taw. letter), ed. Sommer, AU 16f.; also in

KBo 4.10 obv. 35 (treaty); *šuḫḫa le-e warḫūi* cf. section a 3′ b′.

e. as a categorical negative: "In a meadow there stands a *šišiyamma*-tree. Beneath it sit a blind man and a deaf man." *tašwanza aušzi le-e duddumiyanzama ištamašzi le-e ikniyanza pid⸗dai le-e* UḪ$_x$.ḪI.A-*ašša uddananteš* EN.SISKUR *QATAMMA le-e uwanzi* "Does the blind man see? Absolutely not! (lit. 'Let it not be!') Does the deaf man hear? Absolutely not! Does the lame man run? Absolutely not! In the same way let the words of sorcery not see the man for whom this ritual is performed!" KUB 12.62 + 1696/u (ZA 63:87f.) rev. 7-10 (rit., pre-NH); on the use of *lē* after rhetorical questions as a form of categorical negation see Hoffner, JCS 29:151f.

Hrozný, SH (1917) 92 n. 4, 184; JSOR 6 (1922) 69 n. 1; Sommer, HAB (1938) 91 with n. 3, 189; Hoffner, JCS 29 (1977) 151f.

[*liḫaya-*] in KUB 5.1 ii 17 is probably to be read ⸢URU!⸣*Li-ḫa-ia-*. See under *laḫḫiyai-* 2 a.

liḫša[. . .] n.; bison; NH.†

In a lexical text: Sum. ALIM = Akk. *kar-ša-nu* = Hitt. *ti-ša-nu-u*[*š*], ALIM = *ku-ša-ri-iḫ-ḫu* = *li-iḫ-ša*-x[. . .] KBo 1.52 i 11-12, ed. MSL 3:64; the trace and space in 12 allow for -*a*[*š*], -*n*[*a-aš*], or -*n*[*u-uš*]; cf. [. . .]x(-)*li-iḫ-ša*[- . . .] KBo 14.21 i 2 (oracle, NH).

lila- A n. com.; conciliation, pacification; from MH.

sg. acc. *li-la-an* KUB 39.45 obv. 1 (MH?/NS); **gen.** *le-e-la-aš* KUB 9.15 ii 24 (NH), KBo 2.8 i 15 (NH), IBoT 2.106 i (8); *li-la-aš* KBo 2.1 i 43, iv 8, KUB 31.53 obv. 9, IBoT 2.23:3 (all NH); **all.** *li-i-la* KUB 46.38 ii 24 (NH); **Luw. abl.** [*l*]*i*(coll.)-*la-ti* KUB 39.12:9.

a. with EZEN or É: EZEN *le*(-*e*)-*la-aš* "the festival of conciliation" KBo 2.1 i 43, iv 8, KBo 2.8 i 15, IBoT 2.106:(8) (all cult inv., NH); KUB 31.53 obv. 9 (Pud. vow, NH), ed. StBoT 1:20f.; *nan INA* É *li-la-aš ped*[*anzi*?] "They carry him (or it) to the house of conciliation" IBoT 2.23:3 (fest., NH).

b. *naš li-i-la pedanzi naš līlanti*[. . .] "They carry them (two deities) to the conciliation (house?) and they conciliate them" KUB 46.38 ii 24 (rit., NH), cf. also *lilai-* v., 1; *INA* UD.6.KAM *li-la-an anda appanz*[*i*] "On the sixth day they include the conciliation" KUB 39.45 obv. 1 (outline of royal funeral rit., MH?/NS), ed. Otten, WO 2:477f.; cf. KUB 30.27 obv. 1, KUB 39.12:10 and KUB 39.41 obv. 14 with *lilauwar . . . anda appanzi*; [. . . *l*]*i*(coll.)-*la-ti ḫandan* KUB 39.12:9; *mānma le-e-la-aš* UD.KAM.ḪI.A *kišandari* "When the days of conciliation arrive" KUB 9.15 ii 24 (instr., NH).

c. in personal names: ᵐ*Li-la*-⸢UR.MAḪ⸣ KUB 7.20 rev. 6 (also ᵐ*Li-la*-PIRÌG KUB 25.25 left edge 5b and ᵐ*Li*-<*la*?->PIRÌG KUB 13.32 left edge 1).

The translations are based on the assumption that the action of *lilai-* "conciliate, pacify; heal, renew" is performed during the festival and in the house designated by the genitive *le*/*ilaš*. The "days of *lilaš*" are probably those of the EZEN *lilaš*.

Laroche, RA 43 (1949) 69; Otten, WO 2 (1959) 478; Szabó, THeth 1 (1971) 50f.

Cf. *lilai-* and *lilarešk-*.

lela B n. see *leli* A n.

lilaḫuwa- v.; to pour; OH or MH/MS.†

(He holds out baked-clay cups to the priests) [. . . (-)]*nuwašmaš li-la-ḫu-i* "(s)he pours [. . .] into their [. . .]" KBo 21.47 ii 13 (rit.); cf. *la-a-ḫu-i* in ii 16.

Perhaps an unusual spelling or a different ablaut grade of *lilḫuwa-*, q.v.

Cf. *laḫ*(*ḫ*)*uwai-*.

(:)lilai- v.; **1.** to conciliate, pacify; **2.** to soothe, assuage; from OH.

pres. pl. 3 *li-la-a-an-zi* KBo 15.10 i 1, ii 69 (MH/MS); *li-la-an-zi* KUB 39.6 ii 2 (MH?/NS); :*li-la-an-zi* KUB 30.27 obv. 10 (MH?/NS); **Luw. pres. pl. 3** *li-i-la-an-ti* KUB 46.38 ii 24 (NH); *li-la-an-t*[*i*] KUB 17.32 i 19 (NH).

pret. sg. 3 *li-la-a-it* KUB 41.19 obv. 17 (MH/NS).

imp. sg. 3 *le-e-la-ad-d*[*u*] KUB 41.19 obv. 12 (MH/NS); **pl. 3** *li-i-la-an-du* KBo 20.56 obv.? 6 (NH) in Luw. context.

verb. subst. nom.-acc. *li-la-u-wa-ar* KUB 30.27 obv. 1 (MH?/NS), KUB 39.12 rev. (10); **gen.** *li-la-u-wa-aš* KUB 30.42 i 1 (NH); **inf.** *li-la-u-wa-an-zi* KUB 39.12 rev. 17,

(18) (MH?/NS), KUB 12.26 i 9 (NH).

iter. imp. pl. 2 *li-li-iš/eš-ki-it-ten* KUB 29.1 ii 17, 18 (OH/NS).

1. to conciliate, pacify: [*mā*]*n išḫanāš* ^{d}UTU-*un* ^{d}IM-*na* ⌈EGIR⌉-*pa li-la-a-an-zi* "When they conciliate the Sungod of blood and the Stormgod" KBo 15.10 i 1, see ii 69 (rit., MH/MS), ed. THeth 1:12f; "In case the bones must be brought from a distant land, during the days of *mukeššar* they give sacrifices for him daily as follows" IGI-*ziyan* UD.KAM-*ti kuwapi :li-la-an-zi* "On the first day, when they pacify him (the deceased)," (sheep are offered to the deities of heaven and the netherworld) KUB 30.27 obv. 7-10 (royal funeral rit., MH?/NS), ed. Otten, HTR 98f.; in similar context see fragmentary and obscure KUB 39.12:8, ed. HTR 70f.; *naš līla pedanzi naš li-i-la-an-ti*[...] "They carry them (two deities) to the conciliation (house?) and conciliate them" KUB 46.38 ii 24 (rit., NH), cf. KUB 17.32 i 19; *li-la-u-wa-ar-*⌈*ra anda appanzi*⌉ "They include the pacification (ritual)" KUB 30.27 obv. 1 (outline of funeral rit., MH?/NS), ed. HTR 98f.; reading follows KUB 39.12:10 and KUB 39.41 obv. 14; see KUB 39.45 obv. 1 under *lila-* section b; [*akkantaš*?] *šienan li-la-u-wa-an-zi ḫarkir* "They held an image [of the deceased(?)] in order to pacify (him)" KUB 39.12:17 (royal funeral rit., MH?/NS), ed. HTR 70f.; DUB.1.KAM SÌR *li-la-u-wa-aš ŠA* LÚ.MEŠ ^{URU}*Ištanuwa* "One tablet: the song of conciliation of the men of Ištanuwa" KUB 30.42 i 1 (shelf list, NH), ed. CTH p. 161f.

2. to soothe, assuage: (A glassware bowl of figs is placed before a group of female weavers and a pottery[?] bowl of raisins and *ḫašigga* is placed before a group of male weavers and someone says) LUGAL-*unwa li-li-iš-ki-it-ten*! § *šākuwaššet li-le-eš-ki-it-ten* (var. [*l*]*i-li-iš-ki-it*<*-ten*>) "Soothe the king! Soothe his eyes! (Take sickness from him!)" KUB 29.1 ii 17-18 with dupl. KUB 29.2 ii 9-10 (foundation rit., OH/NS), tr. Goetze in ANET 357.

The basic meaning of *lilai-* is to remove anger, hostility, or pain, which impedes proper functioning. With adverb *appa* KBo 15.10 i 1, ii 69; KUB 12.26 i 9 it means to restore to such functioning. The more specific translations offered above reflect the causes of the disability or disfunction. The verb is derived from the noun *lila-*, which may refer to an object (see *lila-* usage b). In view of this, as well as the use of *ḫimma-* "image" and *šena-* "figurine" in KUB 39.12 and the importance of model tongues in KBo 15.10, it is possible that *anda ep-* (*lilai-* mng. 1, *lila-* usage b 2′) may mean "hold against" rather than "include."

Goetze in ANET 357 ("soothe"); Otten in Bossert, WO 2 (1957) 352 n. 1; Otten, HTR (1958) 143, OLZ 1963:253 ("entsühnen"); van Brock, RHA XXII/75 (1964) 141f. ("délivrer, purifier"); Güterbock, JAOS 88 (1968) 68 and n. 12 ("appease, propitiate"); Kronasser, EHS 478, 509, 571; Szabó, THeth 1 (1971) 48-51, 85 ("entsühnen, versöhnen").

Cf. *lila-* A.

[*lilaimmi-*] KUB 46.18 rev.? 6 reads ^{d}LAMMA *šar-la-im-mi-in* after collation.

lilak- v.; to fell, cut down; pre-NH/NS.†

"He who habitually vindicates honest men" *ḫūwappaš*[*ak*]*an* LÚ.MEŠ-*uš* [(GIŠ-*ru*)] *mān li-la-ak-ki* "who repeatedly fells evil men like trees, (who continually strikes evil men on their skulls like *šakšakiluš*, and destroys them)" KUB 24.8 i 2-6 with dupl. KBo 7.18:1-4 (tale of Appu), ed. StBoT 14:4f.

Friedrich, ZA 49 (1950) 242; Laroche, OLZ 1955:225; van Brock, RHA XXII/75 (1964) 130 and 145 ("maintenir ployé ... ployer de façon définitive"); Hoffner in Goedicke and Roberts eds., Unity and Diversity (Baltimore, 1975) 139-40 with n. 34 (for repeated action).

Cf. *laknu-* mng. 2.

lelaniya- v.; **1.** (mid.) to become furious, become enraged, **2.** (part.) furious, enraged; OH.†

mid. pres. sg. 3 *le-e-*[*l*]*a-ni-at-ta* KBo 6.2 ii 14, with Hrozný, CH plate V (OH/OS); **pret. sg. 3** [*le-e-la*]*-ni-e-et-ta-at* KUB 33.10 obv. 9 (OH/MS), [*le-e-l*]*a-ni-it-ta-a*[*t*] ibid. obv. 15, *le-e-l*[*a-*...] KUB 33.8 ii 12 (OH/NS).

part. sg. nom. com. *le-e-la-ni-ia-an-za* KUB 17.10 ii 33, iv (4) (OH/MS), *li-la-ni-ia-a*[*n-za*] KBo 12.78:4 (OH/NS?), *li-la-ni-i*[*a-an-za*] KUB 33.46 i 8 (OH/NS?).

1. (mid.) become furious, become enraged — **a.** said of people: *takku ḫannešnaš išḫāš le-e-*[*l*]*a-ni-at-ta* [*n*]*u* ^{LÚ}*šardian w*[*alḫzi*] "If the adversary in court becomes enraged and strikes the helper" KBo 6.2 ii 14, with Hrozný, CH plate V (Laws § 38, OS); later copy: *našta* [*ḫanni*]*ttalwas* *kar-tim-mi-ya-*<<*an*>>*-ta-ri nu šardiyan walḫ-z[i* . . .] "the adversary in court becomes angry and strikes the helper" KBo 6.3 ii 32-33.

b. said of gods: [*nuwa* ^{d}*T*]*elipinu*[*š le-e-l*]*a-ni-it-ta-a*[*t*] "Telipinu became furious" KUB 33.10 obv. 15 (Tel.myth, OH/MS), rest. by par. KUB 33.8 ii 12, cf. KUB 33.10 obv. 9.

2. (part.) furious, enraged: ^{d}*Telepinuš le-e-la-ni-ia-an-za uit* "Furious, Telepinu came" KUB 17.10 ii 33 (Tel.myth, OH/MS); ^{d}IM-*aš le-e-la-ni-ia-a*[*n*]*-za uizzi* "Furious, the Stormgod comes" ibid. iv 4; cf. KBo 12.78:4 and KUB 33.46 i 8 (missing god, DINGIR.MAḪ version).

Güterbock, FsFriedrich (1959) 210 n. 5.

lilarešk- v.; **1.** to conciliate, pacify, appease, placate, **2.** to soothe, relieve, assuage; from OH; occurs only in the iterative.†

pres. pl. 1 *li-la-a-ri-iš-ki-wa-n*[*i*] KBo 15.10 i 22 (MH/MS); [*l*]*i-la-ri-iš-ki-wa*!*-ni* ibid. i 27.

imp. sg. 3 *li-la-re-eš*[*-ki-id-du*] KUB 33.38 i 4 (OH/MS); [*li-la-*]*-a*!*-re-eš-ki-id-du* HT 100:8 (OH/NS), *l*[*i-la-re*]*-eš-ki-id-du* KUB 33.74 i 9 (OH/NS).

1. to conciliate, pacify: [*q*]*āša išḫanaš* ^{d}UTU-*un* ^{d}IM-*anna* EGIR-*pa li-la-a-ri-iš-ki-wa-n*[*i*] "Behold, we are about to conciliate the Sungod of blood and the Stormgod" KBo 15.10 i 22 (rit., MH/MS), ed. THeth 1:16f., cf. ibid. i 1 under (:)*lilai-* mng. 1; (with *arḫa*) to placate, propitiate: *natkan ANA BĒLI QADU* DAM-*ŠU* DUMU.MEŠ-*ŠU arḫa* [*l*]*i-la-ri-iš-ki-wa*!*-ni* "We will placate (those 'tongues' which Ziplantawiya has devised) against the lord (Tudḫaliya) as well as against his wife and children" KBo 15.10 i 26-27 (rit., MH/MS), ed. Szabó, THeth 1:16f.

2. to soothe, relieve, assuage: "Behold ^{GIŠ}*leti-* (an oil-producing plant) is lying here for you" *nu ŠA* DINGIR-*LIM* [ZI-*KA karat*]*iešša* NÍ.TE.MEŠ-*uš l*[*i-la-re*]*-*⸢*eš*⸣*-ki-id-du* "O god, let it soothe [your soul] and (your) *k.*'s (and your) limbs!" KUB 33.74 i 8-9 (rit. portion of missing god myth, OH/NS).

lilarešk- is apparently identical in meaning with *lilišk-*, although derived from a longer stem than *lilai-*. The *-r*(*e*)*-* element is unexplained. Güterbock, JAOS 88 (1968) 68 and n. 12.

Cf. *lila-* A, *lilai-* v.

lilḫuwai- v.; to pour out (liquids: water, oil, and wine); from MH.†

pres. sg. 3 *le-el-ḫu-wa-i* KBo 12.112 rev. 3 (MH?/NS) (or imp. sg. 2); *le-el-ḫu-u-wa-i* KBo 15.52 i 5, KBo 15.37 v 11 (MH/NS); [*le*]*-*⸢*el-ḫu-wa*⸣*-a-i* KUB 45.5 ii 21; *li-il-ḫu-wa-i* VBoT 1(= EA 31):14 (MH) (or imp. sg. 2); **pl. 3** *le-e-el-ḫu-an-zi* KUB 32.121 ii 36.

imp. sg. 2 (cf. under pres. sg. 3); **pl. 3** [*l*]*e-el-ḫu-wa-an-du* KBo 23.65:6; **iter. sup.** *li-il-ḫu-uš-ki-w*[*a-an*] KUB 29.48 rev. 18 (MH). The spellings with *li-il-* seem to be older than those with *le-el-*.

a. pouring oil on a bride's head: "I have sent to you Iršappa, my envoy, that we may look upon your daughter whom they will conduct to My Majesty to be (my) wife" *nušši li-il-ḫu-wa-i* Ì-*an* SAG.DU-*ši* "He will pour (or: Pour [imp.]) oil on her head" VBoT 1(= EA 31):11-14 (letter from Amenophis III to king of Arzawa, MH); cf. KBo 12:112 rev. 1-3 with SAG.DU-*SÚ* in line 1, ed. Beckman, Diss. (1977) 83, 85.

b. pouring water: [*nu u*]*wanzi wātar li-il-ḫu-uš-ki-w*[*a-an tianzi na*]*n katkattinuwanzi damešša*[*nziyan*] "[They begin] to pour water (on the horse), they make it tremble [and] restrain(?) [it]" KUB 29.48 iii 18-19 (hipp., MH), ed. Kammenhuber, Hipp.heth. 164f. (lines 39-40).

c. pouring wine from a pitcher: *našta* ^{LÚ}SAGI.A *namma* ^{DUG}[*ḫaniššaz* GEŠTIN] *le-el-ḫu-u-wa-i* "the cupbearer again pours [wine from] a p[itcher]" KBo 15.52 i 4-5 (*ḫišuwaš* fest., MH/NS) and [*n*]*ašta* ^{LÚ}SAGI.A ^{DUG}*ḫāniš-šazpat* [GEŠTIN *le-e*]*l-ḫu-wa-i* KBo 15.69 i 20-21 (*ḫišuwaš* fest.), restoring each other; cf. *nukan* ^{LÚ}SAGI.A ^{DUG}*ḫāniššaza* GEŠTIN *la*[*-a-ḫu-i*] KBo 15.69 i 13; ^{LÚ}SANGA-*makan IŠTU* GÌR.GÁN KÙ.BABBAR GEŠTIN *ḫaniškizzipat* (var. *ḫānieškizzipat*) *naššan katta damēdaš* (var. *tamēdaš*) *ANA* GAL.ḪI.A *le-el-ḫu-u-wa-i* (same in dupl.) "The priest keeps dipping up wine from a silver bowl and pouring it out into other cups" KBo 15.37 v 8-11 (*ḫišuwaš* fest., MH/NS), with dupl. KBo 25.172 iv 5-8 (NS).

d. pouring wine and oil from a ^{DUG}LIŠ.GAL: [*nuš*]*šan* ^{LÚ}AZU GEŠTIN-*an* Ì.DÙG.GA-*ia IŠ*!*-TU* $^{[DUG]}$LIŠ.GAL [. . . *le-*]*el-ḫu-wa-a-i* *našta* DINGIR-*LUM* GÌR.MEŠ-*ŠU arri* "The AZU priest [p]ours out wine and fine oil from a LIŠ.GAL and washes therewith the deity's feet" KUB 45.5 ii 20-21 (Hurr. rit. for Ḫebat's throne).

Friedrich, JCS 1 (1947) 285; Otten, BiOr 8 (1951) 227 with n. 27; van Brock, RHA XXII/75 (1964) 159 n. 13.

Cf. *laḫ(ḫ)uwai-*.

lelḫuwarti[ma]-, lelḫurtima- n. com.; outpourings(?), inundations(?), mist(?), spray(?); NH.†

le-el-ḫu-wa-ar-ti[-ma-aš?]/[ut-ne]-⌜e⌝ anda kārier § *[arā?]er le-el-ḫu-ur-ti-ma-aš* "The outpourings(?) enveloped [the lan]d. The outpourings(?) [ros]e(?)" (They reached up to the sun and moon. They reached up to the stars.) KBo 26.105 iv? 10-12 (myth); cf. IM.GÚ!.A KUR-*e anda kariyazi* "the flood sediment envelopes the land" KUB 8.35 obv. 11ff.

l. is clearly nom. in 12 and probably also in 10-11. Since it takes pl. verbs, it is either a collective sing. or a nom. pl. in *-aš*. Note the mention of *garittiš* "floods" in line 9′.

Cf. *laḫ(ḫ)uwai-*.

^{DUG}lelḫūndai- n. com.; (a vessel); MH?/NS.†

sg. acc. ^{DUG}*le-el-ḫu-u-un-da-in* KUB 30.19 iv 18 (= KUB 30.19 + KUB 20 iv 23).

Only in royal funeral rit., KUB 30.19 iv 10-12, 17-18 (transcribed in *lelḫunda(i)-* article below). Preserved in iv 23 and probably to be restored in iv 15, 27. The dupl. KUB 39.8 has *lelḫuntallin* in the first and third positions in iv 10, (25). The two words therefore designate the same type of container. It is also possible that the correct reading of KUB 30.19 iv 18 is ^{DUG}*le-el-ḫu-un-da<-li>-in*.

Otten, HTR (1958) 47 n. 3; Laroche, RA 52 (1958) 187.

Cf. *laḫ(ḫ)uwai-*.

lelḫunda(i)- v.; to pour(?) (from a *lelḫundai-* or *lelḫuntalli*-vessel); MH?/NS.†

maḫḫanmakan GE₆-*ti wakšur ā[(šzi) nu* ^{DUG}*le-el-ḫu-u-un-da-in*] (var. ^{DUG}*l*]*e-el-ḫu-un-ta-al-li-in*) *udanzi natšan ḫaššī AN*[(*A PANI* ALAM) *dāi*] *nu le-el-ḫu-u-un-da*(var. *ta*)*-an-zi* ... *maḫḫan le-el-ḫu-u-un-da*(var. *ta*)*-u-wa-an-zi z*[*innanz*(*i*)] *našta* ^{DUG}*le-el-ḫu-u-un-da-in arḫa da*[*nzi*] "But when one *w.*-unit in the night remains, they bring the *l.*-vessel and [place] it on the hearth before the statue, and they pour(?) ... When [they] f[inish] pouring(?), [they] take away the *l.*-vessel" KUB 30.19 iv 10-12, 17-18, ed. HTR 46f. lines 15-17, 22-23, dupl. KUB 39.8 iv 9-12, 17-18.

Otten, HTR (1958) 47 n. 3; Laroche, RA 52 (1958) 187.

Cf. *laḫ(ḫ)uwai-*.

^{DUG}lelḫuntalli- n.; (a vessel); MH?/NS.†

sg. acc. [^{DUG}*l*]*e-el-ḫu-un-ta-al-li-in* KUB 39.8 iv 10; [^{DUG}*le-el-ḫu-un-ta-a*]*l-li-in* ibid. 25; probably ^{DUG}*l*[*e-el-ḫu-un-ta-al-li-in*] ibid. 18.

Tr. of KUB 39.8 iv 9f., 17f. above sub *lelūnda(i)-* v.

Cf. *laḫ(ḫ)uwai-*.

lelḫurtima- see *lelḫuwarti[ma]-*.

[*lili-*] adj.; moving(?) posited by Goetze, Tunn. 93 with n. 371, is probably to be read *šar*!*-li-in*.

leli A, lela n.; (mng. unknown); Hurr. term in MH and NH festivals of Hurr. background, all NS.†

le-e-li KUB 27.1 iv 39, KBo 15.37 ii 42, v 47, KUB 12.12 vi 4, KBo 11.58:(5); *li-li* KBo 21.34 i 22, 47; [... *-l*]*i* KUB 27.10 v 13; *le-e-la* KUB 12.12 vi 36.

Occurs only in the phrase *lēli ḫašari ekuzi* "he drinks (to?) *lēli ḫašari*".

Laroche, Gl.Hourrite (1976) 159.

Cf. *lili-* B, n.

lili- B n.; (mng. unknown); NH.†

sg. gen. *li-li-ia-aš* KUB 48.111:10, 11 + KUB 31.121 i! 19, 20 (Murš. II).

At the end of a list of gods: DINGIR.MEŠ LÚ.MEŠ *li-li-ia-aš ḫūmanteš* DINGIR.MEŠ SAL.MEŠ *li-li-*[*i*]*a-aš ḫūmanteš tuliyaš AŠRU* ⌜*A*⌝*-ŠAR DINI* KUB 48.111:10-11 + KUB 31.121 i! 19-20 (prayer of Murš. II); possibly *li-li-ia-aš* is both times a scribal error for *tu*!*-li-ia-aš*. Otherwise, it might be the same word as discussed sub *lēli* A, *lēla*.

lil(l)ipa(i)- v.; to lick, lick up; from MH.†

pres. sg. 3 *le-el-li-pa-a-i* KUB 8.67:20 (MH/NS); **Luw. pl. 3** *li-li-pa-an-ti* KBo 11.14 i 21 (MH/NS); **iter. imp. sg. 3** *li-li-pa-iš-ki-id-du* ibid. i 22; *li-li-pa-aš-ki-id-du* KUB 43.57 i 23 (MH/NS).

[(M)]UN (var. MUN-*an*) GIM-*an* UDU.ḪI.A *li-li-pa-an-ti nu uiddu kūš ḫūkmauš* ᵈUTU-*uš QĀTAMMA li-li-pa-iš*(var. *aš*)-*ki-id-du* "Just as sheep lick salt, in the same way let the Sungod come (and) lick up these spells!" KBo 11.14 i 21f. (Ḫantitaššu rit., MH/NS), dupl. KUB 43.57 i 21-23; "[. . .] eats by the [thou]sands [. . .] swallo[ws] like [hon]ey" [. . . G]IM-*an le-el-li-pa-a-i* "licks up like [. . .]" KUB 8.67:20 (Ḫedammu myth), ed. StBoT 14 (1971) 40f.

Otten, KBo 11 (1961) Inhaltsübersicht to no. 14; van Brock, RHA XXII/75 (1964) 133f.; Hoffner, RHA XXV/80 (1967) 53f. with n. 95, JAOS 87 (1967) 355 (on *lellipāi* in Ḫedammu); Oettinger, StBoT 22 (1976) 31f.

Cf. *lip(p)*-.

liliwaḫḫ- v.; to go quickly, hasten, hurry, fly(?); from MH.†

pret. sg. 3 [*li*]-*li-wa-aḫ-ta* KBo 22.79:5, KUB 36.12 iii 16 (both NH); *li-l*[*i-wa-aḫ-ta*] KUB 33.106 i 34 (NH); **pl. 3** [*l*]*i-li-wa-aḫ-ḫi-ir* KUB 33.102 iii 15, KUB 33.98 iii (6) (both NH).

imp. pl. 2 *li-li-wa-aḫ-ten* KUB 33.98 iii 12, KUB 33.102 iii (22) (both NH); **inf.** *li-li-wa-aḫ-ḫu-wa-an-zi* ABoT 60 rev. 4 (MH/MS); *li-li-wa-aḫ-ḫu-u-an-zi* VBoT 2:11, Maşat 75/10:7, 75/11:12, 75/69:9 (all MH/MS); **iter. act. pret. sg. 3** *li-li-wa-aḫ-ḫe-eš-ki-it* KBo 1.44 i 16 (vocab.).

ù.šir.DI = *iḫ-tám-ṭá-ak-ku* = *li-li-wa-aḫ-ḫe-eš-ki-it-ta* "he kept hurrying to you" KBo 1.44 i 16.

a. used with *nuntarnu-* "to hurry" (NH): *kūn*[*waza* TUR-*an*? *d(a)*]*tten nuwaran* <<*šu*>>*uppe*[(*ššar*)] (var. *uppeššar*) *iyat*[*te(n nuwaran* G)]E₆-*i* KI-*pi petat*[(*t*)*en*] *nuntar-nu*[(*ttenwa li-l*)]*i-wa-aḫ-ten nuwarank*[(*an ANA*)] ᵈ*Upelluri* ZAG-*ni* ᵁᶻᵁZAG.L[(U-*ni* ᴳᴵŠŠ)]U.I *tiyatten* "Take this [child(?)] and treat him as a gift. Carry him to the dark earth. Hurry! Hasten! Put him on Upelluri's right shoulder as a blade(?)" KBo 26.61 + KUB 33.102 iii 20-24 with dupl. KUB 33.98 iii 10-14 (Ullik.), ed. Güterbock, JCS 5:154f., cf. KUB 33.102 iii 15, KUB 36.12 iii 16, KUB 33.106 i 34, ii 28 (restored) (all Ullik.).

b. inf. followed by imperative in letters (all exx. but one are MH): *numukan* ᵈUTU-*ŠI BĒLIYA* ÌR.MEŠ-*K*[*A*] *li-li-wa-aḫ-ḫu-wa-an-zi nai* "Your Majesty, my lord, send your servants to me quickly!" ABoT 60 rev. 3-4, ed. Laroche, RHA XVIII/67:82f.; *numukan* ᵐ*Kalbayan* EGIR-*pa parā IŠTU* LÚ *ṬĒMIYA li-li-wa-aḫ-ḫu-u-an-zi nai* "Send K. back to me quickly with my messenger!" VBoT 2:10-12 (= EA 32), ed. Jakob-Rost, MIO 4:329; cf. KUB 23.103 obv. 8 (Tudḫ. IV), restored by Otten, AfO 19:40-41 with n. 28; *nan MAḪAR* ᵈUTU-*ŠI INA* UD.3.KAM *li-li-wa-aḫ-ḫu-u-an-zi arnutten* Maşat 75/11:10-13; *nu MAḪAR* ᵈUTU-*ŠI li-li-wa-aḫ-ḫu-u-an-zi ūnni* Maşat 75/10:6-7; *nu MAḪAR* ᵈUTU-*ŠI li-li-wa-aḫ-ḫu-u-an-zi ūnništen* Maşat 75/69:8-10; *nan MAḪAR* ᵈUTU-*ŠI li-li-wa-aḫ-ḫu-u-an-zi*! *uwateddu* Maşat 75/45:10-12; all Maşat passages cited without copy from S. Alp, VIII. Türk Tarih Kongresi Bildiriler Kitabı I. Cildi (1978) 177-80.

Friedrich, ZA 35 (1924) 20f.

Cf. *liliwant-*.

liliwant- adj.; **1.** traveling swiftly, flying, winged(?); **2.** urgent(?); from OH.†

sg. nom. com. *li-li-wa-an-za* KBo 3.21 ii 15 (OH?/NS), KUB 4.5 iii 11 (NH), KUB 41.8 ii 8 (MH/NS), KUB 33.33:5 (OH/NS), KBo 10.45 ii (44) (MH/NS); *li-li-wa-az* KUB 33.24 i 26 (OH/NS); **sg. nom. neut.** *li-li-wa-an* KUB 12.65 iii 7, KUB 33.122 iii 4, KUB 33.116 iii? (12) (all MH?/NS); **sg. acc. com.** *le-e-li-wa-an-da-an* KUB 17.10 i 24 (OH/MS), *li-li-wa-an-da-an* KUB 33.24 i 23 (OH/NS), KUB 33.33:(8) (OH/NS), KUB 33.4:(12) (OH/NS); **pl. acc. com.** *li-li-wa-an-du-uš* KUB 17.7 iii 11, KUB 33.96 i 14, KUB 33.106 ii (3), KUB 33.106 + KBo 26.65 i (31), KUB 36.24 ii (6) (all NH).

1. traveling swiftly, flying, winged(?) — **a.** qualifying flying/winged creatures — **1′** the eagle: ᵈUTU-*uš ḫāranan*ᴹᵁŠᴱᴺ *le-e-li-wa-an-da-an IŠPUR* "The Sungod sent the swiftly flying eagle (saying: Go, search the high mountains!)" KUB 17.10 i 23f. (Tel.myth) and passim in missing god myths.

2′ the bee: NIM.LÀL *li-li-wa-an-da-*[*an piet*] "[He/she sent] the swiftly flying bee" (to search for the Stormgod) KUB 33.33:8 (missing god myth), ed. Laroche, Myth 65.

b. qualifying deities: ^d*IŠTAR-iš li-li-wa-an-za našta* ^{URU}*Ninuaz* SUR_x.DÙ.A^{MUŠEN} IGI-*anda* (var. *men[aḫḫand]a*) *pāit* "Ištar is able to fly (or: is winged), she went (i.e., flew) from Nineveh to meet the falcon" KUB 41.8 ii 8-9 with dupl. KBo 10.45 ii 44-45 (rit. for infernal deities), ed. Otten, ZA 54:124f.; note that at Yazılıkaya the goddess Ištar-Šauška is depicted with wings.

c. describing the winds as "winged shoes": ŠU-*za* ^{GIŠ}PA-*an dā I[N]A* [GÌR.MEŠ-]*KA!* (text:-*ŠU*)-*maza* ^{KUŠ}E.SIR.ḪI.A-*uš li-li-wa-an-du-uš* IM.MEŠ *šarku[i]* "Take a staff in your hand! On your [feet] put the winds as winged (or: flying) shoes!" KUB 36.7a iii 40-41 + KUB 17.7 iii 10-11 (Ullik.), ed. Güterbock, JCS 5:154f. and passim in Ullik.; cf. Güterbock, JCS 6:34; cf. also in broken context [^{KUŠ}E.SIR.ḪI.A] *li-li-wa-an-za* IM. MEŠ *šarku* KUB 24.7 iii 65.

2. urgent(?) (qualifying *uttar* "word, matter"): *uddanimawatt[a] kuedani ḫalziššai nuwa uttar li-li-wa-an nuwa ḫūdak eḫu* "The matter about which he calls you is an urgent(?) matter. Come quickly!" KUB 12.65 iii 6-7 (Ḫedammu), with dupl. KUB 33.116 iii 11f. and KUB 33.122 iii 3f.; ed. StBoT 14:50f.

Since *liliwant-* seems to be derived from the same stem as the verb *liliwaḫ-* "to go quickly, hasten", its meaning should be similar. In most cases it describes a being which moves through the air (i.e., flies). It is tempting to translate it "winged" in view of the Yazılıkaya depiction of Ištar-Šauška as winged, the winged shoes of the messenger-god Hermes-Mercury, and the Homeric expression ἔπεα πτερόϝεντα "winged words". It is noteworthy that, like the participles and the adjectives *ḫumant-* and *dapiyant-*, but unlike most other adjectives, *liliwant-* regularly follows the noun which it qualifies.

Goetze, Tunn. (1938) 93 n. 371.

Cf. *liliwaḫḫ-*.

(:)lim(m)a- n. neut.; (a beverage); from OH.†

sg. nom.-acc. *li-im-ma-an* KBo 23.90 i 8 (MH/MS), KUB 27.70 iii 4 (OH/NS), Bo 3158 obv. 14 (KlF 1:138 with n. 5); :*li-im-ma* KBo 4.14 iii 8 (NH); **sg. inst.** *li-im-m[i-it]*

Bo 3158 obv. 18; *li-[mi?]-id-da* KBo 20.34 rev. 6 (cf. *li-i-ma-*x[...] in rev. 3) (OH/MS); **unclear** [...]*li-im-m[a]-a[š]* KUB 12.16 i? 2 (NH?).

a. poured as a libation together with beer, wine: KAŠ GEŠTIN *li-im-ma-an* BAL-*zi* "They pour libations of beer, wine, (and) *l.*" KUB 27.70 iii 4 (fest. of Karaḫna, OH/NS); [...] NINDA.Ì.E.DÉ.A *li[-mi?]-id-da išpanzakizi* "She makes sacrifices with sweet oil cake and *l.*-beverage" KBo 20.34 rev. 6 (Ḫantitaššu rit., OH/MS).

b. drunk: KAŠ-*itmaza* GEŠTIN-*it li-im-m[i-it tawalit] walḫit ninkanteš ēšten* "Be satisfied with beer, wine, *l.*, [*t.*], (and) *w.*" Bo 3158 obv. 18-19, rest. following obv. 14, Ehelolf, KlF 1:138.

c. poured on the ground to make magic circles: [*šum]ašmakan kāš memiyaš gulšan* :*li-im-ma* [o o] *ANA* ^dUTU-*ŠI-za agganaš* TI-*annaš* UN-*aš ēš* "For you(pl.) this word is *l.* which has been used to draw a magic circle. Be(sg.) a person of death (and) life for His Majesty!" KBo 4.14 iii 8-9 (treaty, Šupp. II). □ Magic circles or drawings were occasionally made (verb *gulš-*) with beverages such as beer (KBo 20.34 obv. 12).

Ehelolf, KlF 1 (1930) 138 with n. 5.

link-, linka-? v.; to swear, take an oath; from OH/OS.

pres. sg. 3 *li-ik-zi* KBo 6.2 iv 3 (OH/OS), KBo 3.29:16 (OH/NS), KUB 36.127 rev. 16 (MH/NS), KUB 40.88 iii 17 (NH); *li-in-[⌈]ga[⌉]-zi* KBo 6.3 iii 75 (NS var. to KBo 6.2 iv 3 above; according to photo could be *li-in-[⌈]ik[⌉]-zi*); *li-in-ga-zi* KBo 15.1 ii 7 and KUB 43.76 rev. 5 in broken context not clear if 3 sg. or pl.; **pl. 1** *li-in-ku-e-ni* KUB 31.42 iii 16 (MH/NS); *li-ku-wa-an-ni* HT 1 i 34 (MH/NS), KUB 9.31 i 42 (MH/NS); **pl. 3** *li-in-kán-zi* KUB 17.21 iv 15 (MH/MS).

pret. sg. 1 *li-in-ku-un* KBo 9.73 obv. 3 (OS), KUB 30.10 obv. 12 (MH/MS), KUB 14.3 i 33 (NH); **sg. 3** *li-ik-ta* KBo 9.73 obv. (2) (OS), KUB 14.1 obv. (27) (MH/MS) (contra Götze, Madd., who says sg. 2), KUB 26.32 i 4 (NH); *li-in-ik-ta* KBo 4.3 ii 28 (Murš. II); *li-in-kat-ta* KUB 6.41 iii 52 (Murš. II); *le-en-kat-ta* KUB 21.37 obv. 25 (NH); *li-in-kán*(sic)*-ta* KUB 13.35 i 9 (NH); *li-in-ke-eš-[⌈]ta[⌉]* KUB 14.14 obv. 15 (Murš. II) coll. W.; **pl. 1** *le-en-ga-u-en* HT 1 i 43 (MH/NS); [⌈]*li-in*[⌉]-*ku-u-en* KUB 23.29:8 (NH); **pl. 3** [*li-i]n-ki-ir* KBo 8.35 ii 28 (MH/MS); *li-in-kir* KBo 16.27 ii 3 (MH/MS).

imp. sg. 2 *li-i-ik* KBo 4.14 i 41 (NH); *li-in-ki* KUB 14.3 ii 6 (NH); **sg. 3** *li-ik-du* KBo 4.14 iv 54 (NH); **pl. 2** *le-e-ek-te-en* 942/z rev.? 2 (OH/NS); *li-ik-te-en* KBo

16.27 ii 5 (MH/MS); *le-en-ik-ten* KUB 26.1 iii 54, i 3! (Tudḫ. IV); **pl. 3** *li-in-kán-du* KUB 13.35 i 8 (NH).

part. *li-in-kán-za* KUB 7.41 i 15; *li-in-ga-an* KUB 14.1 obv. 79 (MH/MS); *li-in-kán* KUB 30.45 ii! 15 (NH).

iter. pret. sg. 3 *li-in-ki-iš-ki-it* KUB 14.1 rev. 51 (MH/MS); *li-in-kiš-ki-it* KBo 6.34 iii 14 (MH/NS); **pret. pl. 3** *li-in-ki-iš-ki-ir* KUB 48.110 iii 7 (MH/NS); **imp. pl. 2** *li-in-ki-iš-ki-ten* KUB 13.3 ii 26 (MH/NS).

The forms written *li-in-ga-zi* in themselves are no evidence for a longer stem **linga-*. *le-en-ga-u-en* and *li-in-ke-eš-*⌈*ta*⌉, however, would suggest the existence of a stem *linga-* of the *ḫi*-conjugation (so Götze, KlF 1:181).

a. taking an oath to assure truthfulness of a statement of fact by the oath-taker: "If someone harnesses an ox, horse, mule, or ass and it dies, ... if he says, 'It died by the (hand of) a god,'" *nu li-in-*⌈*ga*⌉*-zi* (photo: *li-in-*⌈*ik*⌉?*-zi*; var. A: *li-ik-zi*, var. B: *li-in-kán-*[*zi*]) "he must take an oath (to that effect)" KBo 6.3 iii 73-75 (Law § 75, OH/NS), ed. Friedrich, HG 42; dupl. A: KBo 6.2 iv 1-3 (OS), dupl. B: KUB 13.13 rev. 1-5 (NS); (If a person is found guilty of harboring a fugitive and cannot give the proper compensation, he must give whatever he has. If, however, he has nothing) [...]*-an li-ik-zi* "he must take an oath" KUB 36.127 rev. 13-16 (treaty with Kizz., MH/NS); (after the Hittite king has recounted events involving persons who dispute his understanding of the situation he asserts) "How these things which I wrote to you [happened]" *nu* LUGAL.GAL *li-in-ku-un* "I, the Great King, have sworn" KUB 14.3 i 32-33 (Taw. letter, NH), ed. Sommer, AU 4f., 69. □ Also in NH depositions, where witnesses must confirm their testimony with oaths KUB 13.35 i 8, 9, KUB 40.88 iii 17 (both depos., NH), ed. StBoT 4:4f., 24f.; cf. *lingai-* mng. 1 a.

b. binding oneself by oath to a future course of action: *nuza uwanzi* NÍG.BA.MEŠ *danzi namma li-in-kán-zi* (The deceitful Kaška) "will come, take (our) gifts (exchanged in an oath ceremony), and swear (but when they come back, they will violate their oaths, despise your words, O gods, and do dishonor to the seal of the oath of the Stormgod)" KUB 17.21 iv 15-19 (prayer of Arn. and Ašmunikkal, MH/MS), ed. von Schuler, Kaškäer 160f.; after an extended description of promised good behavior is recited by the vassal, the Hittite king says *nu* ⌈*li*⌉*-ik-ta nuza kē uddār ŠAPAL NĪŠ* DINGIR-*LIM* [*dai*]*š* "(thus) he swore and placed these words under the oath" KUB 14.1 obv. 27 (MH/MS), ed. Madd. 6f., 110; *kāša* ERÍN.MEŠ SA.GAZ-*aš* [*mēnaḫḫanta lingai*]*n li-in-ku-un* "I have taken the [oa]th [vis à vis] the Ḫabirū people" KBo 9.73 obv. 2-3 (treaty with Ḫabirū, OS), ed. Otten, ZA 52:220f., cf. in same treaty *nušše kiššan* [...]x [URU]*Ḫattuši mēnaḫḫanta li-in-ku-en* KUB 36.106 obv. 5-6, ed. ibid. 217f.; *nu ANA* LUGAL SAL.LUGAL *ANA* [m]*T*[*ud*]*ḫaliya* DUMU.LUGAL [LÚ]*tuḫukanti katta AN*[*A* DUMU.M]EŠ-*ŠU* DUMU.DUMU.MEŠ-*ŠU* ... *šer ANA PANI* [d]⌈U⌉ [URU]*Ḫarranašši kuitman li-in-ku-u-e-ni* "While we are swearing allegiance to (*šer*) the king and the queen, to Tudḫaliya, (who is) the prince and *tuḫukanti*, and subsequently (*katta*) to his [son]s and grandsons, in the presence of (*ANA PANI*) the Stormgod of Ḫarranašši" KUB 31.42 iii 11-16 (protocol for dignitaries, MH/NS), ed. von Schuler, OrNS 25:227f., 231; nine men representing the village of Tešenippa take the oath KBo 8.35 ii 25-29 (treaty, MH/MS), cf. also KUB 26.1 + KUB 23.112 i 1-5 (instr. for LÚ.MEŠ SAG, Tudḫ. IV), ed. von Schuler, Dienstanw. 8, without join, KUB 13.3 ii 25-26 (MH/NS), ed. Friedrich, MAOG 4:47ff.

c. swearing without any intention of fulfilling the promise, or swearing to attest something known to be false (i.e. perjury): *nu* ⌈*ANA*⌉ DINGIR-*YA UL kuššanka li-in-ku-un lingain-našta UL kuššanka šarraḫḫat* "I never swore to my god (falsely); I never violated an oath" KUB 30.10 obv. 12 (Kantuzzili prayer, MH/MS), ed. Güterbock, JNES 33:325, with Akk. parallel [*k*]*īma ša nīš ilišu kabtu q*[*alliš*] *izkuru* Lambert, ibid. 278f. line 87; *naššu* DUMU.LÚ.U$_{18}$.LU *li-in-kat-ta našma ēšḫar i*[*yat*] "(if) a person either swore (falsely) or committed murder (and then shook out his cloak over this house)" ... *našmakan ēšḫaškanza li-in-kán-za an*[(*da uit*)] "or (if) a murderer (or) perjurer entered (the house)" KUB 7.41 i 12, 15, with dupl. KBo 10.45 i 1-5 (rit., MH/NS), ed. Otten, ZA 54:116f.; tablets of rituals to help various offenders, including one who *li-in-kán ḫarzi* "has sworn (falsely)" KUB 30.45 ii! 15 (shelf list, NH).

d. active participle *linkant-* "perjurer", cf. above under usage c.

Friedrich, ZA 36 (1925) 53, SV 1 (1926) 173f.; Götze, Madd. (1928) 110; Sommer, AU (1932) 96f.

Cf. *lingai-*, *linganu-*.

lingai- n. com. and neut.; **1.** oath, **2.** oath deity, **3.** perjury, **4.** (model of an oath), **5.** (a location named in the snake oracles), **6.** curse (in *lingaiš appašiwattaš* "a permanent curse"); from OH; written syll. and NAM. ERÍM, *MĀMĒTU*, *NĪŠ* DINGIR.MEŠ, *NĪŠ* DINGIR-*LIM*.

sg. com. nom. *li-in-ga-iš* KUB 35.148 iv 18 (OH/NS), KUB 29.7 rev. 17 + KBo 21.41 rev. 26 (MH/MS), KUB 29.9 i 7 (NH).

sg. com. acc. *li-in-ga-in* KUB 30.10 obv. 12, KBo 17.54 i 15, KUB 14.1 rev. 20 (all MH/MS), KBo 2.5 iv 13 (Murš. II); *li-in-ga-en* KUB 36.108 obv. 10 (OH/OS), KUB 23.78(Bo 2826):4 (MH/MS), KUB 26.76 rev. iii 6 (NH); *li-in-qa-en* KUB 40.79:2 (NH); *li-in-qa-in* KBo 24.47 iii 22, 24.

sg. neut. nom. *li-in-g[a-]*⌈*e*⌉ KUB 29.7 rev. 41 (MH/MS); *apāt-wa NI-EŠ* DINGIR-*LIM* KUB 26.92:7 (NH); *ki-i NI-IŠ* DINGIR-*LIM* KUB 43.38 rev. 19 (NH).

sg. neut. acc. *ki-i NI-IŠ* DINGIR-*LIM* KUB 43.38 rev. 29, *ki-i MA-ME-TUM* KUB 26.1 iv 46 (both NH).

sg. erg. ⌈*li*⌉*-in-ki-ia-an-za* KBo 11.72 ii 40 (MH/MS?), *li-in-ki-ia-az* KUB 30.34 iv 7 (MH/NS), cf. Laroche BSL 57:26, 32.

sg. gen. *li-in-ki-ia-aš* KBo 15.10 iii 63, KUB 17.21 iv 18 (both MH/MS), KBo 6.34 i 14 (MH/NS), KBo 5.3 ii 61 (Šupp. I), KBo 4.14 ii 32 (Šupp. II); *le-en-ki-ia-aš* KUB 36.89 rev. (18), KUB 22.38 i 6, KBo 10.12 iii 24, ABoT 56 i 26 (all NH); *li-in-ki-aš* KBo 8.35 ii 10, 17 (MH/MS), KUB 23.75 iv? 4 (MH?/NS), KUB 40.94 rev.? 7 (NH); *le-en-ki-aš* KBo 6.34 iv 11 (MH/NS), KBo 10.12 ii 33 (NH); *li-in-ga-ia-aš* KBo 4.4 iv 60, 68, KUB 14.17 ii 13 (both Murš. II).

sg. loc. *li-in-ki-ia* KBo 8.35 ii 13 (MH/MS), KUB 14.1 obv. 13, rev. 21 (MH/MS), KUB 41.8 iv 24 (MH/NS), ABoT 56 i 16 (Šupp. II); *le-en-ki-ia* KBo 6.34 iv 18 (followed by erased sign; but note *li-in-ki-ia* in ii 45 (MH/NS); *li-in-ki-i-ia* KUB 14.14 obv. 4 (Murš. II); *li-in-ga-i* KUB 9.31 ii 4 (MH/NS), KUB 19.49 i 61, KBo 12.31 iv 16 (Tudḫ. IV); *le-en-ga-i* HT 1 i 57 (MH/NS); *le-en-qa-i* KUB 4.3 obv. 10 (NH); *le-en-qa-a-i* KUB 43.72 ii 7 (NH), KUB 43.47:8 (NH); *li-in-ga-e* KUB 43.58 i 55 (MH/MS).

sg. abl. *li-in-ki-az* KBo 16.47:23, KUB 43.58 ii 21, 40 (both MH/MS), KUB 30.31 i 16! (NH); *li-in-ki-ia-az* KBo 16.47:14 (MH/MS), KUB 15.42 ii 10 (MH/NS), KBo 5.3 iv 33 (Šupp. I); *le-en-ki-az* KBo 9.146 rev. 18 (NH); *li-in-ki-ia-za* KUB 12.61 iii! 10 (NH), HT 18:5 (NH?); *le-en-ki-ia-za* KUB 41.22 iii 4 (NH), KBo 13.131 iii (9) (MH/NS).

pl. com. acc. *li-in-ga-a-uš* KUB 17.21 iv 16, KUB 23.78(Bo 2826):10, 12 (both MH/MS), KUB 17.26 i 11 (MH/NS); *l[i-i]n-ga-u*!(text: *nu*)*-uš* KBo 4.4 i 45 (Murš. II); *li-in-ga-uš* KBo 6.34 iii 40 (MH/NS), KBo 4.4 ii 9 (Murš. II), KUB 7.56 i (6) (NH); *le-en-ga-uš* KUB 14.3 ii 52 (NH).

pl. neut. nom. (*ke-e*) *MA-MIT* ḪI.A KUB 26.25 ii 2, 5 (Šupp. II); possibly (*ku-i-e*) *MA-ME-TE* MEŠ (*dapiyanda*) KBo 16.98 iv 21 (NH).

pl. neut. acc. (*ke-e*) *MA-MIT* ḪI.A KUB 26.25 ii 7.

pl. erg. *li-in-ki-ia-an-te-eš* KUB 36.106 rev. 6 (OH/OS), KBo 6.34 iii 16, iv 1 (MH/NS), KUB 14.14 obv. 18 (NH).

broken *li-in-ga-i*[-. . .] KUB 30.45 ii! 10 (NH).

On inflection of syll. writings cf. Sommer, AU 356f.

Sumerogram NAM.ERÍM.ḪI.A KUB 15.1 ii 34 (NH); **Akkadogram** *MĀMĪTU* or *MĀMĒTU* variously spelled: *MA-ME-TUM* KBo 15.7:6 (NH); *MA-MI-TUM* KUB 21.42 iv 32 (NH); *MA-ME-DU* KUB 5.6 v 1, 3 (NH); *MA-MI-DU* KBo 5.9 ii 37 (NH); *MA-A-ME-TI* KUB 40.33 rev. 16 (MH); *MA-A-MI-TI* KUB 4.3 obv. 10 (NH); *MA-ME-TI* KUB 7.56 i 9 (NH); *MA-MI-TI* KBo 2.5 iii 32, iv 14 (Murš. II); *MA-MIT* KBo 4.14 ii 51, 72, 77 (NH); *MA-MIT* ḪI.A KUB 26.25 ii 2, 5, 7 (NH); (cf. Hoffner, in FsOtten 102); *MA-ME-TE* MEŠ KUB 15.1 ii 13 (NH); *MA-ME-TI* ḪI.A KUB 5.6 v 6 (NH); *NI-IŠ* (or *NI-EŠ* or *NI-ŠI*) DINGIR-*LIM* (or DINGIR.MEŠ) (cf. Oettinger, StBoT 22:95f., 124). Note *NI-IŠ* DINGIR-*LÌ-ŠU* KBo 16.25 iv 16.

Akk. [*ù akāša i-š*]*a-dá*!*-du-ka a-na ma-a-mi-ti* = Hitt. *tukma le-en-qa-i šallanniyanzi* "They will drag you off to (the place of?) the oath" KUB 4.3 obv. 10-11 (proverbs); dupl. of Akk.: *ù a-ka-š*[*a*] *ú-še-ṣu-*[*ú*] *ina māmīti* Ugar. V:279 iii 9; ed. of Akk. by Nougayrol, ibid. 279, 282, 288f.; ed. of Hitt. by Laroche, ibid. 781; cf. also below under 1 c 3′ for other exx. of this usage in Hittite.

1. oath. — **a.** purpose of oath: — **1′** to confirm the veracity of a statement of fact (such as testimony): "Ukkura, the queen's decurion, took an oath" *nuzakan li-in-ki-ia anda kišan pēdaš* "he brought in the following (testimony) under oath" (followed by quoted testimony) KUB 13.35 i 9-10 (deposition, NH), ed. StBoT 4:4f.

2′ to promise certain future behaviour: cf. many exx. below, and under *link-* d.

b. terminology used to describe taking/administering the oath — **1′** with *iya-* "to make, draft(?)": *nu kāša li-in-ga-i*[*n*] *iyawen* "we have just made the oath" KBo 8.35 ii 8 (treaty, MH/MS), with dupl. KUB 40.36 + KUB 23.78(Bo 2826):4, ed. von Schuler, Kaškäer 110 (line ii 8); *ŠA* LÚ*MU*[*NNABTI-ma ŠAP*]*AL NI-EŠ* DINGIR-*LIM kišan i*[(*yanun*)] "I made the (regulation) of the fugitive (and put it) under the oath as follows" KUB 21.1 iii 61 (Alakš.), with dupl. KUB 21.5 iv 6, ed. SV 2:74f.

2′ *linkiya kattan dai* — **a′** obj. is person sworn: [. . .] *li-in-ki-ia* 3[0] ERÍN.MEŠ *daiēr* KBo 16.29 obv.? 16-17 (cf. 20) (Kaška treaty, MH/MS); *nuza li-in-k[i-i]a kattan* ERÍN.MEŠ-*an dāiēr* "they placed troops under oath to themselves (-*za*)" KBo 16.27 iii 9 (Kaška treaty, MH/MS), ed. von Schuler, Kaškäer 137, *nu kēa QATAMMA [li]nkir nuza li-in-ki-ia kattan QATAMM[A] daiēr* "and these too swore and placed themselves (-*za*) under the oath" KBo 8.35 ii 28-29 (MH/MS), ed. Kaškäer 111, KUR ^{URU}*Ḫapalla*⸗*ma*⸗*z li[-in]-ki-ia kattan kiššan zikkeš* KUR ^{URU}*Ḫapālla*⸗*ma*⸗*z* ^{m}*Madduwattaš li-i[n-ki-ia kattan] kiššan zikkit* "You put the land of Ḫapalla under oath to yourself (-*z*) thus, but M. put the land of Ḫ. under oath to himself (-*z*) so" KUB 14.1 rev. 21-22 (MH/MS), ed. Madd. 24f.

b′ obj. is words: *nuza li-in-ki-ia takšulaš uttar kattan QATAMMA-pat daiēr* "In the very same manner they placed the 'word(s) of alliance' (the pact) under the oath for themselves (-*za*)" KBo 8.35 ii 31 (Kaška treaty, MH/MS), ed. Kaškäer 111; cf. KBo 16.29(+)KUB 31.104 obv. 15-16, 18-19; *nu likta nuza kē uddār ŠAPAL NI-IŠ* DINGIR-*LIM [da-i]š* "he took the oath and [pla]ced these words under oath for himself (-*za*)" KUB 14.1 obv. 27 (MH/MS), ed. Madd. 6f.; cf. *[nutta lin]gan[u]t nu[tta] li-in-ki-ia [ka]ttan kē uddār daiš* ibid. obv. 13-14; *nutta kāša kē uddār ŠAPAL NI-IŠ* DINGIR-*LIM teḫḫun* KBo 5.3 i 38-39, cf. iv 34-35 (Ḫuqq.), ed. SV 2:110f., 134f. (lines 50-51); "When we killed a sheep" *nu li-in-ki-ia [ka]ttan kiššan daiwen* "we put the following words under oath" KBo 16.47:15-16 (treaty, MH/MS), ed. Otten, IM 17:56f.; cf. KUB 23.72 rev. 2, 36-37 (Mita, MH/MS), KUB 14.1 obv. 43, rev. 44, 48 (Madd., MH/MS).

3′ *linkiya tettanu-* (obj. persons): *nuza* DAM. MEŠ-*KUNU* DUMU.MEŠ-*KUNU* ... [. . . *ked]ani li-in-ki-ia tettanutten* "make your own wives and children and [. . .] stand by [th]is oath!" KUB 23.68+ rev. 25-26 (treaty, MH/NS), ed. Kempinski & Košak, WO 5:198f.; with *linkiya tettanu-* cf. *šaḫḫani luzzi tittanu* sub *luzzi* b 2′ c′.

4′ *linkiya kattan* (or *ŠAPAL NĪŠ* DINGIR-*LIM* or GAM *MA-MIT*) *ki-* (mid.) (subj. always the obligation/command): *ŠAPAL NI-IŠ* DINGIR-*LIM-i[a]-at-ta kittaru* "let it be placed (or lie) under the oath for you" KBo 5.3 iii 43 (Ḫuqq.), ed. SV 2:126f.; *[ŠA]* ^{LÚ}*MUNNABTI-ma ŠAPAL NI-IŠ* DINGIR-*LIM QATAMMA kittaru* "let the (regulation) of the fugitive (cf. sub 1 b 1′) likewise be placed under the oath" KBo 5.4 obv. 35 (Targ. treaty, Murš. II), ed. SV 1:58f.; *nu apāšša memiaš ŠAPAL NI-IŠ* DINGIR-*LIM kittaru* ibid. rev. 15; *kāš*⸗*ta memiaš ŠAPAL NI-EŠ* DINGIR-*LIM kittaru* KUB 23.1 ii 7, cf. iv 22 (Šaušgamuwa treaty, Tudḫ. IV), ed. StBoT 16:8f., 16f.; GAM *MA-MIT* GAR-*ru* KBo 4.14 ii 72 (treaty, Šupp. II); *li-in-ki-ia-an-na-ša-at* (*linkiya*⸗*naš*⸗*at*) *[ka]ttan kittaru* KBo 16.50:20-21 (Ašḫapalla oath, MH/MS), ed. Otten, RHA XVIII/67:121f.; *[nušš]i apaddaya* GAM *NI-EŠ* DINGIR-*LIM* GAR-*ru* "let this too be put to him under the oath!" KUB 21.42 i 25 (cf. 28) (instr., NH), ed. Dienstanw. 24 (lines 32, 35).

5′ *linkiya ar-* (mid.): *[šum]ēša* LÚ.MEŠ KUR ^{URU}*Išmirika ḫūmanteš li-in-ki-ia ardumat* "all you men of I. must stand by the oath" KUB 23.68 rev. 11 (treaty, MH/NS), ed. Kempinski & Košak WO 5:196f.

c. *linkiyaš* (gen.) used to identify aspects of the oath and its ceremony — **1′** *linkiyaš uddār* "words of the oath": KUB 31.44 ii 24 with dupl. KUB 31.42 ii 26 (instr. for LÚ.MEŠ DUGUD, MH/NS), ed. von Schuler, OrNS 25:227, 230; KUB 26.19 ii 40 (treaty, MH/NS), ed. Kaškäer 132; Akk. *AWĀTĒ*^{MEŠ} (*ANNĪTI*) *ŠA RIKSI U ŠA MA-ME-TI* KBo 5.9 iv 21, 23, 27f. (Dupp.), ed. SV 1:24f.

2′ *linkiyaš tuppi* "tablet of (i.e., containing) the oath": *[li-i]n-ki-ia-aš tuppi i[yan]un* "I made a tablet of the oath" KUB 26.29 + KUB 31.55 obv. 8 (protocol of Arn., MH/NS), Klengel, ZA 57:227; "(Because we don't find the word, and)" *natš[an kēd]ani li-in-ki-ia-aš tuppiya UL kitta[ri]* "it doesn't stand on this tablet of the oath" KBo 5.3 + KBo 19.43 ii 61 (Ḫuqq.), with dupl. KBo 19.44 obv. 1-2; (in colophon:) DUB.2.KAM ^{m}*Tudḫaliya* ⌜LUGAL.GAL⌝ *ŠA MA-ME-TI* "second tablet of T. relating to the oath" KUB 13.7 iv 1-2; *ṬUPPU MA-MIT-ma-mu kuit TAŠPUR ṬUPPU MA-MIT-wa-mu arḫa* [. . .] *nu zik waštaš nukan ANA ṬUPPI MA-MIT kuit* DÙ-*an* [. . . ?] *nu* URU.DIDLI.ḪI.A *zik* *wedaš kinuna≪na≫ wetumman[zi] iyattati nu waštaš zik MA-MIT-iakan z[ik šarrattat?] ammukma* ⌈*waš*⌉*tumma[nz]i* EGIR-*an zikkiš[i?]* [*TU*]*PPU MA-MI[T INA* ^{URU}*Ḫatti? INA*] É.DINGIR-*LIM* ⌈GAR-*ru*⌉? "The tablet of the oath concerning which you wrote to me, '[You took] away from me the tablet of the oath.' It was you who sinned. Because it was written on the tablet of the oath, you were going to build (i.e., fortify/repair) cities. But are you now proceeding to build (them)? It was you who sinned. It was yo[u who transgressed] the oath. But you keep attributing the sin to me? (Therefore) let the tablet of the oath be deposited [in Ḫatti in] the temple." KBo 18.28 iv 13-18 (letter from Hittite king to a subordinate, NH).

3′ "place of the oath(-taking)" written *linkiyaš pedan*: [*k*]*inunan kāša* [...] *li-in-ki-ia-aš pedi dašuwaḫḫir* "Now they have blinded him (who had broken his oath) in the place of the oath(-taking)" KBo 6.34 i 13-14 (Soldiers' Oath, MH/NS), ed. StBoT 22:6f. (lines 19-20); written *lingai-*: cf. ex. above in bil. sec., and: DUB.2.KAM *mān* ERÍN.MEŠ-*an le-en-ki-ia pēḫudanzi* (colophon:) "Second tablet: when they conduct the troops to (the place of) the oath" KBo 6.34 iv 18-19 (MH/NS), ed. StBoT 22:14f.; *nuwaraš li-in-ki-ia ḫarweni* "We hold them (the women's garments) at (the place of) the oath" ibid. ii 45, ibid. 10f.

4′ *linkiyaš* ^{NA_4}KIŠIB "seal of the oath(-tablet?)": (The Kaškaeans will break their oaths, will despise the words of you gods) *nu ŠA* ^{d}IM *li-in-ki-ia-aš* ^{NA_4}KIŠIB *arḫa ḫullanzi* "and they will nullify(?) the seal of the oath of the Stormgod" KUB 17.21 iv 16-19 (prayer of Arn., MH/MS), ed. von Schuler, Kaškäer 160f.

5′ *linkiyaš* (alone), *linkiyaš antuḫša-*, *linkiyaš* ÌR "person under oath, sworn ally, sworn vassal": *nammaz uit ABI* ^{d}UTU-*ŠI tuk* ^{m}*Madduwattan l[i-i]n-ki-ia-aš-ša-aš iēt* "the father of His Majesty made you, M., his own sworn ally, (he made you take an oath and put these words to you under oath)" KUB 14.1 obv. 13, ed. Madd. 4f.; *nuza kāša šumeš* LÚ.MEŠ KUR ^{URU}*Išmirika ḫūmanteš IT[TI* ^{d}U]TU[-*ŠI l*]*i-[in]-ki-ia-aš-ša-aš* ... *kattama šume[nzan* DUMU.MEŠ *IT*]*TI* DUMU.MEŠ LUGAL *li-in-ki-ia-aš-ša[-aš]* DUMU.DUMU.MEŠ-*KUNU-mašmaš ITTI* DUMU.DUMU.MEŠ LUGAL *li-in-ki-aš-pát* "All you men of I. are sworn allies of His Majesty ... afterwards your sons will be sworn allies of the sons of the king, and your grandsons will likewise be sworn allies of the grandsons of the king" KUB 23.68 + ABoT 58 rev. 7-9 (Išmerika treaty, MH/NS), ed. Kempinski & Košak, WO 5:196f.; *našmaza kuiēš* EN.MEŠ DUMU.MEŠ LUGAL-*ia nuza ŠA MA-ME-TI lē kuiški kuedani[kki] kišari* "Let none of you lords and princes become a sworn ally of anyone (else)" KUB 21.42 iii 3-5 (instr., NH), ed. von Schuler, Dienstanw. 26; (My father made Mašḫuiluwa take an oath to protect the Hittite king and us, his sons,) *nanzan li-in-ga-ia-aš* ÌR-*DUM iyat* "and he made (M.) his own sworn vassal" KBo 4.4 iv 59-60, cf. 68 (Murš. II), ed. AM 140f.; [KUR ^{URU}]*Kalāšmamamu li-in-ki-ia-aš kuit* [UN.M]EŠ-*YA ešir* "since (the men of) the country of K. were my sworn allies" KBo 2.5 iv 12-13 (Murš. II), ed. AM 192f.; ^{m}PÍŠ.TUR-*ašwamu li-in-ki-ia-aš antuḫš[aš] ēšta* KUB 6.41 i 46-47 (Kup.), ed. SV 1:112f.; *našmatta karū ku[ieš] li-in-ki-ia-aš* UN.MEŠ-*uš ešir* KBo 4.14 ii 31-32 (treaty, Šupp. II).

6′ *linkiyaš* ^{NA_4}ZI.KIN: KUB 22.38 i 6 (snake oracle, NH).

7′ *linkiyaš eš-*: *le-en-ki-i[a-aš-w]a-ta ēšdu nuwazakan āršanu lē waḫnuši* "Let it be (a matter) of oath for you: don't change the direction of your (the Maraššanda River's) flow!" KUB 36.89 rev. 18-19 (myth narrative within a rit., NH), ed. Haas, KN 152f., tr. Güterbock in S. N. Kramer, MAW 153.

d. symbolic actions/gestures and metaphors connected with taking the oath: ⌈Ì⌉[-*an-za* GIM-*an katta*] *iškiškiši kēyatakkan MA-MIT*$^{HI.A}$ *Q[ATAMMA* ...] *katta iškiyan ēšdu* TÚG-*an-za* GIM-*an* [NÍ.TE.MEŠ-*KA anda*] *waššiškiši kēyaza MA-MIT*$^{HI.A}$ *QATAMMA wašši[ški]* "[Just as] you anoint [yourself with oil, so also] let these oaths be smeared [on your body!] Just as you put a garment [on your body], so also put these oaths on yourself!" KUB 26.25 ii? 4-7 (oath formula, Šupp. II); note too all of the symbolic gestures and implements employed in the ritual KBo 6.34 and dupls.　ed. StBoT 22.

e. *lingain/lingauš paḫš-* "to keep the oath(s)": (corresponds to Akk. *adê/māmīta naṣāru*): *nu NI-ŠI DINGIR-LIM ŠA LUGAL U ŠU LUGAL paḫši* "keep the oath of the king and the hand of the king" KBo 5.9 i 23 (Dupp.), ed. SV 1:12f.; *kīma NI-IŠ DINGIR-LIM paḫḫašteni* KUB 43.38 rev. 29 (rit., NH); cf. *mān kēlma tuppiaš uddār paḫḫašti . . . nutta kūš NI-EŠ DINGIR.MEŠ . . . SILIM-li paḫšan[du]* KBo 4.10 rev. 8-10 (Ulmi-Tešub treaty); *[NI]-EŠ DINGIR-LIM PAP-aḫšantaripat* KUB 23.94:10.

f. *lingain/lingauš šarra-* "to transgress the oath(s)" (corresponds to Akk. *ištu māmīti etēqu*): *nu mān kūš li-in!(text: li)-ga-a-uš paḫḫašduma šumāša DINGIR.MEŠ-eš paḫšandaru . . . mānašta kūša li-in-ga-a-uš šarradduma šumāšakan li-in-ki-aš DINGIR.MEŠ-eš ḫūmanteš . . . ḫarninkandu* "If you keep these oaths, the gods will keep you . . . if you transgress these oaths, all the oath-gods will destroy you" KBo 8.35 ii 14-18 (treaty with Kaška, MH/MS), translated by von Schuler, Kaškäer 111; cf. the treaty of Šupp. I with Tette of Nuḫašše probably composed in Hittite and translated into Akkadian: *šumma RN awāte annāti ša riksi u māmīti lā inaṣṣar u ištu māmīti īteteq* "If RN does not keep (corr. to Hitt. *paḫš-*) these words of treaty and oath, but transgresses (corr. to Hitt. *šarra-*) the oath" KBo 1.4 iv 40-42, cf. ii 32, ed. Weidner, PD 68f. (lines 48-50), 62f.; cf. CAD E 389a and M/1 192, from which it appears that Hitt. *paḫš-* = Akk. *naṣāru*, and Hitt. *šarra-* = Akk. *etēqu*; ᵐ*Madduwattašaka[n AN]A ABI* ᵈUT[U-ŠI l]*i-in-ga-in šarrattat* "M. transgressed the oath (sworn) to the father of His Majesty (and took all the land of Arzauwa)" KUB 14.1 rev. 20 (MH/MS), ed. Madd. 24f., cf. obv. 42; *li-in-ga-in-na-aš-ta UL kuššanka šarraḫḫat* KUB 30.10 obv. 12 (prayer, OH?/MS), treated sub *link-* d; *nu* ᵐ*Mitaš mekki kuit waštaškit . . . NI-IŠ DINGIR-LIM-kán apāšša šarraškit* "Because M. offended greatly, . . . , and he too kept transgressing the oath" 1684/u + KUB 23.72 obv. 36-37 (Mita, MH/MS), ed. Hoffner, JCS 28:61; *našta li-in-ga-a-uš šarranzi nuza šumenzan ŠA DINGIR.MEŠ memiyanuš tepnuwanzi nu ŠA* ᵈ*IM li-in-*

ki-ia-aš ᴺᴬ⁴*KIŠIB arḫa ḫullanzi* KUB 17.21 iv 16-19, cf. above under 1 c 4'; □cf. Neu, StBoT 5:153 no. 1, where however one must eliminate "brechen, verletzen" and retain only "übertreten" with the object "oath, command, word" (so correctly Oettinger, StBoT 22:112). Exx. show variation between act. and mid. of the verb, as well as the presence and absence of the particles *-ašta, -kan*.

g. violating or rejecting oaths (with verbs other than *šarra-*): (If someone forces you to swear allegiance to a brother of His Majesty,) *nu apūn MA-ME-TUM arḫa peššiyatten* "disregard that oath (and show allegiance only to His Majesty)" KUB 21.42 iv 9-22 (instr., NH), ed. von Schuler, Dienstanw. 28; for *ANA PANI NIŠ DINGIR.MEŠ wašta-* cf. below under 2 f.

h. becoming exempt from oaths — **1'** *linki-yaz parkui-* see below sub 3 b.

2' *ANA NĪŠ DINGIR-LIM kattan arḫa ki-* (mid.): KBo 4.3 i 27, iv 19 (Kup.), ed. SV 1:118f. (line 18), 144f.; KBo 4.10 rev. 16, 17 (treaty with Ulmi-Tešub, NH), translation by Cavaignac, RHA II/10 (1933) 71.

i. canceling or terminating oaths: *[(našmaza)] kī MA-ME-TUM šeknuš pippuwar [(kuiški i)]yazi našmazat arḫa aniyazi* "if anyone makes this oath into a 'garment . . . -ing' or removes it from himself" KUB 26.1 iv 46-48 (instr., NH), ed. Dienstanw. 16f., dupl. KUB 26.8 iv 33-34. □*arḫa aniya-* had the positive connotation "discharge, fulfil (an oath)" with vows which foresee a limited payment and a definite term. But the oath of allegiance to kings could not be so terminated. Therefore with such an oath *arḫa aniya-* described illegal behaviour. The *pippuwar* of the garment is a gesture of disclaiming responsibility for the oath.

2. oath deity — **a.** in the ergative form of *lingai-*, which is *linkiyanza, linkiyanteš* cf. Laroche, BSL 57 (1962) 32: "He took an oath before the gods and then transgressed the oath" *nan li-in-ki-an-te-eš ēppir* "the oath-deities seized him" KBo 6.34 iii 15-17 (Soldiers' Oath, MH/NS), ed. StBoT 22:12f., 41ff.; *šumāša li-in-ki-ia-an-te-eš anda QATAMMA appandu* "Likewise let the oath-deities seize you" ibid. iv 1-2; cf. KUB 36.106 rev. 6 (treaty with Ḫabiru, OH/OS); KUB 14.14 obv. 18 (1st Plague Prayer, Murš. II), ed. Götze, KlF 1:166f.; *nutta uittu kēl ŠA SISKUR.SISKUR [l]i!-in-*

ki-ia-an-za ēpdu "let the oath-deity of this ritual come and seize you!" KBo 11.72 ii 39-40 (rit., MH?/NS); *mānatkan UL-ma ašnuši nutta uidd*[(*u*)] *kēl* (dupl. *kī*) *ŠA* SISKUR.SISKUR *NI-EŠ* DINGIR-*LIM tuk taknaš* ᵈUTU-*uš* (dupl. -*un*) *ēpdu* "But if you don't make it good, the oath-deity of this ritual (dupl.: this oath of the ritual) will seize you, O Sungod of the Netherworld" KBo 11.72 iii 7-9 (dupl. KBo 11.10 iii 19-21); *nu ešḫananza li-in-ki-ia-az* ᴱ*ḫalinduwa* É.DINGIR.MEŠ *lē ēpzi* "Let not the blood (or) oath-deity seize the palace (or) temples!" KUB 30.34 iv 7 (rit., MH/NS).

b. written logographically — **1′** *NIŠ* DINGIR.MEŠ (usual form, esp. in OS or MS), *NIŠ* DINGIR-*LIM* (esp. in NH and in NS copies of OH or MH): *nuš*[*m*]*aškan NI-IŠ* DINGIR.MEŠ DUMU.ḪI.A-*KUNU andan kardišmipa*[*t a*]*zzikkandu* "Let the oath-deities devour your children within you (lit. 'in your heart')!" KBo 8.35 ii 23-24 (treaty, MH/MS); note that dupl. KBo 16.29 i? 11′ has *li-in-ki-ia-aš* DINGIR.ME[Š], see below; *NI-EŠ* DINGIR.MEŠ *ḫarnin⸗kandu* "Let the oath-deities destroy (the offender)!" KUB 13.20 iv 6 (MH); *nan kē NI-IŠ* DINGIR.MEŠ [*QADU* ... -*Š*]*U* É-*ŠU ḫarnin⸗kandu* KBo 19.61 iv? 9-10 (treaty, MH/NS); cf. also KBo 16.28 iii 8; □even in NH or in pre-NH/NS careful scribes tended to distinguish *NIŠ* DINGIR-*LIM* (for syll. *lingain*/*lingauš*, the oath as object of the verb *šarra-*) from *NIŠ* DINGIR.MEŠ (for syll. *linkiyanteš* or *linkiyaš šiuneš*, the oath deities as agents): KBo 6.34 ii 46, 48; KBo 5.13 iii 21 (Kup.); KBo 4.7 iii 29-30 (Kup.); KBo 4.3 iii 7 (Kup.); KUB 21.1 iii 55-56 (Alakš.). When NH scribes began to abandon the distinction, *NIŠ* DINGIR.MEŠ was used for both: KUB 7.59 ii 10, 12 (Soldiers' Oath); KBo 19.74 + KUB 21.5 iv 3, 6 (Alakš.); KUB 23.68 rev. 27 (Išmerika treaty, MH/NS); KBo 6.34 iv 7-8 (Soldiers' Oath, MH/NS); and much more rarely, *NIŠ* DINGIR-*LIM*: KBo 5.3 iv 52 (Ḫuqq.); KBo 6.34 i 15, 18; or the reversed distribution: ibid. i 34, 37; ii 23, 26; in KUB 43.38 rev. 19-20 *kī NI-IŠ* DINGIR-*LIM INA* [ŠÀ?] *RAMANI* ᴹᴱŠ[-*KU*]*NU* [*anda QATAMM*]*A immeattaru* "Let this oath likewise be mixed together in (i.e., be united with?) your bodies". The combination of *kī* (subj.) and *immeattaru* (sg.) indicates that *lingai* (neut. sg.) underlay the logogram.

2′ *MĀMĒTUM* (personified oath; oath deity) without divine determinative: KBo 15.7:6, 13 with discussion by Kümmel, StBoT 3:38ff.

c. written syllabically *linkiyaš* DINGIR (.MEŠ), or *ŠA MĀMĪTI* DINGIR.MEŠ "god(s) of the oath", utilizing a genitive construction: *nan le-en-ki-aš* DINGIR.MEŠ ḪUL-*lu ḫurtandu* "Let the gods of the oath curse him" KBo 6.34 iv 11-12 (Soldiers' Oath, MH/NS); ⸢*nuš*⸣*maškan li-in-ki-ia-aš* DINGIR.ME[(Š DUMU.ḪI.A-*KUNU andan*)] *kardišmipat* <*azzikkandu*> KBo 16.29 obv.? 11 (+) KUB 31.104 left col. 11 with dupl. KBo 8.35 ii 23-24 on which cf. above 2 b 1′; *nukan* PN *kuit NI-EŠ* DINGIR-*LIM šarrit nan ŠA MA-MI-TI* DINGIR.MEŠ *ēppir* KBo 2.5 iii 31-33 (Murš. II), ed. AM 190 (lines 56-58).

d. named (discussed by Kümmel, StBoT 3:38f. and Oettinger, StBoT 22:41f.): ᵈ*Išḫaraš li-in-ki-aš išḫāš* KBo 8.35 ii 10; ᵈ*Išḫara* SAL.LUGAL *NI-EŠ* DINGIR-*LIM* KUB 21.1 iv 14; ᵈ*SIN* EN *MA-M*[*I-TI*] KUB 26.36 iv 5 (dupl. ᵈ*SIN NI-EŠ* DINGIR-*LIM* KUB 19.50 iv 10); ᵈ*SIN MA-ME-TI* KUB 26.50 rev. 10; *li-in-ki-ia-aš* ᵈIM KBo 15.10 iii 63.

e. bearing witness to oaths: *nat kēdani li-in-ki-ia kutruweneš* (dupl. *kutarweneš*) *ašandu* "Let (the gods who were summoned) be witnesses to this oath" KBo 8.35 ii 13 (treaty, MH/MS), with dupl. KUB 40.36 + KUB 23.78 (Bo 2826) ii 9 + KUB 26.6 ii 10; *nuza kēdani le-en-ga-i kutrueneš ēsten* HT 1 i 57; *apedd*[*ni memiyani ku*]*iēš* DINGIR. MEŠ *tul*[*iya l*]*i-in-ki-i-ia k*[*ut*]*ruwanni ḫalzi⸗*[*yanteš*] *ēšten* "you gods who have been summoned to the assembly for bearing witness to the oath on this matter" KUB 19.1 (+) KUB 14.14 obv. 4-5 (1st plague prayer, Murš. II); Akkadographic: *ANA ANNÎ RIKSI [U] ANA MA-ME-TUM* ᴸᵁ́*ŠĒBŪTUM* "be witnesses to this treaty and oath" KBo 5.9 iv 19 (treaty with Duppi-Tešub, Murš. II), ed. SV 1:24.

f. oaths broken ("sinning") in the presence of the witnessing or enforcing deities: [*l*]*i-in-ki-ia-aš ištarna kuiški waštai* KBo 16.44:11; [. . . *kuit*] *ḫu*[*manteš*] *ANA NI-ŠI* DINGIR[.MEŠ *waštan*]*niškir* KUB 14.1 obv. 50-51 (MH/MS), ed. Götze, Madd. 12-13; *PANI NI-EŠ* DINGIR.MEŠ *waštaš*[*i*] KUB 21.1 iii 30 (dupl. 22/t i 3: *PANI*

DINGIR.MEŠ *waš[taši]*); *ANA PANI NI-EŠ* DINGIR.MEŠ *waštaši* KBo 5.13 ii 23-24. (Kup).

g. oath-deities punish: See exx. given above under 2 a-c. For additional exx. in the Soldiers' Oath see the edition by Oettinger, StBoT 22:6-14 passim. The most commonly used general terms used to describe the punishment are: *ep-* "to seize", *ḫarnink-* "to destroy", *parḫ-* "to chase, pursue". *ni*(sic)-*ni-in-kán-du* KBo 5.3 iv 41 (Ḫuqq.), SV 2:136 line 57 is probably to be corrected to *ḫar*!-*ni-in-kán-du*.

h. oath-deities protect/keep those who keep their oaths: cf. above sub 1 e.

3. perjury — **a.** in lists of evils to be purged: *NI-IŠ* DINGIR-*LIM* often in the incantation of Netherworld Deities (KUB 7.41 and dupls.), ed. Otten in ZA 54:116-41 cited here according to cumulative line count of edition: i 18, 31, 55, ii 2, 33, iii (55), iv 3, 10, 14, 52; KUB 29.7 rev. (31), (34), 45, 59 (Šamuḫa rit.); KUB 30.34 iv 17, 28; KUB 30.33 i 11!; *MA-MIT* KBo 13.131 rev. 16 (rit.); syll. *lingai-*: nom. *lingaiš*: KBo 21.46 rev. 26 + KUB 29.7 rev. 17; acc. *lingain*: KUB 9.34 i (27); iv (4); gen. *linkiyaš*: KUB 7.41 i 2; KUB 30.35 iv 6; loc. *linkiya*: KUB 41.8 iv 24; abl. *linki*(*y*)*az*(*a*): KUB 30.33 i (10); KUB 41.22 iii 4; KUB 12.61 iii! 10 (Ašertu myth); KUB 15.42 ii 10 (rit.); KUB 43.58 ii 21 (rit., MH/MS).

b. alone: *nukan kāšma NĪŠ* DINGIR-*LIM zik šarratta* URU*Ḫattušaša li-in-ki-ia-az parkuiš ēštu* "You will be trespassing the oath, but Ḫ. shall be free (lit. 'pure') from (violation of?) the oath" KBo 16.47:13-14 (treaty, MH/MS); "If you do evil (i.e., violate your oaths), and I, My Majesty, harm you" *nuza* dUTU-*ŠI apēz li-in-ki-ia-az ANA PANI* DINGIR.MEŠ *parkuiš ēšlit* "let me, My Majesty, be free from (violation of?) that oath before the gods" KBo 5.3 iv 31-33 (Ḫuqq.), ed. SV 2:134f. (lines 47-49).

4. models of oaths: *li-in-g[a-]e-ma ḫurtaišša ŠA* KÙ.BABBAR KÙ.GI TUR-*TIM iyan[teš]* "small models of the oath and curse (are) made of silver and gold" KUB 29.7 rev. 41; 1 *li-in-ga-in-na* URUDU KBo 24.47 iii 17, cf. 20, 22, 24.

5. (a location named in the snake oracles:) TA *MA-ME-TI uit :luluti* KI.MIN (= *munnait*) "it came from the 'oath' and hid at the *:lulu-*" IBoT 1.33:27 (Laroche, RA 52:152, 156).

6. curse (in *lingaiš appašiwattaš* "a permanent curse", translating an Akk. terrestrial omen apodosis): *li-in-ga-iš-ši-kán* (var. [*li-*]⌈*in-ga*⌉-*ši-kán*) EGIR-*pa*-UD.KAM-*aš* (var. [*appašiw*]*attaš*) *parnišši andan kišari* "a permanent curse (lit. oath of the end-of-days) will occur in his house" KUB 29.9 i 7-8 with dupl. 29.10 i 2-4, ed. Güterbock, AfO 18:78-79; compare NAM.ERÍM *ana bīt amēli īrub* "a curse will enter (lit. entered) the man's house" CT 38.31 rev. 17 (terrestrial omen) cited in CAD M/1 194b.

Hrozný, SH (1917) 16; Friedrich, ZA 36 (1925) 53; ad 2a: Oettinger, StBoT 22:41f. calls into question Laroche's interpretation of *linkiyanteš* as erg., BSL 57 (1962) 32, but his objections are not convincing.

Cf. *link-*.

linganu- v.; to make someone swear or take an oath; from MH/MS.

pres. sg. 1 *li-in-ga-nu-mi* KBo 16.24 i 11 (MH/MS); **sg. 3** *li-in-ga-nu-zi* KUB 21.42 iv 20 (Tudḫ. IV); **pl. 1** *li-in-ga-nu-ma-ni* KUB 17.21 iv 12 (MH/MS); **pl. 3** *li-in-qa-nu-an-zi* KUB 5.4 i 52 (NH).

pret. sg. 1 *li-in-ga-nu-nu-un* KUB 23.72 obv. 35 (MH/MS), KBo 5.12 iv (5) (Šupp. I), KBo 15.24 ii (2), KUB 31.55:7 (MH/NS), KBo 16.17 iii 28, KBo 4.4 iii 14, 16, KBo 5.9 i 18, 22 (all Murš. II), KUB 14.3 i 66, ii (34); *le-en-ga-nu-nu-un* KUB 26.1 iii 47 (Tudḫ. IV); **sg. 3** *li-in-ga-nu-ut* KUB 14.1 obv. (13), (43), (74) (MH/MS), KBo 16.27 iii (12), iv 32 (MH/MS), KBo 4.4 iv 60 (Murš. II); *le-en-ga-nu-ut* KUB 26.1 iii 17 (Tudḫ. IV); **pl. 1** *li-in-ga-nu-me-en* 1121/u:2′; **pl. 3** *li-in-qa-nu-e-er* KUB 40.88 iv 10 (Ḫatt. III?).

iter. pres. pl. 3 *li-in-ga-nu-uš-kán-zi* KUB 21.42 i 10 (Tudḫ. IV); **pret. sg. 3** *li-in-ga-nu-uš-ki-it* KUB 6.41 iii 53 (Murš. II); **pl. 3** *li-in-ga-nu-uš-ki-ir* KBo 16.25 iv (9) (MH/MS), KUB 21.42 i 9 (Tudḫ. IV).

part. sg. nom. com. *l*[*i-i*]*n-ga-nu-wa-an-za* KBo 5.3 ii 36 (Šupp. I); *li-in-qa-nu-wa-an-za* KBo 4.14 ii 47 (Šupp. II); *le-en-qa-nu-an-za* ibid. ii 47; **pl. nom. com.** *li-in-ga-nu-wa-an-te-eš* KUB 14.8 obv. 17, KUB 14.11 ii (2), (41); *li-in*!-*ga*!-*nu-an-te-eš* KUB 14.8 obv. 34 (all Murš. II).

a. to make someone swear (in absolute construction without adv./postpos.): "We will summon the Kaška men and give gifts to them" *nammaš li-in-ga-nu-ma-ni* "and we will make them swear (saying to them: ...)" KUB 17.21 iv 11f. with dupl. KUB 23.117 iii 5f. (prayer of Arn. and Ašm.,

MH/MS), ed. von Schuler, Kaškäer 160f.; *nušmaš[za k]āša* ᵈUTU-*ŠI li-in-ga-nu-nu-un* "I, His Majesty, have made you swear to me (and have made a tablet of the oath)" KUB 26.29 + KUB 31.55 obv. 7f. (treaty/protocol of Arn., MH/NS); "The father of My Majesty made you, Madduwatta, his sworn vassal" *nu[tta li-in]-ga-n[u-u]t* "he made you swear (and put these words to you under the oath)" KUB 14.1 obv. 13f. (MH/MS), ed. Madd. 4f.; cf. also ibid. obv. 43, rev. 14; "I made him (Aparru of Kalašma) a lord and gave him Kalašma to govern" *[na]mman li-in-ga-nu-nu-un* "and I further made him swear (loyalty to me)" KBo 16.17 iii 26-28 (detailed annals Murš. II), ed. Otten, MIO 3:172-74; *nušmaš* ᵈUTU-*ŠI kuit le-en-ga-nu-nu-un* "Because I, His Majesty, made you swear, (saying: ...)" KUB 26.1 iii 46f. (instr., Tudḫ. IV), ed. Dienstanw. 14; "They will go and instruct the kitchen personnel ... " *nammaš li-in-qa-nu-an-zi* "and they will further make them swear" KUB 5.4 i 51f. (oracle, NH); *le-en-ga-nu-ut-wa-mu kuiš nuwa karū :ḫalliya weḫtat* "He who made me swear allegiance has already died" (so that the oath is no longer binding) KUB 26.1 iii 17-18 (instr., Tudḫ. IV), ed. Dienstanw. 13; *naš li-in-ga-nu-nu-un nutta memian šakuwašar memandu* "I put them under oath. Let them tell you the truth!" KUB 14.3 i 66-67 (Taw.), ed. Sommer, AU 6-7; (if a vassal hears of a plot against the Hittite king, and instead of promptly reporting it to him, lets it pass, saying) *ammukwaza l[i-i]n-ga-nu-wa-an-za nuwa UL kuitki memaḫḫi i[yamiy]awa UL kuitki ašimawa [ma]ḫ[ḫ]an ie[zzi nu QATAMMA?] ieddu* "I am sworn to allegiance: I will say and do nothing. But let that man do as he wishes." KBo 5.3 ii 36-38 (Ḫuqq.), ed. SV 2:116-19; *nu* LÚ.MEŠ ᵁᴿᵁ*Ḫatti kuit* LÚ.MEŠ ᵁᴿᵁ*Mizriya IŠTU* ᵈIM ᵁᴿᵁ*Ḫatti li-in-ga-nu-wa-an-te-eš ešer* "because the Hittites and Egyptians had been made to swear by the Stormgod of Ḫatti" KUB 14.8 obv. 16-17 (plague prayer, Murš. II), ed. Götze, KlF 1:208f.

b. to make someone swear allegiance to someone as overlord: — **1′** with *šer*: "Mašḫuiluwa of Arzawa came as a fugitive to my father. My father made him a son-in-law, and gave him his daughter, my sister, Mūwatti in marriage" *nammanzan ANA* SAG.DU-*ŠU šer anzāšša [ANA* DUM]U.MEŠ-*ŠU šer li-in-ga-nu-ut* "And (my father) made (him) swear allegiance to his (my father's) person and to us, his sons" KBo 4.4 iv 56-60 (det. annals Murš. II), ed. AM 140f.; "I, His Majesty, installed you in the place of your father" *nutta [t]uk* x-x-*uš* ŠEŠ.MEŠ-*KA* KUR ᵁᴿᵁ*Amurri-ya šer li-in-ga-[n]u-nu-un* "and I made ... your brothers and the land of A. swear allegiance to you" ... *nutta kāšma ANA* LUGAL KUR ᵁᴿᵁ*Ḫatti* KUR ᵁᴿᵁ*Ḫatti U ANA* DUMU.MEŠ-*YA* DUMU.DUMU.MEŠ-*YA šer li-in-ga-nu-nu-un* "and I made you swear allegiance to the king of Ḫatti, the land of Ḫatti, and to my sons and grandsons" KBo 5.9 i 16-22 (Dupp.), ed. SV 1:10-13; "I gave you, Kup., to Mašḫuiluwa as a son" *namma* KUR ᵁᴿᵁ*Mirā* KUR ᵁᴿᵁ*Kuwaliyaya ANA* ᵐPÍŠ.TUR[(-*wa* (var. ᵐ*Mašḫuiluwa*) ᶠ*Muwa)ttiya*] *tuqqa ANA* ᵐ*Kupanta*-ᵈLAMMA-*ya šer li-i*[(*n-ga-nu-nu-un*)] "Further I made the lands of Mira and K. swear allegiance to Mašḫ. and Muw., and to you, Kup." KUB 6.41 i 28!-30 with dupl. KUB 6.42:5-7 + KUB 6.43:10-12 (Kup.), ed. SV 1:110f.; "Protect only His Majesty with respect to lordship, and after him his sons and grandsons!" *ANA* ŠEŠ.MEŠ ᵈUTU-*ŠI-yašmaš kuēl šer li-in-ga-nu-zi* "(cast away that oath/curse) with which he shall make you swear allegiance to the brothers of His Majesty!" KUB 21.42 iv 19-21 (instr., Tudḫ. IV), ed. von Schuler, Dienstanw. 28; (Murš. II says: I made [x-x-]šarma king in the land of Carchemish,) *nušši* KUR ᵁᴿᵁ*Kargamiš šer li-in-ga-*⌜*nu-nu*⌝*-un* ... "and I made the land of Carchemish swear allegiance to him," (I made Talmišarma, the son of Telepinu, king in Aleppo,) *nušši* KUR ᵁᴿᵁ*Ḫalpa šer li-in-ga-nu-nu-un* "and I made the land of Aleppo swear allegiance to him" KBo 4.4 iii 12-16 (detailed ann. of Murš. II), ed. AM 124f.; (Hittite princes say: Is there no seed of My Lord in the sons of our lords?) *nuwannaš kēdan[i* (GIM)-*an šer li-in-ga-nu-uš-ki-ir kēdaniyaw*[(*anna*)*š QA*]*TAMMA šer li-in-*⌜*ga*⌝*-nu-uš-kán-zi nuwannaš kā*[(*š* E)N]-*ašpat* "Just as they made us swear allegiance to the one, they will make us swear allegiance to the other, (so that) he will be our lord" KUB 21.42 i 8-11 with dupl.

KUB 26.13 i 18-20 (instr., Tudḫ. IV), ed. Dienstanw. 23:14-18; (let a vassal not say:) *:allallā pāuwanziwaza* UGU *li-in-qa-nu-wa-an-za kīmawaza UL le-en-qa-nu-an-za* "I was made to swear with regard to desertion, but I was not made to swear this" KBo 4.14 ii 46-47 (treaty, Šupp. II).

2′ with *menaḫḫanta*: ^{m}*Madduwatt[ašmaz]* [*ŠA*] KUR ^{URU}*Pītašša* $^{\ulcorner LÚ \urcorner}$*tapariyall[iuš U* LÚ.MEŠ Š]U.GI ^{URU}*Pītaššaya menaḫḫanta li-in-ga-nu-uš-k[i-it]* "M. made the rulers of P. and the elders of P. swear allegiance to himself" (saying: Be mine! ... Attack the land of Ḫatti!) KUB 14.1 rev. 38-39 (MH/MS), ed. Götze, Madd. 28f.

c. to take an oath against someone (with postpos. *kattan*): (Mašḫuiluwa allied himself with É.GAL-PAP) [*(nu)*]*šši menaḫḫanda linkta natza* 1-*NŪTIM kišantat* [*(numu)*] ÌR.MEŠ-*YA kattan li-in-ga-nu-uš-ki-it*(var. *-ir*) "He swore allegiance to him, and they united. He (var. they) made my subjects take oaths against me" KUB 6.41 iii 52-53 (Kup.), ed. SV 1:128f. with dupl. KBo 4.3 + KUB 40.34 ii 28-30.

Hrozný, SH (1917) 114; Friedrich, ZA 36 (1925) 53.

Cf. *link-*.

linkiyant- see *lingai-*.

lip(p)-, lipai- v.; to lick, lick up; from OH.†

pres. sg. 3 *li-ip-zi* KUB 35.148 iii 15 (OH/NS); *li-pa-iz-zi* 774/u:(2), 3 (StBoT 22:31); **pl. 3** *li-ip-pa-an-zi* KBo 6.34 ii 20 (MH/NS); *li-pa-a-an-zi* ibid. i 29; **pret. sg. 3** *li-ip-ta* KBo 14.98 i 9 (OH/NS); **pl. 3** *li-i-pí-ir* KBo 24.51 obv.? passim; KBo 24.52:5, (6), (7) (OH/MS?); **imp. sg. 3** *li-ip-tu* KBo 17.17 obv.? 6 (OH/OS); *li-ip-du* KUB 35.148 iii 18 (2x), 19, 22 (OH/NS), KUB 35.149 i (7) (NH); **broken** *li-pa-a-an*[(-)...] 1111/v:6 (StBoT 22.31).

UR.TUR-*ašza maḫḫan* 9 ^{UZU}*ḫappeššaršet li-ip-zi ... ki-i-el-la ḫappešnaš inan QĀTAMMA li-ip-du* ^{UZU}ZAG.LU-*aš inan li-ip-du* "Just as the puppy licks its nine body parts ... in the same way let it lick up the illness of this one's body parts also! Let it lick up the illness of (his) shoulder!" KUB 35.148 iii 14-18 (Zuwi rit., OH/NS), with other body parts in ibid. iii 19, 22-27, 33-35; *ḫar-nammar INA QĀTIŠUNU dāi nat li-pa-a-an-zi* "He puts yeast in their hands and they lick it" KBo 6.34 i 29 (Soldiers' Oath, MH/NS), ed. StBoT 22:8f. (line 35); *nušmaš* BULÙG BAPPIR *INA QĀTI-ŠUNU dāi nat li-ip-pa-an-zi* "He puts malt (and) 'beer bread' in their hands and they lick it" ibid. ii 19-20, ed. StBoT 22:10f.; *ḫūm*[*(andaš alwanzenaš* E)]ME-*an li-ip-d*[*u*] "Let him/it (the sheep of line 26?) lick up the injurious speech of all the sorcerers" KUB 35.149 i 6-7 (SAL.ŠU.GI rit.), with dupl. KBo 9.125 i 5; KI.MIN in HT 6 i 5-20 + KBo 9.125 i 1-5 is to be read *lipdu* "let him lick", objects of which form a catalogue of ills and evils; compare KUB 9.34 iv 7-18, where *mutaiddu* "let him remove!" alternating with KI.MIN is used in nearly identical context; *ešḫaršet li-ip-ta* KBo 14.98 i 9 (incant. frag.); with inst.: [*lalit*]*atkan li-ip-tu* KBo 17.17 obv.? 6, for rest. cf. ibid. 8-12; long sequence of clauses in OH incant. in which verb *li-i-pí-ir* "they licked" takes various ills and evils as obj. KBo 24.51 obv.? 4-14, KBo 24.52:5-8.

The only unambiguous exx. of the stem *lipai-* (774/u:(2), 3) are in a broken context and may prove to be a different verb.

Friedrich, HW 342, AfO 17 (1956) 152f.; Oettinger, StBoT 22 (1976) 31f. ("mit der Zunge berühren").

Cf. *lil(l)ipa(i)-*.

lipšai- v.; (mng. unkn.); from OH.†

pres. sg. 3 *li-ip-ša-iz-zi* KUB 12.52 i 2 (NH); **part. neut. nom.** *li-ip-ša-an* KBo 3.41 obv.! (14), 15, 18 (OH/NS).

a. in an OH legend about the Hurrian wars: "... became a bull" *našta karāwaršet tēpu li-ip-š[a-an ...] punuškimi karāwaršet kuit ḫanda li-ip-ša-an* "and his horn is a little *l.* [...] I ask 'Why is his horn *l.*?' (He says '... when I was traveling ..., the mountain was (too) steep for us. This bu[ll] was ..., but when he came, he lifted that mountain ... We conquered the ... and the sea')" *nu karāwaršet apeda li-ip-ša-an* "And that's why his horn is *l.*" KUB 31.4 obv. 15-19 + KBo 3.41 obv.! 14-18, ed. Otten, ZA 55:160-61.

b. in a fest. frag.: [... *ḫam*]*ešḫi INBAM* [...] *li-ip-ša-iz-zi* [...]x ^{URU}*Tauriša* "[...] in the [spr]ing he breaks off(?)/splits open(?) the fruit" KUB 12.52 i 1-3.

In usage a, *lipšan* appears to indicate some sort of damage to the bull's horn from lifting the mountain (bent, broken, split, or scratched).

Sommer, OLZ 1941:60 (verbogen??).

leššai-, liššai-, lišai- v.; to pick up, gather up, clear; from MH.†

pres. sg. 3 *li-i-ša-iz-zi* KUB 15.31 ii 15 (MH/NS); *li-ša-iz-zi* KUB 15.32 ii 9 (MH/NS); **pl. 3** *li-iš-ša-an-zi* KBo 2.8 iii 1 (NH), KBo 15.25 rev. 18 (MH/NS); **inf.** *le-eš-šu-u-wa-an-zi* KUB 30.15 obv. 1, 7, 17 (MH/NS).

a. objects: bones, fruit: *nu ḫaštāe [šarā] li-iš-ša-an-zi nat ḫaššī awan katta tianzi* "They pick up the bones and put them down on(?) the hearth" KBo 15.25 rev. 18 (rit. against Wišuriyanza, MH/NS), ed. StBoT 2:6-7; *nu* SAL.MEŠ *uktu[riy]a? ḫaštiaš le-eš-šu-u-wa-an-zi pānzi* "The women go to the pyre to pick up the bones" KUB 30.15 obv. 1-2 (royal funeral rit., MH?/NS), ed. Otten, HTR 66-67, cf. ibid. obv. 7, 17; SAL.MEŠ GURUN *li-iš-ša-an-zi* "The women gather up the fruit" KBo 2.8 iii 1 (cult inv., NH).

b. without expressed object: (He digs with a hoe and then with a pectoral) EGIR-*ŠU-maza* GIŠ*šatta* (var. [...*š*]*attan*) GIŠMAR GIŠ*ḫūp-paranna dāi nukan šarā li-i-ša-iz-zi* (var. *li-ša-iz-zi*) "Then he takes a *š.*, a spade, and a *ḫ.*-vessel, and he clears out" (the loose soil, stones, etc. from the holes) KUB 15.31 ii 13-15 with dupl. KUB 15.32 ii 8-9 (rit. of drawing paths, MH/NS), ed. Haas and Wilhelm, AOATS 3:156-57.

Sommer, OLZ 1939:680 n. 2 (auflesen, sammeln, aufräumen).

MULleššalla- n. com.; (a celestial phenomenon); NH.†

In celestial omens: *takkukan* MUL*le-eš-šal-la-aš uizzi nuššikan ḫapparnuwataršet parā mekki lalukešzi* "If a *l.* comes, and its *ḫ.* shines very brightly" KUB 8.16:7-9 + KUB 8.24 rev. 8-10; *takku* MUL*le-eš[-šal-l]a-aš* d*SIN-mi manin-kuwan tiyazi* "If a *l.* comes close to the moon" KUB 8.16:10f. + KUB 8.24 rev. 11.

The above readings differ from the MUL-*li-eš* assumed by Friedrich (HW 286 sub MUL) and are based on the collation made by Laroche and reported by Leibovici.

Laroche apud Leibovici, Syria 33 (1956) 144 (une certaine étoile ou planète; no Akk. equivalent proposed); van Brock, RHA XX/71 (1962) 102 with n. 1 (nom d'une étoile).

Cf. *ḫašter(a)-*, MUL*wannupaštali-*.

leši-, lišši- n. neut.; liver; from OH.†

sg. nom.-acc. *le-e-ši* KUB 12.58 i 24 (NH); **loc.** *li-iš-ši* KBo 3.21 (BoTU 6) iii 10, 12, 16, 22, 26 (OH/NS); **uncertain case** *le-eš-ši* KUB 22.4:6 (coll.).

Akk.-Hitt. vocab.: *li-ib-bu* = ŠÀ[*-er*], *ku-ut-mu* ŠÀ*-ib-bi* = Š[À*-aš*...], *ga-bi-du* = *li-[iš-ši]* KBo 1.51 ii 7-9 (NH).

nutta ke-er-ti minuwandu li-iš-ši-ma-at-ta war(a)šnuwandu "Let them soothe you in your heart! Let them assuage you in (your) liver!" KBo 3.21 (=BoTU 6) iii 16f. (translation of Akk. hymn to Adad, OH/NS) and passim in this text. (In a list of items for a rit.): [...*t*]*epu le-e-ši tepu iššanaš* ŠAḪ.TUR "a little [...], a little liver, a piglet of dough" KUB 12.58 i 24, ed. Goetze, Tunn. i 48.

Goetze, Tunn. 71f.

Cf. *liššiyala-*.

liššiyala- adj.; pertaining to the liver, oracular; OH/NS.†

li-iš-ši-ya-la-at-ta-ma nepišaš daganzipašša uddār kattan arḫa pētummanzi "The oracular words of heaven and earth are for you to take along" KBo 3.21 (= BoTU 6) ii 6-7 (hymn to Adad). □The above interpretation assumes that *liššiyala-* is derived from *lišši-* "liver", and that "pertaining to the liver" means "oracular". For the use of *-ma* after *-ta* see Houwink ten Cate, FsOtten (1973) 133 and footnote 77.

Goetze, JCS 2 (1948) 149-50 ("pertaining to, contained in the liver" means "on one's mind").

Cf. *leši-*.

(GIŠ)leti-, liti- n. com. and neut.; (an oil-producing plant); OH/NS.†

sg. nom. GIŠ*li-i-ti* KUB 17.10 ii 22; *li-i-ti* KUB 33.69:6; GIŠ*le-e-ti* KUB 29.1 iv 7, 139/d i 10 (Otten, HTR 134); *le-e-ti-iš* KUB 33.74 i 8; *le-⸢e⸣-*[...] KUB 17.13:13.

a. in rit. portion of the OH missing god myths: *kāša* GIŠ*li-i-ti kitta nu ŠA* d*Telipinu*[...] *iškiddu* "Behold *l.* is lying here. Let it anoint the [...] of (the god) Telepinu" KUB 17.10 ii

22-23; [*kāš*]*atta le-e-ti-iš k*[*ittari*] *nu ŠA* DINGIR-*LIM* [ZI-*KA karat*]*iešša* NÍ.TE. MEŠ-*uš l*[*ilare*]*škiddu* "Behold *l.* is lying here for you. Let it soothe [your soul] and (your) *k.*'s (and your) limbs, O god!" KUB 33.74 i 8′-9′; cf. KUB 17.13:13 and HT 100:7 + KUB 33.69:6.

b. in lists of materials for rituals: "They take the following from the palace"... GIŠ*šamama* GIŠGEŠTIN.È.A GIŠ*le-e-ti* GIŠ*šuwaitar* KUŠ. GUD... "*šamama-*, raisin(s), *l.*, *šuwaitar*, a cow hide..." KUB 29.1 iv 4-7 (rit. for the founding of a temple), cf. 139/d i 8-10 (Otten, HTR 134).

Güterbock, JAOS 88 (1968) 68.

NINDA**luwammi-** n. com.; (a type of bread); OH/NS.†

In a fest. for Hurrian deities: [... 1?] NINDA(coll.)*lu-wa-am-me-i-en* 1 NINDA.GÚ. GAL 1 NINDA*lattarīen* 1 NINDA*wištatnimmen ANA* d*Iprimuša paršiya* "He breaks [... 1?] *luwammi*-bread, 1 chick-pea bread, 1 *lattari*-bread, (and) 1 *wištatnimmi*-bread for (the god) Iprimuša" KUB 25.50 ii 8-11. Also to be restored in ibid. ii 3: [NINDA]⌈*lu-wa*⌉*-am-me-i-en*.

luwanni- see (TÚG/GAD)*lupan*(*n*)*i-*.

luwarešša/i- n.; (a topographic feature); NH.†

sg. loc. *lu-wa-re-eš-ši* KUB 42.1 iii? 8; **Luw. acc.** *lu-u-wa-re-eš-ši-ia-an* Bo 69/88:7.

Always in lists of fields: 1 A.ŠÀ *lu-wa-re-eš-ši-kán pariyan* "one field beyond the *l.*" KUB 42.1 iii? 8, ed. Souček, ArOr 27:38f.; *lu-u-wa-re-eš-ši-ia-an ŠA* TÚL*Limadduš*[(-)...] Bo 69/88:7 + KBo 19.20 ii? 1′, cf. ZA 68:150f.

Cf. *lūwariššašši-*.

lūwariššašši- Luw. gen. adj.; (describes topography); NH.†

lu-u-wa-ri-iš-ša-aš-ši-iš 14 *PA* NUMUN-*ŠU ŠA* PN Bo 69/88:9 + KBo 19.20 ii 3, cf. Bo 69/88:11 + KBo 19.20 ii 5 and KBo 19.20 ii? 7 (cumulative line 13), cf. ZA 68:150f.; *lu-u-wa-re-eš-ša-aš-ši-iš* ibid. 7.

For semantic treatment see under *luwarešša/i-* n.

(:)lūḫa- n. com.; light(?); NH.†

sg. nom. *:lu-u-ḫa-aš* KUB 17.20 ii 11, :(?)*lu-u-ḫa-aš* 1516/u:4; **acc.** *:lu-u-ḫa-an* KBo 3.65(= BoTU 22Bβ) obv. 4; **uncertain** *lu-u*!(text *nu*)*-ḫa* IBoT 3.83:5.

In a list of good things: EGIR-*ŠU-ma kariyašḫa*<*š*> (dupl. -*ḫ*]*a-aš*) *:lu-u-ḫa-aš* (dupl. :(?)*lu-u-ḫa-aš*) MU.KAM.SIG₅ *a-a-an-ni-iš apašduš ḫattulatar :ušašša ašanzi* KUB 17.20 ii 11-12 (dupl. 1516/u:4) (rit. for the ancient gods). Cf. [*kar*]*iyašḫi lu-u*!(text: *nu*)*-ḫa* MU.KAM.S[IG₅] IBoT 3.83:5 (rit. for the ancient gods).

The suggested meaning "light" is based on the similarity of this word to the root of Hittite *lalukkima-*, *luk-*, and *lukatta*. For the correspondence of Hittite *-k-* with Luwian *-ḫ-* see Laroche, DLL 135.

Bossert, MIO 4 (1956) 208; Laroche, DLL (1959) 63 (lumière?).

luwili adv.; in Luwian (the language of the land of Luwiya); from MH.

lu-ú-i-li IBoT 1.36 iv 45 (MH), KBo 5.11 i 22 (MH), KBo 12.89 ii 12 (NH); *lu-i-li* KUB 35.7 i 8 (NH), KUB 35.8 i 2 (NH); *lu-u-i-li* KUB 32.8 iii 9, 24 (NH); *lu-ú-*<*i*>*-li* KBo 12.100 obv. 3 (NH); *lu-ú-i-li*!(text *-zi*) KUB 35.43 ii 28 (NH).

Always with a verb of speaking: SAL.ŠU.GI-*ma lu-u-i-li kiššan ḫūkkiškizzi* "The Old Woman recites spells as follows in Luwian" KUB 32.8 iii 9-10, 24-25 (SAL.ŠU.GI rit., NH); *nu* LÚÌ.DU₈ *lu-ú-i-li kišš*[*an*] *tezzi* "The gatekeeper says as follows in Luwian" KBo 5.11 i 22-23 (protocol of the gatekeeper, MH), cf. Otten, Luv. 21-22.

Forrer, SPAW 1919:1030; Hrozný, BoSt 5 (1920) 35-42.

(GIŠ)luešśar n. neut.; (a product of a tree or shrub used as incense); from MH.†

sg. nom.-acc. GIŠ*lu-u-e-eš-šar* KUB 45.57 i 28 (MH/MS), 1885/u i 2, 14, KUB 39.70 i 3, (6) (NH), KUB 39.71 ii 46, iv 33 (NH), *lu-u-e-eš-šar* KBo 23.34 iv 6 (MH/MS), [GI]Š?*lu-u-eš-šar* KBo 24.57 i 11, GIŠ*lu-e-eš-šar* KUB 39.71 ii 7 (NH), GIŠ*lu*!*-i-eš-šar* KUB 7.37:12 (NH), *lu-u-e-eš-ša* KBo 21.33 + KUB 32.49a i 9, ii 14, iii 32 (in 49a:23) (NH), KBo 23.42 i 11 (NH), KBo 23.44 i 8 (with GIŠ erased); **erg.** GIŠ*lu-u-e-eš-na-an-za* KUB 39.71 ii 44 (var. GIŠ*lu-u-e-eš-šar* KUB 39.70 i 3 above) (NH); **d.-l.** GIŠ*lu-u-e-eš-ni* KUB 39.71 ii (33), 35, 38; KUB 39.70 i (12); KUB 39.73:6 (NH); **sg. or pl. gen.** *lu-u-iš-na-an* KUB 12.51 i? 15

with var. [GIŠ?l]u(coll.)-*u-e-eš-na-aš* KUB 42.99:7; **broken** GIŠ*lu-ú-i-eš-na*-x[...] KUB 47.35 iv 12.

a. GIŠ*lueššar* — **1′** in the *babilili* ritual: [(1 DUG*PURSĪ*)]*TUM dāi šermakan* GIŠ*lu-u-e-eš-šar* [(*ḫantai*)]*zzi ANA* DUG*PURSĪTI-ma* [*katta*(*n* 1 SÍ)]G *kišrin dāi šermakan* [(1 TÚG)*kureš*]*šar* BABBAR *dāi namma* SÍG ZA.GÌN [(SÍG *ḪAṢARTUM* SÍG S)]A5-*ya anda tarnāi* [(*natkan* GIŠ*lu-u-e-eš-ni*)] *šer dāi* "He takes one bowl and arranges *l.* on it, but [under] the bowl he puts a *kišriš* of wool. On top he puts one white *kureššar*. Then he entwines blue, green and red wool and puts that on the *l.*" KUB 39.71 iv 33-38 with dupl. KUB 39.73:2-6; □KUB 39.71 i 37-42 can be restored to the same wording. This is followed, after a gap and some recitation, by: [*nu* LÚ*šakun*]*eš* GIŠ*lu-e-eš-šar katta tarna*[*i*] "The priest 'lets down' the *l.*" (meaning?) ibid. ii 7; after more recitation: *kuitmanma* GIŠ*lu-u-e*[(*-eš-šar w*)]*arani* "But while the *l.* is burning (the singer sings in Babylonian)" ibid. 18-19 with par. 1885/u (+KUB 39.70+), i 2′-3′; "When the singer has finished singing in Babylonian, the priest begins to make offerings" *nuza* LÚ*šakuneš* NINDA[.SIG *dā*]*i nat arḫa paršiyazzi n*[*atkan* GI]Š*lu-u-e-eš-ni š*[*er*] *dāi* "The priest [take]s a [thin] bread, breaks it, and puts it on the *l.*" ibid. ii 29-33 (omitted in par.); Then two fishes are put upon or over the *l.* (GIŠ*lu-u-eš-ni šer*), ibid. 34-38 with par. 1885/u i 11-14; *nu* DUG*PURSĪTUM šarā dāi kattanma* SÍG*kišrin epzi nan ANA* EN.SISKUR *parā epzi* "Then he lifts the bowl up, but under it he holds a *kišriš* of wool, and he holds it out to the patron of the sacrifice" ibid. 38-40; □the par. 1885/u i 14 has GIŠ*lu-u-e-eš-šar* instead of DUG*PURSĪTUM* (i.e., the contents instead of the bowl); *maḫḫanmaza* GIŠ*lu-u-*⌈*e*⌉*-eš-na-an-za* (var. GIŠ*lu-u-e-eš-šar*) *arḫ*[*a* ...] *nat ANA* DINGIR-*LIM šer arḫa waḫ*[*nuzzi*] § [*kuitmanm*]*a* GIŠ*lu-u-e-eš-šar waḫn*[(*uškizzi*)] LÚNAR-*ma* URU]*papilili ki*[(*š*)*š*(*an* SÌR-*RU*)] "But when the *l.* [burns(?)] out, he waves it over the deity. [While] he is waving the *l.*, the singer sings in Babylonian as follows" ibid. ii 44-47 with par. (1885/u+) KUB 39.70 i 4″-7″. "[When the singer] has finished [singing] the words in Babylonian," *nuka*[*n* LÚ]SANGA-*niš* [(GIŠ*lu-e*)-*eš-šar*] GI*kurši katta dāi* [*nu AN*]*A* EN.SISKUR [(ZA.ḪUM) *ŠA*] KAŠ *arḫa dai nukan* GIŠ*lu*[*-u-e-e*]*š-ni* [(*anda šippan*)]*ti* (var. *šippandāi*) *natkan kištanuzi na*[*t š*]*arā* [(*dāi na*)]*tkan* IZI-*i išḫuwai* "Then the priest puts the *l.* down on the wicker tray(?), takes the pitcher of beer from the patron, pours (the liquid) into the *l.*, and extinguishes it. Then he lifts it up and throws it into the fire" KUB 39.70 i 9″-14″ with par. KUB 39.71 ii 50-57 and HT 5:1-6.

2′ In other rituals: *nu ḫuprušḫin iya*[*zi*] *nuš-šan* GIŠ*lu-u-e-eš-šar katta ḫandaiz*[*zi*] "He makes a burner(?) and arranges *l.* on it" KUB 45.47 i 27-28 (MH/MS); [x + ?]6 GIŠ*zuppariyašša*[*n* GIŠ?*l*]*u*(coll.)-*u-e-eš-na-aš* (var. *lu-u-iš-na-an*) *awan* [(*katta dāi*)] "He puts 6(?) torches under (or: next to) the *l.*" KUB 42.99:7 with dupl. KUB 12.51 i 15; cf. [... GI]Š*zuppari*ḪI.A GIŠ*lu*!-*i-eš-šar dāi* KUB 7.37:12.

b. *luešša*(*r*) without det. together with GIŠERIN: *nuššan ANA* DUGGAL.ḪI.A *wātar* GEŠTIN-*ya tamai ANA* DUG*aḫrušḫiyaššan* Ì.GIŠ *tamai lāḫui* GIŠERIN-*yakan lu-u-e-eš-ša* [*a*]*nda dāi* "Then he pours other water and wine into the cups, and other oil into the censer, and puts cedar (wood, shavings, or resin) (as?/and?) *l.* into it" KUB 32.49a (+ KBo 21.33) ii 12-15 (rit. w. Hurr.), cf. ibid. iii 32 (in 49a iii 23) and ibid. i 7-9 with dupl. KBo 23.44 i 6-8; KBo 23.42 i 9-12 with dupl. KBo 24.57 i 9-11 (rit. w. Hurr.); GIŠERIN *lu-u-e-eš-šar* KBo 23.34 iv 6 over erasure.

The det. GIŠ argues for a tree or one of its products: its wood, shavings, fruit or resin. The sequence of activities under usage a 1′ and the connection with *aḫrušḫi-* "censer" under usage a 2′ point to a material burned as incense.

Laroche, RHA XIX/69 (1961) 85 ("un nom de plante indéterminée"); Laroche, BiOr 21 (1964) 321 n. 6 ("une espèce de bois à encens"); Friedrich, HW 3. Erg. (1966) 22f. ("eine Art Weihrauchholz?"); Laroche in Ugar. V (1968) 506 ("un végétal"); Otten, StBoT 15 (1971) 9 ("Weihrauch?").

luk(k)- A v. act. and mid.; to grow bright, dawn; from OH/OS.

active pres. sg. 3 *lu-uk-zi* KUB 9.15 ii 17, 18 (NH), KUB 24.5 obv. 28 (NH), FHG 13 ii (31) (NH); **active pret. or mid. historical pres. sg. 3** *lu-uk-ta* KBo 5.8 i 26 (Murš. II).

luk(k)- A

mid. pres. sg. 3 *lu-uk-ta* KBo 17.13 "obv.?" 1 (OH/OS), *lu-uk-t*[*a*?] KBo 25.68 rev. 6 (OH/OS); *lu-uk-kat-ta* KBo 17.1 ii 30, iv 7 (OH/OS), VBoT 58 iv 40 (OH/NS), KBo 4.2 i 38 (OH?/NS), KUB 13.1 i 29 (MH/MS), KUB 7.1 i 19 (pre-NH/NS), KUB 24.9 + JCS 24:37 ii 48, iii 4 (MH/NS), KUB 21.10:13, KUB 14.20:14 (Murš. II), KUB 1.13 i 59 (NH) and often in hipp., KUB 17.3 iii 7 (NH), etc.; see StBoT 5:109; *lu-ug-ga-at-ta* KBo 17.3 iv 21 (OH/OS), 911/z ii 9 (NH) (translit. in StBoT 5:109 to be corrected); *lu-uq-qa-ta* KBo 10.41:6 (MH/NS); *lu-kat-ta* KUB 10.91 ii 2, KBo 2.4 i 27, KUB 27.70 ii 11 (all NH); *lu-uk-ka-ta* 789/z 8 (NH).

mid. pret. sg. 3 *lu-uk-kat-ta-ti* KBo 3.38 obv. 2 (OH/NS); *lu-uk-ta-at* KBo 3.34 i 19 (OH/NS), with dupl. KUB 36.104 obv. 17 (OH/OS), KBo 5.8 iii 22 (Murš. II).

a. with expressed subject: *maḫḫanma* GE$_6$-*anza lu-uk-zi* MUL.UD.ZAL.LI-*kan uizzi lu-uk-zi nāwi* "But when the night grows brighter and the morning star rises, (while) it hasn't yet become (really) bright, (let him promptly leave the city; let the sun not find him inside the city!)" KUB 9.15 ii 16-20 (instr., NH), ed. StBoT 3:32f.; [(G)E$_6$-*a*]*n-za lu-u*[(*k-kat-ta* ^{d}UTU-*uškan kal*⸗*maraz uit*)] KUB 36.62:1 with dupl. KUB 17.1 ii 14 (Keššì myth, NH), ed. Friedrich, ZA 49 (1949) 238f.; KUB 17.1 ii 14 collated reads G[E$_6$-*an-za l*]*u-uk-kat-ta* contra Friedrich; □ *maḫḫan*⸗*ma*⸗*aš lu-uk-kat-ta šakruwanzi* KBo 3.2 obv! 47, *maḫḫan*⸗*ma*⸗*aš lu-uk-kat-ta tūriyanzi* KBo 3.5 ii 27, iii 47, *maḫḫan*⸗*ma*⸗*aš*⸗*kan lu-uk-kat-ta IŠTU* É.^{LÚ}IŠ [*parā*] *uwadanzi* KUB 1.13 iv 71, cf. iv 58 (all Kikkuli) are single clauses with adv. *lukkatta*; the -*aš* is acc. pl. Otherwise (*lukkatta* as verb): Kammenhuber, Hipp.heth. 91 n. 72, 94 n. 96, and Neu, StBoT 5 (1968) 110 with n. 3-4.

b. without expressed subject — **1′** with *mān*: *mān lu-uk-ta-at nu ABI* LUGAL *ḫalzaiš* "When it dawned, the father of the king called" KBo 3.34 (= BoTU 12A) i 19 ("Palace Chron.", OH/NS), with dupl. KUB 36.104 obv. 17 (OH/OS); UD.2.KAM *mān lu-uk-ta t*[*a* . . .] KBo 25.68 rev. 9 + KBo 17.13 "obv." 1 (OH/OS); [*ma*]-⌜*a*⌝-*an lu-uk-kat-ta-ti* KBo 3.38 obv. 2 (Zalpa story, OH/NS), ed. StBoT 17:6f., 36; cf. KUB 28.74 obv. 1 (fest., OH/NS); *mān INA* UD.x.KAM *lu-uk-kat-ta*/*lu-uq-qa-ta*/*lu-kat-ta* KUB 7.1 i 19 (Ayatarša rit., pre-NH/NS), KUB 30.15 obv. 1 and KUB 39.4 obv. 1 (royal funeral rit., MH?/NS), ed. HTR 66f., 24f.; KBo 15.8:11 (subst. rit., NH), ed. StBoT 3:68f.; KBo 15.37 ii 47 (EZEN *ḫišuwaš*, NH), KUB 20.84:5 (fest.), KBo 11.5 vi 22 (colophon to rit.), etc.; *INA* UD.x.KAM *mān lukkatta* KUB 24.9 + JCS 24:37 ii 48 (rit. of Alli, MH/NS) and dupl. KBo 10.41:6 with *lu-uq-qa-ta*, ed. THeth 2:38f.; KUB 29.55 i 1 (older, rit.-introduced hipp., MH/MS), ed. Hipp.heth. 150f.; KUB 39.10 i (1) (royal funeral rit., MH?/NS), ed. HTR 54f.; KBo 12.96 iv 4 (rit., MH/NS); KBo 20.72 iii! 14; *mān luggatta*⸗*ma*/*lukkatta*⸗*ma* (all examples OH or MH) KBo 17.3 iv 21, KBo 17.1 ii 30, iv 7, 24 (both rit. OH/OS), ed. StBoT 8:28f., 36-39, KBo 17.74 i 30 (weather fest., OH/MS), ed. StBoT 12:14f., JCS 24:37 + KUB 24.9 iii 4 with dupl. KUB 41.1 iii 12 (rit. of Alli, MH/NS), ed. THeth 2:42f.

2′ with *maḫḫan*/GIM-*an*: *INA* UD.x.KAM-*ya maḫḫan lukkatta* KUB 29.49 + KBo 14.62:5 ("Third Hipp. Treatise", MH/MS), ed. Hipp.heth. 198f., cf. KUB 29.40 ii 2 (MH/MS), ed. Hipp.heth. 178f.; *maḫḫann*⸗*a lu-uk-kat-ta* KBo 4.2 i 38 (rit., pre-NH/NS); *maḫḫan*⸗*ma lu-uk-kat-ta* (from MH), KUB 13.1 i 29 (*Bel Madgalti*, MH/MS); Kikkuli hipp. (all NH): KUB 1.13 + KUB 2.12c i 37, 59, ii 12, 60 (tablet 1), KBo 3.5 ii 49(!), iii 29 (tablet 2), KUB 1.11 ii 1, iii 49 (tablet 3), etc.; GIM-*an-ma lu-uk-kat-ta* (all NH): KUB 17.3 iii 7 (Gilg. epic), KBo 2.4 iii 8 (EZEN.ITU), KUB 21.10:13; KUB 14.20:14 (Murš. II), AM 194f.; GIM-*an-ma lu-uk-zi* KUB 24.5 obv. 28 (subst. rit., NH), ed. StBoT 3:10f., 32.

3′ without introductory temporal conj.: *nu išpandan ḫūmandan iyaḫḫat numukan INA* ^{URU}*Šapidduwa* A.ŠÀ *kueri anda lu-uk-ta-at* "I traveled the entire night. It dawned for me in the fields in Š. (But when the sun rose, I went against him in battle.)" KBo 5.8 iii 21-24, ed. AM 158f.; *nu* GE$_6$-*az iyaḫḫat numu INA* ^{URU}*Kat*⸗*titimuwa lu-uk-ta* (var. *lu-uk-kat-ta*) ibid. i 25f. with dupl. KUB 19.36:21f., ed. AM 148f.

luk(*k*)*atta* forms pertinent to the verb, as opposed to the adverb, can be detected only syntactically: verbal *luk*(*k*)*atta* concludes its clause. Therefore *luk*(*k*)*atta* forms followed immediately by explicit marks of clause boundary are verbal. Others are treated under the adverb. The adverbial *luk*(*k*)*atta* could be derived from a frozen mid. form. Adverbial *luk*(*k*)*atti*, on the other hand, must be a locative of a noun **luk*(*k*)*at*-. No clear examples of active forms of *luk*- have been found in OH or MH. The verb *luk*- is confined to describing the faint but growing sunlight in the atmosphere at dawn just before the sun rises. Only once (sub a) does it possibly describe light emitted from a star. Kümmel's claim, StBoT 3 (1967) 32f., that one should distinguish active *lukzi* "es wird hell" from mid. *lukkatta* "es ist hell" and that the latter includes sunrise seems contrary to the available evidence.

Sommer, Heth. 2 (1922) 22-29; Götze, AM (1933) 255-57; Friedrich, HW (1952) 130; Neu, StBoT 5 (1968) 109f.; Otten and Souček, StBoT 8 (1969) 53, 79f., Neu, StBoT 18 (1974) 79.

Cf. *lalukki-* v., *lalukkima-*, *lalukkeš-*, *lalukkešnu-*, *lalukkiwant-*, *luk-* B, *lukkanu-*, *lukat*, *lukki/a-*, *lukkeš-*.

luk(k)- B v.; to set fire to; NH.†

pres. sg. 3 *lu-uk-zi* KBo 19.137 i 8; **pret. sg. 1** *lu-uk-ku-un* KBo 12.38 iii 9 (Šupp. II), **imp. pl. 2 (or pret. pl. 2)** *lu-uk-ten* 2619/c:6 (StBoT 15:37); **part.** *lu-uk-kán-ta* KBo 19.137 i 6.

GIŠMÁ.ḪI.A-*ma eppun naškan* ŠÀ A.AB. BA *lu-uk-ku-un* "(I annihilated them:) I captured the ships and set fire to them on the high sea" KBo 12.38 iii 7-9 (Šupp. II account of Tudḫ.'s conquest of Alashiya), ed. Otten, MDOG 94:20f., Güterbock, JNES 26:76, 78; [. . .]*zuppāri lu-uk-ten* x[. . .] 2619/c cited by Otten in StBoT 15:37. Perhaps *lu-uk-zi* in KUB 44.21 iii 10 is a form of this word.

The forms *lukkanzi*, *lukker*, *lukkan*, *lukkanta*, and *lukkešk-*, treated under *lukki/a-*, could belong here. But since the only unambiguous datable form of *lukk-* B is from late NH, the ambiguous ones from OH and MH have been interpreted as *lukki/a-*.

Friedrich, HW 3. Erg. (1966) 23; Neu, StBoT 5 (1968), 110 n. 1, StBoT 18 (1974) 79.

Cf. *luk(k)-* A.

lukka- v.; see *lukki/a-*.

lukkanu- v.; to pass the night (sleepless?); NH.†

pres. pl. 3 *lu-uq-qa-nu-wa-an-zi* Bo 2562 iv 22, KUB 46.27 obv. 22; *lu-ug-ga-nu-wa-an-zi* Bo 2998 i 12; **broken** *lu-u[k- . . .]* KUB 39.8 iii 14.

Always in construction with GE$_6$/*išpant-* "night": GE$_6$-*an dapian lu-uq-qa-nu-wa-an-zi* "They pass the whole night (in cult activities?)" Bo 2562 iv 22 (cult inv.); cf. GE$_6$-*an lu-ug-ga-nu-wa-an-zi* Bo 2998 i 12 and GE$_6$-*za lu-uq-qa-nu-wa-an-z[i . . .]* KUB 46.27 obv. 22 (cult inv.).

Replaces earlier GE$_6$-*an laknu-* "to pass the night": *nu kuitman* GE$_6$-*an la-ak[-nu- . . .]* "while (they?) pass the night" KUB 39.7 iii 53 (royal funeral rit.) corresponds to [. . . *išp]andan lu-u[k- . . .]* in the dupl. KUB 39.8 iii 14, if this is restored correctly. One cannot be positive which of the two forms of this idiom has priority. But it is likely in view of the attestation of *išpantan laknu-* in the omens and the royal funeral rituals, compositions which may possibly go back to OH or MH prototypes, and *išpantan luqqanu-* in the cult inventories which are quite late, that the *laknu-* form is the original. "To make the night fall" was not an obvious choice to later scribes for the idiom which means continuation of daytime activities in the nighttime. So the phrase was transformed to "to make the night light/bright".

Neu, StBoT 18 (1974) 79-80.

Cf. *laknu-*, *luk(k)-* A.

lukat, luk(k)atta, luk(k)at(t)i, lukta adv.; at dawn, (by extension:) the following morning, the next day; from OH.

lu-uk-kat-ta KBo 15.33 ii 29 (OH/MS), KBo 13.164 i 8 (OH/NS), KBo 23.8:5, 21 (OH or MH/NS), KBo 22.122 iv? 12 (OH), KBo 15.34 ii 9, 14, 20 (MH?/NS), VBoT 24 iv 11 (MH/NS), KBo 4.4 iii 40, 52, iv (17) (Murš. II), KBo 3.5 i 21, 40, etc., KUB 36.90 obv. 14, 15, KBo 24.130 i 11, 16 (all NH), etc.

lu-uk-kat-ti (not found in OS or MS; probably a NH innovation) KBo 10.20 i 15, (19), etc. (NS) (dupl. KBo 24.112 + KUB 30.39 obv. 14, 18, etc. has *lu-uk-kat-ta*) *lu-uk-kat-ti-ia-kán* KUB 10.31 vi 7 (OH/NS), KUB 9.16 i 4, 8, 12, etc. (OH/NS), KUB 25.51 iv 11 (OH/NS), all other exx. NH: KBo 10.12 ii 6, KBo 4.4 iii 43, KUB 13.4 iii 72 (dupl. KUB 13.5 iii 42 *[l]u-uk-kat-ta*), KUB 36.90 obv. 18, etc.

lu-uq-qa-ti KBo 13.208:2.

lu-uk-kat-te KBo 13.168:8 (MH/NS), KUB 20.80 iii? 1′ (NH).

lu-kat-te KUB 25.21 iv 2′, KUB 1.12 obv. (8) (both NH).

lu-kat-ti (all NH, many late NH) KBo 2.7 obv. 29, KUB 38.32 obv. 11, KUB 25.24 ii 1, KUB 25.23 i 10, etc.

lu-kat KUB 38.26 obv. 8, KUB 25.27 iii 17, 28, KBo 20.87 i 6, KUB 38.32 rev. 15, 27, KUB 46.38 ii 19, KUB 17.32:17, KBo 2.7 obv. 11, 15, etc. (all NH).

lu-uk-kat KUB 25.27 i 20 (NH).
lu-uk-ta-ma KUB 29.4 i 55 (NH) in text which otherwise uses verbal *lukkatta* (cf. *luk(k)*- A).

a. sentence initial *lukkatta/i-ma* — **1′** "If it is feasible (ZAG-*an*) for the lord of the house, he drives into Kuliwišna on that (same) day and bathes himself. But if it is not feasible for him, he bathes himself in the same place where he spends the night" *lu-uk-kat-ta-ma anda* URU*Kuliwišna unnāi* "But in the morning he drives into K." KBo 15.34 ii 17-21 (rit., OH/NS); *lu-uk-kat-ta-ma-kán kuit[man* dUTU-*u]š nāwi uizzi* "But at dawn, whi[le the s]un has not yet 'come' (i.e. risen)" KUB 7.1 + KBo 3.8 ii 45; *lu-uk-kat-ta-ma-kán* dUTU-*uš upzi* "But at dawn, (when) the sun rises" ibid. ii 25; *lu-uk-ta-ma INA* UD.2.KAM *kuitman* dUTU-*uš nu-u-a* (emend to *nawi*) *artari* KUB 29.4 i 55 (rit., NH), ed. Kronasser, Schw.Gotth. 12-13, 45; *[(lu-u)]k-kat-ti-ma-kán* (var. *lu-uk-kat-ta-*) UD[(*-az i*)]*štarna paiz*[(*zi*)] "On the morrow, when the day reaches its midpoint (noon?)" KBo 23.1 + KUB 30.38 i 58 with dupl. KBo 23.2 ii 8f. (Ammiḫatna rit., NH).

2′ beginning §§ in enumerations of activities stretching over many days, "at dawn" meaning "the next day": KBo 24.112 + KUB 30.39 obv. 14, 18, 20, 22, KBo 10.20 i 19, 24, 28, 32 (both AN.TAḪ.ŠUM fest. outline, OH/NS), ed. Güterbock, JNES 19:80-87; KBo 4.4 iii 40, 43, 52, KBo 16.8 i 6 (both Murš. II ann.); KBo 3.5 i 21, 40 (hipp., NH); KBo 24.130 i 11, 16 (bird oracles, NH); KUB 38.32 obv. 11, 29, KUB 25.23 i 10, 26, 32 (cult inv., NH).

3′ beginning §§ and followed immediately by *INA* UD.(number).KAM: KBo 17.105 iii 1 (rit., MH/MS); KUB 30.31 + KUB 32.114 i 56, 68, iv 29, 36 (rit., NH); not at beginning of §: KUB 32.123 i 20, ii 28 (fest., NH); followed by *karuwariwar*: KUB 1.13 iv 1, KBo 3.2 obv.! 64, ed. Hipp.heth. 68f., 134f.

b. not sentence-initial: *nu lu-uk-kat-ta* UD.KAM-*aš ANA* EZEN-*KA eḫ[u] lu-uk-kat-ta-aš-kán* UD.KAM-*ti* m*Dudḫaliyan tuedaš aššiyantaš pedaš* URU*Ḫakmiš* URU*Nerik AŠŠUM* LÚSANGA-*UTTIM iškanzi nu lu-uk-kat-ti* UD-*ti ANA* EZEN-*KA eḫu* "Tomorrow come to your festival! Tomorrow they will anoint D. to the priesthood in your favorite places, Ḫ. and N. Tomorrow come to your festival!" KUB 36.90 obv. 14-19 (prayer, NH), ed. Haas, KN, 176-79; (A vassal said to the Hittite king:) "I have no son. The people are grumbling(?) against us." *nuwa lu-uk-kat-ti* [(*kiššan našmawa ki*)]*ššan* "Tomorrow will it be this way or that way?" KUB 6.43:5-7 with dupl. KUB 6.41 i 24-26 and KBo 4.7 + KBo 22.38 i 23-25 (Kup.), ed. SV 9:108; *našta kuitma*<*n*> (var. *kuitman*) dUTU-*uš šarā nuza* ⌜*ḫudak*(?)⌝ *war*[*ap*]*du naškan lu-uk-kat-ti* (var. *-ta*) DINGIR.MEŠ-*aš* [(*adann*)]*aš meḫuni ḫudak aru* "While the sun is (on its way) up, let him promptly(?) bathe! And at dawn, at the time of the gods' eating, he shall promptly be present!" KUB 13.4 iii 71-73, with dupls. KUB 13.5 iii 41f. and KUB 13.19:14 (instr., NH), ed. Sturtevant, Chrest. 160f., tr. ANET 209; "When I left Uda, did I not say to my lord:" UN-*ašwa lu-uk-kat-ti* EGIR-*anda uiddu* "Let a man come after me tomorrow, (while the men of Assur are here)!" *kinunaš lu-uk-kat-ti* KASKAL-*aḫta* "Now he took the road at dawn (but your man didn't catch them)" KBo 9.82 obv. 4-9 (letter, NH); *maḫḫanmaš lu-uk-kat-ta tūriyanzi* "When on the following day they hitch them up" KBo 3.5 ii 27, iii 47; *maḫḫanmaškan lu-uk-kat-ta IŠTU* É LÚIŠ [*parā*] *uwadanzi* "When on the following day they bring them out of the stable" KUB 1.13 iv 71 (all hipp., NH), ed. Hipp.heth. 90f., 96f., 74f.; □the *-aš* is not the subject of a verb *lukkatta* here, but the object (acc. com. pl.) of the verb which follows it (cf. also *luk(k)*-A, v.).

As observed by Kümmel, StBoT 3 (1967) 32f., *lukkatta/lukkatti* denotes primarily a time of day, namely dawn. Only from the viewpoint of the preceding day does it require the translation "on the morrow, on the following day".

The forms assembled here, which share a common meaning and function (adv.), are apparently of diverse origins. Probably *lu(k)katta* and *lukta* are originally mid. pres. sg. 3 verb forms of *luk(ka)-*. *lukat* could be an abbreviated writing of *lukatta*, but more likely is endingless loc. of noun **lukkat-* "dawn", as *lukkatti* is the loc. in *-i* of the same. *lukta* and *lukkatta* are the oldest forms, while *lukkatti* is probably a NH innovation, and *lukat* occurs only in late NH.

Zimmern, OLZ 1922:300f., Sommer, Heth. 2 (1922) 22-32; Götze, AM (1933) 255f.; Kammenhuber, Heth.u.Idg. (1979) 141f.

Cf. *luk(k)*- A.

lukki/a- v.; to set fire to; from OH/TOS.

pres. sg. 3 *lu-uk-ki-iz-zi* KBo 6.2 iv 53, 56, 59 (OH/TOS), KUB 29.38 left col. 1 (OS), KBo 25.14 ii 7 (OH/MS); KUB 20.10 iii 5 (OH/NS), KBo 15.48 ii 14 (MH/NS), KUB 32.8 iii 23 (MH?/NS), KBo 22.236:9 (NH); **pl. 3** *lu-uk-kán-zi* KBo 20.34 rev. 10, 11 (OH/MS), KUB 33.45 + FHG 2 iii 9, KUB 33.11 iii 10, KBo 10.26 i 2 (all OH/NS), KUB 32.128 ii (10) (MH/NS), KBo 8.72 obv.? 10 (NH); *lu-kán-zi* Bo 1709:7 (StBoT 15:18).

pret. sg. 3 *lu-uk-ki-it* KUB 26.71 (= BoTU 30) i 13 (OH/NS), KUB 23.20:13 (OH/NS), KUB 19.12 ii (6) (NH); **pl. 3** *lu-uk-ke-e-er* KUB 14.1 rev. 54 (MH/MS).

part. neut. sg. acc. *lu-uk-kán* KUB 20.96 iv 2 (OH/NS), KBo 6.11 i 6 (OH/NS), KBo 17.61 rev. 21 (OH/OS or MS), KBo 23.10 iv 23 (MH/MS), IBoT 3.119:4, KUB 20.2 iii 38 (NH), KUB 10.91 ii 9 (NH); **com. pl. acc.** [. . . *l*]*u-uk-kán-du-uš* KUB 33.49 iii 6 (OH/NS); **neut. pl.** *lu-uk-kán-ta* KBo 19.137 i 6; **iter.** *lu-uk-ke-eš-ki*[- . . .] KUB 44.42 obv. 19 (NH).

Only the forms *lu-uk-ki-iz-zi* and *lu-uk-ki-it* belong unquestionably to *lukki/a-*. The others could belong to *luk-* B. See Kronasser, EHS p. 385. The decision to treat the ambiguous ones under *lukki/a-* was based on the dates of the examples. Cf. discussion at end of *luk-* B.

a. obj. houses or buildings: *takku taišzin kuiški lu-uk-ki-iz-zi* "If someone sets fire to a shed" KBo 6.3 iv 59 (Law §100, OH/NS), ed. Friedrich, HG 48f. with *lu-uk-ki-iz-zi* in dupl. KBo 6.2 iv 59 (OH/TOS), dupl. KBo 19.5:4 has scribal error *lu-uk-ki-iš-zi*; *takku* LÚ-*aš ELLUM* É-*er lu-uk-ki-iz-zi* "If a free man sets fire to a house" KBo 6.2 iv 53 (Law §98, OH/TOS), cf. Law §99, ed. Friedrich, HG 48f.

b. obj. cities: *nu* [U]RU-*ŠU* (var. URU.DIDLI-*ŠU*) *lu-uk-ki-it* "and he set fire to its cities" KUB 26.71 (= BoTU 30) i 13 (Anitta text, OH/NS), with dupl. KBo 3.22:69 (TOS), ed. Neu, StBoT 18:14f.; ^{URU}*Maraša*[*n* URU-*a*]*n kattan lu-uk-ke-e-er nan a*[*rḫa warnue*]*r* "They set fire to the city of M. and [burned] it do[wn]" KUB 14.1 rev. 54 (Madduwatta, MH/MS), ed. Götze, Madd. 32f., cf. also KUB 23.20:13 (Ḫatt. I annals, OH/NS) with Melchert, JNES 37 (1978) 21, and KUB 19.12 ii 6 (DŠ frag. 4, B ii 6), ed. Güterbock, JCS 10:60.

c. obj. fields, trees, plants, twigs, fibers, chips of kindling: [(*takku p*)]*aḫḫur AN*[(*A* A.ŠÀ)]-*ŠU kuiški pēdai* [(*ta tame*)]*lla* / [(A.ŠÀ)]-*ŠU lu-uk-ki-i*[(*z-zi*)] *kuišat lu-uk*[(*-ki-iz-zi nu-za lu-u*)]*k-kán* / [(A.ŠÀ-*L*)]*AM apaš dāi* [(SI)]G$_5$-*andanna* [(A.ŠÀ-*LUM ANA* EN)] A.ŠÀ / [(*pa*)]*i taz wa*[(*rši*)] "If someone carries fire onto his field, and sets fire to another's field also, he who set it afire shall take the burnt-over field, and give a good field to the field owner, and he shall reap it" KUB 29.23:1′-4′ (+) KUB 29.21:17-20 (+) KUB 29.22 i 8-11 (Law §106, copy o, OH/NS), ed. Friedrich, HG 62f.; □other copies vary considerably and none is completely intact; KBo 6.11 (b) i 6 and KUB 29.22 (o$_2$) i (9) have neut. part. *lu-uk-kán* modifying A.ŠÀ; [*takku* A.ŠÀ-*LAM*(?) *kui*(*šk*)]*i lu-uk-ki-iz-zi* KBo 6.12 i 17 (Law §105, OH/NS), ed. Friedrich, HG 60f.; □space between *takku* and *kuiški* requires about three signs, but not likely *pa-aḫ-ḫur* as in Friedrich, HG p. 60 with n. 18, since elsewhere *lukki/a-* does not take *paḫḫur* as its object; any three-sign word denoting a field, leaves, trash, etc. would be suitable; [^{GIŠ}*pá*]*r*!-*aš-du-un lu-u*[*k-k*]*án-zi* "They light a twig" KUB 44.57:7 (OH or MH/NS?) cf. *pár-aš-tu* (eras.) *lu-uk-ki-iz-zi* KBo 25.14 ii 7 (OH/MS); [*n*(*u* ^{GIŠ}*waršaman maḫ*)]*ḫan lu-uk-kán-zi n*[(*ašta anda* 4-*taš ḫ*)]*alḫaltumariya*[*š* (*laluk*- *kišz*)*i*] "As they ignite the kindling, and it becomes bright in the four corners" KUB 33.45:9 + FHG 2 iii 4f. with dupl. KUB 33.51:5-7 (disappearance of DINGIR.MAḪ myth, OH/NS), translit. Laroche, Myth. 80; "In the clay cup into which honey and olive oil have been poured" *nuššan* ^{GIŠ}*waršaman šēr lu-uk-ki-iz-zi nat arḫa urāni* "she lights a chip of kindling wood on top, and it (neut., the oil and honey) burns up" KUB 32.8 iii 20-23 (MH?/NS), ed. LTU 21; [. . .]x-*an ḫaššī lu-uk-ki-iz-zi* [1 ^{GIŠ}*e*-]*a-an* ZAG-*ni*<-*it*> ŠU-*it* 1 ^{GIŠ}*e-a-an-ma* [GÙB-*i*]*t* ŠU-*it ḫarzi* "(The Man of the Stormgod) ignites (something, perhaps the chips of fir) on the hearth; he holds one (chip of) fir with his right hand and one with his left" KBo 22.236:9-11, traces in line 9 do not permit reading ^{GIŠ}*e*-] ⌈*a*⌉-*an*; *ta* 8 ^{GIŠ}*e-ia-an* [. . .] *nat lu-uk-ki-i*[*z-zi*] IBoT 2.121 rev. 10-11 (Nerik cult, OH/TOS), ed. Haas, KN 136f.

d. obj. torches: *apāšša damai zuppari* ^{SÍG}*alit* SA$_5$ *anda išḫiyanda lu-uk-ki-iz-zi* "And he lights other torches bound up with red wool" KBo 15.48 ii 12-14 (EZEN *ḫišuwaš*, MH?/NS); describing a procession: (various classes of women march in front,) ^{GIŠ}*zupparu lu-uk-kán pē ḫar-kanzi ḫarnain piran papparškanzi* EGIR-*anda* DINGIR-*LUM iyatta* "they hold lighted torches and sprinkle *ḫ*.-fluid in front, and the deity goes behind" KUB 10.91 ii 9-11 (fest., NS); ^{GIŠ}*zupari* 2-*ŠU* 9-*an ki-iz*! 9-*an lu-uk-kán-zi* [*k*]*izziya* 9-*an lu*-[*u*]*k-kán-zi* "torches, two sets of nine — they light nine on this side, and they light nine on this side" KBo 20.34 rev. 10-11 (Ḫantitaššu rit., OH/MS); $^{LÚ.MEŠ}$ŠU.I ^{GIŠ}*zupparu danzi ta lu-uk-kán-zi taššikan wātar lāḫūwanzi tašta pānzi* "The barbers take a torch, light (it), pour water upon it, and go out" KBo 10.26 i 1-4 (KI.LAM fest., OH/NS), ed. Singer, Diss. 345 ("11th Tablet"), and many other passages cited in Otten, StBoT 15 s.v. *zupparu*/*i*.

Instead of *lu-ki-iz-zi* read DIB-*ki-iz-zi* in KBo 10.37 i 26 (*appiškizzi* in dupl. 572/t i 6); cf. *piran* DIB-*zi* ibid. i 27.

Zimmern, OLZ 1922:300f.; Sommer, Heth. 2 (1922) 30-32 ("in Brand stecken, verbrennen"); Kronasser, EHS (1965) 385; Neu, StBoT 18 (1974) 79f., 89.

Cf. *luk*(*k*)- A v.; *warnu-* v.

lukkeš-, lukiš- v.; to become bright, dawn(?); NH.†

pres. sg. 3 *lu-ki-iš-zi* KBo 21.20 rev. 14 (NH); **pret. sg. 3** *lu-uk-ke-eš-ta* KUB 8.48 i 1 (NH).

nu lu-uk-ke-eš-ta [*nu*] ^{d}*E*[*nk*]*ituš ANA* ^{d}GILGAMEŠ EGIR-*pa memišk*[*iuwan daiš*] "It dawned(?), and E. said to G." (telling his dream of the previous night) KUB 8.48 i 1-2 (Gilg. epic, NH), ed. Friedrich, ZA 39 (1930) 16f., and Stefanini, JNES 28 (1969) 40, 45; □ Friedrich's "hell werden" (HW 130) is appropriate here, since *lukkešta* takes no direct object and seems to indicate the advent of the morning after Enkidu's dream; [GIM-*an*?] *lu-ki-iš-zi nu* EN. [Š]UKUR SI-⌜*ra*⌝ [. . .] "[when?] it becomes light, and the spearman [blows] the horn, (he/she draws pure water)" KBo 21.20 rev. 14f. (med. rit.), ed. StBoT 19:44, frag. L.

Friedrich, ZA 39 (1930) 49f., Stefanini, JNES 28 (1969) 40, 45 ("then daylight came"); cf. van Brock, RHA XXII/75 (1964) 129, 160 n. 20 (attributed *lukkešta* to *lukk*(*ai*)-), and Otten, AfO 21 (1966) 10f.

Cf. *lukki*/*a-* for *lu-uk-ki-iš-zi* KBo 19.5:4 (Law §100); cf. also *luk*(*k*)- A.

lukta adv.; see *lukat*.

[*lu-ku-ut-ri*] is probably to be read UDU *KU-UT-RI* or UDU *ku-ut-ri* in KBo 6.29 iii 20 and KBo 6.28 rev. 24.

$^{(LÚ)}$**lulaḫ(ḫ)i-** n. com. and adj. (all exx. com. gender); (generic designation of uncivilized mountain dwellers); from MH.

sg. nom. ^{LÚ}*lu-la-ḫi-iš* KUB 30.34 iv 30 (MH/NS); **pl. nom.** DINGIR.MEŠ *lu-u-la-ḫi-e-eš* KUB 23.75 iv? 12, KUB 23.77a obv. (8) (MH/MS); DINGIR.MEŠ *lu-la-a-ḫi-i-e-eš* KUB 39.49:9 (NH); DINGIR.MEŠ *lu-la-ḫi-e-eš* KUB 19.50 iv 19 (NH); DINGIR.MEŠ *lu-la-*⌜*ḫi*⌝*-iš* KBo 12.31 iv 7; [DINGIR.ME]Š *lu-la-ḫi-ú-uš* KUB 38.17 iv 7 (NH); DINGIR.MEŠ *lu-la-ḫi-ia-aš* KUB 6.45 i 53 (NH), DINGIR.MEŠ ^{d}*lu-la-ḫi-ia-aš* KBo 4.10 rev. 3 (NH); **pl. gen.** $^{LÚ.MEŠ}$*lu-la-ḫi-ia-aš* KUB 9.34 ii 7, iv 13 (NH), KUB 18.63 iv (16); $^{LÚ.MEŠ}$*lu-u-la-ḫi-ia-aš* HT 1 i 31 (NH); DINGIR.MEŠ *lu-la-ḫi-ia-aš* KUB 20.23 iv 6 (MH/NS); DINGIR ⌜*lu*⌝*-la-ḫi-ia-aš* KUB 47.73 iii 2′.

Akkadographic nom. pl. DINGIR.MEŠ *lu-la-aḫ-ḫi* KBo 5.9 iv 12 (NH); DINGIR.MEŠ *lu-la-ḫi* KUB 21.1 iv 20 (NH).

in Luw. texts (from DLL 64): **sg. nom.** ^{LÚ}*lu-la-ḫi-*(*i-*)*iš*, **acc.** ^{LÚ}*lu-*(*ú-*)*la-ḫi-ia-an*, **dat.** *lu-ú-la-ḫe-e-ia*, **inst.** [^{LÚ}*lu-ú-l*]*a-ḫi-ia-t*[*i*], **pl. gen.(?)** ^{d}*Lu-u-la-ḫi-in-za-aš*.

in divine-witness lists in Akk. treaties (Weidner, PD 30f., n. 4): DINGIR.MEŠ *lu-la-ḫi-i* KBo 1.1 rev. 50 = DINGIR. MEŠ *nu-la*!(text *ù*)*-aḫ-ḫi* KBo 1.2 rev. 27 = DINGIR. MEŠ *lu-la-ḫi-e-eš* KUB 3.1b rev. 16 (PD 30f.), DINGIR. MEŠ *ša nu-la-aḫ-*[*ḫi*] KBo 1.3 rev. 4 (PD 50f:21), DINGIR.MEŠ *lu-la-aḫ-ḫi* KBo 1.4 rev. 29 (PD 68f:37).

a. with LÚ: *naššu* ^{LÚ}*lu-la-ḫi-iš našma* ^{LÚ}SA.GAZ *kuiški ēšta* "(If) it was either a mountain dweller or a desert dweller" (who caused the contamination) KUB 30.34 iv 30f. (purif. rit. for town, MH/NS), dupl. KUB 39.104 iv 8f.; "We interrogated the exorcists(?) ([$^{LÚ.MEŠ}$M]E. SAG), and they said," *ANA* DINGIR-*LIM-wa* [$^{LÚ.MEŠ}$*lu*]*-la-ḫi-ia-aš* GAL $^{LÚ.MEŠ}$*tapri* ^{m}*Du-wattazit*[*išša BIBR*]*I*$^{ḪI.A}$*-uš kar*(*a*)*ššanuir* "'The chief *t*.-man of the mountain dwellers and D. left out the rhytons for the god'" KUB 18.63 rev. iv 5-7, cf. iv 16f. (oracle, NH); $^{LÚ.MEŠ}$⌜*lu*⌝*-u-la-ḫi-ia-aš-ša-an* (var. [o].MEŠ *lu-u-la-ḫi-ia-*[*aššan*]; corresponds to Luw. ^{d}*Lu-u-la-ḫi-in-za-aš-tar* in ii 24 of the dupl.) *ḫupruš kuiēš išḫiyantiš* "(The Innarawanteš) who have bound on (themselves) the sashes(?) of the mountain dwellers" HT 1 i 31 with dupl. KUB 9.31 i 38 (rit. against plague, NH), cf. KUB 31.32 rev.? 7, 11; $^{\text{LÚ.MEŠ}}$*lu-la-ḫi-ia-aš* . . . <EME-*an*> KI.MIN (= *mutaiddu*, cf. iv 7 and 9) "Let him/it remove <the 'tongue'> of the mountain dwellers!" KUB 9.34 iv 13f. (EME-*an* in iv 8-13), cf. i 34f., ii 7 (rit., NH).

b. with DINGIR: (They take loaves, sheep, cheeses and *ḫaššuwawanni*-vessels) *nat INA* É ^{d}*Pišanuḫi* ⸢*I*⸣-*NA* (dupl. ⸢*A*⸣-*NA* KUB 42.90 rev. 17) É DINGIR.MEŠ *lu-la-ḫi-ia-aš* (dupl. DINGIR ⸢*lu*⸣-*la-ḫi-ia-aš* KUB 47.73 iii 2′) *arḫa uppanzi* "They send them back to the temple of the mountain-dweller gods (which is) in the temple of P." KUB 20.23 iv 5-7 (*ḫišuwaš* fest., MH/NS), with dupl. KUB 47.73 iii 1′-3′ and KUB 42.90 rev. 17; [DINGIR.ME]Š *lu-la-ḫi-ú-uš* ŠÀ.BA 2 *ú-i-l[a-na-aš]* "(Statues of) mountain-dweller gods, including 2 of clay" KUB 38.17 iv 7 (cult inv., NH), ed. Jakob-Rost, MIO 8:208; □for the place of the DINGIR.MEŠ *l.* in the lists of gods in treaties and prayers see Goetze, Kl. (1957) 131.

The tentative translation "mountain dweller" is based on the articles by Landsberger and Klengel cited below.

Landsberger, KlF 1 (1930) 325-28; Goetze apud Bottéro, RAI 4 (1954) 81f.; Goetze, Kl. (1957) 123; Klengel, MIO 11 (1965) 358.

^{GIŠ}**lulai[. . .]**, $^{\text{[GI]Š?}}$**lulaišša** (something made of wood, or a tree and its products); from OH.†

^{GIŠ}*lu-u-la*[- . . .] KBo 20.8 rev.? 12, 13 (fest., OH/OS); ^{GIŠ}*lu-la-a-i*[- . . .] KBo 14.23:2 (birth rit.?); $^{\text{[GI]Š}}$*lu-u-la-iš-ša*(*-ma-aš-ši*-x[. . .]) KBo 13.100:7 (rit.); all three in fragmentary contexts.

luli-, luliya- n. com.; **1.** lake, pond, **2.** well, spring, basin, **3.** vat, pithos, from OH; wr. syll., log. TÚL only in RN ^{m}KÙ(.GA).TÚL-*ma* = Šuppiluliyama (II).

sg. nom. *lu-li-iš* KBo 13.58 iii 19 (MH), KUB 12.62 obv. (7) (OH?/NS); **acc.** *lu-li-in* KBo 23.74 obv. 10 (OH/MS); *lu-ú-li-in* KUB 19.18 i 14 (NH); *lu-li-ia-an* KUB 27.13 iv 21 (NH; Luw. form?); **gen.** *lu-li-ia-aš* KBo 6.14 i 6 (OH/NS), KUB 42.1 iii 12, KBo 23.92 ii 12, 14 (OH/MS), KBo 25.14 ii 6 (OH/MS); *lu-ú-li-aš* KBo 16.49 i 6, 9, 11 (MS?); *lu-ú-li-ia-aš* KBo 2.12 ii 33 (OH/NS), KBo 17.100 i 12; **loc.** *lu-ú-li* KUB 2.3 ii 15 (OH/NS), KUB 8.75 iv 16, 20, 57, KUB 33.98 i (12), (13), KBo 25.66 i 2 (OH/NS); **all.** *lu-li-ia* KBo 6.2 i 56 (OH/OS), KBo 23.74 obv. 9 (OH/MS), KBo 25.66 i 11 (OH/NS), IBoT 2.90:6, 10; *lu-ú-li-ia* KUB 2.3 ii 14, 19, iii 20, 33 (OH/NS), KUB 43.29 iii 7; **abl.** *lu-ú-li-ia-az* KUB 29.21:3, KUB 2.3 ii 28 (both OH/NS), KBo 12.98:6; *lu-li-ia-za* KUB 13.4 iii 33 (MH?/NS); *lu-ú-li-az* KBo 21.22:39 (MS); **inst.** *lu-li-*⸢*it*⸣ KBo 21.22:37 (OH/MS).

pl. nom.(?): *lu-ú-li-ia-aš* KUB 13.2 ii 24 (MH/NS).

The longer stem *luliya-* attested in the (Luwian influenced?) acc. sg. *lu-li-ia-an* KUB 27.13 iv 21 is perhaps also found in the form of the second component of the RN *Šuppiluliyama* (cf. Laroche, NH p. 166f.). Note also that the hieroglyphic sign (Laroche 215 = Meriggi 191) which represents this second component of the RN is read by Laroche *luliya-* (HH pp. 118, 166) and translated "bassin?", HH (1960) 118 or "étang", NH (1966) 167.

1. pond or lake — **a.** in general: *takku lu-li-ia-aš* MUŠEN-*i*[*n annanu*(*ḫḫan*) *našma* (*kak*~~*kapan*)] *annanuḫḫan kuišk*[*i taiezzi*] "If someone [steals] a trained pond bird or a trained *k*." KBo 6.14 i 6-7 (Law §119, OH/NS), with dupl. KUB 29.36 obv. 7 + KUB 29.25:3 (OH/OS), JCS 16:18; keep the drains clear) *maniyaḫiyayatakkan kuieš* MUŠEN.ḪI.A-*aš lu-ú-li-ia-aš anda* (var. *andan*) *nat* SIG$_5$-*anteš ašandu* "and the bird ponds that are in your domain, let them be kept in good condition" KUB 13.2 ii 24-25 with dupl. KUB 31.90 ii 5f. (instr., MH), ed. Dienstanw. 45, translated differently; cf. *lazziyaḫḫ-* 1 a; *paimi* ÍD-*p*[*a mu*]*-u-uḫ-ḫi lu-l*[*i-ia*] *mūḫḫi* "I shall go, I shall fall into a river, I shall fall into a pond (or lake)" KUB 43.60 i 33f. (OH/NS); [1] A.ŠÀ *lu-li-ia-aš* (a field bordering on a pond or lake) KUB 42.1 iii? 12 (list of fields), ed. Souček, ArOr 27:38f., Text F.

b. "pond" or "lake" in GNs: *naš :ikunta* (var. without gloss) *lu-ú-li-kán anda araš nukan* [:(?)]*ikunta lu-ú*[-*li a*]*nda šalliš* $^{\text{NA}_4}$*peruna*[*š*] *kittari* "He arrived at the Cold Lake, and in the Cold Lake a large rock was lying" KUB 33.98 + KUB 36.8 i 12-14, with par. KUB 33.96 i 16-18 (Ullik., NH), ed. Güterbock, JCS 5:164f.; *nu* $^{\text{ḪUR.SAG}}$*Ammuna* KUR ^{URU}*Tupaziya* [. . . -*n*]*a lu-ú-li-in walḫta* "He attacked Mt. A., the country of T. and the [. . .] Lake" KUB 19.18 i 14-15 (DŠ), ed. Güterbock, JCS 10:76; ḪUR.SAG.MEŠ ^{URU}*Ḫupi*<*š*>*na* ḪUR.SA[G.MEŠ . . .] ḪUR.SAG.MEŠ *šalliyaš lu-l*[*i-* . . .] "The mountains of Ḫ., of [. . .] (and) of the Great

L[ake] (*luli*[*yaš*])/Great M[arsh] (*luli*[*yašḫaš*]) KBo 12.140 rev. 10f. (cult inv.); 1 A.ŠÀ :*tapašuwanti lu-ú-li* "one field at Fever-infested(?) Lake" KUB 8.75 iv 20; 2 *karšattar* :*tapašuwanti lu-ú-li* ibid. iv 16, cf. ibid. iv + KBo 19.11:57 and 59 (list of fields), ed. Souček, ArOr 27:20-25; cf. GNs: URU*Lu-li-*x[...] KBo 7.24 rev. rt. col. 1′ (inv. of tin); URU*Šup-piluliyan* KUB 22.51 obv. 11; ÍD*Šuppiluliya* KUB 17.20 iii 14 and PN *Šuppiluliuma, Šuppiluliyama*. On GNs cf. RGTC 6:368, 550f.

2. connected with, or part of, a spring or well, possibly a basin — **a.** in an OH incantation the spring (*wattaru*) of the Sungod is described: *waršedakan* x[... *l*]*u*(!)-*ú-li-az ar-aš-zi* "but its water flows [...] from a/the *l.*" KBo 21.22:38-39 (MS), with par. KBo 12.98:6, cf. [...] *lu-li-*⌜*it*⌝(?) ibid. 37; in a cult inventory for the cult of various springs (or wells): TÚL*Kuwannaniyan ša*[*r-ḫ*]*u*?-*li-ia-an lu-li-ia-an* LÚ.MEŠ AN.TAḪ^AḪ^.ŠUM^SAR^ ... *eššan-z*[*i*] "The men of the *a.*-plant (and other functionaries) provide for the spring (or well) K., (namely its) pole(?) (and) basin(?)" (a list of offerings follows) KUB 27.13 iv 21-23 (NH); note the Luwian acc. forms in *-an* (cf. DLL 137, §27).

b. uncertain whether pond, spring, well, or basin: [*takku* o o o o] *lu-ú-li-ia-az* (var. [*takku lu-ú-li-i*]*a-az*) GIŠ-*ru kui*[(*ški taiezzi*)] "If someone steals timber from a [...] *l.*" (he shall give 3 shekels of silver for 1 talent of wood, etc.) KUB 29.21:3 (Law §102), dupl. KBo 6.12 i 8 (both OH/NS); *namma ŠA* DINGIR-*LIM* [*k*]*uiš lu-li-iš kungaliyaš nukan* LÚNIMGIR *ḫalenzu šer arḫa daškizzi* "The 'herald' shall remove the leaves (or water plants?) from the surface of the *luliš kungaliyaš* that belongs to the deity" KBo 13.58 iii 18-20 (*ḪAZANNU* instr.), ed. Daddi Pecchioli, OA 14:104f., cf. Otten, BagM 3:94f.; ⌜LÚ.MEŠ⌝ URU*Ḫallapiya lu-li-ia-aš še-e-er aranta* LÚ.MEŠALAN.ZUₓ *pānzi ta lu-li-ia-aš še-er zaḫḫanda* "The men from Ḫ. are standing above the *l.*; the performers go and fight (with them) above the *l.*" KBo 23.92 ii 12-14 (fest., OH/NS); *lu-ú-li-ia-aš še-e-er kuiuš* [GUD.ḪI.A-*uš*] *ḫukanzi* "The [oxen] which they slaughter above the *l.*" KBo 2.12 ii 33f. (fest., OH/NS); cf. *lu-ú-li-ia-aš* (gen.) *šer* KBo 17.100 i 12 (OH/MS?) and younger *lu-li-ia šer* IBoT 2.90:6, 10; named: *nu watar* 3-*ŠU Labarnaš lu-li-ia-za INA* É.DINGIR-*LÌ-ŠU pedau* "let him carry water three times from Labarna's *l.* to his temple" KUB 13.4 iii 33f. (instr., MH), ed. Chrest. 158f.; d*Taḫašta* KÁ.GAL-*az pān*[*zi*] d*IŠTAR-aš lu-ú-li-aš* KÁ.GAL-*az uwa*[*nzi*] GEŠTIN-*aš išpanduz-ziya lu-ú-l*[*i*(-) ...] *tianzi* UDU.ḪI.A-*uš* LÚ.MEŠMUḪALDIM *appanz*[*i*] *tuš edi lu-ú-li-aš arḫi* LUGAL-*i* [...] *iškaranzi* § LUGAL-*uš uizzi lu-ú-li-aš šer AŠARŠ*[*U epzi*] "They leave by the Gate of Daḫa, they come (back?) by the Gate of Ištar's *l.* They put the libation vessels of wine [by] the *l.* The cooks seize the sheep and line them up on the far side of the *l.* [opposite/before] the king. The king comes and [takes] his place above the *l.*" KBo 16.49 i 5-11 (cult of Mt. Daḫa, OH/NS).

3. vat or pithos — **a.** "When the king comes out of the tent" *taš tiyazi* GUNNI-*aš kattan marnuwandaš lu-ú-li-ia* (var. *lu-li-ia*) 2 LÚ.MEŠALAN.ZUₓ *nekumanteš lu-ú-li-kán anda paršnanteš* § SALAMA.DINGIR-*LIM* d*Tittiutti* UGULA SAL.MEŠKAR.KID *mar-nuwandaš lu-ú-li-ia* (var. *lu-li-in*) 3-*ŠU ḫuyanzi* "the king steps near the hearth to a vat of (for?) *m.*-beer. Two performers are squatting naked inside the vat. The priestess of T. (and) the overseer of the harlots run three times around(?) the *m.*-vat" (later, a priest pours *m.*-beer three times on the backs of the performers); LÚ.MEŠALAN.ZUₓ *lu-ú-li-ia-az ariyan*[*z*]*i* "The performers rise from the vat (blow the horns three times and leave)" KUB 2.3 ii 11-19, 28-31, with par. KBo 23.74 obv. 8-11 (KI.LAM fest., OH/NS), cf. KUB 28.101 iii 3-4, KUB 43.29 iii 6-8; [*nu*] LÚ.MEŠMUŠEN.DÙ.ḪI.A NINDA.ḪI.A *lu-ú-li-ia tarnanzi nuš* LÚ.MEŠḪUB.BÍ appanzi "The augurs put the bread loaves into the vat, and the dancers seize them" KUB 2.3 iii 19-21 (same fest. as above); LUGAL-*uš lu-ú-li-ia šer tiyazi* "the king takes his stand above the vat" ibid. iii 33-34.

b. uncertain whether vat, well, or spring: [*takku*] LÚ.U₁₈.LU-*aš* DUGUTÚL-*i našma lu-li-ia paprizzi* "If a person causes contamination in a bowl or a vat (or: well?)" KBo 6.2 i 56′ (Law

§25, OH/OS); ed. Friedrich, HG 22f., often discussed, most recently Starke, StBoT 23 (1977) 56 ("Wenn sich ein Mensch in einem Bottich oder in einem Bassin als unrein erweist"); [*l*]*u-li-iš artari* "a *l.* is standing" KUB 12.62 obv. 7f. (incant.), cf. *altanniš arta andanašta* GIŠ-*ru arta* ibid. obv. 16.

Hrozný, CH (1922) 19, 111; Götze NBr (1930) 65 n. 1; Ehelolf, KlF 1 (1930) 144 n. 3 (PN ᵐKÙ.TÚL-*ma*); Forrer, Glotta 26 (1938) 183-86; Kammenhuber, OrNS 39 (1970) 559f. (different distribution).

Cf. *luliyašḫa-*.

luliyašḫa- n.; marsh, marshland; NH.†

sg. gen. *lu-li-ia-aš-ḫa-aš* KUB 8.75 ii 10, 13, 16.

Akk. *erṣetu ša mātikunu lū sà-a-ḫu ša ni-IB-ḫu-u lū tašallâma lā tebbirā* "May the terrain of your country become a swamp of *n.*, may you sink in and not be able to cross it!" KBo 1.1 rev. 67-68, ed. Weidner, PD 34f., cf. CAD E 11b = Hitt. [. . .] *lu-ú-li*[- . . .] KUB 21.18 rev. 19-20 (Šupp. I treaty with Šattiwaza), ed. Laroche, Ugar. VI:372f.; *lu-ú-li*[- . . .] probably belongs to *luliyašḫa-* rather than *luli-*.

1 A.ŠÀ *lu-li-ia-aš-ḫa-aš* 2 KASKAL.ḪI.A-*kan ištarna arḫa panzi* "One field of marshland, two roads run through it" KUB 8.75 ii 13 (NH); 1 A.ŠÀ *lu-li-ia-aš-ḫa-aš ANA* KASKAL ᵁᴿᵁ*Taqqapašuwa*-x[-*kan* ZA]G-*za* "One field of marshland to the [rig]ht of the road to T." ibid. ii 16; 2 *karšattar lu-li-ia-aš-ḫa-aš* "Two sections of marshland" ibid. ii 10 (list of fields), ed. Souček, ArOr 27:12f.; for possible rest. ḪUR.SAG.MEŠ *šalliyaš lu-l*[*i-ya-aš-ḫa-aš*] KBo 12.140 rev. 11 see *luli-*, 1 b.

Laroche, RA 52 (1958) 188 ("marécage").

Cf. *luli-*.

lulim(m)i- Luw. adj.?; (epithet of ᵈLAMMA); from MH.†

sg. nom. *lu-li-mi-eš* VBoT 24 i 28 (MH/NS); **acc.** *lu-li-mi-in* ibid. iv 35, *lu-li-im-mi-in* KUB 30.65 ii 4, 11 (NH); **gen.** *lu-li-mi-ia-aš* VBoT 24 i 2; *lu-li-mi-ia-š*[*a-* . . .] 335/w:8; **stem form** *lu-ú-li-mi* VBoT 24 ii 2; *lu-li-mi* 108/e:5.

a. in the rit. of Anniwiyani, paired with ᵈLAMMA *innarawanza*: "On this tablet two rituals are copied down" [1 S]ISKUR *mān* ᵈLAMMA *lu-li-mi-in* ᵈLAMMA *in<na>rau-wandanna šipanti* "[one r]itual, when one sacrifices to ᵈLAMMA *l.* and ᵈLAMMA *i.*, (and one ritual, when one sacrifices to ᵈLAMMA ᴷᵁᔆ*kuršaš*)" VBoT 24 iv 33-36 (colophon), ed. Sturtevant, Chrest. 116f.; "From the midst of the house they bring forth a virgin(?) and make her stand in the gate. She holds in her hand a bird (made) of dough, and the maiden calls out" *parāwakan eḫu* ᵈLAMMA *lu-li-mi-eš andawakan* ᵈLAMMA *innarauwanza uizzi* "Come out (of the city through the gate), O ᵈLAMMA *l.*, (so that) ᵈLAMMA *i.* may come in" ibid. i 25-29; □from the latter passage it appears that ᵈLAMMA *lulimiš* represents an undesirable quality — e.g., impotence, effeminacy, weakness — and ᵈLAMMA *i.* a desirable one.

b. in shelf lists: KUB 30.65 ii 4, 11; KUB 30.50 + KUB 30.49 + 1963/c v 18-20, ed. CTH p. 169f., 167.

c. on a label: "Two tablets, of which one tablet is" *mān* ᵈLAMMA ᴷᵁᔆ*kuršaš mān* ᵈLAMMA *lu-li-mi muganzi* "whether they invoke the Patron Deity of the Fleece or ᵈLAMMA *l.*" 108/e:1-6 (entire).

d. in onomastics: ᵐ*Lu-lim-me* RŠ 17.244:9 (PRU IV:232) in Akk. document from Ugarit, father of ᵐ*Lilli* (Laroche, NH no. 705).

KUB 15.22:12 is to be read as Akkadogram *LU-LI-IM*ᴹᴱᔆ.

Sturtevant, TAPA 58 (1927) 7, 9, 18 ("effeminate"); Friedrich, HW 130 (unklares Beiwort des Schutzgottes); Laroche, DLL 64 (part. louv. en hitt.); Laroche, NH (1966) 336 (hitt. ou louv., adj. de sens inconnu; épithète d'un ᵈKAL peut être antonyme de *innarawant-*).

lulu- see (:)*lulu*(*t*)-.

luluwai- v.; **1.** (act.) to sustain, **2.** (mid.) to be sustained, survive; from OH.

pres. act. sg. 2 [*l*]*u-lu-wa-i-ši* KUB 31.135:16 (OH/MS), **pres. mid. sg. 3** *lu-lu-wa-it-ta* KBo 6.34 iv 15 (MH/NS), KUB 8.34 iii 19 (NH), **pret. act. sg. 1** *lu-lu-wa-*⸢*nu-un*⸣ KBo 19.51:10 + KBo 19.49 iv 1 (NH), **pret. act. sg. 3** *lu-lu-wa-it* KUB 14.14 obv. 29 (Murš. II), **pret. act. pl. 3** [*lu*]-*ú-lu-wa-a-ir* KUB 26.74 i 5 (OH/NS), **pret. mid. pl. 3** *lu-lu-wa-an-da-at* KUB 14.14 obv. 32 (Murš. II), **imp. act. sg. 2** *lu-lu-wa-a-i* ABoT 44 i 49 (OH/NS), KBo 2.9 i 35, KBo 21.48 obv.? 8 (MH/NS), **pl. 2?** *lu-lu-wa-it*[-*ten*?] KUB 23.43:5, **iter. imp. act. sg. 2** *l*[*u*]-*lu-wi₅-iš-ki* KBo 5.13 iv 4,

KUB 6.41 iv 12, *lu-lu-ú-i-i[š-k]i* KBo 5.4 obv. 26 (all Murš. II), **inf.** *lu-lu-wa-u-an-zi* KUB 31.130 rev. 8 (OH/MS).

1. to sustain — **a.** act. noniter.: "Afterwards care for the king, the queen, the sons of the king (and) the grandsons of the king in well-being, life, health, vigor, (and) long years forever" *nat lu-lu-wa-a-i ḫappinaḫḫiyat* "Sustain it (Ḫatti) and make it rich!" KBo 2.9 i 33-34 with par. KBo 21.48 obv.? 6-7 (rit. for Ištar, MH/NS); *luluwai-* is also paired with *ḫappinaḫ-* in KBo 19.51:10f. + KBo 19.49 rev. 1'f. (DŠ?) and KUB 26.74 i 5 (Muršili I against Babylon, OH/NS); *nammayaza damāi araḫzena* KUR.KUR.MEŠ LUGAL-*ueznann[i anda tarḫta?] nu* KUR ^{URU}*Ḫatti lu-lu-wa-it nušši* ZAG.ḪI.A-*uš kez kezziya [daiš]* "And furthermore he (Šupp. I) [conquered?] other foreign lands [during] his reign. He sustained Ḫatti and [established] its borders on this side and that." KUB 14.14 obv. 28-29 (plague prayer of Murš. II), ed. Götze, KlF 1:168f.; *kūnna* LÚ.NAM. U$_{18}$.LU-*aš* ÌR-*KA* ^{d}UTU-*uš lu-lu-wa-a-i* "O Sungod, sustain also this mortal, your servant, (that he may proceed to offer bread and beer to the Sungod)" ABoT 44 i 49-50 (prayer, OH/NS), ed. Güterbock, JAOS 78:241, cf. KUB 31.135 obv. 16 and KUB 31.130 rev. 8, two fragments of the same tablet (prayer, OH/MS), and 544/u (+ KUB 24.3) ii 4f., (prayer, Murš. II), tr. ("segne") by Güterbock in Neues Handbuch der Literaturwissenschaft, 230.

b. (act. iter.): *nammaza zik* ^{m}*Kupanta-*^{d}LAMMA-*aš tuel* ZI-*an tuella* (var. *tuel*) É-*KA tuel* LÚ.MEŠ.AMA.A.TU-*KA maḫḫan eššatti* ^{d}UTU-*ŠI-yatta kuin* ERÍN.MEŠ LÚ.MEŠ (var. omits LÚ.MEŠ) *ašandulan kattan daliyanun nanzan katta QATAMMA uški nan [l]u-lu-wi$_5$-iš-ki nanzan* SIG$_5$-*in ešša idalawaḫtiman l[e]* "Moreover, Kupanta-^{d}LAMMA, just as you treat yourself and your house (and) your servants, in the same way watch the garrison which I, His Majesty, have left with you; sustain it, treat it well, and don't do it any harm." KBo 5.13 iv 1-5 with dupl. KUB 6.41 iv 9-13 (Kup.), ed. SV 1:132-35; □in place of *nan luluwiški* another duplicate, KBo 4.3 iii 15, may have *nan le da[m-me-eš-]*⌈*ḫa-*⌉*ši* "don't harm them", but this restoration is uncertain; cf. KBo 5.4 obv. 26 (Targ.), ed. SV 1:56f.

2. (mid.) to be sustained, survive: NAM.RA. MEŠ-*yaza kuiēs IŠTU* KUR LÚ.K[ÚR *wetan-teš ešir?*] *nat lu-lu-wa-an-da-at UL kuitki ḫarkta* "And the civilian prisoners who [were brought] from the land of the en[emy] survived; they did not perish (literally: nothing perished)." KUB 14.14 obv. 31-32 (plague prayer of Murš. II), ed. KlF 1:168-69; LÚ-*aš lu-lu-wa-it-ta* "the man will survive" KUB 8.34 iii 19 (omen apod.); *nuššiššan welluš ḫālišši ašaunišši šuplešši le lu-lu-wa-it-ta* "Let the meadow not survive for his herd, his flock, or his cattle" KBo 6.34 iv 13-15 (soldiers' oath, MH/NS), ed. StBoT 22:14-15.

The verb *luluwai-* in its act. forms denotes the action of providing someone with all the support which he needs in order to survive and to fare reasonably well. Its semantic range overlaps somewhat with *ḫuišnu-* "to save, preserve alive". In its mid. forms the verb is similar in meaning to the idiom *lulu auš-* "to experience *l.*, be sustained" treated under (:)*lulu(t)*-.

Friedrich, ZA 35 (1924) 188 and SV 1 (1926) 79f.

Cf. (:)*lulu(t)*-.

$^{(NA_4)}$**lulluri-** n. com.; (a mineral).†

sg. nom. *lu-ul-lu-ri-iš* HT 3:7; Frankfurt text: (5) (both NH); **stem form** (in lists): ^{NA_4}*lu-ul-lu-u-ri* KUB 27.67 ii 60 (MH/NS); ^{NA_4}*lu-ul-lu-ri* ibid. iii 62, iv (35); *lu-ul-lu-u-ri* KBo 11.11 iii 3 (NH); *lu-ul-lu-ri* KBo 15.10 i 8 (MH/MS); KBo 22.142 iv 4; KUB 43.60 iv 13 (OH/NS).

a. in rituals, listed with various metals and minerals: KÙ.BABBAR KÙ.GI ^{NA_4}ZA.GÌN NA$_4$.KÁ.DINGIR.RA ^{NA_4}*parašḫaš* ^{NA_4}DU$_8$. ŠÚ.A *lu-ul-lu-ri* AN.NA URUDU *kuitta parā tepu dai* "silver, gold, lapis lazuli, 'Babylon stone', *p.*-stone, quartz, *l.*, tin, copper — he takes a little of each" KBo 15.10 i 8-9 (rit. to pacify the gods of blood, MH/MS), ed. THeth 1:12f.; cf. KUB 27.67 ii 60, iii 62, iv 35 (rit. of Ambazzi, MH/NS); 1 GÍN AN.NA 1 GÍN *lu-ul-lu-u-ri* "one shekel-weight of tin, one shekel-weight of *l.*" KBo 11.11 iii 3 (rit., of Uruwanda, NH); [1?] MA.NA AN.BAR 1 MA.NA *lu-ul-lu-ri* "[one?] mina-weight of iron, one mina-weight of *l.*" KBo 22.142 iv 3-4 (rit.); *nuššan* KÙ.BABBAR KÙ.GI AN.NA AN.BAR URUDU A.GAR$_5$ *lu-ul-lu-ri* "on (a table) are silver, gold, tin, iron, copper, lead, (and) *l.*" KUB 43.60 iv 12-13 (rit., NH).

b. in lists of ingredients for making glass: *tarnaš uzapiliaš tarnaš lu-ul-lu-ri-iš tarnaš* URUDU HT 3:6-8; ed. Rosenkranz, ZA 57:238f. and A. L. Oppenheim, Glass and Glassmaking in Ancient Mesopotamia 67f.; *ḫulubaš lu-ul-lu-ri-i[š] ḫulubaš uzabiliaš ḫulubaš turiš ḫulubaš* URUDU Frankfurt text: 5-8, ed. Riemschneider, FsGüterbock 267f.; □*tarnaš* is a unit of volume; *ḫu-lu-ba-aš* (or *ḫu-ib-ba-aš*?) is elsewhere unknown; note that *l.* is nom. here, not gen.

Rosenkranz, ZA 57 (1965) 239.

(:)lulu(t)- n. neut. (Luw.); **1.** (a desirable condition, such as flourishing, thriving); in construction *lulu auš-* "to be sustained"; **2.** (the name of a location mentioned in snake oracle texts); from MH.

sg. nom.-acc. *lu-ú-lu* KBo 5.3 ii 13 (Šupp. I, MH/NS), KBo 5.4 l.e. 4 (Murš. II), KUB 21.5 iv 49 (Muw.), KBo 19.145 ii 20 (NH), KUB 43.2 iii 8 (NH); *lu-lu* KUB 34.15:11 (NH), KUB 19.28 iv 11 (NH) (coll. confirms copy that traces preceding are not gloss); *lu-lu-ú* KUB 21.4 iv 16 (Muw.); *lu-lu-u(š-se-et)* KBo 6.34 iv 10 (MH/NS); *:lu-ú-lu* KUB 1.1 i 20; KUB 1.2 i 18; KBo 3.6 i 17 (all Ḫatt. III).

(Luw.) d.-l. *lu-lu-ti* KUB 18.6 ii (7), iv 1; KUB 22.38 iv 14; *lu-lu-u-ti* 1472/u obv.? 11; *:lu-lu-ti* IBoT 1.33:5, 27, 49, 92, (94), 103, 105 (all NH).

See Carruba, RHA XXV/81 (1967) 154 for discussion of the form of the stem.

1. (a desirable condition) — **a.** *lulu auš-* to see (or experience) *l.*, be sustained (cf. *luluwai-* 2): *nutta kēma NĪŠ* DINGIR.MEŠ *aššuli paḫšandaru našta ANA QĀT* ᵈUTU-*ŠI anda aššu lu-ú-lu uški* "(If you are loyal to My Majesty) let these oaths keep you in well-being. May you experience good *l.* in the hand of (i.e., may you be sustained by) My Majesty" KBo 5.3 ii 11-13 (Ḫuqq., MH/NS), ed. SV 2:114f.; *nuttakan QADU* DAM-*KA* ... *aššu[(li paḫ)]šantaru nukan ANA* ᵈU[(TU-*ŠI*)] ŠU-*i anda a-aš-š[(u lu-ú-l)]u* (var. *lu-lu-ú*) *au nukan ANA* ᵈ[(UTU-*ŠI* Š)]U-*i anda miya[(ḫuwan)t]aḫut* "Let (these oaths) keep you and your wife (etc.) in well-being. May you experience good *l.* in the hand of (i.e., may you be sustained by) My Majesty, and may you grow old in the hand of My Majesty" KUB 21.1 iv 42-46 with dupl. KUB 21.5 iv 47-50 and KUB 21.4 iv 11-17 (Alakš.), ed. SV 2:82f.; cf. KBo 5.4 left edge 4 (Targ.), ed. SV 1:70, rest. from Alakš., *nuzakan ANA* ŠU ᵈ*IŠTAR* GAŠAN-*YA :lu-ú-lu uḫḫun* "And so I experienced *l.* at the hands of (i.e., I was sustained by) my lady Ištar" KBo 3.6 i 17 with dupl. KUB 1.1 i 20 and KUB 1.2 i 18 (Ḫatt., NH); *nuza apāš* UN-*aš* [...]x *lu-lu aušdu* KUB 19.28 iv 10'-11' (treaty?, NH); *[(našta* KUR-*a)]n-ti kuedani anda [(nanakušz)]i nuza lu-ú-lu* (var. *lu-lu*) *aušzi* "The land in which it ... -s will experience *l.* (i.e., will be sustained)" KUB 43.2 iii 7-8 with dupl. KBo 9.68 right col. 10f. and KUB 34.15:10f. (omen apod.).

b. Listed with other nouns: "Just as this burning fire was extinguished, so let these divine oaths seize whoever transgresses these oaths" *našta apella* TI-*taršet* ᴸᵁ́GURUŠ-*taršet lu-lu-uš-še-et INA* EGIR U₄-*MI QADU* DAM.MEŠ-*ŠÚ* DUMU.MEŠ-*ŠÚ QATAMMA kištaru* "And let also his life, his youth, his *l.* and (that of) his wife and his sons be extinguished forever in the same way!" KBo 6.34 iv 5-11 (Soldiers' Oath), ed. StBoT 22:14f.

2. (The name of a location mentioned in snake oracle texts): MUŠ.SAG.DU-*kan :lu-lu-ti ŠUM-uen* "we named/assigned(?) the Snake of the Head for/to the (place called) *l.*" IBoT 1.33:5; 91f.; ed. Laroche, RA 52:152, 155f., 158; cf. *lamniya-* 4 d; TA *MAMETI uit :lu-lu-ti* KI.MIN (=*munnait*) "(the snake) came from Oath and hid at '*l.*'" ibid. 27, cf. ibid. 49, 94; MUŠ.SAG.DU ᵈUTU-*ŠI-kan ANA* MU.ḪI.A GÍD.DA *ŠUM-en naškan* TI-*ni :lu-lu-ti nu šarā epta* ... *ANA* GUNNI KU₆ *epta :lu-lu-ti ezza*<*š*> "We named/assigned the Snake of the Head of His Majesty to the (place called) Long Years, and it (went?) to Life (and) '*l.*' and emerged(?) ... At the Hearth it caught a fish (and) ate (it) at '*l.*'" ibid. 102-105; [...]x *lu-lu-ti pait* KUB 22.38 iv 14; [G]IM-*ankan lu-lu-ti pedaš* KUB 18.6 iv 1.

The association of the phrase "experience *lulu*" with "grow old" — i.e., "live long" — in some treaties, and the passage in Ḫatt. where the statement "I experienced *lulu* at the hand of Ištar" follows the explanation that Ḫattušili had been entrusted to that goddess because he was dying, may be adduced in favor of the translations "recovery" or "survival". Similarly the mid. of the verb *luluwai-* seems to mean "to be sustained, survive", and may be nearly synonymous with the idiom *lulu auš-*. On the other hand, the association of active forms of *luluwai-* with the near synonym *ḫappinaḫḫ-* "make rich" may be cited in favor of "make prosperous", if simple juxtaposition of the two verbs implies a similar meaning. A more general translation like "good fortune, doing well, thriving" might cover all uses.

Friedrich, ZA 35 (1924) 188 and SV 1:79f.

Cf. *luluwai-*.

:lumpašti-, :luppašti- n. com.; something unpleasant, displeasing, offensive, or annoying; NH.†

sg. nom. [*:l*]*u-um-pa-aš-ti-iš* KUB 21.38 rev. 11; *:lu-up-pa-aš-ti-iš* KUB 36.97 iv? 1; **acc.** *:lu-um-pa-aš-ti-in* KUB 21.38 rev. (12), 13; *:lu-pa-aš-tin* ibid. obv. 65; [:]*lu-up-pa-aš-ti-in* KUB 36.97 iv? 2.

a. in a letter of Puduḫepa: *mānmat ANA* ŠEŠ-*YA UL* ZI-*za nu ANA* ŠEŠ-*YA* ZI-*ni :lu-pa-aš-tin* DÙ-*mi* "If my brother doesn't want it, will I do something offensive to my brother's mind?" KUB 21.38 obv. 65, ed. Helck, JCS 17:92; *ANA* ŠEŠ-*YA kuiš* ZI[-*ni :l*]*u-um-pa-aš-ti-iš ammukman ANA* ŠEŠ-*YA UL namma iyami* [*m*]*ān UL kuit IDI nu ANA* ŠEŠ-*YA :lu-um-p*[*a-aš-ti-i*]*n apūn* DÙ-*mi karūma kuit IDI nu A*-[*N*]*A* ŠEŠ-*YA :lu-um-pa-aš-ti-in UL-pat iy*[*ami* . . .] "I will not do to my brother again that which is offensive to my brother's mind. If I didn't know something, then I might do such an offensive thing to my brother. But since I already know, I won't do anything offensive to my brother." ibid. rev. 11-13.

b. in a fest.: *nu kuedani* DINGIR-*LIM-ni kuiš* ZI-*aš :lu-up-pa-aš-ti-iš nuza idālun* [:]*lu-up-pa-aš-ti-in* ZI-*ni piran* [*a*]*rḫa uiyaddu* "Let the god in whose mind there is annoyance send away the evil annoyance from his mind." KUB 36.97 iii? 8-iv? 3 (New Year's fest.), ed. Otten, OLZ 1956:103.

Laroche, DLL 64 ("chagrin").

luntarni- n.; (a body part?).†

In an *IZBU* omen: *takku IZBU lu-un-tar-ni-iš*[. . .] "If the *luntarni-* of a malformed fetus[. . .]" KUB 34.19 i 5; cf. the following omen: *takku IZBU* IGI.ḪI.A-*ŠU* UR.MAḪ-*aš* GIM-*a*[*n* "If the eyes of a malformed fetus are like those of a lion[. . .]" ibid. 6.

KUB 34.19 lists omens describing various body parts. Therefore *luntarni-* is probably a body part. The word occurs before a break and may not be complete.

Riemschneider, StBoT 9 (1970) 54-56.

[*lu-nu-ḫa*] in IBoT 3.83:5 should be read *lu-u*!-*ḫa*; cf. *:lūḫa-*.

:lūpannauwant- adj.; wearing a cap; NH.†

1 ALAM KÙ.GI LÚ [G]UB-*an :lu-u-pa-an-na-u-w*[*a-an-za*] "One gold figure of a man, standing, wearing a cap (he [stands?] on a leashed sphinx of gold)" KUB 38.1 ii 7-8 (cult inv.), ed. Bildbeschr. 14f., Jakob-Rost, MIO 8:180; the name of the god is not preserved.

von Brandenstein, Bildbeschr. (1943) 44f.

Cf. (TÚG/GAD)*lupan*(*n*)*i-*.

(TÚG/GAD)lupan(n)i-, luwanni- n. com. and neut.(?); **1.** (a type of headdress) cap, **2.** (part of a dagger, sword, or knife); from MH.

sg. nom. TÚG*lu-pa-an-ni-iš* KUB 29.4 i 45, KUB 42.59 rev.? 9, KUB 42.13 vi? (6) (all NH); *lu*!-*pa-ni-iš* IBoT 1.31 obv. 9 (coll.) (NH); TÚG*lu-pa-an-ni-eš* KUB 42.59 rev.? 12 (NH); *lu-pa-an-ni-eš* ibid. rev.? 15, KUB 12.1 iii 13, KUB 42.42 iv? 5, 6 (all NH); **acc.** TÚG*lu-u-pa*[*-an-ni-in*] KBo 15.15 iii? 5 (MH/MS); *lu-u-pa-an*[*-ni-i*(*n*)] KUB 35.145 obv. 17 with dupl. KUB 17.15 ii 14 (both NH); [TÚG]*lu-pa-an-ni-n*(*a-wa-kán*) KUB 9.13 obv. 9 (NH); **neut. or stem form** 6 TÚG*lu-pa-an-ni* KUB 42.22 rt. col. 11 (NH); [. . . *lu*]-*pa-an-ni* KBo 18.175 i 16 (NH); TÚG*lu-pa-ni* Bo 6989 obv. 2′ (NH); **pl. nom.** *lu-pa-an-ni-eš* KUB 12.1 iii 10, KUB 38.38:5, VBoT 87 iv 2′ (all NH); **sg. or pl. nom.** TÚG*lu-pa-an-ni-i*[*š*] KUB 42.51 obv.? 4 (NH); GAD*lu-pa-an-ni-eš* KBo 18.186 l.e. 2 (NH); *lu-pa-an-ni-eš* KUB 12.1 iii 12 (NH).

Note the unusual spellings *lu-wa-an-ni-eš* KBo 18.170 rev. 2 (NH); *lu-ba-a*[*n-* . . .] KUB 12.1 iii 9 (NH).

1. (a type of headdress) cap (mostly with det. TÚG) — **a.** of the king: "Behold, this one is king! [I have bestowed] the title of kingship upon this one, I have clothed this one in the [garments] of kingship" $^{[TÚG]}$*lu-pa-an-ni-na-wa-kán kedani šiyanun* "and I have put the cap on this one" KUB 24.5 + KUB 9.13 obv. 20-22 (subst. king rit., NH), ed. StBoT 3:10f.; cf. ^{GAD}*lu-pa-an-ni-eš* LUGAL-*UTTI* KBo 18.186 l.e. 2; 6 ^{TÚG}*lu-pa-an-ni* LUGAL-*a*[*n*?-*na-aš*] KUB 42.22 rt. col. 11 (inv., NH); *ŠA* LUGAL-*R*[*UTTI*. . .]x-*an* ^{TÚG}*lu-u-pa*[-. . .] KBo 15.15 iii 4f. (rit., MH/MS); 1 ^{TÚG}*lu*[-. . .] KUB 42.98 i 11 (inv., NH) among ^{TÚG}NÍG.LÁM.MEŠ LUGAL-*UT-TI* (i 10); KBo 15.15 iii 4f. rest. by Kümmel, StBoT 3:136 and 31.

b. of the Sungod: *našta anda* ^{d}UT[U-*aš*] (var. *ŠA* ^{d}UTU) [(*lu-u-pa-an*)-*ni-i*]*n kištanunun* [*našta and*]*a* ^{d}U-*aš naḫšarada*[(*n ki*)*štanun*]*un* "Then I extinguished therein the 'cap' of the Sungod, then I extinguished therein the fear of the Stormgod" KUB 17.15 ii 13-16, with dupl. KUB 35.145 obv. 17f. (rit. with Luw., NH).

c. of a woman: 1 TÚG *šarā ḫuittiyanza* 1 ^{TÚG}E.ÍB *MAŠLU* 1 ^{TÚG}*kariulli* 1 ^{TÚG}*lu-pa-an-ni-iš* 1 ^{TÚG}*kaluppaš* 1-*NUTIM* ^{TÚG}E.ÍB *TAḪAPŠI* 1-*NUTIM TUDITTUM* KÙ.BABBAR *kī ŠA* SAL-*TIM* KUB 29.4 i 44-46 (rit., NH), ed. Schw.Gotth. 10-11.

d. listed in invs., with and without det. TÚG, with indication of color: IBoT 1.31 obv. 9, KBo 18.175 i 16 (ZA.GÌN "blue"), KUB 42.13 vi? 6, KUB 42.59 rev.? 9, 12, 15, Bo 6989 obv. 2′ (*ḪAŠMANNI* "blue-green"), frag. KBo 7.25:7, KUB 42.51 obv.? 4 (all NH).

2. part of a dagger (sword, knife); without det.: 21 GÍR ŠÀ.BA 1 GÍR ^{URU}*Ḫ*[*a*-. . .]. . . 2 EME AN.BAR.GE$_6$ GAB *lu-pa-an-n*[*i-eš*. . .] ANA 1 EME ZABAR *lu-ba-a*[*n-ni-iš*. . .] 11 EME ZABAR *lu-pa-an-ni-eš* GAB x[. . .] . . . GAB *lu-pa-an-ni-eš* AN.BAR § 1-*EN šikkiš* AN.BAR.GE$_6$ GAB *lu-pa-an-ni-eš* ^{NA_4}ZA[. . .] "21 daggers, among them:. . . two (with) blades (EME) of black iron, (their) front(?) (GAB) (and their) 'caps' (*lupanneš*) [of. . .]; on one blade of bronze the *l.* [is . . .]," etc. KUB 12.1 iii 6-13 (inv. of Manninni, NH); □EME "blade", *lupanni-* "cap" and GAB "front(?)" are here understood as parts of a GÍR "dagger"; cf. KUB 42.42 iv? 3, 5, 6; x [E]ME ZABAR *lu-wa-an-ni-eš* GAB AN.BAR.G[E$_6$ . . .] KBo 18.170 rev. 2′, [. . .]x 2 *lu-pa-an-ni-eš* KÙ.GI.GAR.[R]A VBoT 87 iv 2, *lu-pa-an-ni-eš* KÙ.GI NA$_4$ KUB 38.38:5 (all NH).

The employment of the verb *šāi-*/*šiya-* with *lupanni-* characterizes the latter as a type of headdress (Götze, NBr 77f.). The det. TÚG indicates it was made of cloth (once GAD, "linen", KBo 18.186 l.e. 2). According to reliefs, the headdress worn by the king and the Sungod was a round cap. Metal *l.*'s are mentioned in descriptions of daggers (swords) and may have been caps (or cappings) on the pommel. The alleged interchange with ^{TÚG}BAR.SI claimed by Goetze is based on insufficient evidence.

Goetze, Cor.Ling. (1955) 61f.; Kümmel, StBoT 3 (1967) 30f.

Cf. *lūpannauwant-*.

luppašti see *lumpašti-*.

luri- n. com. and neut.; **1.** loss of honor, disgrace, humiliation, **2.** embarrassing predicament, **3.** financial loss, **4.** deficiency(?), shortage(?); from OH/OS.†

sg. nom. com. *lu-ú-re-eš* KUB 13.4 iii 34; *lu-ú-ri-iš* KUB 13.18 iii 6; *lu-u-ri-iš* KUB 13.5 iii 5 (MH/NS); **sg. acc. com.** *lu-u-ri-in* KUB 31.68:32 (NH), IBoT 2:121 obv. 8 (OH/OS), IBoT 1.33:91 (NH); **sg. nom.-acc. neut.** *lu-u-ri* KBo 1.42 iv 8 (NH), KUB 30.32 i 12 (MS or early NS); **sg. loc.** *lu-u-ri* KUB 31.68:44 (NH); **sg./pl. abl.** *lu-ri-ia-az* KBo 18.57 l.e. 2 (MH/MS).

pl. nom. com. *lu-u-ri-e-eš* IBoT 2:121 obv. 14 (OH/OS); **pl. acc. com.** *lu-u-ri-uš* KBo 17.15 obv.? 7 (OH/OS).

(Sum.) i-bí-za = (Akk.) [*i-bi-sú*]-⸢*ú*⸣ = (Hitt.) *lu-u-ri*; Sum. and Akk. terms denote "(financial) loss" KBo 1.42 iv 8 (vocab., NH), cf. MSL 13.140:235.

1. loss of honor, disgrace, humiliation: "If they do not kill him, let them subject him to public ridicule (*luriyaḫḫandu*)! Naked . . . let him convey water three times from Labarna's pond to his temple!" *nušši apāš lu-ú-re-eš* (var. A: *lu-u-ri-iš*, var. B: *lu-ú-ri-iš*) *ešdu* "Let that be his humiliation!" KUB 13.4 iii 31-34, with dupl. A: KUB 13.5 iii 2′-5′ and B: KUB 13.18 rev. iii 6 (instr. for temple officials, MH/NS), ed. Chrest. 158-59; *mānza lu-*

u-ri-in tepnummarra UL uḫḫi SIG₅*-ru* "If I shall not experience humiliation and degradation, let (the oracle) be favorable!" IBoT 1.33:90f. (oracle, NH).

2. an embarrassing predicament: *zikmawa-kan innarā lu-u-ri anda tiyaši* "But on your own you will get yourself into an embarrassing predicament" KUB 31.68:44 (depos., NH); [. . .] *lu-ri-ia-az kuinki daḫḫun* "I extricated someone from an embarrassing predicament" KBo 18.57 left edge 2 (letter, MH/MS); cf. also *innarawa-kan lu-u-ri-in* [. . .] KUB 31.68:32.

3. financial loss, see bilingual section above.

4. deficiency(?), shortage(?): É*ḫeštā šarazzi kattēr kuwapi w*[(*etešnaš*)] GIŠ*-ru naššu lu-u-ri kuitki našma pur-aš-ta-an* [(*kuitk*)*i*] "Where/when there is construction(?) timber for the upper (and) lower *ḫ*.-building — (if there is) either a deficiency(?) or some . . . ," KUB 30.32 i 11-12 (inv., MS?), with dupl. KBo 18.190:6′-8′; [. . .]*-nuš lu-u-ri-uš* 2 K[UŠ]*annanuzziuš* 2 K[UŠ . . .] "The . . . shortages(?): two leather bridles, two le[ather . . .-s]" KBo 17.15 obv.? 7 (fest., OH/OS), cf. also IBoT 2.121 obv. 7-14 (cult of Nerik, OH/OS) and esp. pl. form *lu-u-re-e-eš* in line 14.

The unifying idea seems to be "loss", whether of possessions, honor, or station. Attending such a loss is embarrassment or humiliation.

Weidner, Studien (1917) 126 ("Unglück"); Sturtevant, Chrest. (1935) 159 ("humiliation").

Cf. *luriyaḫḫ-*, *luriyatar*.

luriyaḫḫ- v.; to humiliate, embarrass, disgrace, defame, subject to public ridicule; NH.†

pret. sg. 3 *lu-ri-ia-aḫ-ta* KUB 19.5 obv. 7; **imp. sg. 2** *lu-u-ri-ia-aḫ* KUB 36.35 i 21; **imp. pl. 3** *lu!-ri-ia-aḫ-ḫa-an-du* KUB 13.4 iii 32; **iter. pret. sg. 3** *lu-u-ri-ia-a*[*ḫ-ḫe-eš-ki-it*] KUB 21.37 obv. 20; **iter. pret. pl. 2** *lu-u-ri-ia-aḫ-ḫe-eš-ki-it-ten* KUB 21.37 obv. 15.

a. to subject to public ridicule as a punishment for misdeeds: "If they don't kill (the offender)," *lu!-ri-ia-aḫ-ḫa-an-du-ma-an* "let them subject him to public ridicule." (Naked . . . let him convey water from the pond to the temple) KUB 13.4 iii 31f. (instr.), ed. Chrest. 158f., cf. discussion under *luri-*; the god Elkunirša instructs the Stormgod how to punish the goddess Ašertu: *itwaran :šaššūmāi* :x-x[. . . d*Ašerdun* DA]M*-IA* [*n*]*uwaran lu-u-ri-ia-aḫ* "Go! Bereave(?) her! [. . . A.,] my [w]ife! And (thereby) disgrace her!" (Whereupon the Stormgod reports to her that he has killed all her sons) KUB 36.35 i 20f. (Hitt. translation of West Semitic myth), ed. Otten, MIO 1:126f., tr. Goetze, ANET (1969) 519.

b. to destroy someone's reputation by scandal (in order to be able to remove him from office): (spoken by Ḫatt. III about Urḫi-Tešub) *apāšma ammuk tepnummanzi š*[*e*]*r lu-u-ri-ia-a*[*ḫ-ḫe-eš-ki-it*] "But he subjected me to constant scandal in order to demote me" KUB 21.37 obv. 20 (decree of Ḫatt. III), cf. ḪUL*-aḫten lu-u-ri-ia-aḫ-ḫe-eš-ki-it-ten-mu* ibid. obv. 15; (spoken by Manapa-dU, king of Šeḫa River Land and Appawiya); [m*Piyam*]*aradušmamu* GIM*-an lu-ri-ia-aḫ-ta* "When [P]. had defamed me, (he set up Atpa in authority over me)" KUB 19.5 obv. 7-8 (letter), ed. Forrer, Forsch. I/1:90, cf. sequence *lūrin tepnummarra* IBoT 1.33:91 and discussion under *luri-*.

Forrer, Forsch. I (1926) 90 ("ins Unglück stürtzen"); Sturtevant, Chrest. (1935) 159 ("humiliate").

Cf. *luri-*.

luriyatar n. neut.; disgrace, humiliation, loss(?); NH.†

Only in Elkunirša story: (The Stormgod, having been instructed by Elkunirša to bereave(?) (*:šaššūmāi-*) and disgrace (*lūriyaḫḫ-*) E.'s wayward wife Ašertu, goes to her and tells her that he has killed all her sons) d*Ašerduš* [*kī l*]*u-u-ri-ia-tar IŠME nuššikan* ZI*-za anda* ḪUL*-ue*[*š*]*t*[*a*] "A. heard (of) [this] disgrace (or: the loss [of her children]), she was grief-stricken" KUB 36.35 i 24-25, ed. Otten, MIO 1:126f.; Hoffner, RHA XXIII/76:9; Laroche, Myth. 140f.; tr. also by Goetze, ANET (1969) 519.

Otten, MIO 1 (1953) 126f.; Friedrich, HW 1. Erg. (1957) 13 ("Demütigung, Kränkung").

Cf. *luri-*.

luššanu- v.; (mng. unkn.); NH.†

a. in a medical rit.: [. . .] *dai natkan lu-uš-ša-nu-wa-an-zi* (long break) *nat papparšanzi*

"He takes [. . .] They *l.* it . . . They sprinkle it" KUB 44.61 rev. 15-16, ed. StBoT 19:20-21.

b. in an inv. for the cult of dPirwa: *nu* LÚ.MEŠ*lapanallie*[*š*] 1 UDU *ḫūkanzi* LÚSANGA *ŠA* DUMU.NITA LÚ.M[EŠ*lap*]*analli*ḪI.A*-ša*? [*Š*]*A* DUMU.SAL.MEŠ *nu lu-uš-ša-nu-an-zi* IBoT 2.131 rev. 10-12 (NH).

(É)luštani- n. com.; side door(?), postern(?); from MH.

sg. acc. É*lu-uš-ta-ni-in* 174/t iii 13; **sg. (or pl.) gen.** *lu-uš-ta-ni-ia-aš* KUB 40.57 i 12 (MH/NS), KUB 13.1 i 26 (MH/MS); **loc.** *lu-uš-ta-ni-ia* IBoT 1.36 i 51 (MH/MS); É*lu-uš-ta-ni-ia* ibid. iv 35; **abl.** *lu-uš-da-ni-ia-az* ibid. i 61; *lu-uš-ta-ni-ia-az* ibid. i 53, iv (7); KBo 25.171 obv.? ii 4 (OH?/NS).

pl. nom. *lu-us-ta-ni-e-eš* KUB 31.89 ii 3 (MH/NS); *lu-uš-ta-ni-ia-aš* KUB 31.86 ii 13 (MH/NS) or pl. gen. against parallel 31.89 ii 3; **acc.** *lu-uš-ta-ni-i-e-e*[*š* . . .] KUB 40.57 i 10 (MH/NS).

namma KÁ.GAL-*TIM lu-uš-ta-ni-e-eš* (var. *lu-uš-ta-ni-ya-aš*) GIŠ*ilana*[(*š* SAG.DU.MEŠ)] BÀD.ḪI.A-*aš* GIŠAB.ḪI.A-*uš* GIŠIG-*anteš ḫat-talwant*[(*eš*) *aša*(*ndu*)] "Let the gates, the posterns(?), the heads of the staircases (var. same translation, or the heads of the stairs of the posterns [gen. pl.?]), and windows of the fortifications be provided with doorleaves(?) and bars!" KUB 31.89 ii 3ff. (Bel Madg. instr., MH/NS), ed. von Schuler, Dienstanw. 43, parallel KUB 31.86 ii 14, instead of BÀD.ḪI.A-*aš* GIŠAB.ḪI.A-*uš*, has [*I-NA*?] URU.DIDLI.ḪI.A; "Furthermore let the scouts . . . go up to the city" *nu* KÁ.GAL.ḪI.A-*TIM l*[(*u-uš-ta-ni-i-e*)*-eš* . . .] *ḫatalwandu nu zakkiēš pēšš*[(*iyandu*) . . .] *lu-uš-ta-ni-ia-aš* ERÍN.MEŠ (var. EN.M[EŠ] KUB 40.57 i 12′) EGIR-*an ḫandā*[*ndu*?] "and let them bar the gates (and) *l.*'s, and let them throw the bolts! And let them post(?) troops (var. lords) of the *l.* behind (them)!" KUB 13.1 i 23-26, with dupl. KUB 40.58:1-3 and par. KUB 40.57 i 9-12 (Bel Madg., MH/MS, par. KUB 40.57 is NS), ed. von Schuler, Dienstanw. 60, Goetze, JCS 14:70; "The guard shall not enter the gate building on his own. But if he does appear on his own, the gateman will confront him (saying), 'Either go up or go down!' If the guard proceeds through the gate building, he will hold the spear throughout the gate building." *lu-uš-ta-ni-ia-ma-aš ari* "But (when) he arrives at the side door(?) (or postern?)," (he leaves the spear with the gateman, and he goes down) IBoT 1.36 i 48-52 (*Mešedi* protocol, MH/MS), ed. Jakob-Rost, MIO 11:178f., cf. iv 35f.; "If a guard steals away" *našta* GIŠŠUKUR *lu-uš-ta-ni-ia-az katta pidai* "and he carries (his) spear down through the postern(?), (and the gateman catches him in the act, he shall remove a shoe from the guard)" ibid. i 53f., cf. Hoffner, Tyndale Bulletin 20 (1969) 42-4 for the significance of the shoe removal; "Guards (and) palace personnel shall not go down through the great city gate" *natkan lu-uš-da-ni-ia-az katta paiš*[*kand*]*a* "They shall go down through the side door(?)/postern(?)" ibid. i 60-61; *maḫ-ḫanma* LUGAL-*uš* KUR-*e weḫzi naškan* É d*Mizzulla* EGIR-*an arḫa paizzi naškan ŠA* É d*Mizzulla* É*lu-uš-ta-ni-in katta paizzi naškan* É*ḫalentūaš anda paizzi* "But when the king tours the land, he passes behind the temple of M. and descends the *l.* of the temple of M. and enters the *ḫ.*" 174/t iii 8-15 (fest. frag., OH/NS).

Laroche, RHA X/51 (1950) 25f.; Güterbock, Oriens 10 (1957) 354 (translating "side door" and concluding "might be a postern").

(GIŠ)luttai- n., neut. in sg. (KUB 30.29 obv. 17), com. in pl. (KBo 26.83:8); window; from OH; written syll., GIŠAB, and *A-AP-TI.*

sg. nom.-acc. GIŠ*lu-ut-ta-i* KUB 17.10 iv 21 (OH/MS); *lu-ud-da-a-i* KUB 33.52 ii 10 (OH/NS); GIŠAB-*i* KUB 33.32 ii 4 (OH/NS); [GIŠAB]-*e* KUB 33.17 i 3 (OH/NS); **erg.** GIŠ*lu-ut-ta-an-za* KUB 17.10 iv 10 (OH/MS); **gen.** *lu-ut-ti-ia-aš* KBo 17.74 i (12), (15), 24 (OH/MS); **loc.** *lu-ut-ti-ia* ibid. ii (5), 11, KBo 21.85 i 51; GIŠ*lu-ut-ti-ia* VBoT 58 iv 25 (OH/NS); GIŠAB-*ia* VBoT 24 i 35 (MH/NS); dAB-*ia* (sic) KUB 20.45 i 17 (NH); GIŠAB-*i* KBo 11.32 obv. 17 (OH/NS); **abl.** GIŠ*lu-ut-ti-ia-az* KBo 20.61 iii 46 (OH); *lu-ut-ti-ia-az* KBo 21.85 iv 12 (OH/MS); GIŠ*lu-ti-ia-az* IBoT 2.131 rev. 13 (NH); *lu-ut-ti-ia-za* KUB 26.1 ii 60 (Tudḫ. IV); GIŠAB-*az* KBo 5.3 iii 55 (Šupp. I); GIŠAB-*za* KBo 4.13 v 14 (NH); GIŠAB-*ia-az* KBo 21.95 i 14 (OH/NS); [GIŠ*l*]*u-ut-ta-an-za* KUB 17.5 i 24 = GIŠ*lu-ut-ta-an*[*-za*] KUB 17.6 i 19 (OH/NS); GIŠ*lu-ut-ti-an-za* KBo 21.95 i 11 (OH/NS).

pl. nom. GIŠAB.MEŠ-*uš* KBo 26.83:8 (NH); GIŠAB.ḪI.A-*uš* KUB 31.89:4 (MH/NS); **pl. acc.** GIŠ*lu-ut-ta-a-uš* KUB 17.10 i 5 (OH/MS); **pl. loc.** GIŠ*lu-ut-ti-aš* KBo 14.80:11 (OH/NS); *lu-ut-ti-ia-aš* KBo 17.74 i 24 (25) (OH/MS); GIŠAB.ḪI.A-*aš* KBo 22.186 ii 14 (NS).

uncomplemented Sumerogram ^{GIŠ}AB: covering Hitt. **nom. sg.** VBoT 58 iv 16, **acc. sg.** ibid. iv 28, **loc.** KBo 4.9 iii 7; **pl.** usually ^{GIŠ}AB.ḪI.A KUB 33.36 ii 5, occasionally ^{GIŠ}AB.MEŠ with or without Hitt. ending, e.g., KBo 26.83:8.

Akkadogram *IŠ-TU A-AP-TI* AT 454 ii 9.

a. as object of various verbs — **1′** *ep-* to seize: ^{GIŠ}*lu-ut-ta-a-uš kammaraš IṢBAT* "Mist seized the windows" KUB 17.10 i 5 (Tel. myth), also KBo 13.86 obv. 8f. where *e-ep-ta* "seized" is used, and passim in the missing god myth; cf. ^{GIŠ}AB. ḪI.A *tuḫḫuiš IṢBAT* KUB 33.36 ii 5.

2′ *ḫaš-* to open: *nu* ^{GIŠ}AB.ḪI.A EGIR-*pa ḫaššanzi* "They open up the windows" KBo 5.1 i 5-6 (rit. of Papanikri, NH); ^{d}NIN.TU *lu-ud-da-a-i ḫašta* "(The goddess) NIN.TU opened a window" KUB 33.52 ii 10 (myth of Inara, OH/NS).

3′ *ḫašḫaš-* to scrape(?): [... ^{GIŠ}]ÙR.MEŠ $^{\text{[G]IŠ}}$AB.ḪI.A-*ya arḫa ḫašḫaššanzi* "They scrape off(?) the rafters and the windows" KUB 7.13 obv. 8 (rit.).

4′ *ištap-* to close: *nu* ^{LÚ}Ú.ḪÚB ^{GIŠ}AB. ḪI.A *anda ištāpi* "The deaf man closes the windows" KBo 5.11 iv 14 (protocol of the gateman).

5′ *dai-* to put: 2 ^{GIŠ}AB ZABAR *INA* 1 ^{GIŠ}BANŠUR *ANA* ^{d}UTU *da-*[*a-i*] "She (the Old Woman) puts two bronze windows on one table for the Sungod" VBoT 58 iv 28 (rit. of missing god).

6′ *tarna-* to let go: ^{GIŠ}*lu-ut-ta-i kammaraš tarnaš* "Mist let go of the window" KUB 17.10 iv 21 (Tel.myth) and passim in missing god myths.

b. for looking through: *ziggawarašta* ^{GIŠ}*lu-ut-ta-an-*[(*za*)] *arḫa le autt*[*i*] "Don't look out of the windows!" KUB 17.6 i 19f. with dupl. KUB 17.5 i 24, cf. KUB 17.6 i 23f. (Illuyanka myth, OH/NS); *ABI* ^{d}UTU-*ŠI-makan imma* ^{GIŠ}AB-*az a*[*r*]*ḫa aušzi* "The father of His Majesty looked (hist. pres.) out of a window" KBo 5.3 + KUB 40.35 iii 55 (Ḫuqq.), ed. SV 2:128f.; cf. LUGAL-*uškan* ^{GIŠ}AB-*za* [*a*]*rḫa aušzi* KBo 4.13 v 14 (ANTAḪŠUM fest., NH). ^{d}U-*wa UL uškanzi nu*[*w*]*akan* SAL-*TUM IŠTU A-AP-TI andan aušta* "They don't (i.e., one isn't supposed to) look at the Stormgod, (but) a woman looked in (at him) through a window" AT 454 ii 9-10 (oracle, NH).

c. as a location for activities in rituals and cults — **1′** one of the parts of the sanctuary (together with throne, hearth, door bolt, etc.) which receives offerings: ^{GIŠ}AB-*ia* 1-*ŠU šipanti* KUB 25.18 iv 28′ (ANTAḪŠUM fest.); "the chief cook makes the rounds of the (sacred) places with groats, and he pours them ..." ^{GIŠ}AB-*ia* 1-*ŠU* "once on/at the window" KUB 11.21 iv 16-21.

2′ to put things on or near: *nanšan naššu* ZAG.GAR.RA-*ni* [*dai n*]*ašmankan* ^{GIŠ}AB-*ia dai* "she puts it (a bird made from dough) either on the altar or on the window" VBoT 24 i 34-35 (rit. of Anniwiyani, MH/NS); cf. KUB 20.92 vi 5.

3′ to pour or throw libations out of (abl.): LUGAL-*uškan* ^{GIŠ}AB-*az arḫa kūšpat* DINGIR. MEŠ-*aš* 13-*ŠU šipanti* "the king pours a libation from/through the window thirteen times to these gods" KUB 2.13 i 47f. (fest. of the month), cf. ibid. iv 18, KBo 20.61 iii 46, and KBo 21.85 iv 12; *nukan* Ì.NUN.NA ^{GIŠ}*lu-ti-ia-az arḫa peššiyanzi* "They throw butter/ghee out of the window" IBoT 2.131 rev. 13 (NH).

4′ other activities in rituals and cults: [*n*]*aš PANI* ^{GIŠ}AB *UŠKÊN* "(the king) bows before the window" KBo 17.75 i 27 (fest.); UGULA LÚ. ^{GIŠ}BANŠUR ^{GIŠ}BANŠUR ^{GIŠ}AB-*ia piran dāi* "the chief of the table-men puts a table in front of the window" KUB 2.13 iii 9 (fest. of month); LÚ.MEŠ ^{URU}*Tiššaruliya* ^{GIŠ}AB.ḪI.A-*aš* EGIR-*an* SÌR-*RU* "the men of T. sing behind the windows" KBo 22.186 ii 13f. (fest.).

d. special uses — **1′** as (erg.) subject of transitive verb: ^{GIŠ}*lu-ut-ta-an-za-at tarnau* "Let the window release it (the anger of the deity)!" KUB 17.10 iv 10 (Tel.myth, OH/MS).

2′ in the phrase *šarazzi luttai* "upper window": *naš šarazzi* ^{GIŠ}AB-*ya tapušza tiyazzi* "she (the queen) steps next to the upper window" KUB 27.69 v 4-5 (fest. of month); cf. KBo 19.138 obv. 7 (fest.).

Friedrich, ZA 37 (1927) 297-99.

[*lu-ta-al-la*] in KUB 38.3 ii 14 should be read: UDU *ta-al-la*.

luzzi- n. neut.; corvée; from OH.

sg. neut. nom.-acc. *lu-uz-zi* KBo 6.2 ii 39, 40, 43, etc. (OH/TOS), KBo 20.13 rev. (13) (OH/TOS), *lu-u-zi* ABoT 56 iii 10 (Šupp. II); **loc.** *lu-uz-zi-ia* Meskene 127 + 107:13 (NH); *lu-uz-zi* ibid. 25, KUB 1.1 iv 85, KUB 1.3 iv 6, KUB 26.58 obv. 13, KBo 4.10 obv. 45, KUB 21.15 iv 11 (all NH); **abl.** *lu-zi-ia-za* KUB 13.8:6 (MH/NS); *lu-uz-zi-ia-z(a-at)* ABoT 56 iii 5 (Šupp. II); *lu-uz-zi-ia-az* KUB 26.43 rev. 11 (NH); **inst.** *lu-uz-zi-it* KBo 10.2 iii 18 (OH/NS), KUB 17.21 i 25 (MH/MS).

Akk. *ina šapal šamê* AMA.AR.GI-*šunu* (= Akk. *andurāršunu*) *aštakan* "Under heaven I effected their liberation" KBo 10.1 rev. 13-14 = Hitt. *naškan šaḫḫanit lu-uz-zi-it arawaḫḫun* "I freed them from *š.* and *l.*" KBo 10.2 iii 18-19 (deeds of Ḫatt. I, OH/NS); cf. further below under b 1′ b′.

a. nature of the obligation (examples of the services required): *e-ki* (later var. B: *A-NA*, var. D: omits) BÀD-*ni* LUGAL-*aš* KASKAL-*ša* (var. B and D: KASKAL LUGAL) *takšu-anzi* (var. D: *pāuwanzi*) ^{GIŠ}KIRI₆.GEŠTIN-*aš* (var. B and D: lack -*aš*) *tuḫḫušuanzi* ⌈*ŠA*⌉ [(^{LÚ}URU)]DU.⌈NAGAR⌉ *natta kuiški arauaš* $^{LÚ.MEŠ}$NU.^{GIŠ}KIRI₆ *ḫūmantiyapat lu-uz-zi* [(*karp*)]*ianzi* "No copper-worker shall be exempted from being assigned to a royal expedition for (work) on ice(-cutting) (vars. omit "ice") or on fortification work, (or) from harvesting of vineyard(s). The gardeners too shall perform corvée in all the same (-*pat*) (duties)" KBo 22.62 iii 24f. + KBo 6.2 iii 21f. (Law §56, OH/OS) with dupls. KBo 6.3 iii 24f. (B) and KBo 6.6 i 30-32 (D); cf. Starke, StBoT 23:58f., Melchert, JCS 31:57-59; for ice-cutting as an obligation see Hoffner, JCS 24:34; "In the future let only 200 (men) of his go on a military expedition of Ḫatti! Let them no longer demand (lit. seek) troops from the store house(?) (of the Ḫulaya River Land)!" *apāt-maššì* KARAŠ *ŠA* DINGIR-*LIM šaḫ*[(*ḫani*)] *lu-uz-zi* EGIR-*an* SUM-*er kuinši AŠŠUM* $^{LÚ.MEŠ}$KISAL.LUḪ-*UTTI* EGIR-*an* SUM-*er kuinmašši AŠŠUM* $^{LÚ.MEŠ}$APIN.LÁ-*UTTI* EGIR-*an* SUM-*er kuinmašši AŠŠUM* x[. . .] EGIR-*an* SUM-*er* "But they have given those troops (exempted from military duties) over to a god's *š.* and *l.*: they gave over some to do the temple maintenance (lit. courtyard sweeping), some to do plowing, and some to do [. . .]" KBo 4.10 obv. 43-46 (Ulmi-Tešub treaty), with par. ABoT 57 obv. 16-24, ed. Götze, NBr 55-56.

b. exempt from the obligation — **1′** under ordinary terms of existing law (i.e., not special cases) — **a′** recipient of fields given as dowry, if not given in their entirety (Law §46); **b′** buyer of a large part of "craftsman's" fields (Law §47); **c′** *ukke* people of Nerik (Law §50); **d′** priests in Arinna and Zippalanta (Law §50); **e′** eleven-month resident of Arinna with fir tree (or pole of fir?) erected in his gate (Law §50); **f′** weavers in Arinna and Zippalanta (Law §51).

2′ persons exempted by special royal decree — **a′** mentioned in laws: *mānankan* LUGAL-*uš-ma arauwaḫḫi nu lu-uz-zi UL iyazzi* "If the king, however, exempts him, he shall not perform *l.*" KBo 6.4 iv 13-14 (Laws, par. series §XXXVI, NH); *mānankan IŠTU* É.GAL-*LIM arawaḫḫi lu-uz-zi UL kar-ap-zi* . . . LUGAL-*un punuššanzi nu kuit* LUGAL-*uš tezzi nu apāt lu-uz-zi kar-ap-zi* "If he exempts him from the palace, he shall not render *l.* ... (in another case) they shall ask the king, and he shall render that *l.* which the king specifies" ibid. 29-33 (Laws, par. series §XXXIX, NH).

b′ mentioned in historical texts: (in narration of defeat of the city of Ḫaḫḫa) "I took the hands of its maidservants from the millstone(s); I took the hands of (its) manservants from the sickle(s)" *naškan šaḫḫanit lu-uz-zi-it arawaḫḫun* "I freed them from (inst.) *š.* and *l.*" KBo 10.2 iii 16-19 (deeds of Ḫatt. I, OH/NS). This seems to correspond in Akk. vers. to: *ina šapal šamê* AMA.AR.GI-*šunu* (= Akk. *andurāršunu*) *aštakan* "Under heaven I effected their liberation" KBo 10.1 rev. 13f., cf. Saporetti & Imparati, SCO 14 (1965) 52f., 79, 82.

c′ in decrees, land grants, concessions, treaties: "Thus says Ašmunikal, the Great Queen: Regarding the Stone House which we established, the towns which were given to the Stone House, the craftsmen . . . , the farmers, oxherds, shepherds . . . ," *natkan šaḫḫanaza lu-zi-ia-za arawēš ašandu* "let them (all) be exempt from *š.* and *l.*!" KUB 13.8:1-6 (decree, MH/NS), ed. Otten, HTR 106f.; *šaḫḫaniyaš lu-uz-zi lē* *kuiški epz*[(*i*)] "Let no one lay hold of them (com. pl., the descendants of Ḫatt.) for *š.* and *l.*!" KUB 1.1 iv 85 with dupl. KUB 1.3 iv 6f. (Ḫatt.); "Let the house of Ištar of Šamuḫa be exempted" *šaḫḫanaza* [*lu-u*]*z-zi-y*[*a-z*]*a* "from *š.* and *l.*" (and from many other itemized obligations) KUB 21.12 (+ KBo 6.29) iii 20 (decree, Ḫatt. III), ed. Götze, NBr 48f.; *n*[*uka*]*n AN*[*A* ᵈ*IŠTAR* ᵁᴿ]ᵁ *Šamuḫa šaḫḫani lu-uz-z*[*i-ia l*]*ē kuiški tiyazz*[*i*] "And let no one appear before (the temple of) Ištar of Š. for *š.* and *l.*" KBo 6.29 iii 25-27, cf. KUB 26.43 rev. 10-14 with dupl. KUB 26.50 rev. 2-6 + KBo 22.60:6-9 (land grant to Šaḫurunuwa, Tudḫ. IV), ed. Imparati, RHA XXXII (1974, pub. 1977) 34f.; "Whoever keeps these words ... (and)" É-*erma šaḫḫani lu-uz-zi UL tiddanuzi* "doesn't make the house stand (liable) for *š.* and *l.*" (let Ištar favor him) KUB 21.15 + 715/v iv 6-11 (decree, Ḫatt. III), ed. Götze, NBr 52f., Otten-Rüster, ZA 63:85; "I have exempted *ḫegur pirwa*;" *n*[*at šaḫḫani*] *lu-uz-zi* [*Š*]*A* UD.KAM-*MI ḫaršuwanz*[*i*] *te*[*ri*]*ppūwanzi* ... *lē kuiški p*[*i*]*ran* EGIR-*p*[*a ēpz*]*i* "let no one lay hold of it ... for *š.* and *l.*, daily plowing and tilling," (delivery of various agricultural products, etc.) KBo 6.28 rev. 22-25 (decree, Ḫatt. III), ed. Götze, NBr 54.

c. abuses in application of laws concerning *luzzi* are termed "oppression": (in a royal prayer text Arn. and Ašmunikal accuse the Kaškaeans) *namma ŠA* DINGIR.MEŠ SAG.GEMÉ.ÌR.MEŠ-*KU-NU* UR[(U.DIDLI.ḪI.A-*K*)]*U-NU šaḫḫanit lu-uz-zi-it dammišḫiškir* "Furthermore they oppressed your servants and your cities, O gods, by means of *š.* and *l.*" KUB 17.21 i 24f. with dupls. KUB 31.124 i 5 and 398/u + 1945/u:9f. (MH/MS); abuse in application of *šaḫḫan* and *luzzi* is also the subject of the letter Meskene 127 + 107 (transliteration courtesy of E. Laroche), cf. *nan lē kuiški dammišḫaizzi* in its lines 31-32. Since the Meskene letter is more significant for *šaḫḫan* than for *luzzi*, see there.

According to Götze the distinction between *šaḫḫan* and *luzzi* is that while *š.* denotes an obligation incurred through land tenure, *l.* can be incumbent upon persons not holding land.

A. Götze, NBr (1930) 54-59, Kl (1957) 108f.

Cf. *šaḫḫan*.

M

-ma enclitic conj.; (relates words or clauses to each other through pairing or opposition); from OH.

- **a.** marking the correlation of single words in adjacent clauses
  - **1′** appended to all but the first member of a series
    - **a′** with more than two members
    - **b′** with only two members
      - **1″** complementary pairs of adjectives, adverbs, nouns, or verbs
      - **2″** complementary *kuiš*
      - **3″** complementary demonstratives
      - **4″** expressing alternatives in double questions
  - **2′** appended to both members in a bipartite construction
- **b.** marking correlation of clauses without focus on a particular pair of words
  - **1′** clauses showing opposition, where "however" or "but" is an appropriate translation
  - **2′** clauses showing positive-negative opposition
  - **3′** correlative clauses showing alternatives, employing *naššu=ma* (>*našma*)
  - **4′** correlative negative clauses, employing *natta*(=*ma*) ... *natta=ma* "neither ... nor"
  - **5′** correlative dependent clauses (often with change in grammatical subject) followed by a main clause which does not contain *-ma*
  - **6′** correlation of words or phrases within a dependent clause with parts of a following main clause
  - **7′** correlation of clauses showing concurrent action
  - **8′** in *namma=ma*
- **c.** marking an explanation or elaboration (NH)
- **d.** marking anaphora (from OH)
- **e.** marking continuation
  - **1′** in general
  - **2′** with specific adverbs
- **f.** position of *-ma* in the clause

In passages rendered in broad transcription in this article only those *-ma*'s which represent the usage under discussion are set off with ⸗.

The *a* of *-ma* is lost before a following vowel: *ta-a-i-mu-uš-za* KBo 20.32 ii 9, *i-en-zi-mu-uš* KBo 16.78 i 10 (cf. HW[2] 42a).

a. marking the correlation of single words within adjacent clauses — **1′** appended to all but the first member of a series — **a′** with more than two members: [^{d}UT]U-*ušza* ^{URU}ZIMBIR-*an eš*[*zi* ^{d}]*SIN-aš⸗ma⸗za* ^{URU}*Kuzinan eš*[*zi* ^{d}]U-*ašza* ^{URU}*Kummiyan eš*[*zi*] ⸢^{d}⸣*IŠTAR-iš⸗ma⸗za* ^{URU}*Nenuwan eš*[*zi*] ⸢^{d}⸣*Nanayaš⸗ma⸗za* ^{URU}*Kiššinan* [*ešzi* ^{UR}]^{U}KÁ.DINGIR.RA-*an⸗ma⸗za* ^{d}AMAR.UTU-*aš e*[*šzi*] KUB 24.8 iv 13-18 (Appu story, pre-NH/NS), ed. StBoT 14:12-13, □the first two deities, "sun" and "moon" form a natural pair and a separate sub-series; 3 *wattaru iet kedani ... kedani⸗ma ... kedani-ma* KUB 33.59 iii 7-9 (myth, OH/MS), translit. Laroche, Myth. 89; cf. KBo 5.6 i 10-13 (DŠ frag. 28 A), ed. Güterbock, JCS 10:90.

b′ with only two members — **1″** complementary pairs of adjectives, adverbs, nouns, or verbs: ⸢*šarazzi*⸣ ... *kattirra⸗ma* "above ... below" KUB 31.127 ii 1, 3 (prayer, OH/NS); ZAG-*aztet* ... GÙB-*laz⸗ma⸗tta* "on your right ... on your left" ABoT 44 i 59-60 (prayer, OH/NS); GIBIL ... LIBIR.RA⸗*ma* "new ... old" KUB 13.35 i 48 (depos., NH); *UL* GUD-*uš UL⸗ma⸗wa* UDU-*u*[*š*] KUB 36.51 obv. 7 (myth, OH/NS); *IŠTU* GÍD.DA 230 DAGAL⸗*ma⸗šši* 60 KI.MIN (i.e., *gipeššar*) "(a field) with a length of 230 (*gipeššar*) and a width of 60 'ditto'" KUB 8.75 iv 10, cf. lines 13, 18, 19, etc. (list of fields, NH); GUD-*ušza* AMAR-*un UL kappuwaizzi* [UD]U-*uš⸗ma⸗za* SILA$_4$-*an UL kappuwaizzi* "the cow doesn't take care of her calf, the sheep doesn't take care of her lamb" KUB 33.37+ KUB 39 iv 4-5 (lost god myth, OH/NS); [*I*]*NA* ŠÀ É.GUD-*kan* ... [Š]À TÙR⸗*ma⸗kan* "in the cowshed ... in the sheepfold" ibid. 1-2; *et⸗za ... eku⸗ma* "eat ... drink" KUB 46.52:4-5 (OH/NS); ⸢^{d}⸣IM-*aš* ... [*uizzi nan* LÚ ^{d}U] *araizzi* ^{DUG}UTÚL⸗*ma⸗k*[*an uizzi n*]*an* ^{GIŠ}*tipaš ara*[*izzi*] "The Stormgod comes, and the Man of the Stormgod stops him; the bowl comes, and the *t.* stops it" KBo 12.78:4-6 (OH/ NS?); *ḫamešḫi⸗ya⸗z* BABBAR-*TIM wašš*[*aši*] BURU$_{14}$⸗*ma⸗z išḫarwand*[*a w*]*aššaši* "In the spring you (the hawthorn) wear white, at harvest time you wear red" KUB 33.54 ii 13-14 + KUB 33.47:1 (OH/NS); *šieššar* ... NINDA.KUR$_4$.R[A]⸗*ma* "beer ... bread" KUB 7.1 iii 35-36 (rit., NH); (The queen already took up two minas of silver) *nu* 1 MA.NA KÙ.BABBAR *ANA* ^{SAL}*ḫarnawaš* ^{m}*Lulluš* ^{LÚ}*patiliš pedaš* 1 MA.NA KÙ.BABBAR⸗*ma ANA* DINGIR.MEŠ ^{URU}*Urikina ḫališšuanzi* EGIR-*anda pier* "L., the *p.*-priest, transported one mina of silver to the Woman of the Birthstool; the other (*-ma*) mina of silver they gave to plate the deities of U." KUB 26.66 iii 10-13 (list of metals, NH); [*ANA* 1]4? *dammuri* ŠÀ.BA 7 *dammuriš ŠA* 3 MA.NA [7 *d*]*ammuriš⸗ma* ⸢*ŠA*⸣ 4 MA.[N]A KUB 42.79 iii 3-4 (list of metals, NH); — **2″** complementary *kuiš*: [*n*]*uza kuišš⸗a* (var. 6: [*ku*]*iš*) DUMU.NITA-*li* (var. 6: DUMU-*iš-š*[*i*]) N[INDA-]*an* UZU.Ì-*ya pai* [*kui*]*š⸗ma⸗za* DUMU.NITA-*li* (var. 7: [...-]*ši*) *aku*[(*wa*)]*nna pai* [^{m}*A*]*ppušma* NINDA-*an UL kuitanikki pai* "One gives bread and fat meat to his son, another gives his son something to drink, but A. gives bread to no one" KUB 24.8 i 19-21 (Appu story, pre-NH/NS), with dupl. KUB 43.70b:6-8, ed. StBoT 14:4-5, □*-ma* on [^{m}*A*]*ppušma* is usage b 1′; *nukan antuḫšatar* ^{URU}*Ḫatti ANA* URU.DIDLI.ḪI.A ^{URU}*Gašga* EGIR-*an kuieš* ^{É}*arzanan ḫarkir kuieš⸗ma⸗kan ḫappiri* EGIR-*pa panteš* KBo 5.6 i 15-17 (DŠ frag. 28 A); further exx. sub *kui-* relative; — **3″** complementary demonstratives: *kez ... kez⸗ma* e.g., KUB 19.37 ii 20, 21, 24 (AM 168), and *kedani ... kedani⸗ma* e.g., KUB 33.59 iii 7-9 (myth, OH/MS); — **4″** expressing alternatives in double questions (which pose contrary or opposing alternatives): BAL *andurza kuiški* DÙ-*yazi* ... *nu* BAL *araḫza⸗ma kuiški* DÙ-*zi* "Will someone rebel inside (i.e., domestic insurrection) ... or will someone rebel outside (i.e., foreign insurrection)?" KUB 5.4 i 33, 35 (oracle question, NH), cf. HW[2] 237 rt. col.; *nat panzi ANA* DINGIR-*LIM IŠTU* NA$_4$ *pianzi ... nat ANA* DINGIR-*LIM IŠTU* KÙ.GI⸗*ma pianzi* "Shall they proceed to give it to the deity with gems ... or shall they give it to the deity with gold?" KUB 22.70 obv. 51-53 (oracle question, NH); ⸢DAM⸣-*IA* SAL.LUGAL *idalawaḫta ku*⸢*itki*⸣ *nan tepnutta⸗ma ku*⸢*it*⸣*ki*

"Did my wife do the queen some harm/wrong, or did she demote her in some way?" KUB 14.4 iii 21-22 (Murš. II prayer, NH); cf. Hoffner, JCS 29:153; *nuwarat* ŠE[Š-*IA IDI nuw*]*arat UL⹋ma IDI* "Does my brother know it, or does he not know it?" KUB 14.3 i 52 (Taw., NH).

As can be seen from the exx. quoted above, the first alternative question may or may not be introduced by *nu*, while the second one is always so introduced. The -*ma* is appended to that element in the second question which is central in the opposition to the first alternative: e.g., NA₄ ... KÙ.GI⹋*ma, andurza* ... *araḫza⹋ma, idalawaḫta* ... *tepnutta⹋ma, IDI* ... *UL⹋ma IDI*. The -*ma* serves within the clauses to focus the attention on the central elements in the opposition while the *nu* ... *nu* or *φ* ... *nu* conjunctions relate the juxtaposed clauses. Contrast the indirect double questions posing the same kind of opposition, where *mān* introduces both, and -*ma* does not occur in the second clause (see sub *mān* and Friedrich, HE §333).

While it is true that the second clause of a direct double question posing alternatives seems always to be introduced by *nu* and to contain -*ma*, not all *nu* ... -*ma* clauses serve this function: cf. *nutta ke⹋ma* ... KBo 5.3 ii 11, *nuwamukan zik⹋ma anda* [*le*] *daliyaši* KUB 21.16 i 19-20 both marking a change of subject, *nan karu* ... *nu kinun⹋ma* KBo 4.8 iii 17-18 with contrast such as in a 1′b′1″, [*n*]*u tuk maḫḫan⹋ma* ... KBo 5.9 i 19, *nu ammuk⹋ma* GIM-*an nakkešta* KBo 4.14 i 7, *nuwa tuppa*ᴴᴵ·ᴬ⹋*ma kue ŠA*[...] KUB 43.76 rev. 6, [*n*]*ašta IŠTU* ᴵᴹŠᵁ·NÍGᴺÍGÍN.NA. GIM-*an⹋ma welku ša*[*r*]*a UL uizzi* KBo 6.34 + KUB 48.76 iii 42-43 (StBoT 22:14).

2′ appended to both members in a bipartite construction: *ḫuišwatar⹋ma⹋pa anda ḫingani ḫaminkan ḫingan⹋a⹋ma⹋pa anda ḫuišwanniya ḫaminkan* "life is bound up with death, and death is bound up with life" KUB 30.10 obv. 20 (Kantuzili prayer, pre-NH/MS), □note that ⹋*a* "and" or "but" in this passage does not seem to exclude ⹋*ma* in the same chain of enclitics. Since this would be our only example of -*ma* appended to both members, we should note that it is possible that the first -*ma* relates the entire bipartite construction to the preceding context.

b. marking correlation of clauses without focus on a particular pair of words — **1′** showing opposition, where "however" or "but" is an appropriate translation: (the queen of Egypt says:) LÚ-*ašwamukan* BA.ÚŠ DUMU-*IA⹋mawamu* NU.GÁL *tuk⹋ma⹋wa* DUMU.MEŠ-KA *meggauš memiškanzi mānwamu* 1-*an*

DUMU-*KA paišti manwarašmu* ᴸᵁ*MUTIYA kišari* ÌR-*YA⹋ma⹋wa nuwan para daḫḫi* "My husband (lit. man) has died. And while I have no son, they say that you, on the contrary (-*ma*), have many sons. If you give one of your sons to me, he would become my husband. One of my subjects, on the other hand (-*ma*), I do not wish to take (and make him my husband)" KBo 5.6 iii 10-14 (DŠ frag. 28 A), ed. Güterbock, JCS 10:94; (The people, cattle and sheep of the cities of Ḫalila and Duddušga I brought back to Ḫattuša,) [(ᵁᴿᵁᎵᴴ*a*)]*lilan⹋ma* ᵁᴿᵁ*Dudduš⹋gann⹋a arḫa warnunun* "but the cities Ḫ. and D. (themselves) I burned down" KBo 3.4 i 35 with dupl. KBo 16.1 i 52 (ten-year annals of Murš. II), ed. AM 22f.; "I ruled the Upper Land," *piran⹋ma⹋at⹋mu* ᵐᵈ*SIN*-ᵈU-*aš* DUMU ᵐ*Zida maniyaḫ⹋ḫiškit* "before me, however, Arma-ᵈU, son of Zida, had been administering it" KUB 1.1 i 27-28 (Ḫatt.); ᵁᴿᵁ*Ḫattušanma kuin pe ḫarta nankan arḫa daḫḫun nan ḫumandan* EGIR-*pa ašeša⹋nunun* ᴸᵁ·ᴹᴱŠ*piran ḫuiyattalluš⹋ma eppun naš ANA* ŠEŠ-*IA ḫinkun* "I took away (from the enemy) the Hittites which he held and resettled them all; but the leaders I seized and presented them to my brother (Muw.)" KBo 3.6 ii 10-13 (Ḫatt. ii 26-29); (The loyal vassal must not say:) :*allala pauwanzi⹋wa⹋za* UGU *linqanuwanza ki⹋ma⹋wa⹋za* UL *lenqanuanza* "I have been made to swear concerning desertion(?), but concerning this I have not been made to swear" KBo 4.14 ii 46-47 (treaty of Šupp. II); ⸢KA×U?⸣-*i⹋at memišta ANA ṬUPPI⹋ma⹋at⹋šan* UL *kittat* "He said it with (lit. in) his mouth, but it wasn't put on the tablet" VBoT 2(= EA 32):5-6 (Arzawa letter to Amenophis III); *AŠŠUM* EN-*UTTI* ᵈ*UTU-ŠI paḫḫašten kattama* NUMUN ᵈ*UTU-ŠI paḫḫašten dammeda⹋ma le autteni tamaimaš⹋*<*maš*> EN-*UTTA le ilaliyatteni* [*ku*]*iš⹋ma⹋* ⸢*za*⸣ *ilaliyazi* "(For the present) protect His Majesty with respect to lordship! And in their turn protect the seed of His Majesty! To another (ruler), however, do not look! Do not desire for yourselves another lordship! He who nevertheless desires (one), (let it be put to him under oath!)" KUB 21.42 i 29-32 (instr. for princes and lords, NH), ed. Dienstanw. 24; see also KUB 24.8 i 19-21 quoted and translated above a 1′b′2″.

-ma, b

2′ clauses showing positive-negative opposition (most often found in the *takku/mān natta⸗ma* ... clause): (If the owner of a field or vineyard kills a pig which wanders onto his property,) *nan išḫi⸗šši* EGIR-*pa pai takku⸗an UL⸗ma pai naš* LÚNÍ.ZU-*aš kiša* "he shall give it back to its owner; if, however, he does not give it, he becomes a thief" KBo 6.3 iv 20-21 (law §86, OH/NS); *takku* ÌR-*iš* (var. A iv 56: ÌR-*aš*) É-*er lukkizzi išḫaš⸗šeš⸗a šer* (var. B 1: [E]N-*ašša šer⸗š[et]*) *šarnikzi* ... *takku UL⸗ma* (var. A iv 58: *natta⸗ma*) *šarnikzi* "If a slave sets fire to a house, his master/owner shall make compensation for him ... If, however, he does not make the compensation," (he will forfeit the slave) KBo 6.3 iv 55, 57 (law §99, OH/NS), with dupls. KBo 6.2 iv 56, 58 (A), KBo 19.5:1 (B); (If you do something wrong,) EGIR-*zian⸗ma⸗at išdu⸗wari* ... *mān⸗ma⸗at UL⸗ma išduwari* "and subsequently it becomes known, (to you it will be a 'sin of the head'); but if it does not become known, ..." KUB 13.17 iv 8-9 (instr., NH), ed. Chrest. 164-65; further exx. sub *natta*.

3′ correlative clauses showing alternatives, employing *naššu⸗ma* (>*našma*): *mānkan ABU* DUMU-*RU-ya našma* (<*naššu⸗ma*) *MUTU* DAM-*SÚ-ya naššu⸗ma* ŠEŠ NIN-*ya ḫallu⸗wanzi* "If/whenever father and son, or husband and wife, or brother and sister quarrel" 2Mašt. iv 33-34 (MH/MS); □contrast: *[mā]nkan* ... *[našma?]* ... *našma* KBo 2.3 i 2-3 (1Mašt. A), *mānkan* ... <*našma*> ... *naš*<*ma*> iv 15-16; *mān ŠA* ITU.1.KAM *naššu⸗m[a] ŠA* ITU.2.KAM KBo 23.8: 19-20 (rit.); *[n]aššu gašza kiša naššu⸗m[a]* LÚ-*aš kuiški aki* "Either a famine will occur, or some man will die" KUB 34.10:7-8 (apodosis of lunar omen, NS); further exx. sub *naššu*.

4′ correlative negative clauses, employing *natta(⸗ma)* ... *natta⸗ma* "neither ... nor" (for *natta⸗ma* in opposition to a positive, see b 2′): *aliyašwa UL wai UL⸗ma⸗wa waki UL⸗ma⸗wa išparrizzi* "the *a.*-creature neither ...-s, nor bites, nor tramples(?)" KUB 14.1 rev. 91 (Madd., MH/MS); *UL iyat kuitki UL⸗ma waštaš kuitk[i] UL⸗ma⸗kan daš kuedanikki kuit⸢ki⸣* "He neither did anything, nor committed any sin, nor took anything from anyone" KBo 10.37 iii 46-47 (rit., OH/NS); DUMU.LÚ.U$_{18}$.LU *UL innara uwanun UL⸗ma šullanni uwanun* "I, the mortal, did not come here presumptuously, nor did I come to pick a quarrel" KBo 10.45 i 45-47 (rit. for netherworld deities, MH/NS), ed. Otten, ZA 54:120f.; (eight winds arose against Ḫuwawa and blew against his face) *nušši UL para i[y]anni⸗yauwa[nzi]* (erasure) *kišari UL⸗⸢ma⸣⸗šši* EGIR-*pa ti[yauwanzi] kišari* "he can neither advance nor retreat" KUB 8.53:18-20 (Gilg., NH); further exx. sub *natta*.

5′ correlative dependent clauses followed by a main clause which does not contain *-ma* (often with change in grammatical subject): *takku* LÚ-*aš MAḪAR* DAM ŠEŠ-*ŠU šeškizzi* ŠEŠ-*ŠU⸗ma ḫuišwanza ḫurkil* "If a man sleeps with his brother's wife, and his brother (*-ma*) is (still) living, it is the crime of incest" KBo 6.26 iii 49-50 (law §195); □for this translation of *ḫurkil* see Hoffner, AOAT 22:83; *takku* SAL-*an ku[(išk)]i pittenuzzi* EGIR-*anda⸗m[a⸗šma]š⸗⸢kan⸣ [ša]rdiyaš paizzi* "If someone elopes with a woman, and a *š.*-troop goes after them, ..." KBo 6.3 ii 29 (law §37); *našmakan ANA* ^{d}UTU-*ŠI aššuwanni kuiški ⸢andan⸣ neanza tuk⸗ma⸗kan ŠA* ^{d}UTU-*ŠI* LÚKÚR-*aš* EGIR-*pa* UGU *dai ašiwakan PAN* ^{d}UTU-*ŠI laknut zik⸗ma⸗a[t iy]aši nankan laknuš[i]* "Or if someone enjoys the good favor of His Majesty, and an enemy of His Majesty solicits(?) you (saying): 'Make that one fall from His Majesty's favor!' and you do it and you cause him to fall out of favor, (let these gods destroy you)" KUB 26.1 iii 37-41 (instr. to eunuchs, NH), ed. Dienstanw. 13-14; *[mān* L]Ú*aranma kuiš UL ḫant[i tiyazi]* ^{d}UTU-*ŠI⸗ma⸗at išdammašmi* "But if someone will not denounce his friend, and I, His Majesty (*-ma*), hear it, ..." ibid. iv 38-39; *maḫḫanmaza ABUYA* ^{m}*Mu[rš]iliš* DINGIR-*LIM-iš kišat* ŠEŠ⸗*YA⸗ma⸗za⸗kan* ^{m}NIR.GÁL *A[N]A* GIŠGU.ZA *ABIŠU ešat ammuk⸗ma⸗za ANA PANI* ŠEŠ[-*Y*]*A* ⸢EN⸣ KARAŠ *kišḫaḫat numu* ŠEŠ-*YA ANA* GAL.*MEŠEDIUTTIM tittanut* "But when my father M. died, and my brother M. (*-ma*) sat down on his father's throne, and I (*-ma*) had become the commander of the army in the reign of my brother, my brother installed me in the office of the Chief

-ma, b

Mešedi" KUB 1.1 i 22-25 (Apology of Ḫatt. III), ed. Ḫatt. 8f.

6′ correlation of words or phrases in a dependent clause with parts of a following main clause (although *-ma* appears in main clauses immediately following dependent clauses, it is not quite correct to speak of the particle as functioning to introduce main clauses; the conditions for its occurrence are unrelated to the sequence dependent clause + main clause): *nuza ABUYA kuwapi* DINGIR-*LIM-iš* DÙ-*at* ^{m}*Ar⸗nuandaš⸗ma⸗za⸗kan* ŠEŠ-*YA ANA* ^{GIŠ}GU.ZA *ABIŠU ešat* "When my father died, my brother A. sat down on the throne of his father" KBo 3.4 i 4-5 (AM 14-15); similarly: *mānmaza* ^{m}NIR.GÁL-*išma* ŠEŠ-*YA* DINGIR-*LIM-iš* [*kišat*] *ammuk⸗ma ŠA* ŠEŠ-*YA nakkianni ḫa*[*ndaš*] *UL manqa iyanun* KUB 21.19 + 1303/u ii 23-25 (Ḫatt. III prayer), ed. Otten, Puduḫepa 18 n. 41, □the *-ma* following *Arnuwandaš* in KBo 3.4 i 4-5 and following *ammuk* in KUB 21.19+ ii 23-25 marks a change in subject; LÚ-*LUM-ma kuiš piran ḫuiyanza ešta nankan* GIM-*an kuenun* ^{LÚ}KÚR⸗*ma⸗za pid⸗dait* KBo 3.6 ii 23-24 (Apology of Ḫatt. III); *nu* EGIR-*pa*-UD-*ti kuwapi* ^{m}*Abiraddaš aki* LUGAL-*UTTAŠU⸗ma⸗za⸗kan* ^{GIŠ}GU.ZA-*ŠU* KUR-*SÚ* É-*SÚ-ia ANA* ^{m}IR.^{d}U-*up* DUMU-*ŠU katta talešdu* KBo 3.3 ii 7-9, cf. ibid. iii 19; "If a girl is betrothed to a man, and he pays the bride-price (*kušata*) for her," *appezzin⸗at attaš annaš ḫullanzi nankan* LÚ-*ni tuḫšanzi kušata⸗ma* 2-*ŠU šarninkanzi* § *takku* LÚ-*ša* DUMU.SAL *nawi dai nanza mimmai kušata⸗ma kuit piddait naškan šamenzi* "and subsequently the parents abrogate it and withhold her from the man, they shall repay double the aforementioned brideprice. If, however (*-a*), the man hasn't yet taken the girl, and he refuses her, he must forfeit the brideprice which he paid." KBo 6.3 ii 12-15 (laws §§29-30, OH/NS), ed. HG 24-27; □the OS copy KBo 6.2 does not have these two laws; cf. also KBo 6.4 iv 28-29, ed. HG 58f.; the two *kušata⸗ma*'s are probably examples of the anaphoric use, see usage d.

7′ correlation of clauses showing concurrent action (often with a change in the grammatical subject) — **a′** without *kuitman* in the first clause: *nu apunna šara danzi memai⸗ma kiššan* "They take that up, while he speaks as follows" KBo 4.2 ii 17 (rit., pre-NH/NS); *memiškizzi⸗ma kiššan* ibid. i 44, 50, 58; *nat para tianzi* ^{LÚ}Ì.DU$_8$⸗*ma⸗aš⸗kan ḫa*[*tti*]*li lamnit ḫalziššai* (Those who spend the night up in the palace) "step forward, while the gateman calls them by name in Hattic" KBo 5.11 i 6-7.

b′ with *kuitman* in the first clause and *-ma* in the second: *nu kuitman ABUYA INA* KUR ^{URU}*Kargamiš kattan ešta* ^{m}*Lupakkin⸗ma⸗kan* ... *para naišta* KBo 5.6 iii 1-3 (DŠ); *nu kuitman ABUYA INA* KUR *Middanni ešta* ^{m}*Piḫḫuni⸗yaš⸗ma* LÚ ^{URU}*Tipiya iyattat* KBo 3.4 iii 67-68 (AM); *kuitm*[*a*]*n* ŠEŠ ^{d}UTU-*ŠI* LUGAL-*uš ešta uk⸗ma⸗za BĒLU ešun* KUB 26.32 i 9-10 (Šupp. II); *nu kuitman* 8 *MŪŠU šara tittanuanzi* ḪA.LA.MEŠ-*ŠU⸗ma azzikkanzipat* KBo 3.5 i 61-62 (Kikk.); *nu kuitman* $^{m.GIŠ}$PA.LÚ-*iš IŠTU* KUR ^{URU}*Mizri* EGIR-*pa uit* EGIR-*az⸗ma⸗za ABUYA* ^{URU}*Kargamiššan* URU-*an tarḫta* KBo 5.6 iii 26-27 (DŠ); *kuitman eniššan memiškir* ^{d}UTU-*uš⸗ma⸗šmaš* [o]x *tiyat* KBo 26.58 + KUB 36.7a iv 51 (Ullik.); further exx. sub *kuitman*.

8′ in *namma⸗ma* "over and above, in addition": (this adv. has its own particular syntactic environment and nuance distinct from, though related to, clause initial *namma* "next" and clause internal *namma* "again". Frequently it is associated in the same clause with the adjective *tamai-* "other, additional"): DUMU-*YA-ya kuin* ^{d}UTU-*ŠI temi* ... *nuza ziqqa* ^{m}*Ḫuqqanaš apun šak* § *namma⸗ma kuieš ammel* DUMU.MEŠ-*YA* ŠEŠ.MEŠ-*ŠU ammella* ŠEŠ.MEŠ[-*YA*] *našza aššuli AŠŠUM* ŠEŠ-*UTTIM U AŠŠUM* ^{LÚ}*TAPPUT*[*TIM*] *šak namma⸗ma⸗za damain BĒLAM kuiešaš kuiš* [UN-*aš*] *ANA* ^{d}UTU-*ŠI* EGIR-*an arḫa le kuinki šakti* "You, Ḫ., must recognize (as lord) my son, whom I, His Majesty, designate. In addition (*namma⸗ma*) you must gladly recognize as brothers and peers my sons, his brothers and also my brothers. But over and above this (*namma⸗ma*) you must not recognize any additional lord, whoever he may be, behind the back of His Majesty" KBo 5.3 i 9-15 (Ḫuqq., Šupp. I), ed. SV 2:106-09; *nu zik* ^{m}*Ḫuq⸗qanaš* ^{d}UTU-*ŠI-pat aššuli paḫši* EGIR-*panna ANA* ^{d}UTU-*ŠI-pat arḫut namma⸗ma⸗za damain le kuinki šakti* ibid. i 31-33, ed. SV 2:108-11; *nuwaza* *apunpat eši namma⸗ma⸗wa*[*z*] *para tamain ḫapatin tamai* KUR-*e* ZI[-*i*]*t le e*[*š*]*tari* KUB 14.1 obv. 19-20 (MH/MS), ed. Madd. 4-7; *nu mān uniušpat waškuš namma⸗ma⸗ka*[*n*] DINGIR-*LUM* ŠÀ É.DINGIR-*LIM damain waškuin UL kuinki uškiši* "If (you see) only these offences/omissions, but over and above them you see no further offence in the temple, O god" KUB 18.63 i 20-22 (oracle question, NH), and often in other oracle questions; □in KUB 14.1 rev. 23 (Madd. 26f.), however, *namma⸗ma* must be translated "but after that".

c. marking an explanation or elaboration (which interrupts the normal flow of the context); NH: *mānnaza ŠA* ᵈUTU-*ŠI* ḪUL-*lu k*[*uwapi kišari*] (var. [*kuwa*]*pi* ḪUL-*lu* [*k*]*iša⸗r*[*i*]) *ANA* ᵈUTU-*ŠI⸗ma* ŠEŠ.MEŠ *meqqae*[(*š*)] "If at some time evil befalls His Majesty — for His Majesty has many brothers — . . ." KUB 26.1 i 17-18 (instr. for eunuchs), with dupl. KUB 26.8 i 7-8; □von Schuler, Dienstanw. 9, uses dashes in his translation to set this phrase off as an interruption.

d. marking anaphora (to resume and more completely describe or define a word just mentioned; on the resuming word at the head of its clause); from OH: ᴷᵁᴿ*Alašiyanmazakan pedešši* [ÌR-*aḫḫu*]*n arkammanaḫḫun arkamman⸗ma⸗ši⸗kan* [*kū*]*n*? *išḫiyanun* "The land of A., however, on the spot I [subjugat]ed and obligated to tribute. As tribute I imposed [thi]s upon it" KBo 12.38 i 7-9 (conquest of Cyprus, NH), ed. Güterbock, JNES 26:75, 77; ᵈUTU-*š⸗at aruni peda*[*š*] § *aruni⸗ma* URUDU-*aš palḫaeš kianda*[*ri*?] "The Sungod too[k] it off to the sea. Now in the sea copper vessels are lying" KUB 33.66 ii 8-9 (myth, OH/MS?); translit. Laroche, Myth. 70; *ANA* DINGIR-*LIM peran* ᴳᴵŠ*eyan a*[*rta*] ᴳᴵŠ*eyaz⸗ma⸗kan* UDU-*aš kuršaš kank*[*anza*] "Before the deity a fir tree st[ands], and from that fir tree a sheepskin is han[ging]" KUB 33.38 iv 6-7 (myth, OH/MS), translit. Laroche, Myth. 85; L[UGAL-*uš*] ⌈3⌉-*ŠU* SAL.LUGAL-*ašša* 3-*ŠU* ERÍN.MEŠ-*an allappaḫḫanz*[*i* ERÍN.MEŠ]-*ti⸗ma⸗ššan šer* GÍR ZAB[AR] *kitta* KBo 17.1 ii 18-20 (OH/OS), ed. StBoT 8:26f.:32-34; *nu ḫurtiyallan ḫarmi ḫurtiyali⸗ma* [AN.B]AR-*aš nepiš* 1-*EN kitta* ibid. i 7-8; *nu kenupi uda kenupi⸗ma⸗ššan anda ŠA* UR.MAḪ *šiešai* . . . *šumumaḫ* KUB 29.1 ii 41-43 (OH/NS); another example above in b 6′.

e. marking continuation — **1′** in general: often *-ma* has no detectable sense of opposition, but serves to relate a large segment of new material to what has preceded. In most instances *-ma* in this usage is attached to the first word of a new paragraph or section. To illustrate one may follow the opening lines of the paragraphs of KUB 13.4 and duplicates ed. Chrest. 148ff.: *mān⸗ma⸗šta* (§3), *anda⸗ma* (§§4, 8, 16, 17), *anda⸗ma⸗šta* (§19), *anda⸗ma⸗za* (§§9, 10, 12, 13, 14, 18). Only three of the 15 paragraphs of the Apology of Ḫattušili ed. Ḫatt. lack *-ma* in the opening word; note *maḫḫan⸗ma* (§§4, 5, 6, 9, 10, 11), *uit⸗ma* (§7), *ammuk⸗ma* (§12), *kuiš⸗ma* (§14). In the ten-year annals of Muršili II ed. AM, of the approximately 39 paragraphs whose opening words are preserved, eight begin with *maḫḫan⸗ma*, six with MU-*anni⸗ma*, and one each with *kinun⸗ma*, *ABUYA⸗ma*, and KUR ᵁᴿᵁ*Arzau⸗wa⸗ma*, making a total of 17 paragraphs certainly containing *-ma* in the opening word. 11 paragraphs begin with *nu*, *namma*, *kuitman* or no conjunction at all, and the opening paragraph begins with *UMMA*. In the Hitt. translation of the Sum.-Akk. hymn of praise of Ludingirra to his mother (signalement lyrique) after the introduction of each new section ("first . . . second . . . third sign") all metaphors after the first in the series are introduced by . . . *⸗ma⸗aš* "she is a . . ." Hitt. text ed. in Ugar. V:773-79.

2′ with specific adverbs — **a′** *anda⸗ma* which is paragraph initial, and which is not properly the local preverb "in, into, together" but an adverb of transition which connects the new paragraph with the preceding, was first correctly identified by Otten, RHA XVIII/67 (1960) 123 and von Schuler, Kaškäer (1965) 126. Neither, however, noticed that its diachronic distribution was OH and MH, passing out of use in early NH. Kammenhuber in FsOtten (1973) 149 with n. 12 distinguished OH clause initial *anda* from "jungheth. Neubildung mit Adv. *anda-ma*(-)", and 150 n. 12 gave many